Securitization Theory

This volume aims to provide a new framework for the analysis of securitization processes, increasing our understanding of how security issues emerge, evolve and dissolve.

Securitization theory has become one of the key components of security studies and IR courses in recent years, and this book represents the first attempt to provide an integrated and rigorous overview of securitization practices within a coherent framework. To do so, it organizes securitization around three core assumptions which make the theory applicable to empirical studies: the centrality of audience, the co-dependency of agency and context and the structuring force of the dispositif. These assumptions are then investigated through discourse analysis, process-tracing, ethnographic research, and content analysis and discussed in relation to extensive case studies.

This innovative new book will be of much interest to students of securitization and critical security studies, as well as IR theory and sociology.

Thierry Balzacq is holder of the Tocqueville Chair on Security Policies and Professor at the University of Namur. He is Research Director at the University of Louvain and Associate Researcher at the Centre for European Studies at Sciences Po Paris.

D1352462

LIVERPOOL JMU LIBRARY

3 1111 01543 2550

Series: PRIO New Security Studies

Series Editor: J. Peter Burgess, PRIO, Oslo

The aim of this series is to gather state-of-the-art theoretical reflexion and empirical research into a core set of volumes that respond vigorously and dynamically to the new challenges to security scholarship.

The Geopolitics of American Insecurity

Terror, power and foreign policy
Edited by François Debrix and Mark J. Lacy

Security, Risk and the Biometric State

Governing borders and bodies
Benjamin Muller

Security and Global Governmentality

Globalization, governance and the state
Miguel de Larrinaga and Marc G. Doucet

Critical Perspectives on Human Security

Rethinking emancipation and power in international relations
Edited by David Chandler and Nik Hynek

Securitization Theory

How security problems emerge and dissolve
Edited by Thierry Balzacq

Securitization Theory

How security problems emerge and dissolve

**Edited by
Thierry Balzacq**

Routledge
Taylor & Francis Group

LONDON AND NEW YORK

First published 2011
by Routledge
2 Park Square, Milton Park, Abingdon, Oxon OX14 4RN

Simultaneously published in the USA and Canada
by Routledge
711 Third Avenue, New York, NY 10017

Routledge is an imprint of the Taylor & Francis Group, an informa business

© 2011 Thierry Balzacq for selection and editorial matter,
individual contributors; their contributions

Typeset in Baskerville by Swales & Willis Ltd, Exeter, Devon

All rights reserved. No part of this book may be reprinted or
reproduced or utilised in any form or by any electronic,
mechanical, or other means, now known or hereafter
invented, including photocopying and recording, or in any
information storage or retrieval system, without permission in
writing from the publishers.

British Library Cataloguing in Publication Data
A catalogue record for this book is available from the British Library

Library of Congress Cataloging-in-Publication Data
Securitization theory: how security problems emerge and
dissolve/edited by Thierry Balzacq.
  p. cm.
  1. Security, International. 2. National security. I. Balzacq, Thierry.
JZ5588.S4283 2010
355´.033001—dc22
              2010003574

ISBN13: 978-0-415-55627-9 (hbk)
ISBN13: 978-0-415-55628-6 (pbk)
ISBN13: 978-0-203-86850-8 (ebk)

Contents

Tables

Figures

Contributors

Thierry Balzacq is holder of the Tocqueville Chair on Security Policies and Professor at the University of Namur. He is Research Director at the University of Louvain and Associate Researcher at the Centre for European Studies at Sciences Po Paris. He specializes on critical approaches to security, IR theories and the external dimensions of EU internal security. His articles have appeared, inter alia, in the *European Journal of International Relations*, *Journal of Common Market Studies*, *Security Dialogue*, *Review of International Studies*, *Cultures & Conflits*. His most recent book is *The External Dimension of EU Justice and Home Affairs* (Palgrave Macmillan, 2009). He is currently working on two projects, one in French titled *Théories de la sécurité* (Under contract with Presses de Sciences Po) and another provisionally titled *The Nature and Origins of Security Ideas*. Thierry Balzacq has taught at Aberystwyth, Cambridge, and Sciences Po Paris.

Christian Kaunert holds a PhD in International Politics and an MSc in European Politics from the University of Wales Aberystwyth, a BA (Hons) in European Business from Dublin City University, ESB Reutlingen and a BA (Hons) Open University. Dr Kaunert also lectured at the University of Wales Aberystwyth before joining Salford University in January 2007 as Lecturer. In 2004, he was a University Association of Contemporary European Studies (UACES) Research Fellow at the Université Libre de Bruxelles, Brussels, Belgium, where he examined the role of European Institutions in counter-terrorism and the broader security field. He will be a visiting research fellow at IBEI Barcelona, a joint research institute on international relations for the universities in Barcelona, Spain, from February until September 2010. He has studied, travelled and researched widely in Europe, Asia, and especially Latin America, including one six-month stay in Cali, Colombia, as well as further trips to China, Puerto Rico, and the United States. He is the author of several articles on European counter-terrorism, and wider homeland security matters. His articles have appeared in journals, such as *European Security*, *Journal of European Integration*, *Terrorism and Political Violence*, *Studies in Conflict and Terrorism*, *European Political Science* and *Journal of Contemporary European Research*. His monograph *EU Internal Security: towards supranational governance* is forthcoming with Manchester University Press (2010). He is joint editor of the *Journal of Contemporary European Research* (JCER) and a member of the executive committee of UACES. He has frequently commented for UK and international media (Al-Jazeera, USA Today) on terrorism and European Union issues.

Sarah Léonard holds a first degree in International Relations and a Master's degree in European Studies from the University of Louvain (UCL, Belgium), as well as an MA in Russian and Eurasian Studies from the University of Leeds. She received her PhD in International Politics from the University of Wales, Aberystwyth. In 2004, she was a University Association of Contemporary European Studies (UACES) Research Fellow at the Université Libre de Bruxelles, Belgium, where she examined the 'securitization' of asylum and migration in the European Union. She will be a visiting research fellow at IBEI Barcelona, a joint research institute on international relations for the universities in Barcelona, Spain, from February until September 2010. Building upon the Copenhagen School's work on the social construction of security threats, her research examined the ways in which the European Union has increasingly placed migration issues in the realm of security. Her main research interest and area of expertise is the European Union's response to non-traditional security threats such as irregular migration and terrorism, including the development of the EU's external cooperation on these issues. She has published on international security, including NATO and European security, and on the European Neighbourhood Policy. She is the joint editor of the *Journal of Contemporary European Research* (JCER).

Mark B. Salter is Associate Professor at the School of Political Studies, University of Ottawa. He is editor of *Mapping Transatlantic Security Relations: The EU, Canada, and the War on Terror*, *Politics at the Airport*, and *Global Policing and Surveillance: Borders, Security Identity* with Elia Zureik. He is the sole author of *Rights of Passage: The Passport in International Relations and Barbarians and Civilization in International Relations* (also published in Chinese). Recent research appears in *Geopolitics*, *Citizenship Studies*, *International Political Sociology*, *Alternatives*, *Security Dialogue*, the *Journal of Air Transport Management*, and the *Journal of Transportation Security*. He teaches courses on globalization, security studies, territory, and IR theory.

Dirk Schmitchen has completed a Master's degree in International Relations with the Department of War Studies at Kings College London and previously, he gained a Magister in Linguistics, Politics and History from the University of Hildesheim, Germany. He is currently undertaking his PhD with the Faculty of Social Sciences at Frankfurt University on constructivist approaches to International Relations and US-Iranian relations. He has published articles on German military and security policy and several works examining rogue states and their meaning for US foreign and security policy.

Roxanna Sjöstedt is a Doctoral candidate at the Department of Peace and Conflict Research, Uppsala University. She will defend her dissertation in the Fall of 2010. Her research primarily concerns security studies and the construction of threat images. Particular focus is on the broadened security agenda and the issue of HIV/AIDS in the United States and Russia. Previous articles by the author on discourse, securitization, identity, and norms, in the empirical settings of Russia, Estonia, and the United States, have been published in *Journal of Peace Research, Foreign Policy Analysis* and *Security Dialogue*.

Holger Stritzel is Lecturer of International Relations at the University of St Andrews, UK, specializing in International Relations, International Security, New European Security Theory and European Security. He has published on securitization theory, German foreign policy and critical approaches to security. Recent articles appeared in *European Journal of International Relations, Security Dialogue* and *Zeitschrift für Internationale Beziehungen*.

Fred Vultee is Assistant Professor of journalism at Wayne State University, where he teaches content analysis, editing, journalism history, and other courses. His research concentrates on the performance, functions, and impact of mass media in conflicts and crises, and he has published in journals such as *Media, War, and Conflict; Journalism Studies; Visual Communication Quarterly; The Journal of Mass Media Ethics;* and the *International Journal of Mass Emergencies and Disasters*. Before completing his PhD at the University of Missouri, he was an editor at US newspapers for 25 years.

Juha A. Vuori is a Senior Research Fellow at the Department of Political Science at the University of Turku in Finland. His research has focused on the critical development of securitization theory through illocutionary logic and through applying the approach to the study of politics in the People's Republic of China. His other research interests include online techniques of government, the politics of technology, and issues related to nuclear weapons. He has published in journals such as *European Journal of International Relations, Asian Journal of Political Science, Issues and Studies,* and *Politologiske Studier*. He is the current editor-in-chief of *Kosmopolis*, the journal of the Finnish Peace Research Association. He has co-edited volumes on Chinese politics and International Relations Theory development in Finnish, and is currently co-authoring an introductory book on Chinese contemporary history and politics.

Maria Julia Trombetta is a researcher at the Delft University of Technology. She has a PhD in International Politics from the University of Wales, Aberystwyth and degrees from the University of Pavia and from Bocconi University, Milan. She has been a Fulbright Scholar, working on comparative environmental politics. Her main research interests are critical approaches to security, environmental and energy politics. Recently, she has published on climate change and security in the *Cambridge Review of International Affairs* and is finalizing a monograph on environmental security. Maria Julia Trombetta is currently working on a project on energy security in Europe. She has taught at Aberystwyth and Oxford Brookes.

C. Wilkinson is currently a Lecturer in Russian at the Centre for Russian and East European Studies, University of Birmingham, UK. Her PhD (University of

Birmingham, 2009) was entitled "Interpreting Security: Grounding the Copenhagen School in Kyrgyzstan" and explored understandings of security in post-Akaev Kyrgyzstan with reference to the concepts of securitization and societal security within a broadly interpretivist methodology. Claire's work has previously been published in *Security Dialogue* and she has contributed chapters to books on fieldwork and the localization of international agency in Central Asia.

Michael C. Williams is Professor in the Graduate School of Public and International Affairs at the University of Ottawa. His research interests are in International Relations theory, security studies, and political thought. He is the author of *The Realist Tradition and the Limits of International Relations* (Cambridge University Press, 2005) and *Culture and Security: Symbolic Power and the Politics of International Security* (Routledge, 2007) and the editor of several books, including most recently, *Realism Reconsidered: The Legacy of Hans J. Morgenthau in International Relations* (Oxford University Press, 2007). His articles have appeared in journals including the *European Journal of International Relations, International Organization, International Studies Quarterly, Millennium,* and the *Review of International Studies.* He is currently completing a major research project with Dr Rita Abrahamsen on the globalization of private security. Prior to joining the University of Ottawa, he was Professor of International Politics in the Department of International Politics at Aberystwyth, and has been a visiting fellow at the Universities of Cape Town, Copenhagen, and the European University Institute in Florence.

Preface

This book is about securitization as a theory, a policy, and a framework.[1] Since the publication of Buzan, Wæver and de Wilde's *Security: A New Framework for Analysis* in 1998, securitization has become one of the dominant approaches to security. Building upon a mixture of theories of International Relations, securitization addresses the following interdependent questions: What counts as a security problem? Why do certain challenges become security issues while others do not? How are threat images realized in policies? Are the realms of security and politics compatible or mutually exclusive?

Provisionally, I define securitization as *a set of interrelated practices, and the processes of their production, diffusion, and reception/translation that bring threats into being*.[2] The innovation of securitization theory is important for changing the attitude of security theorists toward language. For securitization theory, language is not only concerned with what is "out there" as mainstream theories of International Relations hold, but is also constitutive of world politics. It is not only "representational". The natural tendency of mainstream approaches to international relations, such as Realism or Liberalism, is to explain insecurity by identifying an objective situation as threatening to an objective entity. To students of securitization, by contrast, threats are not separable from the intersubjective representations in which communities come to know them. In short, insecurity partakes of a distinctive type of shared knowledge.

There is one fundamental political consequence to this. Traditional approaches to security often limit the responsibility of political leaders to their ability in curbing a given menace. The realist argument of external threat, for example, masks the construction of threat images, and the equally important political functions it serves. On this view, leaders can only be held accountable for failing to take appropriate steps in confronting a threat. To students of securitization, by contrast, the very way threats are tackled depend upon how they are perceived which is not always commanded by the objectives features of what is called a "menace". Instead, the social design of a security problem conditions and legitimates the kind of means used to stop it. Thus, defining a menace is a normative political act. In other words, those who define a threat can be held accountable, as threats are also the product of their entrepreneurship.

Securitization is a popular area. The volume of articles produced in the last decade is impressive. There is now a rich (and growing) body of conceptual intuitions, theoretical claims, and hypotheses. In this context, the book argues that the main task facing students of securitization is not to add to the already long list of arguments and conjectures but instead to unpack and re-present these diverse approaches into a coherent set of assumptions guiding empirical research.

Securitization Theory aims to restructure securitization theory by developing a common theoretical ground upon which empirical studies can be grounded. To do so, it designs a new framework for analysis, which provides a sociological twist to understanding how security issues emerge, evolve and dissolve. My hope is that even when the contributions in this volume emphasize, in different ways, the three core assumptions offered in *A Theory of Securitization* (chapter 1 of this volume), or push them in a specific direction, students of securitization will have acquired some analytically rigorous means, in the form of a common language, which allows them to contribute to the construction of a comprehensive theory of securitization.

After a first round of (electronic) exchanges, the book began to take life in May 2009, at a workshop convened at the Centre for European Studies – Sciences Po Paris. This gave us the opportunity to test and improve the arguments of the chapters and to strengthen the book's coherence. I thank Renaud Dehousse and Linda Amrani respectively, the Director and the Administrative Manager of the Centre, who offered invaluable logistic support. During that Workshop, and even after, contributors fully played the game of delving into other authors' work and provided clear, often incisive, but always very helpful suggestions. The final product presented here owes much to their insights. They cannot, however, be blamed for all of what, as editor, I have done with their comments. I must acknowledge the impressive contribution of Stéphane Baele, Marjorie Legendre, Elisabeth Meur, and Léon Sampana, my research and teaching assistants. For so generously supporting my travels to places where the progress of the book and its results were discussed, I owe thanks to the Belgian National Fund for Scientific Research (FRS–FNRS). I would not have contemplated the book without Peter Burgess's encouragement to submit it to PRIO's New Security Studies series. Finally, I thank three anonymous reviewers for Routledge.

Thierry Balzacq
Lille (France)

Notes

1 The concept of "securitization" which was coined in the banking system was initially transposed into International Relations by Ole Wæver (1989).
2 For a comprehensive definition of securitization, however, see Chapter 1 of this volume.

1 A theory of securitization

Origins, core assumptions, and variants

Thierry Balzacq

This chapter reformulates the assumptions of securitization in a form appropriate to empirical studies and to the development of a comprehensive theory. Drawing on a variety of IR theories—constructivism, poststructuralism, critical theory—students of securitization aim to explicate the structures and processes that constitute security problems.[1] Securitization theory elaborates the insight that no issue is essentially a menace. Something becomes a security problem through discursive politics.[2] However, within securitization theory there are various ways to characterize this insight. On one side, those working in a poststructuralist tradition believe in a "social magic" power of language, a magic in which the conditions of possibility of threats are internal to the act of saying "security." "The *word* "security"', argues Waver (1995: 55), a pioneer of securitization studies, 'is the act . . . by saying it something is done.' In short, 'security is a speech act' (Ibid.).[3] In essence, the basic idea of the speech act theory is, simply expressed: certain statements, according to Austin, do more than merely describe a given reality and, as such, cannot be judged as false or true. Instead these utterances realize a specific action; they "do" things: they are "performatives" as opposed to "constatives" that simply report states of affairs and are thus subject to truth and falsity tests. This view, which is part of the philosophy of language fold, provides foundations for the Copenhagen School (CS) approach to securitization. Thus, I call it "philosophical."[4]

Others, including those with a social theory influence, talk about securitization primarily in terms of practices, context, and power relations that characterize the construction of threat images. The argument is that while discursive practices are important in explaining how some security problems originate, many develop with little if any discursive design. This variant is termed "sociological." It inspires most of the contributions of this volume.

There are three key differences between the philosophical and the sociological view of securitization. First is that the philosophical variant *ultimately* reduces security to a *conventional procedure* such as marriage or betting in which the "felicity circumstances" (conditions of success of speech act) must fully prevail for the act to go through. The sociological view argues, on the contrary, that securitization is better understood as a strategic (pragmatic) process that occurs within, and as part of, a configuration of circumstances, including the context, the psycho-cultural disposition of the audience, and the power that both speaker and listener bring to the interaction. In other words, if the strategic action of discourse operates at the level of persuasion and uses various artefacts (metaphors, emotions, stereotypes, gestures, silence, and even lies) to reach its goals, the speech act seeks to establish universal principles of communication, the value of which is to be functional whatever the context, culture, and whatever the relative power of the actors. In fact, this contrast between the strategic and speech act view of security parallels the difference between "pragmatics" and "universal pragmatics."[5] While the first deals with language usage, including a colourful use of language to attain a goal, universal pragmatics is primarily concerned with fundamental principles (or rules) underlying communicative action.[6]

Second is that, for the sociological variant, performatives are situated actions mediated by agents' *habitus*; that is, a set of dispositions that informs their perceptions and behaviors (Bourdieu 1990, 1991). Performatives are thus analyzed as nodal loci of practices, results of power games within the social field or context on the one hand, and between the latter and the *habitus* on the other. In this instance, the discourse of securitization manifests a distinct kind of agency, i.e., a 'temporally constructed engagement by actors of different structural environment—the temporal relational contexts of action—which, through the interplay of habit, imagination, and judgment, both reproduces and transforms those structures in interactive response to the problems posed by changing historical situation' (Emirbayer and Mische 1998:970).

Third is that audience is important for both philosophical and sociological approaches to securitization, but it is conceived in different terms by each. For the philosophical view, the audience is a formal—given—category, which is often poised in a receptive mode. The sociological view emphasizes, by contrast, the mutual constitution of securitizing actors and audiences. In this respect, audience is not necessarily a fully constituted entity, across the board, as the speech act tends to assumes, but an emergent category that must be adjudicated empirically, before being set as a level of analysis. This does not mean that the sociological model subscribes to the argument that speech act "creates" the audience, because this would transform audience into a pure byproduct of a speech act event.

Taken together, these three differences open a new avenue not available to the philosophical view. Securitization can be discursive and non-discursive; intentional and non-intentional; performative but not 'an act in itself'. In short, security problems can be designed or they can emerge out of different practices, whose initial aim (if they ever had) was not in fact to create a security problem. As Pouliot (2008: 261) puts it, following Bourdieu, 'social action is not necessarily preceded by a premeditated design. A practice can be oriented toward a goal without being consciously informed by it.' In this light, securitization consists of practices which instantiate *intersubjective* understandings through the *habitus* inherited from different, often competing social fields (Balzacq *et al.* 2010). The *dispositif* weaves these practices. Thus, in addition to discourse analysis, the sociological view argues that the study of securitization is compatible with other methods currently available in social sciences (see Chapter 2).

On the surface, the difference between the two variants seems rather stark. On closer inspection, however, the two variants are primarily ideal types, meaning that studies of securitization do not necessarily fall neatly within a particular category. In other words, examining the development of threats combines philosophical and sociological insights, with the proviso that statements about the "magical power" of speech acts are moderated. This is what Bourdieu attempted, if in a different domain, by insisting on the *symbolic power* of words, that is

the power of constituting the given through utterances, of making people see and believe, of confirming and transforming the vision of the world and, thereby, action on the world and the world itself, an *almost* magical power which enables one to obtain the equivalent of what is attained through (material) force . . ., by virtue of the specific effect of mobilization.[7]

In this citation, the qualification "almost" (in French: *presque or quasiment*) has been dropped by many commentators, but it is probably more important than often thought. In fact, for Bourdieu, the symbolic power *does not* pertain to the illocutionary force (in which case it will be absolute magic), but is, on the contrary, associated with the 'belief in the legitimacy of words and those who utter them.'[8] It is, therefore, mainly at the intersection of the legitimacy of agents involved and words used, that the symbolic power of security lies.

Securitization is not a self-referential practice but an *intersubjective* process.[9] Recall the definition proposed in the preface, whereby securitization was understood as *a set of interrelated practices, and the processes of their production, diffusion, and reception / translation that bring threats into being*. The strength of this definition is its parsimony. It has two main weaknesses, however. One, this definition is not so different from other conceptualizations of the construction of security problems. Two, it overlooks one of the fundamental constituents of securitization, namely time constraint or the sense of criticality (i.e., the time left before something purportedly irremediable, happens). I propose, in this light, to consolidate it.

I define securitization as *an articulated assemblage of practices whereby heuristic artefacts (metaphors, policy tools, image repertoires, analogies, stereotypes, emotions, etc.) are contextually mobilized by a securitizing actor, who works to prompt an audience to build a coherent network of implications (feelings, sensations, thoughts, and intuitions), about the critical vulnerability of a referent object, that concurs with the securitizing actor's reasons for choices and actions, by investing the referent subject with such an aura of unprecedented threatening complexion that a customized policy must be undertaken immediately to block its development*. Beginning with a critical investigation of its lineages (section I), this chapter codifies securitization theory in terms of three core assumptions from which the structure of the volume will be constructed: 1) the centrality of audience; 2) the co-dependency of agency and context; 3) the structuring force of the *dispositif*, that is, a constellation of practices and tools. This is the subject of section II. Facing the difficulty of mapping out different variants of securitization theory, section III reframes the distinction between the philosophical and the sociological variants of securitization in relation to their commitment to our three assumptions. In particular, it outlines how the association of the speech act (philosophical) view with "poststructuralism" leads to methodological impasses. The purpose of the chapter is to contribute to the development of a comprehensive theory of securitization, stripped of some of its original tensions, so that it can be easily deployed to explicate the development of specific security problems.[10]

Speech act protocols and the evolution of securitization

It is widely recognized that the commitment of securitization theory to speech act is inspired by Austin and Searle, probably the most prominent figures in developing the performativity of language in philosophy.[11] Thus, any attempt at revising, regrounding, and expanding the theoretical procedure of securitization requires a clarification of the central premises of the philosophy of speech acts. Such an undertaking risks disparagement, however: 'It is rather to insist,' warns Quentin Skinner (2002: 106), 'that we shall miss the relevance of speech act analysis if we think of it as just another piece of philosophical jargon that we can brush aside if we happen not to like the sound of it.' Therefore, heading this caveat, this section provides the reader with the conceptual instruments needed to proceed, I hope, smoothly through the remainder of the article. Basically, it seeks to shed light on how I reevaluate the CS study of security, the manner in which I try to remedy its weaknesses, and how, in practical terms, the position adopted here leads us to a concept of security as a pragmatic act.

Locutionary, illocutionary, perlocutionary[12]

The enterprise of speech act philosophy can be interpreted as a movement away from descriptive grammar and generative transformational thinking. The first claims that language is a question of "sound and meaning," whereas the second reduces language to truth conditional criteria of meaning. The latter position clearly lines up with logical positivism, with its belief that the meaning of sentences lies in the verifiability principle—whether a sentence can be classified as true or false.[13] Both assume, however, that linguistic communication is concerned with words, sentences and symbols *per se*. Taken together, these commitments pitch descriptive grammars and logical positivism against the speech act theory. In particular, the speech act theory puts emphasis on the function of language—doing things—and thus moves the unit of linguistic communication from symbols, words and sentences so as to locate it in the composition of these elements in 'the performance of . . . speech act(s)' (Searle 1969: 16). Thus, in contrast to logical positivism, that which constitute the primary units of linguistic communication are speech acts, where utterances are able to 'perform' an activity that can transform the way the world currently is.

From Austin's perspective, each sentence can convey three types of acts, the combination of which constitutes the total speech act situation: (i) locutionary—the utterance of an expression that contains a given sense and reference (Austin 1962: 95, 107); (ii) illocutionary—the act performed in articulating a locution. In a way, this category captures the explicit performative class of utterances, and as a matter of fact, the concept "speech act" is literally predicated on that sort of agency;[14] and (iii) perlocutionary, which is the "consequential effects" or "sequels" that are aimed to evoke the feelings, beliefs, thoughts or actions of the target audience. This triadic characterization of kind of acts is summed up by Jürgen Habermas (1984: 289) in the following: 'to say *something*, to act *in saying something*, to bring about something *through* acting in saying something.'[15]

It is important to note that illocutionary and perlocutionary acts diverge in the direction and the nature of consequences they initiate. The first, by convention, is bound up with effects that occur if and only if all four of the "felicity conditions" are met: (i) a preparatory condition determined by the existence of a 'conventional procedure having a certain conventional effect, that procedure to include the uttering of certain words by certain persons in certain circumstances'; (ii) an executive condition to determine whether the procedure has been fully executed by all participants; (iii) a sincerity condition that posits that participants in this 'conventional procedure' must have certain thoughts or feelings, and 'must intend so to conduct themselves'; (iv) a fulfillment condition determined by whether participants 'actually so conduct themselves subsequently' (Austin 1962: 14–15).

The second, perlocution, is 'specific to the circumstances of issuance, and is therefore not conventionally achieved just by uttering particular utterances, and includes all those effects, intended or unintended, often indeterminate, that some particular utterances in a particular situation may cause' (Ibid.).[16] The source of this unfortunate mistake rests on the false assumption that the speech act encompasses both the illocutionary and the perlocutionary act. This might be grounded in a more profound confusion between the term "speech act" that is the illocutionary act, and the "total situation of speech act," namely 'the total situation in which the utterance is issued . . . [and which allows us] to see parallel between statements and performative utterances [also referred to as speech acts, explicit performatives, or illocutionary act]' (Austin 1962: 52, 101–32).[17] Perlocution does not belong literally to speech act since it is the causal response of a linguistic act. Perlocution and illocution are 'often confused because part of the speaker's intent in issuing a speech act is to bring about the perlocutionary effect. Also, confusion comes about because success in achieving illocutionary effect (success in communicating via a speech act) is very often followed by success in achieving the perlocutionary effect (the desired causal result of many speech acts)' (Fotion 2000: 22). Paraphrasing Searle, Fotion argues that confusing illocutionary and perlocutionary leads to "bad philosophy." The reason is simple: the focus of speech acts is the *philosophy of language*; the focus of perlocution is *linguistic philosophy*. In other words, speech acts deal with language itself, how it functions in any language. On the other hand, linguistic philosophy is a mode of enquiry that tries to see how the analysis of language can help establish a link between the nature of reality and how we get to know that very reality. Perlocution falls into this category (Searle 1969: 3–4). Thus, if perlocution does not adhere to rules conditioning the realization of an illocutionary act, which the CS paraphrases for its definition of security and securitization, it becomes plain that viewing security as a speech act is a restrictive theoretical position. Equally, in any *intersubjective* process such as securitization, the purpose is to prompt a significant response from the other (perlocutionary effect); unless this happens there is no securitization. Necessarily, then, perlocution is central rather than tangential to understanding how a particular public issue can change into a security problem.

Recent advances on securitization and performativity

The potential and the weaknesses of the philosophical view of securitization have been exposed by several researchers. For instance, in their writings, Stritzel, McDonald, and Vuori advocate a different reading and/or a sustained revision of securitization theory. The former investigates the 'conceptual tension' which pervades securitization theory, according to which security is at once a speech act *event* and the result of a negotiated process between an actor and the relevant audience (i.e., an *inter-subjective* endeavour). In developing his critique of securitization theory, Stritzel observes, and subsequent research tends to confirm, that this tension undermines the development of a comprehensive theory of securitization most fundamentally. Put simply, it is the contention that 'the (decisionist) performativity of security utterances as opposed to the social process of securitization, involving (pre-existing) actors, audience(s) and context(s), are so different that they form two rather autonomous centres of gravity' (Stritzel 2007: 364).[18] The argument, however, extends beyond finding the right centre of gravity of securitization theory to the difficulty of determining whether securitization has occurred. As he recalls, in 'empirical studies one cannot always figure out clearly which audience is when and why most relevant, what implications it has if there are several audiences and when exactly an audience is "persuaded"' (Ibid.: 363). In recognition of this, McDonald (2008: 573) argues that there is 'a clear need . . . to draw the role of the audiences into the framework more coherently, but in doing so the CS will almost certainly need to downplay either the performative effects of the speech act or the inter-subjective nature of security.' Thus, adds, McDonald (2008: 572): 'how we know when (securitization) happens (is) radically under-theorized . . . ' Though often implicit, then, the performative aspect of securitization (i.e., the productive power of speech act event) is the rule, not the exception.

In one of the most perceptive if radical discussions of securitization theory, Ken Booth (2007) sees comparable difficulties. He argues, for instance, that 'the *existence* and salience of a security issue does not depend on the political success of an actor reaching out a particular audience,' and that 'if security is always a speech act, insecurity is frequently a zipped lip' (emphasis in the original; Booth 2007: 167, 168). The point here is not that Booth is either correct or wrong, but rather to illustrate the idea that the lack of a clear position upon whether securitization is primarily of an *intersubjective* nature or an illocutionary (self-referential) act, is susceptible to lead to different kinds and often contradictory readings of securitization theory.

Vuori (2008) raises different kinds of challenges to securitization theory, at different levels of conceptualization, and sees different strategies available for coping with them. For instance, in order to operationalize securitization processes in a non-democratic context, Vuori (2008: 76) emphasizes the function of security utterances, by distinguishing four strands of securitization: '(1) Securitization for raising an issue on the agenda, (2) the securitization for deterrence, (3) securitization for legitimating past acts or for reproducing the security status of an issue, and (4) securitization for control.' This is justified insofar as these strands shape the framework of analysis, but it means that revising securitization theory relates more to method than to unpacking some of the tensions identified by Stritzel and McDonald, for instance. However, to the extent that conceptual epithets are implicated in the way social processes are studied, questions of methods are ineluctably linked to substantive issues (Little 1991; George and Bennett 2005). In effect, as Wendt (1999: 34) correctly notes, 'while . . . methods do not determine substantive theory . . . they are not always substantively innocent.' In this light, the four strands raise a difficulty as they adjudicate the theoretical leverage of securitization against its political functions (e.g., deterrence, agenda setting, control). This nonetheless allows Vuori to recast the theoretical polemics about whether audience acceptance (i.e., perlocutionary act) should be a matter of concern for students of securitization into a discussion about the logics of illocutionary speech acts, and the different political functions they complete: 'The criteria for successful securitization,' he argues, 'depend on the function security arguments are intended to serve' (Vuori 2008: 73). Thus, he reclaims a privileged theoretical status for illocutionary act, which comports the rare advantage of being applicable to different contexts, but pitches it at a functionalist level by reducing the success of securitization to the function of arguments (Vuori 2008: 66, 68, 75–76).[19]

More recently, a number of scholars have argued for the need to reset audience's role in the process of securitization. Among the theoretical innovations advanced is an attempt to avoid "false generalizations" (Ruzicka 2009; Balzacq and Léonard 2009). The key argument is that both successful and failed securitizations, are best captured by disaggregating the audience, as different audiences are receptive to different kinds of arguments, and have distinct types of power. For instance, Salter (2008) focuses on the importance of developing an analytical capacity to determine whether securitization has occurred. To do so, he dwells on Goffman and Huysmans. From the former, he borrows a concern with dramaturgical analysis and the importance of setting; from the latter, he retains the drive to account for the diversity of audiences. To think in terms of dramaturgical analysis and multiple audiences is to insist upon the variability of securitizing moves. In other words, 'securitizing moves in popular, elite, technocratic, and scientific settings are markedly different—they operate according to different constitutions of actor and audience' (Salter 2008: 329; see also Chapter 6 in this volume).

Contrary to the speech act philosophy, according to which the securitizing actor and the audience remain unchanged, whatever the context, Salter (2008: 329) argues, in Goffman's vein, that 'the presentation of the self changes from different social settings, and that an understanding of the setting can illuminate the exigencies of different performances.' Both the securitizing move and the acceptance of audience are enabled and constrained by the setting (Salter 2008: 328). In turn, argues Salter (2008: 330), 'the relationship between the audience and the performer structures how . . . speech acts are made and received.' This relationship seems particularly apposite for processes of securitization because how securitizing moves are accepted or rejected is function of 'the grand narratives by which truth is authorized, the characters who are empowered to speak, and the relationships between characters and audience' (Ibid.).

These studies all converge around one decisive point: the principle that securitization requires acceptance by an audience is a distinctive feature of securitization theory. Throughout this section, we have made the case that these studies suggest the potential fruitfulness of clarifying the nature, the types, and functions of audience(s). This permitted a focused engagement with existing conceptual literature, but might have suggested that we subscribe to a causal approach to securitization in which all that matters is whether audience "decides" to back up the claims of the securitizing actor, or a tit-for-tat one in which all that matters is the differential power between the securitizing actor and the audience. We advocate neither. That audience subscribes to a threat image for it to produce political effects is important, and the quantum of power is rarely even. However, what empirical evidence we have indicates that the demanding assumption of securitization theory that an—observable—audience must agree with the securitizing claims, generates tremendous problems (compare Abrahamsen 2005; Hansen 2006; Huysmans 2006). There are indeed two main disadvantages. First, threat images that become prevalent in a society, without explicit audience assent, cannot be captured in terms of securitization theory, nor participate in the development of the conceptual apparatuses of the latter. Second, as a consequence, other approaches to understanding the emergence of security issues are treated either as subordinate of, or as substitute for securitization theory. This is unwarranted. On the one hand, keeping the assumption of audience assent in securitization theory yields difficult inference obstacles. On the other hand, dropping it would be fatal to the argument that securitization is an inter-subjective process. Only by restricting this premise is it possible for securitization theory to integrate the ideas of alternative views of the formation of security problems, and propose results that were previously untapped. That means that audience can only be one element of a larger theoretical pattern in securitization studies, one which draws its importance in relation to others.

Core assumptions of securitization theory

In order to improve our empirical studies, securitization studies must generate theoretical assumptions about intersubjectivity, context, and practices. Toward this end, this section presents and discusses three core assumptions of securitization, respectively, the centrality of audience, the co-dependency of agency and context, and the *dispositif* and the structuring force of practices. This restatement of securitization provides foundations on which the development of a coherent theory of securitization can be built.

Assumption 1: The centrality of audience

For an issue to be pronounced an instance of securitization, an 'empowering audience' must agree with the claims made by the securitizing actor. The empowering audience is the audience which:

a) has a direct causal connection with the issue; and b) has the ability to enable the securitizing actor to adopt measures in order to tackle the threat. In sum, securitization is satisfied by the acceptance of the empowering audience of a securitizing move.

Despite pervasive ambiguities surrounding agents' perception of a threatening external development or a state of affairs, it can be argued that the success of securitization is highly contingent upon the securitizing actor's ability to identify with the audience's feelings, needs, and interests (see Edelman 1988). To persuade the audience (e.g., the public), that is, to achieve a perlocutionary effect, the speaker has to tune his/her language to the audience's experience. In fact, identification is the perspective through which the cognitive and behavioral change induced by security utterances can perhaps be accounted for most explicitly. This is demonstrated by the work of Kenneth Burke (1955: 55) for whom an effective persuasion requires that a speaker's argument employs terms that resonate with the hearer's language by 'speech, gesture, tonality, order, image, attitude, idea, identifying (her/his) ways with (her/his).' Indeed, securitizing actors 'develop maps of target populations based on both the stereotypes (of the referent subject) they themselves hold and those they believe to prevail among that segment of the public likely to become important to them' (Schneider and Ingram 1993: 336).

The securitizing actor is sensitive to two kinds of supports, formal and moral (see Roe 2008). They can be congruent or not; nonetheless the more congruent they are, the more likely the public issue will be successfully securitized. Be that as it may, although moral support conditions formal backing, the two should not be conflated; they are of a different status and are unequally distributed depending on whether the target audience is a formal institution. For example, to wage a war against a country to rid the state of a threat—real or perceived—political officials will appeal for moral support from both the public and the institutional body whose attitude has a *direct causal connection* with the desired goals. But while moral support is generally necessary, alone, it is not enough. Often, it is the formal decision by an institution (for instance in the form of a vote by a Parliament, Security Council, or Congress) that mandates the government to adopt a specific policy. This support is, generally, necessary and sufficient. The requirement of a "direct causal connection with desired goals" is important because audiences do not have the same "power over" a given securitizing actor. As we know, states can do without the U.N. Security Council, but generally need the support of their legislative branch to launch a military action. Be that as it may, securitizing agents always strive to convince an audience as broad an audience as possible because they need to maintain a social relationship with the target individual group (Kasper 1990: 205). In common with the desire to transmit information, political officials are responsive to the fact that winning formal support while breaking social bonds with constituencies can wreck their credibility. That explains why, while seeking formal acquiescence, political officials also cloak security arguments in the semantic repertoire of the national audience in order to win support. The following text, articulated by the Greek orator Demosthenes, is particularly useful in understanding the impact of this technique.

Had my opponents urged the right policy in the past, this discussion would be superfluous.

First, then, we must not be downhearted at the present situation, however regrettable it seems. . . . The fact that it is plain dereliction of duty on our part which has brought us to this position. . . . Why mention this? To set this fact firmly before your minds, gentlemen, that if you are awake, you have nothing to fear, if you close your eyes, nothing to hope for. To prove this I point to two things, the past power of Sparta, which we defeated by sheer attention to business, and the present aggression of Macedon, which alarms us because our attitude is wrong. If the belief is held that Philip is an enemy hard to face in view of the extent of his present strength and the loss to Athens of strategic points, it is a correct belief. But it must be remembered that at one time we had Pydna, Potidaea, Methone and the whole surrounding district on friendly terms, and that a number of communities now on his side . . . would have preferred our friendship to his. . . . Consider the facts, consider the outrageous lengths to which Philip has gone. He does not offer us the choice between action and inaction. He utters threats. . . . When are we to act? What is the signal? When compulsion drives, I suppose. Then what are we to say of the present? In my view the greatest compulsion that can be laid upon free men is their shame at the circumstances in which they find themselves.

First, then, gentlemen, I declare the need to provide fifty triremes, and secondly to arouse a spirit in the men of this country which will recognize that . . . they must serve in them in person. Further, transports and sufficient smaller craft for half the cavalry must be provided. This I maintain should be a standing force to use for immediate moves away from home. . . . The idea must be implanted in Philip's mind that Athens has abandoned inaction, and may make a sudden move.

When you vote . . . you will be giving your vote for action against Philip, and action not confined to the words of manifestos and dispatches.

(as quoted in Saunders 1970: 188–89, 190–91, 193–94)

Threatened by Philip of Macedon, Demosthenes tries to get his audience to vote for action and provide necessary means—financing an expeditionary force against Philip—to alleviate the danger he represents to the good life of Athenians. Demosthenes' choice of language to sway audience's attitude and arouse action is characterized by a high sense of urgency—'This I maintain should be a standing force to use *for immediate moves away from home.*' To convince them to stand by his side, Demosthenes connects to his audience by using inclusive plural pronouns like "our," "us," "we." Two modalities affect the semantic repertoire upon which Demosthenes, as any securitizing actor, draws, in order to fuse his/her perspective with his audience's: collective memories, products of social experiences—'it must be remembered that'—and the *Zeitgeist* (spirit of the times) reflected in words that convey the general feeling prevalent among Athenians—'We must not be downhearted at the present situation,' and 'If the belief is held that Philip is an enemy hard to face in view of the extent of his present strength and the loss to Athens of strategic points, it is a correct belief.' Further, although the *Zeitgeist* can be rooted in collective memory, it is mostly constituted by the predominant social views, trends, ideological and political attitudes that pervade the context in which participants are nested—'Consider the facts, consider the outrageous lengths to which Philip has gone. He does not offer us the choice between action and inaction.' In turn, as it appears in the excerpt, collective memory and the *Zeitgeist* condition how a given community perceives and symbolizes urgency, the kind of language likely to induce an audience to change its ideas on a subject and convey political immediacy (Bar-Tal 2000: 87–90; White 1992: 146). The essence of this point of view is the assumption that speaking is an action, and that the question of expedient agency underlies any attempt to securitize a public issue by eliciting a suitable attitude.

Assumption 2: The co-dependency of agency and context

The semantic repertoire of security is a combination of textual meaning—knowledge of the concept acquired through language (written and spoken)—and cultural meaning—knowledge gained through previous interactions and current situations. Thus, the performative dimension of security rests between semantic regularity and contextual circumstances.

Let us restate the baseline assumptions for our treatment of securitization. The CS endorses the postulate that language is performative; in other words, by uttering the term security the previous state of affairs changes. This highlights what the speech act approach to security consists of: modifying the context through the enunciation of utterances, the success of which hangs upon "felicity conditions" (necessary and sufficient rules that must prevail for linguistic acts to produce their effects), and for communication to be practicable. It implies that if the speech act is achieved under prescribed rules, the context alters accordingly; hence, a formerly secure place will become insecure. On this internalist approach, the context is shaped by the use of the concept of security. Thus, security, or at least its illocutionary force, remodels the context in which it occurs. What is key here is the "abductive power" of words; indeed, as an abductive tool, the concept of security permits the activation of a new context, or converts the existing one into something different. In this sense, security utterances operate as 'instructions for the construction and interpretation of the situation. The power of these tools is such that appropriate conditions can be created when they are not textually or contextually erased' (Violi 2001: 187). I would like to follow Patrizia Violi's ideas on this to their logical conclusion. I interpret Violi to mean that words create their own conditions of receptiveness by modifying, or building a fitting context. To illustrate something of what is at stake, consider the story of the Popish Plot that involved Catholics in England in 1678. Eugene E. White (1992: 108) recounts it in remarkable terms:

[A] perjurer, Titus Oates, projected a complex, fabricated story that Catholics were conspiring to murder [King] Charles, substitute his Catholic brother, and restore England to Catholics by rebellion. This tale led much of Protestant society to believe that a provoking crisis of gravest immediacy actually existed. It was widely thought that in coordinated strikes the Catholics were going to massacre thousands of Protestants and that the queen was in league with assassination attempts on her husband's life. Largely on the basis of invented evidence supplied by Oates and testimony given by a known conspirator and confidence man, William Bedloe, seven men were executed for treason and [consequently] a Disabling Act was passed excluding Roman Catholics from both houses of Parliament. Although there was no "real" urgency to the conspiracy, it constituted a very "real" substance to the alarmed Protestants, and through the rhetoric of their Parliament and their Courts they modified the alleged exigency to their satisfaction.

This segment reveals how linguistic content can modify a context by investing an individual group with a specific ominous tone. For members of the CS, this is a clear articulation of the Janus-faced nature of security: a practice and a discourse, or, indeed, a 'discursive politics of security.'[20] Highlighted in this context, the word "security" does not point towards an objective reality; it is an agency in itself to the extent that it conveys a self-referential practice instantiated by discourses on existential threats that empower political elites to take policy measures (sometimes extraordinary) to alleviate "insecurity." Furthermore, this approach reinforces the CS view that "real rhetorical urgency" does not always equal the existence of a "real threat." The radical approach to the relation between language and the facts surrounding it can be described like this: what is decisive for security is what language constructs and, as a consequence, what is "out there" is thus irrelevant (compare Campbell 1992: 1–2; Knudsen 2001).

However, despite important insights, this position remains highly disputable. The reason behind this qualification is not hard to understand. With great trepidation my contention is that one of the main distinctions we need to take into account while examining securitization is that between "institutional" and "brute" threats. In its attempts to follow a more radical approach to security problems wherein threats are institutional, that is, mere products of communicative relations between agents, the CS has neglected the importance of "external or brute threats," that is, threats that do not depend on language mediation to be what they are: hazards for human life. In methodological terms, however, any framework over-emphasizing either institutional or brute threat risks losing sight of important aspects of a multifaceted phenomenon. Indeed, securitization, as suggested earlier, is successful when the securitizing agent and the audience reach a common structured perception of an ominous development. In this scheme, there is no security problem except through language game. Therefore, *how* problems are "out there" is exclusively contingent upon how we linguistically depict them. This is not always true. For one language does not construct reality; at best, it shapes our perception of it. Moreover, it is not theoretically useful nor is it empirically credible to hold that what we say about a problem would *determine* its essence. For instance, what I say about a typhoon would not change its essence. The consequence of this position, which would require a deeper articulation, is that some security problems are the attribute of the development itself. In short, threats are not only institutional; some of them can actually wreck entire political communities regardless of the use of language. Analyzing security problems then becomes a matter of understanding how external contexts, including external objective developments affect securitization. Thus, far from being a departure from constructivist approaches to security, external developments are central to it.

Specifically, a large part of what is going on in securitization is overlooked by an internalist view of the context, the logic of which overstates the intrinsic power of a rule-governed use of concepts. The fact is, to move an audience's attention toward an event or a development construed as dangerous, the words of the securitizing actor need to resonate with the context within which his/her actions are collocated. With this awareness of the limits of an internalist position, I would like to advance a second, externalist approach to connecting security utterances to a context.

While the CS insists that the concept of security modifies the context by virtue of a successful application of the constitutive rules of a speech act (illocutionary act), I suggest, on the contrary, that to win an audience, security statements must, usually, be related to an external reality (Grace 1987: 48–49). Hence success, that is, the possibility of marshalling the assent of an audience (perlocutionary effect), rests with whether the historical conjuncture renders audience more sensitive to its vulnerability. If so, the alarming discourse put on the "marketplace of ideas" by the elites would elicit the required conduct from the masses (Snyder and Ballentine 1996; Kaufman 1996). This means that the success of securitization is contingent upon a perceptive environment. Therefore, the positive outcome of securitization, whether it is strong or weak, lies with the securitizing actor's choice of determining the appropriate times within which the recognition, including the integration of the "imprinting" object—a threat—by the masses is facilitated.[21] This tends to subscribe, moreover, to the view that the public would accept the description of threats deployed by elites, and securitization will successfully take place, if the times are critical enough.

A simple idea underlies this, though the details might be arcane. We agree that when the concept "security" is used, it forces the audience to "look around" in order to identify the conditions (the presumed threats) that justify its articulation. In other words, the context "selects" or activates certain properties of the concept, while others are concealed. This sensitivity to the modeling function of the context is to a large extent that which activates some properties of the concept while at the same time maintains other properties, naturalized parts of the semantic repertoire of security (Williams 1976: 21–22). In this respect, the conditions for success of the Popish Plot can be seen under a fresh light. Of course, the aforementioned internalist interpretation possessed elements of cogency: rhetoric, in short, catalyzed the sense of urgency. Yet, while there may be little harm in relying on the intrinsic properties of words to explain how Titus Oates maneuvered England toward his position, overlooking the broader context of seventeenth century England would be shortsighted. Indeed, research in the success of securitization should also examine the facilitating conditions that predisposed Britons to agree with Oates's ideas. In this respect, two important contextual factors are noteworthy. First, at the domestic level, England was still very traumatized by London's 1666 fire, for which Catholics were thought to be responsible. In addition, many Protestants scorned the prospect of having James who was a Catholic, succeed his brother upon death. Second, at the European level, England felt economically threatened by France's King Louis XIV, a Catholic, who had just invaded the Netherlands and tightened his hold on Spain. Taken together, these circumstances made the masses ripe for persuasion; indeed the context could have served to cause this directly. Oates used the context purposefully by stressing the dangers that were allegedly lurking for Britons, and, as a result, he convinced England to espouse his concerns and take action against the Catholics.

Actually, every securitization is a historical process that occurs between antecedent influential set of events and their impact on interactions; that involves concurrent acts carrying reinforcing or aversive consequences for securitization. Because securitization is the product of such a complex repertoire of causes, an investigation focused on a unique factor (e.g., speech acts) may fail if other elements exert a significant influence on the process. To analyze the construction of a security problem, then, we ought to take note of the fact that any securitization 'encompasses not only the particular piece(s) of persuasion that we are interested in but also all other successful and abortive attempts at modification that are relevant to experiencing that rhetoric' (White 1992: 13).[22] Thus, the semantic repertoire of security rests with overarching consequences for a given community, for instance, the possibility for a people's slaughter. The semantic repertoire of security is, to reiterate, a combination of textual meaning and cultural meaning. Taken together, these two kinds of meanings form a frame of reference through which security utterances can be understood. Chapter 4 reflects on the implications of framing for securitization theory and looks at empirical illustrations through content analysis. Chapter 9 attempts to clarify the work of the semantic repertoire of security not only in the diffusion of threat images, but also in the translation of distinctive dynamics of security, from one cultural context to another. This suggests something close to Bubandt's (2005: 276, 291) argument that the 'concept of security is contextualized in terms of local political histories' and that 'security is conceptualized and politically practised differently in different places and at different times.'

The role of a frame is to structure various properties of an entity or development under the same label—"threat"—by virtue of the conventions governing the use of the concept and the conditions under which its invocation is justified. More pragmatically, the basic idea is this: the performative dimension of security sits between semantic regularity and contextual circumstances. Indeed, security utterances are complex strings of creative and performative arguments pointing toward an external threatening referent subject.[23] It is not necessary, in attempting to understanding a security issue, to have recourse to an abstract definition that functions as formal "barbed wire," and thus constrains its application to different agents' domains of experience. I posit that security utterances are linguistic 'marks intended to recall or direct the attention (of the audience) to some person, object, idea, event or projected activity . . .' (Sapir 1934: 492).[24] This enables us to say that security is a symbol. What is involved in the mediation of the symbolic aspect of security is an elucidation that points to specific features of natural or social development which, in turn, influences the action of the other, or of the assembly, as the case applies.[25] The symbol of security is isomorphic, that is, although it is a naturalized frame, it is also shaped by current information about the context, and the influence of the speaker's discourse (see Balzacq 2004).

In fact, the mobilization of security arguments requires a judgment of best fit between the state of affairs or a development and a voiced utterance. To use Philip N. Johnson-Laird's (1983: 471) words, the manifest content of security discourse 'is usually a blueprint for a state of affairs: it relies on the (audience) to flesh out the missing details.' It is important to note, however, that security utterances can only have a meaning 'for those who know how to interpret them in terms of that which they refer' (Sapir 1934: 492). Therefore the meaning of security derives from the mutual recognition of the content of the threatening object that is symbolically referred to. The configuration of securitization evolves within a symbolic context of forces that define what a conceptual event (security) is for an audience, and when the use of that concept resonates with the context in order to increase or win the support for the enunciator's policy.

Assumption 3: The dispositif and the structuring force of practices

Securitization occurs in a field of struggles. It thus consists of practices which instantiate intersubjective understandings and which are framed by tools and the habitus inherited from different social fields. The dispositif connects different practices.

Securitization is not necessarily the result of a rational design wherein goals are set beforehand, following a predetermined agenda. The thrust of the argument is that beneath and above the discursive "level" loom subtle yet decisive processes of securitization that only an approach through practices can disclose. 'Practices,' writes Reckwitz (2002: 249), are

a routinized type of behaviour which consists of several elements, interconnected to one another: forms of bodily activities, forms of mental activities, 'things' and their use, a background knowledge in the form of understanding and know-how, states of emotion and motivational knowledge.[26]

Security practices are enacted, primarily, through policy tools. Given the thickness of security programs, in which discourses and ideologies are increasingly hard to disentangle, and differences between securitizing actors and audiences are blurred, there is growing evidence that some manifestations of securitization might best be understood by focusing on the nature and functions of policy tools used by agents/agencies to cope with public problems, defined as threats. In other words, the study of tools is not reducible to an analysis of their endogenous, technical functions. Instead, because operating tools activates a specific *dispositif*,[27] they can be regarded as basic elements contributing to the emergence of a security field and in the routinization of practices (i.e., *habitus*). Security tools or instruments are the social devices through which professionals of (in)security think about a threat. They contribute to the taken-for-grantedness of security practices. Tools rest upon a form of background knowledge about a threat, and the way it needs to be confronted. Balzacq (2008: 79) defines the instruments of securitization as 'an identifiable social and technical "dispositif" embodying a specific threat image through which public action is configured to address a security issue' (cf. Linder and Peters 1984; Salamon 2002: 19; Lascoumes and Galès 2004: 13). Put differently, security tools embody practices.

This definition, imperfect as it may be, offers four basic characteristics of the instruments of securitization. First, each tool of securitization has *defining features* that align it with others, and *design traits* that make it unique or, at least, vary from one program to another. For instance, all European Union (EU) Justice and Home Affairs databases require the collection, storage and exchange of information, but they differ significantly in the nature of the information they collect, the duration of the storage, and the conditions under which they can be retrieved. Second, tools configure actions, in the sense that each instrument 'has its own operating procedures, skills requirements, and delivering mechanisms, indeed its own "political economy"' (Salamon 2002: 2). What is involved here, moreover, is the idea that tools are institutions of sorts, which means they are routinized sets of rules and procedures that structure the interactions among individuals and organizations. A nuclear weapon, for example, does not only provide a sense of security or power to the state that acquires the capacity to design one; it also alters the relationships between the latter and other states and thus transforms the configuration of the international system. In short, policy tools shape social relations in decisive ways. In this respect, by their very nature, tools 'define who is involved in the operation of public programs, what their roles are, and how they relate to each other' (Ibid.19). Third, the tools of securitization reconfigure what is called public action, the aim of which is to address issues identified as threats. Fourth and finally, tools embody a specific image of the threat and, to a large extent, what ought to be done about it (Balzacq *et al.* 2010). In this respect, EU Justice and Home Affairs databases, for example, do not only quantify but also categorize individuals entering into and moving within the EU area, as well as commanding a particular method of policing: tracing and localizing those whose marks are stored in the databases.

From what has been said, it follows that knowledge of security instruments and their attributes reflects something of the threat that public action is meant to respond to. Further, it reveals policy preferences and the direction of action. In spite of basic similar attributes, each tools of securitization phases in different effects. In fact, different tools are not equally effective in all cases. Moreover, sometimes, security instruments have limited consequences or indirect effects. It becomes therefore obvious that the function of an instrument has a major impact on securitization. This function rests, in turn, on the nature of the tool.

Thus, the policy instruments of securitization do not represent a pure technical solution to a public problem. Of course, the operational, i.e., technical character of any security instrument, has to be adequately linked with a specific issue that it intends to address. However, a narrow focus on the operational aspect of security tools neglects two crucial features of instruments, namely the political and symbolic elements. On the one hand, the tools of securitization are fundamentally political. To put this point another way, both the selection and use, as well as the effects of security instruments depend on political factors and require political mobilization (Peters 2002: 552). It should thus be kept in mind that while security tools might have technical attributes, why they are chosen, how they operate and evolve, and what their consequences are cannot be reduced to the technical particulars of the instruments. On the other hand, there are symbolic attributes built-in policy instruments 'that [tell] the population what the [securitizing actor] is thinking . . . and what its collective perception of problems . . . [is]' (Peters and van Nispen 1998: 3). In other words, the focus on the political and symbolic aspects of security tools will allow for an imaginative leap into a more robust conceptualization of how 'the intention of policy could be translated into operational activities' (de Bruijn and Hufen 1998: 12).

Broadly speaking, security practices relate essentially to two kinds of tools: regulatory and capacity instruments.

Regulatory instruments

The starting-point here is that regulatory tools seek to "normalize" the behavior of target individuals (e.g., policy regulation, constitution, etc.). Policy instruments of this sort thus aim to influence the behaviors of social actors by permitting certain practices to reduce the threat; by prohibiting some types of political activities which are transformed into a menace; by promoting certain perceptions of threat—e.g., since 2002 almost all of the documents on illegal migration and asylum (in Western countries) have a strong connection to terrorism (Balzacq and Carrera 2005; Balzacq *et al.* 2006). Moreover, what makes regulatory instrument so attractive is that they often provide the framework within which capacity tools operate.

Capacity tools

These are the most contentious tools of the EU strategy on counter-terrorism, yet they are the most preferred. In simple terms, capacity tools often call for enablement skills, that is skills that allow individuals, groups and agencies to make decisions and carry out activities, which have a reasonable probability of success (Ingram and Schneider 1990: 517). Whereas regulative tools relates essentially to the processes of governmentality, capacity tools are specific modalities for imposing external discipline upon individuals and groups (compare Boswell 2007 and Neal 2009). In this sense, capacity tools include, *inter alia*, information (personal and non-personal), training, force, and other resources necessary to attain policy purposes (e.g., nuclear weapons). Finally, capacity instruments are hardly stable. EU internal security databases, for example, are always under pressure to adopt new protocols and practices, to extend their functions, and to mobilize new resources to attend to the transformations of what is perceived as a precarious environment (Bigo and

Tsoukala 2008). Tools change through practices; in turn, tools ineluctably affect practices.

To summarize: the important point that stands out from this section is that the speech act model of security, emphasis the creation, not the construction of security problems. In other words, it conceals more than it reveals about the design, let alone the emergence of security problems. One of the lessons to be drawn is that perlocutionary effect is not *literally* part of the speech act (see Fotion 2000). There are crucial differences, which the philosophical view overlooked. Thus, to palliate this shortcoming and, as a result, strengthen the theory of securitization, I have developed the view that securitization should be understood as a pragmatic (sociological) practice, as opposed to a universal pragmatics (speech act), the aim of which is to determine the universal principles of an effective communicative action of security. Another lesson is that, if from the standpoint of the CS, an effective securitization is derivable from the magical power of the speech act, the sociological approach embeds securitization in a configuration of circumstances, the congruence of which facilitates its realization. Of course, the circumstances leading to securitization vary in form and content; it would therefore be presumptuous to think that they can be grasped comprehensively. However, in order to make the analysis of securitization more tractable, I have narrowed down their number by arguing, in substance, that the conditions underlying the effectuation of securitization fall into at least three set of assumptions, pertaining respectively to the audience, the context and the *dispositif*.

Some may contend that these assumptions cannot tell us what causes securitization. To this I will answer: the problem of a strict causality in securitization dynamics is probably an inaccurate frame. Indeed, rather than looking for a one-directional relationship between some or all of the three factors highlighted, it could be profitable to focus on the degree of congruence between them. This does not mean that I am writing off causality from the analysis of securitization; instead, what I would like to propose is to inquire into causal adequacy rather than causal determinacy. It seems to me that one of the best ways to do this is through an examination of the degree of congruence between different circumstances driving and/or constraining securitization. The advantage is noteworthy: an investigation of *degrees of congruity* enables us to determine the relative status of one of the forces within the *network of causality*. Since it is tricky to identify a precise causal link as the exclusive source of a securitized issue, investigating congruence between, for instance, the strategies of the securitizing actor, the frame of reference of the audience, the immediate context, and the work of the *dispositif*, may yield more credible results. In other words, rather than clinging to set of a priori universal principles, the analysis of the degree of congruence among relevant concurrent forces should better guide attempts at understanding securitization, because how these various factors blend tells us a great deal about the likely outcome of the process.

Two models of securitization

There are many ways of scripting securitization. It is generally assumed that there are two variants of securitization, a linguistic and a non-linguistic. This categorization has gained wide currency, but it is moot because the so-called non-linguistic approach integrates many features of a linguistic view. To put it more precisely, the non-linguistic does not, contrary to what the labels insinuate, negate the linguistic. Moreover, what is regarded as the linguistic approach draws on the philosophy of language, whereas what is said to be "non-linguistic" dwells on linguistic philosophy (see section II above). Ultimately, I argue, the question is not whether an approach is non-linguistic or not. Most of them are. The lines of demarcation are shaped, instead, by the degree to which variants of securitization are committed to the aforementioned assumptions. Drawing on these assumptions, then, I isolate two ideal-typical approaches to securitization, the philosophical and the sociological.

Philosophical securitization: self-referentiality and Derridean speech act

Because the philosophical view has not really given much attention to the non discursive aspects of securitization, this section examines its commitments to two of the three assumptions developed above (i.e., audience and context). It looks in particular at the two issues at the centre of a sociological (pragmatic) reformulation of securitization: 1) the meaning and implications of speech act theory; 2) the conflation of poststructuralism with the speech act view of security. Each addresses a particular vulnerability in the CS theory of securitization. First, it is argued that by mixing perlocutionary and illocutionary acts together, the CS obscures the role of audience(s) in securitization theory. This point actually reiterates the argument made in Section I. Second, by following Derrida, who blends linguistic act theory with poststructuralism, the CS belies the distinctive contribution of each approach to discourse analysis. These two problems are related, because how we understand securitization will depend on two choices—whether to focus on illocutionary or perlocutionary acts, and whether to deploy textual or practice analysis (Neumann and Heikka 2005). Specifically, a focus on the illocutionary has led the CS to skirt the distinctive role of the audience, while an emphasis on textualism has left it unable to account for the impact of context on securitization.

The speech act politics of security

Many works that have come to constitute the standard argument about securitization rest upon the philosophical view. Speech act theory and in some instances, poststructuralist concepts have thus been applied, albeit with varying success, to a broad range of substantive issues such as identity (Buzan, Wæver and de Wilde 1998: 119–40), infectious disease (Elbe 2006; Vieira 2007), transnational crime and human trafficking (Emmers 2003; Jackson 2006), and religion (Laustsen and Wæver 2000). But the transferability of philosophical concepts to such a spectrum of issues has a perverse effect. The problem is essentially one of consistency in their substantive assumptions, as there is a disconnect between the theoretical premises and the method that follows (Léonard 2007). Indeed, within the philosophical model of securitization, most substantive studies fall outside the framework of speech act theory (but see Vuori 2008, for an exception.). In short, the philosophical model scorns methodological consistency (in substance, though not in the basic concepts used). Equally, some proponents of the philosophical approach to securitization are led to build a compromise between philosophical contents that are hardly compatible—for instance, speech act and poststructuralism (Searle 1977a). Still, others thought it useful to conflate pieces of Bourdieu's sociology and Derrida's philosophical intuitions, without consideration for the respective reservations of these authors (cf. Bradford 1993; Bourdieu 1991; Derrida 1982; Kamuf 1991; Taurek 2006).

The basic idea is as follows. The focus on rules of securitization, which enables the CS to hold that security is a *self-referential* practice (or an illocutionary act the validity of which is subject to conditions set forth earlier), poses a great challenge to its model of securitization as an *intersubjective* process (cf. Stritzel 2007; McDonald 2008). As a result, the CS saps its view of security as a "self-referential practice," the utterance of which achieves something by virtue of its illocutionary force in conformity with formal conditions of explicit performatives. The source of this confusion rests on the assumption that the speech act encompasses both the illocutionary act and the perlocutionary effect.[28] To express my concern in this way is to treat the conception of "security as a speech act" with some qualifications. Indeed, to claim that security is a speech act, as I have suggested, is to reduce security to an illocutionary act, i.e., a conventional procedure; an act . . . conforming to a convention' (Austin 1962: 105). In a nutshell, either we argue that security is a self-referential practice, in which case we forsake perlocution with the related acquiesence of the audience (and thereafter the idea that security is a "speech act"), or we hold fast to the creed that using the concept of security also produces a perlocutionary effect, in which case we abandon self-referentiality. I suspect instead that the CS leans towards the first option.

One basic reason supports my position: although the CS appeals to an audience, its framework ignores that audience, which suggests that the CS opts for an illocutionary view of security rather than a full-fledged model encompassing perlocution as well (Buzan, Wæver and de Wilde 1998: 46, note 5). In fact, the CS singles out three units of analysis: (i) the *referent object*—what is the object of securitization? (ii) The *securitizing actor*—who speaks "security"? (iii) *Functional actors*—i.e., those whose activities have significant effects on security making. They are not securitizing actors; nor are they referent objects (Ibid.: 36; emphasis in the original). True, these units draw attention to most of the factors that students of security must be concerned with. The choice sets the matters, however. In sum, the failure to treat audience and context as proper units of analysis makes it difficult to address the practically important question of what the proportionate weight of audience and contextual factors are in securitization theory.

Difficulties with a poststructuralist speech act

The theoretical position of the CS on speech acts stems from a Derridean reappropriation of Austin's philosophy. This is conspicuous in two respects, at least: first, because of the paucity of contextual studies; and, second, as a corollary, because of the overemphasis on textual analysis.[29] A brief look at Derrida's ideas on the matter will make this clear. According to Derrida, what is crucial in performatives is neither the context of their utterance, nor the speaker's intention, but the intrinsic attribute of the enunciation, that is, 'its iterability' or reproducibility. Indeed, performatives can be cited, extracted from their 'context of production,' and grafted onto other ones with little quibble.

Hence, Derrida is amplifying two points. First, the enunciation of a performative cannot be construed as the sheer product of a speaker's intention, since the possibility of the absence of the speaker makes the intentionality claim of any given text void. Second, the possibility of the absence coupled with the iterability and citationality of performatives reveals the worthless nature of contextual analysis. This understanding of enunciation drives us in a telling direction that, if pushed to its basic assumptions, anticipates the primary error of the CS: there is nothing to be gotten out of the text, and the act of writing, as Derrida (1977: 174) puts it, is not a vehicle 'of communication, at least not in the . . . sense of transmission of meaning.' This is a central, though often confusing, claim of poststructuralism; an assumption that leads the CS to maintain that 'the defining criterion of security is textual' and 'discourse analysis can uncover one thing; discourse', as its purpose 'is not to get at something else' (Buzan, Wæver and de Wilde 1998: 76f.). On this view, it is not clear why embarking on discourse analysis is relevant at all, if everything is known before the task is undertaken. Hence, one could argue that in making the aforementioned claims, the CS further strengthens the contention that its method is wholly devoted to the study of 'lists of instances' in texts, instead of meaning. Yet, it is not argued here that a poststructuralist view of the speech act is not, in its own terms, a valid approach to security. Instead it is claimed that the *link* between the speech act approach to security and poststructuralism—in the guise of Derrida's philosophy—creates tremendous difficulties for securitization theory.

This assertion bears directly on a central problem in the epistemology of discourse analysis: to what degree do studies draw on extant theoretical categories as opposed to building conceptual tools that emerge from the relations under scrutiny? A speech act view of security believes that the first challenge is to record securitization practices deductively, i.e., with a theoretical order imposed *a priori* (the rules of speech act and units of analysis). For poststructuralism, by contrast, the main purpose—and the biggest difficulty—is to capture securitization processes inductively, i.e., without a theoretical scheme imposed *a priori* (Sarup 2003; Carroll 1990). The core of such a position is to study the topography of discourse without 'assigning . . . relatively fixed labels to pieces of textual evidence (that) one assume(s) mean the same thing' (Hopf 2002: 36). If, in some sense, speech act philosophy is committed to theoretical categories that are used to structure our understanding of collected discourses (verbal and textual), then the imperative of 'non-categorization' guiding poststructuralism will not fit within a speech act model of security. Perhaps, it dovetails best with a pragmatic scheme, with the important caveat that, in contrast to the speech act view, pragmatism posits that cognitive structure—a coherent but flexible set of modes of thought, motivations, and reasons for action—have a real impact on discourse (Mead 1934; Balzacq 2003).

Sociological securitization: argumentative processes and web of practices

The weakness of a philosophical, speech act approach considered in section I gives us some reason to believe that any approach to securitization called properly pragmatic must at least try to account for 'the constitution of the political field and the relation between this field and the broader space of social positions and processes' (Thompson 1991: 28). This project lies at the centre of the sociological approach to securitization.

The sociological variant of securitization draws upon symbolic interactionism and, to various degrees, on Bourdieu's contribution to the symbolic uses of language and on the sociological features of Foucault's works, in particular the concept of the "dispositif." I would like to add a disclaimer, however: Bourdieu's central assumptions on the social functions of language themselves flow partly from symbolic interactionism, as a kind of social pragmatism (cf. Balzacq 2003; Balzacq 2009a). Yet on other counts, Bourdieu's argument outperforms the latter. For instance, those who build upon Bourdieu recast in new terms how securitizing agents coalesce to form a *social field*, i.e., a configuration of social actors that generates distinctive practices and effects (Bigo 2008; Ceyhan and Tsoukala 2002; Salter 2008; Huysmans 2006; Aras and Polat 2008). The two together work on 'symbolically-mediated' interactions (Abrahamsen 2005).[30] The next section further substantiates the view that securitization is a practice, which can be either discursive or non-discursive. In the first instance, securitization usually takes the form of argumentative processes, rather than that of a self-referential performative. In the second instance, by contrast, securitization is embodied in specific *dispositifs*. I have discussed the latter, under assumption 3. Later, I amplify the former, that is, securitization as a discursive practice, as it connects to premises about the constitutive and causal features of language.

Causality and habitus

We may begin with the stipulation that when talking of performatives, we assume that they are actions, i.e., a specific 'bringing about that *p*,' where the value of "*p*" indicates the new end-state to be achieved as a result of the discursive action.[31] Communication is successful, from this point of view at least, to the extent that the speaker and the hearer attain a mutual knowledge that prompts the receiver to do something. The main implication is that the hearer and speaker are engaged in responsive activity within a dynamic situation. Thus, the power involved in communication is relational, rather than being merely substantial or "self-actional." Indeed, to study securitization is to unravel the process by which a securitizing actor induces an audience to agree with a given interpretation of an event or a set of events. In this sense, a study of securitization blends questions of persuasion and linguistic competence to place the issue of agency at the center of discourse analysis. However, understanding agency in securitization is a complicated process. Therefore, we have to work it out carefully (i.e., schematically).

The essence of a discursive action is its compelling power to cause a receiver or an audience to perform a deed. Thus, discourse and action are linked in two distinct ways. First, discourse is part of agency in that it instantiates a sphere of action wherein agents dealing with defined questions operate "agonistically."[32] This is the constitutive side of discursive action, which is another way of saying that through mutual knowledge, discourse shapes social relations and builds their form and content. Second, on the causative side, as vehicle of ideas, discourse targets and creates the instantiation of a particular communicative action.[33]

Yet to preface words' agency, for utterances to lead to specific actions, the hearer must deliberate first between the sentence's meaning and the speaker's meaning. The former refers to the semantic meaning associated with words syntactically aggregated, whereas the latter is predicated on some aspects of language use that include metaphors, indirect implications, images, metonymies (pragmatics). When this task of decoding is completed, and after a common knowledge is established, normally, a reaction ensues. This gives consistency to Paul Ricœur's (1981: 206) claim that 'discourse leaves "a trace," makes its "marks" when it contributes to the (intersubjective) emergence of such patterns which become the document of human action.' A vivid example of discourse's capacity to leave a trace and *cause* an action can be seen in the consequences provoked by the statement released by Song, the former spokeswoman of the then South Korean President Roh Moohyun. In a press conference held in mid May 2003, she declared that South Korean military preparedness was stepped up to Watchon II—a military move that ensues when North Korea makes a threatening gesture—immediately after the US-coalition started the war on Iraq. Although both South Korea's Defense and Unification ministries were quick to offset this announcement by recalling that the current Wathcon II had been in effect since the naval clash between the two Koreas in the West Sea in 1997, North Korean officials decided to cancel both the 10th inter-Korean ministerial talks and the 5th economic cooperation forum scheduled for June 2003.[34]

The constitutive and causative forces are not the only relevant sides of discursive action; there is indeed another face upon which discursive action is critically salient, which is, the teleological approach. There, we start off with the idea that both causal and teleological explorations answer the question "why." They differ, however, on the object of reference. Put simply, causal explanations have the following logic: "'Y" occurred *because* "X" happened' or '"X" is what *produced* "Y"; teleological explanations, on the other hand, proceed thus: '"X" occurred *in order* that "Y" should happen' or '"Y" is what "X" *was for*.'[35] In discourse analysis, the distinction is nonetheless tenuous. As the Korean case shows, the meetings were cancelled *because* the spokeswoman issued a statement that was construed as an act of threat.

Now, taken from the standpoint of actions and intentions, the North Korean elites reacted as they did because they thought that the articulation of the symbol "Wathcon II" *was intended to* get them to "see" a warning signal. To explain South Korea's statements, North Korean elites used a backward analysis of the inferential link between the spokeswoman's intentions and South Korea's planned actions. In grammatical terms, their aim was to find an answer to a decisive question: 'what was the statement of the spokeswomen for?[36] If, therefore, my analysis of discourse as action is correct, if "X" happens, for instance, because "Y" was uttered, then, in the total speech act, the resulting matrix articulates action-type to action-type, the *communication purpose* (the how-question), the *problem* a securitizing claim intends to solve (the what-question), the *domain of relevance* it pertains to (see Table 1.1).

Two propositions follow from this map. First, when we study securitization, we elucidate how action-types are mobilized in discourse to comprehend and communicate the stakes raised by a threatening development. Second, communicative purposes mediate between the "problem" and the "domain of relevance" as laid out on the "map" (see Table 1.1); they direct our attention to the results and consequences of actions. It can, therefore, be agreed in these cases that an utterance is a distinct action insofar as we can attribute a communication purpose, that is, a real or a potential consequence to it.[38] Our analysis points towards the idea that if we want to consider what is done *in* saying (illocutionary act), we need to give credit to the effects of that specific action—perlocutionary effects (what is done *by* saying). However, when I insist that illocutionary act must be complemented by perlocution, I do not want to commit myself to Searle's view that because communicative purposes are not grounded upon the rules of speech act, we cannot guarantee they will be effectuated. It is true, of course, that constitutive rules of speech acts are central to the power of words. But, it is misleading to hold that because conventional

Table 1.1 A conceptual map of the speech act (Balzacq 2005: 189)[37]

Action-type	Problem	Communicative purpose	Domain of relevance
Assertive	What is the case?	That H shall come to believe that *p*	Extra-linguistic reality
Commissive	What does the speaker S want to do?	That H shall be oriented as to a certain future behavior of S	Future behavior of the speaker
Directive	What shall the hearer do?	That H Shall do *r*	Future behavior of the hearer
Declarative	What shall be the case institutionally?	That the institutional reality W shall be maintained or changed into W'	Institutional reality
Expressive	What has to be done in view of a new social or personal reality?	That the (un)tranquillization connected with a certain personal or social fact shall be dissolved	Social and personal reality

rules do not guarantee the results will be attained *by* producing an utterance, our description of performatives must dismiss communicative or extra-linguistic elements. This is why the insistence on rule-guided security actions fails to capture some factors that may affect the outcome of discursive games. In a lucid book, Mey laments that this view of speech act gave rise to an imbalance between universal illocutionary force of language and the necessary contextual rearticulation. To correct this defect, Mey proposes a theory of pragmatic acts.' The difference is of essence. 'The theory of pragmatic acts,' Mey (2001: 221) argues,

does not try to explain language use from the inside out, that is, from words having their origin in a sovereign speaker and going out to an equally sovereign hearer. . . . Rather, its explanatory movement is from the outside in: the focus is on the environment in which both speaker and hearer find their affordances, such that the entire situation is brought to bear on what can be said in the situation.

Intention and linguistic competence

There are various interpretations of word's agency; but I argue that the expression of the power of words, in the sense relevant here, depends on: (i) the context and the power position of the agent that utters them; (ii) the relative validity of statements for which the acquiescence of the audience is requested; and (iii) the manner in which the securitizing actor makes the case for an issue, that is, the discursive strategy displayed. The first conception derives from a notable expression by Perinbanayagam (1985: 22): 'the force of an utterance,' he states, 'signifies the force of the self being presented discursively in the interaction. . . . [The] signifying force is presented in an organized and creative force embodying the intentions of the [securitizing actor].' Intentions, despite their central status in discourse analysis, are notoriously hard to pin down; they remain problematic because it is very difficult to know whether actors must mean what they say (see Brand 1984; Cavell 2002). Cut to the bone, intentions refer to *what the securitizing actor wants to achieve in articulating a specific utterance* within a societal context (Austin 1962: Lecture VIII).

In the political field, like in many others, the ability of bringing about transformations with words largely depends on the authority that actually articulates sequences of utterances. This is also known in pragmatics as the question of "linguistic competence"—who is allowed to speak about a subject matter or who can partake in the debate? On security issues though, with very few exceptions, not a very sharp line can be drawn between those who can and those who cannot (see Bigo 2000; Doty 1998–1999). Nonetheless, in empirical ways, it can be argued that many discourses can readily marshal the assent of a target audience as a result of the audience's asymmetric access to information. Since the audience is not fully informed, for instance, on the temporal proximity of threats, it usually relies on state officials' discourses because it thinks that the latter, who are the site of constitutional legitimacy, must have "good reasons" to assert, in this case, that "X" represents a threat to a state's survival.[39] Of course, by virtue of "good reasons" (i.e., the claim that they know more than they can say or the argument of secrecy) public officials would find it easier, compared to any other securitizing actor, to securitize an issue, primarily, because they hold influential positions in the security field based on their political capital, and have a privileged access to mass media (see Bourdieu 1990; Foucault 1980; Herman and Chomsky 1989). Moreover, the concept of linguistic competence is also important because it implies that certain issues 'are the legitimate province of specific persons, roles, and offices that can command public attention, trust, and confidence' (Gusfield 1981: 10).

In both cases of linguistic competence, the power to persuade rests with the assumption that a given securitizing actor knows what is going on, and works for common interests. Here, knowledge (a kind of cultural capital), trust, and the power position (political or symbolic capital) are linked (Bourdieu 1979; Lupia and McCubbins 1998: 43–60).[40] This connection suggests something about the "dispositional concept" of power, which is, the ability to induce effects either directly or indirectly—by performing actions or having them done by others.[41] The "power to" secure the compliance of the audience helps the securitizing actor "fuse his/her horizon" with the audience's, which, in turn, has the "power to" acknowledge or ratify the claims put forward by the speaker (Luke 1974: 23). The case remains, nonetheless, that the claims of public officials would, generally, be ascertained against clues coming from the "real world." This attends to the second position that places a word's agency in the logical structure of the securitizing actor's statements. In other words, the determination of evidence for truth claims does not only derive from the authority of the speaker, but emerges also out of the claim itself. If it does, the third position, the discursive strategy displayed by the enunciator, conditions how effective a professed argument will affect the salience of the point at issue. Like any other aspects of word's agency, the manner in which the securitizing actor makes the case for the point at stake follows at least two basic principles: emotional intensity and logical rigor (proving how critical a problem is, how it matters to the audience(s), and point to the consequences). The practical force of discourse falls, therefore, between logical consistency and the dynamics of social power (Weldes *et al.* 1999: 17–19).

This chapter has tried to promote a new understanding of securitization theory, articulated around three core assumptions. To do this, my argument has been put forward in three steps.

First, I have attempted to reconcile the illocutionary force of the concept of security and its meaning through a symbolic scrutiny of security interactions, beginning with a discussion of the main vulnerabilities associated with the centrality of speech act philosophy and their implications for securitization theory. This has provided the baseline for a sociological reformulation of securitization through the development of three core assumptions, which restores the distinctive role of audience, context and *dispositif* in the construction of threat images. Our investigation of the three assumptions provided conceptual materials which, I argue, enable us to understand when and how this happens. Chapter 2 examines the methodological import of these assumptions, drawing particular attention to: how units and levels of analysis are sorted out; how different methods are operationalized; and how methods could be triangulated to account for the intricacies of securitization processes. Moreover, the argument has been made that the status and power of audience, context and the *dispositif* often vary from one issue to another, and from sector to sector. Chapters 3, 4 and 6 reconstruct the operation of audience, respectively, in the light of recent literature on agenda setting, then in terms of media framing, and finally through the Normal Accident Theory developed by Perrow.

Second, I have attempted to develop an alternative scheme for security studies by lifting discourse analysis above the conceit of a textualist model of speech act. In this account, the pragmatic act of security allows scholars to revise the relationship between securitization and poststructuralism. Thus, I argued that the attempt by the CS to pattern itself purely on a poststructuralist speech act (following Derrida) is unfortunate, for two principal reasons. One, it reduces discourse analysis to a merely textualist enquiry. Two, as a result, it tones down the distinctiveness of a pragmatic investigation of security. By contrast, I have amplified the idea that threat images are social facts which acquire a status of objectivity within the relationship between the securitizing actor and the audience, in contexts. To analyze security utterances discursively is to account for their capacity to bring about something desired (and sometimes unintended) by the speaker. In terms of the logic of persuasion, securitization is a meaningful procedure carried out through a strategic (argumentative) use of linguistic impulses that seek to establish a particular development and/or entity as an *intersubjective* focus for the organization of cognition and action. Chapter 5 connects to diverse approaches to context (distal and proximate) in order to reconstruct the extent that resistance of any form to securitization is itself a securitizing move. Each of Chapters 6 through 10 moves considerably further away from a philosophical approach to securitization. They specify the main lines around which securitization theory can be developed. Thus, in order to tease out the theoretical insights of failed cases of securitization Chapter 6 departs from Buzan, Wæver and de Wilde's (1998: 39) admonition that 'security analysis (must be) interested mainly in successful instances of securitization' because, so the argument goes, 'they constitute the currently valid specific meaning of security' (Buzan, Wæver and de Wilde 1998: 39). Chapters 7 through 10 set out the implications of the theoretical revisions and extensions provided in Chapter 1, through rigorous empirical investigations. But they go beyond mere application of Chapter 1, to offer distinctive reformulations of the ways in which the social content and meaning of security can be used to flesh out a theory of securitization.

Third, I have cast aside the exclusivist linguistic view which has dominated securitization studies, by developing an explicitly practice-oriented *complement* which emphasizes the structuring force of the *dispositif* for understanding both the designed and the evolutionary character of securitization. Chapter 8 offers a compelling picture of the complementary relation between the designed and evolutionary nature of securitization, while Chapter 9 covers one expression of the evolutionary feature of securitization that takes the form of diffusion/translation of threat images from one context to another. Finally, Chapter 11 reassembles the arguments in a coherent and compelling story, evaluates the framework put forward and proposes avenues for research, which grow from the current volume. The result is a new set of standards that provide securitization scholarship with the possibility of developing insights that previous pathways were unable to reveal.

Notes

1 We might even add realism and structural realism. On the theoretical lineages of securitization theory see, for instance, Wæver (2004) and Taurek (2006).

2 Campbell (1992); Dillon (1996).

3 Emphasis added.

4 Put succinctly, the two main intellectual pillars of the CS are philosophical: speech act philosophy and Schmittean political theory.

5 Some clarifications are in order, however. Pragmatics is part of pragmatism, and although related, the two are not the same. Simply put, as suggested earlier, pragmatics designates the contextual and interactional use of linguistic symbols in order to construct meaning. Pragmatism, on the other side, can hardly be defined. There is a narrow and a broad characterization. The first is definitional: pragmatism is thus seen as 'that method of reflection which is guided by constantly holding in view its purpose and the purpose of the ideas it analyzes, whether these ends be of the nature and uses of action or thought' Peirce (1931–58). The second, broad approach to pragmatism adopted here avoids this restrictive view by delineating its scope in three respects: (i) ontology—relational and processual, wherein shared language and practices of socially contextualized agents give reality a 'substance'; (ii) epistemology—knowledge is the result of symbolically mediated interactions in which meaning is constructed; and (iii) methodology—the contextual analysis of the symbolic relations between agents and generalization through counterfactuals and cross-contextual enquiries. See Emirbayer (1997). On pragmatism and IR theory, see Cochran (2002).

6 This is extrapolated from Habermas (1984). See also Thompson (1984).

7 Emphasis added. Bourdieu (1984: 170).

8 Ibid.

9 In fact, Nightingale and Cromby (2002: 705) argue that no concept can be wholly self-referential; instead, concepts frequently execute a kind of reference—though this might be partial or biased.

10 This is different from developing a *political theory* of securitization.

11 Different portrayals of the "speech act theory" can be found in Austin (1962; 1970: 233–52; 1971: 13–22; Searle (1969; 1977b: 59–82). There are several aspects and branches of speech act theory. However, in fairness to the CS and in order to limit the scope of my investigation, I will privilege Austin's and Searle's treatment of speech act, authors on which the CS examination of speech act draws.

12 For discussion on the variations of speech act philosophy, see Balzacq (2003).

13 Logical positivism can be considered as an outgrowth of Comtean positivism. Both share three common elements: (i) belief in the cumulation of knowledge; (ii) the uncontaminated view of knowledge as free of metaphysical and normative concerns; and (iii) "naturalism," namely the fact that social and natural science can be subject to the same rules of positivism in scientific enquiry. Yet, logical positivism departs from Comtean positivism by adding three peculiarities: (i) a referential conception of meaning which aims at overcoming the "fuzzy" use of language in science through the "verifiability principle," that is, 'a statement makes sense only if, and to the extent that, its empirical reference can be firmly corroborated'; (ii) the belief that science should follow a deductive-nomological method of explanation and the incumbent hypothetico-deductive scheme of theory construction; (iii) an axiomatic view of theories wherein the latter are 'a structural network of statements from which one could derive specific laws' (Dellmayr 1984: 36–37; Bechtel 1988). It is mainly against the tenets of logical positivism that Ludwig Wittgenstein directed his *Philosophical Investigations*. Indeed, rather that making sense of utterances on a truth-false basis, Wittgenstein insisted that they be accounted for in terms

of language-games, that is in accordance with language usages, thus his famous aphorism: 'meaning is use' (Wittgenstein 2001, para. 43). See the contrast with the *Tractatus Logico-Philosophicus*. Initially published in 1922, it was wedded to a correspondence account of language. Cf. Wittgenstein (1961). However, one of the most elegant works on logical positivism assumptions remains Ayer's (1936).

14 Searle (1977b).

15 For sophisticated attempts at applying Habermas's ideas on rules and language uses into International Relations, see Onuf (1989); Risse (2000).

16 For a rearticulation of this view, see Levinson (1983: 237).

17 This confusion is also perceptible in Schiffrin's (1994: 54).

18 Williams (2003) offers a sophisticated discussion of decisionism as it relates to Schmitt's political philosophy. For a good introduction to the general implications of Schmitt's political theory on IR, see Huysmans (2008).

19 Dwelling on Butler, McDonald (2008: 572) puts this in the following terms: 'the speech act . . . serves to construct or *produce* the audience itself.' Emphasis in the original. In fairness to Vuori, however, he does in fact recognize that audience is necessary for securitization to occur. But in a move that is akin to Wæver's, his empirical illustrations leave it unspecified. The cases give foremost importance to the securitizing actors and to their respective securitizing moves. Audience explicitly pops up at the end of the essay (Vuori 2008: 94).

20 For a treatment of the double hermeneutic in social sciences, see Giddens (1979: 284). In International Relations, this concern is voiced by those endorsing a critical theoretical approach to security studies. See, for instance, Krause and Williams (1996); Krause and Williams (1997: 33–60); Wyn Jones (1995); Smith (1999).

21 In Ethology, the science of animal behavior, "imprinting" means a visual and auditory process of learning. Konrad Lorenz (1981) showed that ducklings learn to follow real or foster parents at a specific time slack, that is, at critical stage after hatchings. As used here, imprinting refers to a learning process conjured up by political discourse. This learning activity is meant to grasp the causal structure of the environment and to categorize the objects that populate it. This process is generally eased by a given state of the political field in which leaders draw to make people believe what they say. It is thus social and cognitive. The German word for imprinting (*Prägen*) was coined by O. Heinroth in 1911. For a recent account see Bateson (2000: 85–102).

22 On the socio-temporal embeddedness of utterances, see Bakhtin (1986).

23 This contradicts the poststructuralist analysis of security as a self-referential concept, the articulation of which "constitutes an (in)security condition." In addition, practices attached to security are inherent to or emerge from its utterance. See Huysmans, (1998b); Wæver (1995).

24 See also Todorov (1983).

25 In many respects, these views are close to the concept of "seeing as" or "aspects of perceptions." On these, see Ludwig Wittgenstein (2001: 165–78); McGinn (1997: 189–204).

26 For a discussion of the ambiguities underwriting the concept of practice in securitization theory, see Ciuta (2009: 311–14).

27 According to Foucault (1980: 194), a *dispositif* is 'a thoroughly heterogeneous ensemble consisting of discourses, institutions, architectural forms, regulatory decisions, laws, administrative measures, scientific statements, philosophical, moral and philanthropic propositions–in short, the said as much as the unsaid. The dispositif itself is the system of relations that can be established between these elements.'

28 This might be grounded upon a more profound confusion between the term "speech act," which is the illocutionary act, and the total situation of speech act, i.e., 'the total situation in which the utterance is issued . . . (and which allows us) to see parallel between statement and performative utterances (also referred to as speech acts, explicit performatives, or illocutionary act)' (Austin 1962: 52). This confusion is also perceptible in Schiffrin (1994: 54).

29 This is demonstrated by a closer look at Wæver's references. See, for instance, Wæver (1995: 80f., endnotes 25 and 35); Buzan, Wæver and de Wilde (1998: 47, endnote 5). Here, Austin's (1962) text is often cited in conjunction with Derrida (1977: 172–97). Interestingly, Searle's (1977a) response to Derrida, which regards this use of speech act as inappropriate, is ignored.

30 On security as a symbol, see Wolfers (1962).

31 See Forguson (1969: 127–47); Eckard (1990: 147–65).

32 This is another way of saying that in discourse actors do not ignore conflict, but integrate it in a consensus. That is to say that the chief aim of discursive exchanges is not to dissolve dissensus, but to create a space wherein such differences can be dealt with. However, this consensus remains a "conflictual consensus," which is to say that that discourse is a "mixed game" partly co-operative and partly confrontational. See Laclau and Mouffe (1985).

33 In connection, see Huysmans (1998b).

34 See 'I Dunno,' *The Korean Times*, 15 May 2003. See also 'Pyongyang Cancellation of Talks,' *The Korean Times*, 15 May 2003.

35 See von Wright (1971: 83ff). For Aristotle (1992), both causal and teleological explanations are causes: the first is the efficient cause—what made the event happen—whereas the second is the final cause—why the event happened.

36 It must be pointed out that the teleological explanation in this point relies on an intentional process driven by desires and beliefs; for instance, the rational choice theory. In turn, the desires and beliefs explain the action by providing us with the agent's reasons for behaving in the way s/he did. Davidson calls this process the "rationalization of action." For the difference between intentional and non-intentional teleology, see McLaughlin (2001). On rational choice theory and teleological explanation, see Davidson (1963: 685, 690–91).

37 Chartered from Eckard (1990: 160, 163).

38 Several inquiries into the philosophy of action that inform my view here include Davidson (1982); Danto (1968); von Wright (1971).

39 This touches on the authoritative knowledge pertaining to the issue and/or the associated moral authority that "incite" the audience to believe that the speaker's statement is accurate and then to act accordingly. See Risse (2000: 22).

40 On trust and securitization, see Balzacq (2009b).

41 The power involved in securitization requires the decision of the securitizing agent to produce its effects. Peter Morris (1987: 20–29) calls this kind of power "ability." The *ability* refers to what the securitizing decides to do. Morris furthermore describes the moral and the evaluative context. The first is the realm of individual responsibility whereas the latter pertains to the evaluation of the social system.

2   Enquiries into methods

A new framework for securitization analysis

Thierry Balzacq

It is generally assumed that the way in which securitization occurs is essentially an empirical question, but, paradoxically, there has been little discussion on methods. To exacerbate the problem, scholars of IR have often been divided in their speculations over whether we should pay attention to method at all (Milliken 1999: 226). Further, there is considerable disagreement over the rationales for choosing a specific method: Why and when, for example, is discourse analysis preferred, rather than participant observation, let alone process-tracing and content analysis, and what differences these choices ultimately make in grasping policy processes (Neuendorf 2002; Herrera and Braumoeller 2004: 15–39). The peculiarities of these approaches to security are compelling, so much so that the hardest and clearest obstacle which students of securitization face is to simply make sense of this diversity.[1] Finally, the distinction between method and methodology is, by itself, grounds for controversy.[2]

This chapter sketches the distinctiveness of four techniques that constitute the methodological repertoire of securitization studies, all of which are used in various degrees in this book. I proceed from discourse analysis, probably the most popular approach to securitization studies, through ethnographic research, down to process-tracing and content analysis, techniques whose potential remains broadly unexplored in the empirical literature of securitization. Using the definition from Chapter 1, this chapter proposes a new framework—organized around three levels of analysis—in order to assist students in sorting out the actors and the factors most relevant for the study of securitization.

A caveat. My aim is not to emulate textbooks on methods (excellent proposals are readily available in different outlets), but to underscore the values and shortcomings of different techniques in an attempt to assist others who might want to write empirical studies of securitization. Obviously, the best way to master a method is through concrete work. In fact, textbooks on methods, however well written they might be, remain call for action. One way to get acquainted with the nuts and bolts of a method is to read "methodological exemplars," i.e., studies which 'exhibit instances of reasoning that the scientist takes to be worthy of emulation or ripe for avoidance' (Kitcher 1995: 86). In short, methodological exemplars (of which this volume provides a few), offer a practical experience with the performance of a given method.

LIVERPOOL JOHN MOORES UNIVERSITY
LEARNING SERVICES

The chapter unfolds as follows. First, I outline the promises, and perils of case study as a primary component of research design in securitization studies. I argue, moreover, that intensive analysis of cases does not necessarily 'define method' (Klotz 2008: 43). 'Too often,' warns Klotz (2008: 43), 'the justification of research design begins and ends with the rationale for number of cases, obscuring key issues, such as the *unit* and *level* of analysis.'[3] Thus, in order to strengthen our research design, the section proposes three levels of analysis for case studies which either "test" or "apply" securitization theory. Second, I provide, the basics of four approaches to the study of securitization (discourse analysis, process-tracing, what is broadly termed "ethnographic research," and content analysis). Finally, I conclude by delineating the practices of methodological pluralism.

Research design and levels of analysis

Understanding processes of securitization involves making hard choices about the substantive focus of the analysis. In fact, there are two fundamental, interdependent layers in securitization studies: the first is to identify the puzzle named "threat"; the second is to determine how to make sense of it. The study of securitization starts from an important, but often neglected prerequisite: How to sort out the issue referred to as a security problem? Two criteria, each of which is sufficient, are of operational salience: 1) it should be a focus of public attention or debate; 2) the issue should be a target for activities related to public opinion or legal and/or political actions; in other words, it should be critically pervasive for the political system.

However, it is in the idea of criticality or emergency that the essence of securitization primarily lies. For instance, states may be convinced that the possession by "A" of weapons of mass destruction poses a threat which besets the good life of organized social communities, but nonetheless sharply disagree on whether the times are as critical as they are purported to be. Where this criticality or shortage of time is shared, the 'issueness' of a public problem is attained and becomes intersubjective; it is then against the backdrop of this common context that an issue reaches the stage of securitization and looms large for political management. In brief, the *shared critical salience* of an issue marked by the *imperative of acting now*, constitute necessary and sufficient conditions for securitization. However, knowing what the problem is does not tell us *what* makes it a threat, for *whom*, *why*, and *why now*? These questions constitute the main quandaries for case study. This section discusses the status of case study in research design for securitization studies. The research design is meant primarily to calibrate the investigation by forcing the researcher to test expected outcomes against what the data finally reveal. It argues, moreover, that it is difficult to make sense of case studies absent "levels of analysis," a point I examine next.

Case study

In the empirical literature of securitization, case study constitutes the primary research strategy. Its use, however, varies from one author to another. Some employ case study for exploratory reasons; others use it for descriptive reasons;

finally, few employ case study for explanatory purposes. The rationale underlying the practice of case study does not, however, fundamentally alter its primary aim, that is, to determine whether a phenomenon is an instance of a class of events (cf. Eckstein 1975; Brady and Collier 2004). Under this heading, Robert Yin (2009: 18) stipulates a twofold technical definition of case study, which I find very useful:

1. A case study is an empirical inquiry that

    *   investigate a . . . phenomenon in depth and within its real-life context, especially when
    *   the boundaries between the phenomenon and context are not clearly evident.

2. The case study inquiry

    *   copes with the technically distinctive situation in which there will be many more variables of interest than data points, and as one result
    *   relies on multiple sources of evidence, with data needing to converge in a triangulating fashion, and as another result
    *   benefits from the prior development of theoretical propositions to guide data collection and analysis.

It should be noted that the definition says nothing about the kind of method which should be used to investigate the case, nor does it says anything about whether the researcher should employ qualitative or quantitative data. These depend upon the research design of the case selected. Three components dominate the research design of a case study. The starting point for all versions of research designs for case study is to specify the study's question and its related propositions—who, how, why, when, where, what (see Figure 2.1). A second related important feature of the design is to isolate the most relevant unit of analysis (see Table 2.1). The third component comprises the 'logic of linking the data to the propositions' and the 'criteria for interpreting the findings' (Yin 2009: 27).

Many students of securitization acknowledge the analytical importance of case study, but few are comfortable with the protocols of case design (Hansen 2006 is, however, a nice exemplar). Though scholars have often privileged single-case designs, the research questions raised by the construction and evolution of threat images can also be addressed by employing multiple-case designs (cf. Emmers 2004). But the decision to conduct either of the two methods should be taken relatively early in the research process as it conditions, or guides, data collection and analysis. Yet, the number of cases cannot be an end in itself. In fact, single- and multiple-case designs are underwritten by distinct rationales. Most of the study in this book use single-case design. This explains why I focus on its potential and pitfalls. Obviously, multiple-case designs will spark different kinds of issues, depending on whether the investigator analyzes several cases in parallel (Buzan, Wæver and de Wilde 1998) or whether the researcher concentrates on one level of analysis that is then scrutinized across different cases. This can lead to various combinations of case study that cannot be (and need not be) spelled out here.

Cut to the bone, three rationales underlie single case designs of securitization: "typical case," "critical case" and "revelatory case" (Yin 2009: 47–48; Denzin and Lincoln 1994; Creswell 2006). To start, typical cases are meant to shed light upon the logic of a given phenomenon. The conclusions drawn from typical cases are informative about the processes analyzed. To some extent, typical cases result from the transformation of critical or revelatory cases, in the sense that they no longer contribute significantly to theory-building via "testing" (which is the objective of critical cases) nor do they shed light upon social phenomena that were previously out of sight (which is the primary aim of revelatory cases).

The commitment to a case design comes with one major challenge: which case to select? Buzan, Wæver and de Wilde (1998: 39) advise that: 'security analysis (must be) interested mainly in successful instances of securitization' because, so the argument goes, 'they constitute the currently valid specific meaning of security.' This admonition has, in some instances, provoked one problem and a consequence. The problem is called "selection bias." Indeed, those who study securitization, although they may emphasize different levels of analysis (agents, acts, contexts), generally share the conviction that we learn something about security logic only if we select cases that have a particular outcome, i.e., successful. We do not argue that selecting case studies on the basis of the dependent variable can never be useful. Actually, especially in the early stages of theory development (e.g., revelatory cases), such a strategy can enable researchers to identify 'potential causal paths and variables leading to the dependent variable of interest' (George and Bennett 2005: 23). Rather, we want to emphasise that a selection of cases on the basis of outcomes can understate or overstate the relationship between dependent and independent variables. One immediate—but by no means unique—consequence of selection bias is, to put it simply, confirmation bias. That is, when researchers focus on outcomes, they often devote their attention to applying (not testing) a theory. As Greenwald *et al.* (1986: 220) argue, 'when the researcher's faith in the theory cannot be shaken by disconfirming data, it is inappropriate to describe the research strategy as theory testing. Rather, the strategy is effectively one of theory confirming.' However, a framework cannot be blamed for all the indirect consequences brought by its success. Thus, it is important for the analysts of securitization to rigorously apply their analytical framework and guard against overgeneralizing their results. In the words of Greenberg *et al.* (1988: 567), 'overgeneralization sometimes occurs not because of problems with the theory but because of inappropriate applications in which theoretically specified conditions are ignored.'

There are significant constraints on what can be called "securitization," and, hence, an effective way of *validating* the results of case studies. I have argued in Chapter 1, for example, that for an issue to be pronounced an instance of securitization, an 'empowering or enabling audience' has to agree with the claims made by the securitizing actor. To reiterate, an enabling audience is the audience which: a) has a *direct causal connection* with the issue; and b) has the ability to empower the securitizing actor to adopt measures in order to tackle the threat. In short, securitization is satisfied by the acceptance of the enabling audience of a securitizing move. If this is correct, then a number of case studies do not qualify as (successful) instances of securitization.[4] It may be difficult to precisely identify the relevant audience as long as different political regimes tolerate and value different kinds of audiences. Nevertheless, the assumption that securitization necessitates the assent of the audience is a stable and decisive condition for drawing and verifying the conclusion that securitization has occurred.

Levels and constituent analytics

The study of securitization requires that we first specify what the units and levels of analysis are. This concern traverses any approach to IR that bears on substantive questions. Does not Wendt (1999: 82) argues that 'before we can be constructivist about anything we have to choose "units" and "levels" of analysis'? Buzan, Wæver and de Wilde (1998: 36) singled out three units of analysis in their book:

1. *Referent objects*: things that are seen to be existentially threatened and that have a legitimate claim to survival.

2. *Securitizing actors*: actors who securitize issues by declaring something—a referent object—existentially threatened.

3. *Functional actors*: actors who affect the dynamics of sector. Without being the referent object or the actor calling for security on behalf of the referent object, this is an actor who significantly influences decisions in the field of security.

What is problematic with this characterization is that it does not integrate two equally important elements, audience and context. Further, most of what is called "units" of analysis here actually fall within one level of analysis, that of the agent. We therefore need an alternative. This search is motivated by two concerns. On the one hand, I find it useful to distinguish levels from units (constituent analytics). On the other hand, I want to draw securitization theory out of the narrow precincts of agents. More specifically, the levels of analysis on which I think securitization theory captures the construction of security problems include not only agents, but also acts and contexts. It might be difficult to account for all of the levels of analysis for each case study, but this should not be taken as an excuse to disqualify other levels a priori. In fact, given that securitization analysis generally emphasizes the retroduction of practices through empirical analysis, we cannot see other features of securitization that a mono-level approach ignores: the way in which the context empowers or disempowers securitizing actors; specific non-discursive approach practices (e.g., tools) which provoke securitization; some heuristic artefacts which induce the audience to built some image of a problem. Thus, I offer a vocabulary articulated around three dimensions which help to isolate different perspectives on securitization analysis. That vocabulary takes the form of three "levels" of analysis and their constituent analytics (units).

Level 1: Agents. This level concentrates on the actors and the relations that structure the situation under scrutiny. It includes four facets:

(i)   those who contribute or resist, either directly or by proxy, to the design or emergence of security issues (securitizing actors, audiences, and "functional actors");

(ii)   the power positions (or rather relations) of actor identified under (i);
(iii) the personal identities and social identity, which operate to both constrain and enable the behaviour of the actors identified under (i);
(iv)   the referent object and the referent subject, or what is threatened and what threatens.[5]

Level 2: *Acts.* This level is interested in practices, both discursive and non-discursive, which underwrite the processes of securitization being studied. The overarching outcome is to open up the politics and methods of creating security, since they involve practice and refers to variables that are extra-linguistic (Williams 2003; Wilkinson 2007). This level has, at root, four sides:

(i)   The first is the "action-type" side that refers to the appropriate language to uses in order to perform a given act—the grammatical and syntactical rules of the language.

(ii)   The second facet is strategic: which heuristic artefacts a securitizing actor uses to create (or effectively resonate with) the circumstances that will facilitate the mobilization of the audience—analogies, metaphors, metonymies, emotions, or stereotypes? What kinds of frames are thus constructed, around which storylines? Which media are favoured—electronic or print media?

(iii) The third facet is expressed by the *dispositif* of securitization (i.e., a constellation of practices and tools).

(iv)   The policy(ies) generated by securitization.

Level 3: *Context.* Discourse does not occur nor operate in a vacuum; instead, it is contextually enabled and constrained. 'Discourse,' according to Fairclough and Wodak (1997: 277), 'is not produced without taking context into consideration.' After all, threats arise out of, and through the work of, specific contexts. As a consequence, to capture the meaning of any discourse, it is necessary, I argue, to situate it both socially and historically. In this light, students of securitization who embark on discourse analysis 'must have a thorough understanding of the context of the discourse they are

Table 2.1 The vocabulary of securitization (revised from Balzacq 2009a: 64)

Levels		Constituent analytics (UNITS)
Agent		• Securitizing actor; audience; functional actor
		• Power positions/relations
		• Personal and social identities
		• Referent object and referent subject
Act		• Action-type
		• Heuristic artefacts
		• Dispositif
		• Policy
Context		• Distal
		• Proximate

analyzing—modes of production, class structure, political formation—in order to situate their analysis and explain relationships' (Crawford 2004: 24). But context itself is difficult to unpack. Fortunately, Wetherell's (2001: 380f.) parsimonious distinction between *distal* and *proximate* contexts makes the matter more tractable.

(i) The proximate context includes 'the sort of occasion or genre of interaction the participants take an episode to be (e.g., a meeting, an interview, a summit).' To a certain extent, the proximate context relates to what Salter (2008) calls, following Goffman, "setting."

(ii) By contrast, the distal context focuses on the sociocultural embeddedness of the text. The distal context has strong *recursive effects*, meaning that persuasive arguments operate in cascade (e.g., people are convinced because friends of a friend are convinced, etc.). It refers to 'things like social class, the ethnic composition of the participants, the institutions or sites where discourse occurs, ecological, regional, and cultural' environments.

This vocabulary is a source of both the strengths and the limitations of a comprehensive securitization analysis. On the one hand, the distinction of three levels offers considerable scope for choice. In fact, the attention of the investigator can focus on the level of analysis necessary to answering the question at hand. On the other side, there are constraints. Given the levels' constituent analytics, it is very difficult for one individual researcher to embrace all the levels. Further, each level points to different sources likely to affect the outcome of securitizing moves and thus explanations of securitization that are distinct, but complementary to other sources. Thus, I translate the three levels into a scheme that enables us to capture securitization processes along two axes (Figure 2.1): vertical (functional/ontological terms), and horizontal axis (pragmatics/semiotics terms).

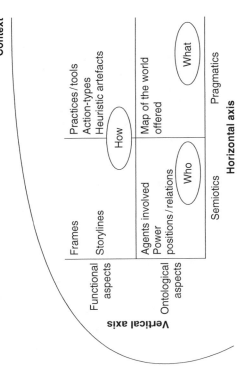

Figure 2.1 Securitization analysis in context (Balzacq 2009a: 66)

Each box contains different factors involved in categorizing public problems as threats. Similarly, the two axes are rough sets, not clean dichotomies. Each intersection between the two axes indicates different ways of capturing the process of securitization. Although we could confine the scope of inquiry to one of the boxes or one single intersection, we need to be aware that a more credible study of securitization requires an account of all three dimensions, i.e., "how," "who" and "what." Beneath these three dimensions lies that which determines the most relevant material of scrutiny. Put differently, the three dimensions, embedded in a defined context (e.g., "when" and "where"), grasp the main preoccupation of securitization analysts: to understand the political structuring of a threat image.

The capacities of methods

There seems to be an overriding myth in IR that students come to methods intuitively and as such methods do not deserve absorbing part of our research time. Even in book length manuscripts, few scholars lay down how data were collected, which strategies were employed to trace their meanings, and how they verified that the conclusions drawn were reliable (see Hopf 2002, for a notable exception). This section leans the other way, in defence of methodological awareness. It is thus a plea for teaching and learning methods and their underlying epistemologies, as no research can attend to substantive questions only through gut feeling. Intuition does not preclude discipline; instead, by keeping it focused, it reinforces its overall productivity.

In this section, then, I identify four techniques to the task of analyzing securitization processes: discourse analysis, ethnographic research, process-tracing, and content analysis. I do not claim, however, that these are the only methods available to students of securitization. As the theory grows, new techniques (or new combinations of techniques) could be mobilized to apply, or better, test its premises. I think, however, that the methods I discuss in this section are probably those with the highest potential as regards the development of a comprehensive theory of securitization. These methods could be employed alone or in combination. In other words, although one method could help grasp the main features of securitization, I also think that some of them could be mutually supportive in accounting for the nuances of the design and evolution of a security problem. This might raise concern among orthodox scholars of various camps, but I want students of securitization to be open to the possibility. Finally, the development of these methods is riddled with controversies of which we should be aware, since they are pertinent to securitization analysis, even though we cannot and need not resolve them. I follow a generous reference policy which will allow students of securitization to understand both the strengths and the limits of the method(s) they might want to adopt. The publications I dwell upon offer detailed account of the methods they discuss and often provide relevant illustrations. In short, a book chapter is not well equipped to undertake intensive analysis of such a range of methods. But, I attempt to suggest sufficient guidelines for using specific methods, in the context of securitization theory.

Discourse analysis

In the literature of securitization, discourse analysis has impressive credentials. In fact, the design of threat images is generally captured by mapping meaning through discourse analysis. Members of the CS themselves explicitly use a discursive approach to account for processes of securitization in different sectors. Unfortunately, the method promoted by the CS seems to restrict discourse analysis to spoken or, to be more precise, written utterances. Thus, in dealing with discourse analysis, it is helpful to start from a specification of its boundaries. Next, I will provide an overview of different approaches to discourse analysis in securitization studies. Coming last, the section on "features of discourse analysis" will narrow down our discussion to the appropriate basic steps to follow when using discourse analysis in understanding processes of securitization.

Definitions. Part of the reason for the debates surrounding discourse analysis is that it is difficult to craft a generic definition of the concept "discourse." In fact, the word "discourse" means different things to different people. Take, for instance, van Dijk's discussion of the concept (1997a, 1997b). It surveys numerous ways of coming to terms with "discourse" and the resulting method, "discourse analysis." In IR scholarship, there is no paucity for choice either (compare Duffy, Federking and Tucker 1998; Fierke 1998; Hansen 2006; Hopf 2002; Larsen 1997; Milliken 1999; Neumann 2008; Ringmar 1996; Laffey and Weldes 2004). Probably, one way to channel these competing arguments is to specify why students of securitization resort to discourse analysis in the first place. Put simply, the answer could run like this: discourse analysis helps students to map the emergence and evolution of patterns of representations which are constitutive of a threat image. In this sense, discourse is a vehicle of meaning, a meaning which is rarely self-evident but has to be charted by the analyst.

According to Hardy *et al.* (2004: 20), discourses are 'bodies of texts . . . that bring . . . ideas, objects and practices into the world.' This suggests that discourses are both *resources* and *practices*. In the first sense, discourses are sociocultural resources activated by people 'in the construction of meaning about their world and their activities' (Ó Tuathail and Agnew 1992: 192–93; cited in Laffey and Weldes 2004: 28). In the second sense, as practices, discourses are 'structures of meaning-in-use' (Laffey and Weldes 2004: 28). The conventional manner in which discourse materializes is text. Discourses are 'created, supported, and contested through the production, dissemination, and consumption of texts . . .' (Hardy 2001: 28). Since it is easy to misinterpret this claim, I should note two things Hardy does not intend by it. First, "text" here does not mean written text or spoken words only. Second, "text" does not indicate any commitment to Derridean analysis, in which the very idea of method would be treated with scorn. The significance of these moves becomes apparent when we specify what text covers. The notion of text points, indeed, to a variety of signs, including written and spoken utterances, symbols, pictures, music. What unites these manifestations of text is their capacity to convey meaning, in a context. This preserves Kress's (1995: 122) original formulation, which treats texts as the sites of the emergence of complexes of social meanings, produced in the particular history of the situation of production, that record in partial ways the histories of both the participants in the production of the text and of the institutions that are "invoked" or brought into play, indeed a partial history of the language and the social system, a partiality due to the structuring of relations of power of the participants.

Thus, the aim of discourse analysis is to establish the meaning of texts shaped by distinct contexts. In fact, patterns of representations embodied by discourse are contextually enabled and/or constrained. Put crisply, it is the recognition that the meanings conveyed by different units are often heterogeneous, and vary across time and place. In this light, the claims made by discourse analysis are modest, but strong as they rest on carefully evaluated sets of historical and geographical assumptions. In Chapter 9 Stritzel and Schmittchen show, for instance, that the use of the concept "rogue state," its relationships to other words in the texts examined, and its position in the American and German culture, are dissimilar. This does not prevent them, however, from offering a reliable account of the traduction/translation of threat images across cultural contexts.

Discourse analysis in securitization studies.

Securitization theory, we have argued, aims to capture a distinct social phenomenon, namely how some public problems become security issues. This premise means that the technique we adopt needs to be tailored to the task of uncovering the structures and practices that produced the threat image whose source, mechanisms, and effects we want to explicate. A survey of empirical works on securitization reveals, however, that the philosophical and the sociological approaches to securitization do not have the same understanding of what discourse analysis is meant to achieve. The first is essentially text-based, in the sense that it does not emphasize context and the power positions/relations which underwrite the text analyzed. These empirical works can be said to fall within a *social linguistic analysis* of texts (cf. Mauws 2000; Stokoe 1998; Dunford and Jones 2000; Gill 1993; van Dijk 1993). In this light, the philosophical approach to securitization has often been called "linguistic."[6] For social linguistic analysis, indeed, the objective of discourse analysis is to examine the 'constructive aspects of texts, to understand not only the discursive microdynamics of individual decisions but also the discursive foundations of the social reality in which those decisions are located' (Philips and Hardy 2002: 23). It should be noted that this focus remains silent about the figures of language that is examined. In fact, it does not matter much. What is useful to outline, however, is that social linguistic is pertinent to securitization because it helps to investigate the production of specific phenomena such as identities, decisions or norms. This explains, in part, why social linguistic analysis is often used in retrieving the rhetorical strategies of texts. However, the weaknesses of social linguistic analysis are that it does not pay attention to power relations underlying texts, and does not account for the context.

The use of discourse analysis by the sociological securitization conforms, if tacitly, to the tradition of *critical discourse analysis* (Fairclough 1992, 1995; Fairclough and Wodak 1997). In many ways, critical discourse analysis has affinities with Foucault's insistence on 'how discourse actively structures the social space within which actors act, through the constitution of concepts, objects, and subject positions' (Philips and Hardy 2002: 25). Researchers who dwell on this perspective focus on dialogical struggles which are nested in power relations. In general, critical approach to discourse will use a diverse body of data including, for example, interviews, participant observation, pictures, archival materials and newspapers coverage of the threat image concerned. This comes with one noteworthy advantage: it offers a "thick description" of the social practices associated with the construction and evolution of threat images. The variety of data and the focus of analysis point to the insight that securitization can reside in practices other than words: bureaucratic procedures and practices, technologies, norms of a given profession, and so forth. In sum, critical discourse analysis is powerful in grasping both textual and non-textual activities of securitization, and the "power tectonics" which enable or silence certain voices (Hansen 2000).

Features of discourse analysis. Not everything can be planned in the study of discourse, but the researcher has to conform to basic, common steps which help to conduct reliable enquiries into the processes of securitization. I tend to subscribe to the belief that a minimum of formalization in discourse analysis is a scholarly requirement not only for the sake of presenting your results to others, but also because it facilitates comparability of insights and enables scholars to learn from others and see where their own study went astray. But my formalism is limited to: What data to collect, how much? How to make sense of the material thus assembled? How to verify that the conclusion drawn allows us to respond to the research question? Obviously, the backdrop of these questions is the theoretical perspective that informs the study or that the study aims to amend or enrich.

The nature of the data to collect will vary from one research question to another. In other words, the analyst must avoid assuming that some data are indispensable once and for all. In fact, many studies often claim that we should start from written text and then triangulate the materials with spoken texts and other kinds of texts. My view is that this is too deterministic. What if the subject of study is already embodied by specific type of texts such as cartoons (Hansen 2007)? Hence, the point is that the research question commands the kind of data collected and the hierarchy, if any, established among them. If the investigator studies, for example, the securitization of migration by the far right in France, the most obvious route will be to start with the far right party's program, its manifestos, in sum, all the official documents in which it expresses its position towards migrants. This might, however, be insufficient because the language could be extremely controlled (due to fears of prosecution, for instance). The researcher could then triangulate by collecting newspapers reports on far right and migration during the relevant period, interview some far right elites on the issue of migration and any issue connected to it (e.g., health, welfare, security, national identity, serious crime, border control...). By the same token, if the researcher is interested, for example, in the securitization of Islam in Switzerland in 2009, a study of cartoons and campaign pictures would definitely constitute one of the basic materials to assemble as these were the main media through which representations of the "menace" during the referendum on banning the minarets, acquired meaning.

However, the data collected could also depend on the moment at which the analysis is carried out and/or the level of analysis that is singled out. Again, if the researcher studied the securitization of Islam in Switzerland during the campaign on banning the minarets, one would have employed some polls data and, accordingly, concluded that the securitizing moves had failed as these indicated that the majority would vote "no." This means, on the other hand, that conducting research on ongoing securitization processes is a risky endeavour. Be that as it may, the results of opinion polls should be treated cautiously. They are generally of limited significance to account for the complex process of securitization. Of course, the literature on agenda setting shows that there is nothing wrong with using public opinion polls as *indicators* (though not as evidence) of the prominence of an issue (cf. McCombs 2004; Wæver 1991). However, I submit, drawing securitization inferences from public opinion polls, without tracing their impact on a visible outcome (e.g., vote, policy), raises serious difficulties. Meynaud (2007) shows, for instance, that public opinion polls are *at once* processes and outcomes. In other words, the results of polls can be instrumentalized and play a role in securitizing moves, but can also be utilized to account for (successful) cases of securitization at the same time. This is definitely one area where much research is still required, precisely because the first task for the researcher is to delimit the conditions upon which inferences are drawn.

The level of analysis might call for different types of data, too. If the analyst examines the securitization of migration by states, not by parties that do exert power, one needs to analyze specific legislative texts of the country concerned. In France, for instance, the law governing the acquisition of French citizenship (*Code de la nationalité*) is an essential data in tracing the evolution of securitization. The changes thereof indicate turns in securitization of aliens (Corollier 2010: 2–4).

Deciding to stop data collection is not an easy task, but it has to be done at a certain point in time, if data overload is to be avoided. Reading sources of various kinds, extensively, is an essential attribute for discourse analysts, but it is just materially impossible to read everything on a given subject. Usually, the more precise a research question is, the easier it is to isolate the texts most appropriate to carry out the analysis. Moreover, experienced researchers are often well trained in deciding that they have read enough. The problem, however, is that the level of training is not the same across the field, and many processes that students of securitization want to capture are not precisely defined from the outset. In various instances, indeed, the contours of the research question emerge more accurately out of data collection. This is so mainly because discourse analysis adheres to the logic of emerging theory. It follows from this line of argument that researchers should not be perturbed a priori by the quantity of data, as this concern is generally coterminous with the delineation of the subject, which is, in turn, related to the data collected. Openness, however, does not mean indecision. Generally speaking, discourse analysts are drawn to support the idea that once the repetitions of the representations investigated tip a certain density (i.e., the intellectual marginal gain decreases or nears zero), then data collection can be suspended with little risk that something relevant has been missed out.

The second step in examining discursive manifestations of securitization is to make sense of the data thus gathered. This warrants a degree of flexibility. This flexibility is, however, inscribed with two main features of the study of texts. The first relates to the examination of actualized sets of specific strings of statements, uttered by the securitizing actor; it focuses indeed on the internal coherence of the text (intratextuality). On this view, intratextuality enquires into the performative dimensions of the text, in which securitizing moves appear:

- What kind of action that a text wants to achieve (assertive, commissive, expressive, directive, or declarative).[7] What representations are created by this or that particular action? What are the communicative purposes and domains of relevance of the text?

- Which heuristic artefacts are favoured, for which meanings (metaphors, pictures, emotions, analogies, and so forth)? What "map" of world politics does it present?

- What kinds of interactions are generated?

The second feature of text analysis emphasizes the relationships among texts (intertextuality). In effect, the distinctively qualitative view of discourse analysis is primarily about the generative power of this intertextuality. The argument here is that patterns of representations are captured in different ways depending upon the text examined. In this light, patterns of representations are understood according to their relationship with others, in different texts. Once we start thinking about meaning as the result of the interplay between bodies of texts, it becomes clear that patterns of representations emanate out of the interrelations between various texts. To pre-empt the argument that will be made in the last section, I want to extract from intertextuality one fundamental consequence for the study of securitization: to capture the breath and depth of securitization processes, the analyst cannot focus on one text, but instead examine various genres of texts, at different points in time, in distinct social contexts (Neumann 2008: 71). In other words, 'discourses are always connected to other discourses which were produced earlier, as well as those which are synchronically and subsequently' enacted (Fairclough and Wodak 1997: 277). The recurrent patterns of linguistic characterization, which is consolidated by intertextualism, constitute what Hajer (1995: 56) calls "storylines," i.e., generative narratives 'that allow actors to draw upon various discursive categories to give meaning to specific physical or social phenomena.' In general, a storyline holds three functions: first, it establishes a link among signifying characteristics that point toward the threatening phenomenon. Second, when reified, a storyline acquires its own momentum by contributing to a cognitive routinization. Third, storylines create contending coalitions around contrasting sets of common understandings. Thus, storylines weave the representations culled from different texts, and give them their overall coherence. In this respect, intertextuality helps to map out what varies and what does not, from one text to another, from one setting to another.

Ethnographic research

Thus far our discussion has indicated if implicitly that the components of ethnographic research are often used as a complement to discourse analysis. It doesn't have to be so. To some extent, ethnographic research can do without discourse analysis and sheds distinctive light upon processes of securitization. In this section, I argue that ethnographic research is a method that is most sensitive to the sociological variant of securitization (cf. Bigo 1994, 2005; Bigo, Bonelli and Olsson 2007; Balzacq 2008; Balzacq *et al.* forthcoming; Guittet 2008; Salter 2008; Scherrer 2009). In this book, some features of the ethnographic approach to securitization are illustrated by Chapters 5, 6 and 10. They combine ethnographic research with critical discourse analysis, for particularly good effect. To develop the argument of this section, it is necessary first to delimit what ethnographic research is. I will then examine its link to case study in order to bring out some practical matters associated with ethnographic research including the use of participant observation and semi-structured interviews.

Conceptual clarification. Clifford Geertz (1968: 4) characterizes ethnographic research as the science of the particular, the concrete or the microscopic. In other words, ethnographic research aims to 'find in the little what eludes us in the large, to stumble upon the general truths while sorting through special cases' (Ibid.). In short, ethnographic researchers are 'the miniaturists of the social sciences' (Ibid.). Some scholars think that ethnographic research is a particularistic description of social phenomena. I do not share that view. At root, in fact, the objective of ethnographic research is to explain "general truths" by examining the concrete and what looks, depending upon the scale, like the microscopic. It may be said, then, that the findings from ethnographic research are generalizable. 'Good ethnography,' says Gusterson (2008: 108), 'gives a rich evocation of the . . . world it describes while also contributing something to theory. . . . It should give a thick enough description that readers could draw their own inferences about (what is) being described.' In my view, ethnography brings out the grammar of a social phenomenon, because studying practices of controls at one site (for instance, the airports), teaches us a great deal about cross-national patterns of securitization (see Salter 2008). The consequence of this position is that if we can unveil the *grammar of securitization*, it means that the prospects of building a theory of securitization are clearly within reach.

Practical matters: participant observation and semi-structured interviews. To some extent, ethnographic research is regarded as a type of case study. Its logic is that of discovery. However, ethnographic research displays different procedures of collecting and sifting data, which depends upon the kind of technique that is mobilized. In fact, students of securitization who employ ethnographic research use essentially two types of methods, participant observation and semi-structured interviews, generally in combination. These two techniques have distinctive features and specific requirements, to which I now turn.

Participant observation requires a peculiar state of mind on the side of the researchers: to be able to give an account of the world from the standpoint of "insiders"; in short, to have the capacity to "participate." This method is appropriate for the study of daily manifestations of securitization or what is often referred to as "micro-practices" of securitization. I am not claiming that participant observation can achieve all analytical purpose. This would be presumptuous, at best. Specifically, participant observation is poorly equipped to account for the causal relation between variables, which is one of the fruitful terrains of process-tracing. By contrast, participant observation is at its best when it comes to the critical assessment of a theory. To be more precise, by employing participant observation, students of securitization would be able to 'describe (1) what goes on, (2) who or what is involved, (3) when and where things happen, (4) how they occur, and why . . . things happen as they do in particular situations' (Jorgensen 1989: 12).

Participant observation is a very demanding technique of generating knowledge claims. It starts with a problem that, certain circumstances, have been proven insuperable for some and thus brought their project to an end, that is, how to enter the field and how do to so without being intrusive. While it might do little harm to your result to tell a refugee that you are investigating how they were portrayed as a threat to the receiving society, it would be imprudent to bluntly inform police officers or border guards that you are studying how they came to construct threat images. The truth, however, is that there are no canonical rules of entry. Each field has its own rules for entry which are sometimes known, but often have to be experienced. Moreover, the entry can be conditioned by genre, race, class or even the reputation of the institution to which the researcher is affiliated. In this respect, participant observation requires a sharpened sense of feeling and the ability of grasping opportunities as they arise.

Participant observation has been especially important to researchers who investigate the "backstage" of securitization, that is, processes of securitization that are obscured from the view of outsiders (cf. Balzacq 2008; Salter 2008). Echoing the view that 'ethnography must be able to bring a people and a place to life in the eyes of those who have not been there,'[8] Claire Wilkinson (Chapter 5, this volume) uncovers day-to-day processes of securitization through direct experiential and observational accounts of a series of mass protests that occurred in Bishkek, the capital of Kyrgyzstan, in October 2005. Via participant observation of the daily moves and counter-moves by audiences and securitizing actors, she elicits the effects of the distal and proximate contexts in which these actors were implicated. This case study opens a possible window in understanding how contexts constantly reallocate power positions to agents and rearticulate their power relations (audience here, securitizing actor there; and vice versa).

In the second variety of ethnographic research, the investigator conducts semi-structured interviews to uncover the meaning people activate to make sense of their daily practices. In this use, many students who have worked on the securitization of migrants in or by the European Union (EU) generally have carried out various rounds of extensive interviews, at different levels of EU institutions. However, they differ in the degree to which they stick to fine-grained protocols. Too often, some analysts insist that the questionnaire must be stable enough to allow comparability of answers. This is understandable, but methodologically unsatisfactory. In recent projects, I found that fixed questionnaires made the interviews less dynamic and actually brought little returns (cf. Balzacq 2004, 2008). To be sure, if securitization is produced by a "discursive community," the more questions framed differently provoke similar answers from different people the more reliable the conclusions become (see also Gusterson 2008: 104). Of course, I trust that a core set of questions might be helpful, if only to create some conviviality at the outset of the interview, but what I think is of limited service are fully controlled questionnaires, timing, formality of context. . . . Interviews are, to some degree, performance of the self. Under these circumstances, the investigator needs to respect the trajectories of interviewees to capture the stories told in the heat of action.

I must finally point out that in (face-to-face) interviews, what is said is almost as important as what remains unspoken; the verbal is supplemented (i.e., the case for it is strengthened or contradicted) by the gestural; and, variations in stories are as useful as stabilities. Furthermore, the difficulty with interviews on securitization processes is that many securitizing actors may be doing their best to manipulate meanings, obscure intentionally or unintentionally or conceal those meanings from the viewpoint of the researcher (Jørgensen 1989: 14). In the field of migration, this is common as some securitizing actors do not want to be depicted as "racists." In part, through semi-structured interviews, Bigo (1986) described the construction of the network of police forces in Europe. In her PhD thesis, Léonard (2007) catches up the extent to which EU insiders' views affected the conception of migrants and refugees as a threat in Europe since 2001. In short, semi-structured interviews evince otherwise inaccessible insiders' world of meaning and reveal new perspectives on the origins of a security problems.

Process-tracing

With process-tracing (along with content analysis), we enter one of the least travelled routes of securitization analysis. The reason is that process-tracing is consistently associated with positivist methodologies, which are regarded as incompatible with securitization theory. I have recently received a friendly critique of a colleague who holds that process-tracing, because of its commitment to causal explanation, is a radical misfit for securitization analysis. Poststructuralists, too, ordinarily sidestep any explanation that lends credence to the idea of causal mechanisms. It is not unreasonable to respond to such interpellations by asking what makes securitization a *domaine réservé* of an interpretive epistemology? Nothing. To start, process-tracing operates essentially with qualitative data (various types of documents, interviews, newspapers, historical memoirs, surveys, etc.). Of course the nature of data is not enough to situate a method in one epistemological stripe or another. But it does indicate that possibilities of connecting methods exist. Making a different argument, then, I hope to show that process-tracing can be a useful method for examining *certain* processes of securitization. In other words, those who are in the—difficult—business of designing a comprehensive theory of securitization have a great deal to learn from process-tracing.

The realm of process-tracing. If the investigator inquires "why a securitizing move was successful?", answering "because an audience accepted" would be a platitude, if not a tautology. For the present purpose, I argue, process-tracing is particularly useful for uncovering the "scope conditions under which" securitizing moves are likely to obtain. In fact, 'to identity the (causal) process', argues Goldstone (1991: 50–62),

one must perform the difficult cognitive feat of figuring out *which* aspects of the initial conditions observed, in conjunction with *which simple principles* of the many that may have been at work, would have *combined* to generate the observed sequence of events.[9]

In this light, the core of process-tracing is to examine social mechanisms which brought a social phenomenon into being. According to Hedstroem and Swedberg (1998: 25), social mechanisms are 'a set of hypotheses that could be the explanation for some social phenomenon, the explanation being in terms of interactions between individuals and other individuals and some social aggregate.' In short, process-tracing deals with issues of interactions, causal chains linking the independent variable(s) to the outcome of the dependent variable, and the conditions under which such causal paths obtain (Checkel 2008). In this sense, process-tracing can be a cure to confirmation bias. In fact, the explanation of process-tracing lies upon the strategy of condition-seeking, which asks: "under what conditions does securitization occur?" Process-tracing fares better than discourse analysis in that regard, as the latter often concentrates on whether securitization has happened or not, and how it has taken shape; less frequently, if ever, does discourse analysis ask why. This is where, I surmise, process-tracing is probably at its best. The point is that the concern with 'has securitization occurred and how?' has led some scholars to assume (among other things) that accumulating facts in order to confirm the desired outcome (i.e., successful) was the *summum bonum* of securitization studies. In brief, discourse analysis is strong in understanding how securitization operates, but weak in uncovering why certain securitizing moves succeed and when. In these circumstances, I argue, the insights brought by process-tracing can contribute to laying the groundwork for developing a comprehensive theory of securitization.

Two techniques capture the significance and specificity of process-tracing: condition-seeking and design strategy. First, condition-seeking aims to sort out 'limiting conditions for a known finding'. The aim of design strategy is, on the other hand, to discover 'conditions that . . . produce a previously unobtainable result' (Greenwald *et al.* 1986: 211). This means, for example, that within the conspectus of process-tracing, failed securitizing moves are outcomes worthy of investigation, in part because they enable us to explain why other moves were successful and, in part, as a consequence, because the knowledge culled from failed securitizing moves can 'enrich the general theory' of securitization (George and Bennett 2005: 215). In this light, process-tracing is decisive both in constructing and testing theories.

Recently, Salter (2008) has examined failed cases of securitization. The net benefit of his work is to cast new light on how the securitizing actor interacts with various types of audiences, in different settings. In this volume, he pursues this work, devoting more attention to the different types of failures which can derail a securitizing move. Through a case study, he tests different assumptions and unveil the social mechanisms upon which they rest. With the help of this analysis, what could be interesting to explain next is which of the failures has the strongest effect on securitizing moves, when?

Tracing social mechanisms. The language of causal mechanisms can be daunting for the "traditional" investigator employing securitization theory. But it should not be for two reasons, both of which have to do with the underlying assumptions of securitization theory. Recall the first and second assumptions of Chapter 1.

Assumption 1: The centrality of audience

For an issue to be pronounced an instance of securitization, an "empowering audience" must agree with the claims made by the securitizing actor. The empowering audience is the audience which: a) has a direct causal connection with the issue; and b) has the ability to enable the securitizing actor to adopt measures in order to tackle the threat. In sum, securitization is satisfied by the acceptance of the empowering audience of a securitizing move.

Assumption 2: The co-dependency of agency and context

The semantic repertoire of security is a combination of textual meaning—knowledge of the concept acquired through language (written and spoken)—and cultural meaning—knowledge gained through previous interactions and current situations. Thus, the performative dimension of security rests between semantic regularity and contextual circumstances.

These two assumptions embody distinct processes whose features and effects could be comprehended via the use of process-tracing techniques. In particular, in the first, there is a distinct social mechanism at play, namely "persuasion." In the second assumption, I isolate *one* possible social mechanism, namely "learning." These two mechanisms are distinct, but interdependent. In fact, learning generally occurs through socialization which, if designed (inducing new actors into the ways of thinking, acting and behaving of a given community) follows the mechanism of persuasion, i.e., 'a social process of communication that involves changing the beliefs, attitudes, or behaviour, in the absence of overt coercion' (Checkel 2008: 117). The problem, however, is that for many sceptics, neither persuasion nor learning is amenable to process-tracing. I demur. Checkel's works on socialization and persuasion (2001, 2005) provide a fine-grained illustration of how process-tracing operates. He uses a series of hypotheses in order to understand the effects of persuasion on the beliefs of agents analyzed. In my view, those who would like to use process-tracing in securitization might start from there.

However, process-tracing does not look for a one-directional relationship between some or all of the factors highlighted by the aforementioned assumptions. It insists, in contrast, on the degree of congruence between them. In this sense, what

I would like to propose is that process-tracing illuminates not only mechanisms of *causal determinacy* but also mechanisms of *causal adequacy*. It does so, more precisely, through an examination of the degree of congruity between different circumstances driving and/or constraining securitization. The advantage is noteworthy: an investigation of *degrees of congruity* enables us to determine the relative status of one of the forces within the *network of causality*. Since it might prove tricky to identify a precise causal link as the exclusive source of a securitized issue, investigating congruence between, for instance, the strategies of the securitizing actor, the frame of reference of the audience, and the immediate context, may yield more credible results. In other words, the analysis of the degree of congruence among relevant concurrent forces should better guide attempts at understanding securitization, because how these various factors blend tells us a great deal about the likely outcome of the process. Indeed, with configuration and congruence one does not need to rely on the normative conditions of securitization; one grasps key concepts that highlight at once causal networks and products of securitization.

There are probably as many process-tracings as there are social mechanisms. Process-tracing can have different names, and many typologies compete (cf. Aminzade 1993; George and Bennett 2005; Roberts 1995). In other words, this is not a one size fits all technique. For instance, Aminzade (1993: 108) develops what he calls 'theory-guided process-tracing', that is, 'theoretically explicit narratives that carefully trace and compare the sequences of events the constituting process' under study. George and Bennett (2005: 210–11), for their part, propose four kinds of process-tracing: detailed narrative, use of hypotheses and generalizations, analytic explanation, more general explanation. The format of this chapter prevents us from discussing these types of process-tracing in depth. Suffice it to point out that what the investigator wants to trace is the sequence of events that brought securitization about. To do so, the researcher uses analytic explanation which 'converts historical narrative into an *analytical* causal explanation couched in explicit theoretical forms' (Ibid.; emphasis in the original).

Thus, in Chapter 8, Roxanna Sjostedt attempts to investigate the securitization of HIV/AIDS by tracing the different causal chains that led to the successful outcome. This is achieved mainly through the examination of the causal effect of context on the securitizing moves, a causality whose significance is assessed by disaggregating context. She does not work one-way, however: from context to securitizing moves. Instead, Sjostedt constantly moves from causes to effects and from effects to causes in order to test her premises and eliminate spurious accounts. In short, the chapter offers a good illustration of how process-tracing could be employed as a reliable tool for theory development and refinement. In this light, the two assumptions on audience, on the one hand, and agency and context, on the other hand, could be translated in theoretical terms. For instance, the common frame of reference and the perceived speaker's knowledge of the security problem would bear more weight in securitizing an issue absent of a sensitive external context. By contrast, if the external context provides potent clues for the existence of a security hazard, the importance of the speaker's knowledge and the influence of the common frame of reference would decrease. In other words, in securitization, the common frame of reference and the perceived speaker's knowledge can be substitutes for external forces (Lupia and McCubbins 1998: 55).

A cautionary note. Process-tracing is not a panacea; no method is. I would therefore be useful to terminate this section by drawing researchers' attention to some of the constraints on conducting process-tracing, in the context of securitization studies. To me, three are essential: specifying the unit of analysis; taking equifinality into account; scrupulously assessing the time available for crafting the work. To start with, the investigator needs to clearly specify the level(s) of analysis at which the causal path(s) will be examined. In section II, I have specified three levels of analysis and their constituent analytics (i.e., units of analysis). Taking the level of agent, the investigator using process-tracing could then decide to test, for instance, the effect of the securitizing agent's personal identity on the likely outcome of a securitizing move. This is not out of reach as one may think. In a compelling study, Abdelal *et al.* (2009) have developed the different ways in which identity could be treated as a "variable." In this book, context is rigorously treated as a variable both by Wilkinson and Sjostedt. The inferences they make from the evidence gathered are compelling, even if the theoretical conclusions remain provisional.

The second constraints on doing process-tracing relates to the issue of equifinality (i.e., the repertoire of causal paths that lead to a given outcome or what I have called earlier the 'degree of congruence among relevant concurrent forces'). The challenge for the researcher is to separate processes which are causal but congruent from those that are not. The result: process-tracing is not a method which is meant to contribute to the construction of what is regarded as "parsimonious theories." Instead, it aims to 'explain more completely the outcome at hand' (Checkel 2008: 123). In other words, process-tracing could help to craft middle-range theories. However, warns Checkel (Ibid.), 'If one is not careful, middle-range theories can lead to over-determined and, in the worse case, "kitchen-sink," arguments where everything matters.' He concludes nonetheless that this risk could be minimized by careful research design.

The last constraint is more material, but no less important. Because process-tracing generates many alternatives explanations that have to be checked out against the data, it will generally require more time than discourse analysis for instance. In my view, in fact, only ethnographic research comes closest to matching the time demand brought by process-tracing. As such, those who embark on process-tracing needs to evaluate their chances of completing their research within the time allotted. This may sound banal, but many projects are financed for a limited period and, as such, require that the results be made available at a particular date.

Content analysis

Students of securitization who use content analysis seek primarily to capture the kind of cues to which audience is likely to be responsive to, and whether this sensitiveness is contextually (in)dependent (Hermann 2008: 167). But the use of content analysis remains rather exceptional. Indeed, primarily because of its commitment to a positivist methodology, content analysis is subject to the same under-use as process-tracing. Whether researchers like it or not, however, securitization studies have something to learn from content analysis. This section focuses its attention on outlining what marks out content analysis from discourse analysis, a method to which it is often fruitfully combined. This is done along three axes: one bears on aims, one relates to the data used, and one concerns the logic of enquiry.

First, according to Moyser and Wagstaffe (1987: 20), the objective of content analysis is to throw 'light on the ways (agents) . . . use or manipulate symbols and invest communication with meaning.' Ultimately, this concern is not distant from what discourse analysis tries to accomplish. Indeed, both methods are concerned with drawing conclusions from a set of texts. But it is worth pointing out that while content analysis concentrates on the text as an independent entity, discourse analysis focuses on the situated and social aspects of the text; in other words, the text emerges out of an intersubjective context. Thus, for discourse analysis the reaction that a text provokes in a given audience is an important element that needs to be accounted for. Second, discourse analysis and content analysis use very similar range of data and the decision to select one type of data depends on the research question. In fact, content analysis and discourse analysis have recourse to data that, broadly put, convey meaning. These, we have shown, are generically called "texts."

The third axis—the logic of enquiry—strikes at the heart of fundamental contrasts between the two methods. It is here that the stakes are higher for students of securitization. While discourse analysis insists on the constructed character of the meaning generated by the analyst, content analysis holds that the meaning of the text can be fixed and, if well coded, be retrieved via replication by other investigators. Put crisply, content analysis proceeds deductively, while discourse analysis operates inductively. For content analysis, in other words, text's meaning is constant and stable across time and place and, hence, differences in interpretations indicate a potential problem that has to be addressed if the results are to be reliable (Hardy *et al.* 2004: 20). On this view, then, content analysis emphasizes the measurability of variables or counting and coding. However, the fact that content analysis uses essentially quantitative methodologies does not mean that it cannot integrate questions whose treatment requires a methodology that is more qualitative in nature. In fact, the procedures used to draw inferences from the materials collected vary. For instance, if the investigator looks for the presence or absence of a "securitization frame" in the materials under scrutiny, the method could be qualitative. If, by contrast, the investigator is interested primary in the "*degree to which* the securitizing frame affects the trust in government," the materials could be subject to a quantitative analysis. Often, however, qualitative and quantitative techniques are triangulated (see Vultee's Chapter 4 in this volume).

A related important aspect, regardless of the logic of enquiry (qualitative/quantitative), is the unit that the investigator aims to code. In fact, content analysis rarely analyzes documents as a whole: interview, newspaper articles or speech. What is coded, instead, are more manageable units such as words, sentences, paragraphs or themes, extracted from the materials that the researcher has available (Neuendorf 2002). In turn, the coding itself should conform to the research question. If the investigator is interested in "securitization frames," s/he codes for words, sentences

. . . having to do obviously with threat images. The matters are more complex when it comes to quantifying the degree to which the securitization frames affect the trust in government (see Vultee, this volume). In sum, the ideal for content analysis rests on the quality of the coding plan that can be drawn upon by any coder.

Towards a reflexive pluralism

I have presented the methods employed in this book without a preconceived notion about the superiority of a method over another. I think, contrary to others, that the methods discussed in this chapter could be combined in various ways and that there are no insurmountable fences around any of the method that would prevent it from being combined with another in the list. In fact, Chapters 3 through 10 use more than one method to carry out the task at hand. Although the combination of discourse analysis with any other method is by far the most dominant, we have expressions of other combinations, too (see Table 2.2).

Most qualitative methods dramatically increase in usefulness to the extent that their features can be related to other areas of enquiry and to other methods. Arguably, the result is to produce a much richer version of securitization processes, that is, a grammar of the relationship between different factors and actors of securitization. It is for this reason that pluralism in methods is said to be "productive," because it generates patterns of understanding that could have gone unnoticed or inappropriately captured by the use of a single method (Lupovici 2009). As Checkel (2008: 126) nicely puts it, 'if we want to offer better answers to the questions we ask . . . then . . . epistemological and methodological boundary crossing is both essential *and possible*' (emphasis in the original).

Pluralism is not syncretism. Indeed, bringing different methods together in the hope that more would be known could prove counterproductive if done recklessly. In fact if one scraps away the surface of some empirical studies, few pass the test of what I call "reflexive pluralism." I define reflexive pluralism as a proactive and non-biased attitude towards methodological dialogue. In other words, reflexive pluralism does not attempt to smuggle through the view that one of the methods employed is superior to the other. If a method fares better than another, it should be stated clearly and justified. Finally, reflexive pluralism recognizes both the strengths

Table 2.2 A cartography of this volume's methodological commitments

	Discourse analysis	Ethnographic research	Process-tracing	Content analysis
Chapter 3	•			
Chapter 4	•	•		
Chapter 5	•			
Chapter 6	•	•		
Chapter 7	•		•	
Chapter 8	•			•
Chapter 9	•			
Chapter 10	•			

and limits of the approaches which are brought together to examine a particular case. Herrera and Braumoeller's (2004: 17) put it thus: 'researchers must be circumspect in their claims, regardless of methods.' For that reason, as the majority of the contributors to this book insist, it is necessary for the investigator to pay close attention to the validity of the results obtained. My understanding of validity here does not—at least not necessarily—refer to the ability of the researcher to forecast what might happen in the future, but instead follows Holsti's (1969: 143): 'Are the results plausible? Are they consistent with other information about the phenomenon being studied?' This is another way of arguing that the chapters that follow are united in the view that the most fundamental issue in securitization analysis is the extent to which the practice of methodological pluralism can enliven our knowledge of processes of securitization.

Notes

1 In the realm of discourse analysis, for instance, the following authors do not often share the same kind of method: Duffy, Federking and Tucker (1998); Fierke (1998); Hansen (2006); Hopf (2002); Larsen (1997); Milliken (1999); Neumann (2008); Ringmar (1996); Laffey and Weldes (2004).

2 For Sartori (1970: 1033), whose view I follow, methodology is 'a concerns with the logical structure and procedure of scientific enquiry.' Methods refer to the different techniques used to collect and examine data (Crotty 1998: 3).

3 Emphases added.

4 We think it is useful to put "successful" in brackets in order to indicate that, strictly speaking, this concept is redundant when attached to "securitization," as the latter refers to successful moves only.

5 The referent subject is my term while the referent object is the CS's. I place them at the level of the agent because they are often regarded as expressing an agency, of sorts.

6 The work of Hansen (2006, 2007) constitute a notable exception in that regard. This shows, parenthetically, that the language of schools is more limited than that of theoretical delineation proposed in this book. See Chapter 1 in this volume.

7 Searle (1977b).

8 Nordstrom (2004: 14).

9 Cited in George and Bennett (2005: 206); italics in original.

Part I
The rules of securitization

3 Reconceptualizing the audience in securitization theory

Sarah Léonard and Christian Kaunert

Securitization theory has attracted much attention since it was first developed by the so-called 'Copenhagen School'. In a nutshell, the Copenhagen School argues that an issue is transformed into a security issue (i.e. *securitized*) after a securitizing actor presents it as an existential threat and this 'securitizing move' is accepted by the 'audience' (Wæver 1995; Buzan, Wæver and de Wilde 1998). The original formulation of securitization theory is heavily influenced by linguistics, and more precisely the concept of 'speech acts', that is, discourses that do not 'report on things', but rather 'do things'. Whilst the potential of this approach for contributing to the debates on the meaning of security in the post-Cold War era has been widely acknowledged, a consensus has also emerged around the idea that securitization theory in its original formulation by the Copenhagen School suffers from several weaknesses, including the significant under-theorization of several aspects of securitization processes (Barthwal-Datta 2009; Balzacq 2005; McDonald 2008; Stritzel 2007; Wilkinson 2007).

This chapter focuses on one of these weaknesses, which concerns the conceptualisation of the relationship between the securitizing actor and the audience or, in other words, the role of the audience in securitization processes. This has been identified as a problematic and under-theorised aspect of the securitization framework by several scholars, as will be discussed later in this chapter. Even the scholar who developed the concept of 'securitization', Ole Wæver, has recognised that the concept of 'audience' '[needs] a better definition and probably differentiation' (Wæver 2003: 26). Indeed, given that an issue *only* becomes securitized after such a representation has been accepted by the audience, it is important for the framework to offer a clear conceptualisation of who constitutes the audience and how its acceptance can be assessed. Otherwise, the application of the securitization framework to empirical case studies remains difficult and open to conflicting interpretations stemming from the uncertain composition and role of the audience.

This chapter starts by analysing how the Copenhagen School initially conceptualised the audience in securitization processes. Then, it examines some of the criticisms that have been levelled at the Copenhagen School's treatment of the audience, before considering some of the suggestions made to remedy these shortcomings. It recognises the strengths of some of these contributions, but argues that they still leave some questions unanswered. In the following section, the chapter argues that incorporating some insights from public policy literature in securitization theory, in particular Kingdon's 'three streams' framework, offers a promising avenue to reconceptualise and refine the role of the audience in the securitization framework. Such a reconceptualisation allows for (1) a clearer operationalisation of key concepts such as 'securitizing actor' and 'audience', (2) an understanding of the audience as actually comprising different audiences, which are characterised by different logics of persuasion, and (3) a more systematic analysis of the linkages between the various audiences and their respective impact on the overall policy-making process.

The role of the audience in securitization processes: the Copenhagen School's view

The Copenhagen School's position on the exact role played by the audience in securitization processes lacks precision and clarity. Its treatment of this issue is at times vague and at other times contradictory. This will be demonstrated by a close critical reading of what remains to date their most systematic and detailed discussion of the securitization framework, namely their book *Security: A New Framework for Analysis*.[1]

First of all, there is significant uncertainty regarding the role of the audience in securitization processes, as there seems to be an important contradiction within the writings of the Copenhagen School on this topic. On the one hand, the Copenhagen School seems to give the audience an important role in securitization processes, as securitization is presented as 'an essentially intersubjective process' (Buzan, Wæver and de Wilde 1998: 30). Buzan, Wæver and de Wilde (1998: 25) argue that '[a] discourse that takes the form of presenting something as an existential threat to a referent object does not by itself create securitization – this is a *securitizing move*', but the issue is securitized only if and when the audience accepts it as such'. On the other hand, the Copenhagen School implicitly downplays the role of the audience in other parts of *Security*. For example, after refuting the idea that the 'security-ness' of an issue can be objectively assessed, Buzan, Wæver and de Wilde (1998: 34) argue that '[thus], it is the actor (...) who decides whether something is to be handled as an existential threat' – 'actor' referring to 'securitizing actor' in this sentence. This contradicts their previous assertion that '[s]uccessful securitization is not decided by the securitizer but by the audience of the security speech act' (Buzan, Wæver and de Wilde 1998: 31).[2]

Despite this contradiction, it appears that, overall, the Copenhagen School grants a significant role to the audience in securitization processes. Nevertheless, this is a dimension of their securitization framework that remains fundamentally under-developed. First of all, it is not entirely clear what the acceptance by the audience means and entails exactly, and therefore how it could be identified in practice. Buzan, Wæver and de Wilde (1998: 25) note that '[accept] does not necessarily mean in civilized, dominance-free discussion'. They rephrase this in the following way: '[since] securitization can never only be imposed, there is some need to argue one's case' (Buzan, Wæver and de Wilde 1998: 25). Other mentions of the role of the audience in *Security* refer to ideas such as 'the existential threat has to be argued and just gain enough resonance for a platform to be made from which it is possible to legitimize emergency measures or other steps that would not have been possible (. . .)' (Buzan, Wæver and de Wilde 1998: 25). Again, it is not clear how the 'resonance' of the securitizing move with the audience or the 'signs of such acceptance' (Buzan, Wæver and de Wilde 1998: 25) could be assessed.

Moreover, and perhaps more fundamentally, the Copenhagen School remains extremely vague on the issue of how to identify the audience of a securitizing speech act. The audience is defined as 'those the securitizing act attempts to convince to accept exceptional procedures because of the specific security nature of some issues' (Buzan, Wæver and de Wilde 1998: 41). However, no precise criteria are outlined to identify who exactly constitutes the audience in practice. Whereas they give practical examples of securitizing actors – 'political leaders, bureaucracies, governments, lobbyists, and pressure groups' (Buzan, Wæver and de Wilde 1998: 40) – Buzan, Wæver and de Wilde do not give any illustrations of audiences in *Security*. In a draft paper written in 2003 and aiming to 'take stock' of the recent developments in securitization studies, Wæver is only marginally more precise in his definition of 'audience'. He argues the following:

Audience is those who have to be convinced in order for the securitizing move to be successful. Although one often tends to think in terms of 'the population' or citizenry being the audience (the ideal situation regarding 'national security' in a democratic society), it actually varies according to the political system and the nature of the issue

(Wæver 2003: 11–12)

Later in the paper, Wæver (2003: 26) argues that the Copenhagen School's original version of the securitization framework may have been too overly informed by the example of Western democratic regimes. It would therefore be necessary to consider cases of securitization taking place in various political and cultural settings in order to develop a more general framework. Wæver (2003: 26) also argues that the securitization framework should take into account the existence of various categories of audience involved in a securitization process, without giving any more details about how this could precisely be done.

Having closely examined the treatment of the audience in *Security*, as well as in a paper subsequently written by Wæver, one therefore reaches the conclusion that the role of the audience in securitization processes remains significantly under-theorised in the Copenhagen School's formulation of securitization theory. Although Buzan, Wæver and de Wilde emphasise that securitization is an *intersubjective* process, in which the audience seemingly plays a crucial role, this concept remains rather vague and under-specified. How it could be operationalised in empirical studies is also far from clear.

Criticisms of the Copenhagen School's conceptualisation of the audience

Given the vagueness of the idea of 'audience' in the Copenhagen School's conceptualisation of securitization, it is therefore unsurprising that it is an aspect of its framework that has been particularly criticised. First of all, several scholars have denounced the lack of clarity and precision in the Copenhagen School's treatment of the audience (Balzacq 2005; Stritzel 2007: 363; Dunn Cavelty 2008: 26; Salter 2008; McDonald 2008: 573) along the lines of what has been elaborated in the previous section. As Balzacq (2005: 173) puts it, 'although the Copenhagen School points out that a "significant audience" must concur with the securitizing actor – who speaks "security" – for a referent object – the threatening event – to be securitized, the nature and status of that audience remains unaccounted for'. Dunn Cavelty (2008: 26) notes that 'it remains largely unclear which audience has to accept what argument, to what degree, and for how long'. Salter echoes this view, by stating that 'the actual politics of the acceptance [by the audience] are left radically under-determined by [the Copenhagen School's securitization] model. It is precisely the dynamics of this acceptance, this resonance, this politics of consent that must be unpacked further' (Salter 2008: 324). According to Vaughn (2009: 273), the lack of precision concerning this specific aspect of the Copenhagen School's securitization framework is particularly problematic. In her view, '[while] there may be a valid reason for this – namely, that "the relevant audience" is always case specific – the omission of detailed criteria for recognizing and delimiting the audience weakens empirical research as the audience plays such an important role for securitization'.

Moreover, it has been questioned whether securitization can be conceptualised as both a speech act and an intersubjective process at the same time. Balzacq argues that there are tensions between these two dimensions of the Copenhagen School's securitization framework. On the one hand, the idea that securitization is a speech act indicates that it is a self-referential activity, governed by discursive rules. On the other hand, the idea that the acceptance of the audience is crucial for successful securitization emphasises that it is intersubjective (Balzacq 2005: 179). This is an ambiguous position. However, according to Balzacq (2005: 179), the lack of attention given to the audience indicates that the Copenhagen School 'leans towards self-referentiality, rather than intersubjectivity'. In the same vein, Stritzel (2007) questions whether the idea of a securitizing speech act taking place at one discrete point in time can be combined and reconciled with the idea of securitization being an intersubjective process, which strongly suggests the existence of some sort of 'negotiations' between the securitizing actor and its audience, or in the Copenhagen School's own words, '*processes* of constructing a *shared understanding* of what is to be considered and collectively responded to as a threat' (Buzan, Wæver and de Wilde 1998: 26, quoted in Stritzel 2007: 363; italics by Stritzel).

Finally, it has been argued that the idea of the 'audience' oversimplifies the fact that there can be multiple audiences, with different characteristics (Balzacq 2005; Stritzel 2007: 363; Salter 2008; Vuori 2008; Roe 2008). The first to elaborate on that point was arguably Balzacq (2005). In his article on 'political agency, audience and context', he criticises the fact that the idea of the Copenhagen School gives the securitizing speech act too high a degree of formality – 'reduc[ing] security to a *conventional procedure* such as marriage or betting' (Balzacq 2005: 172; italics in the original). In his view, Buzan, Wæver and de Wilde neglect the configuration of circumstances in which securitizing speech acts take place, 'including the context, the psycho-cultural disposition of the audience, and the power that both speaker and listener bring to the interaction' (Balzacq 2005: 172). One can therefore conclude that several scholars have argued that the Copenhagen School's conceptualisation of the composition and the role of the audience in the securitization framework lacks precision and that it is problematic with respect to applying the framework empirically.

Re-conceptualisations of the role of the audience in securitization processes

Further to the various criticisms levelled at the way in which the Copenhagen School theorised the role of the audience in *Security*, several scholars have put forward suggestions to develop and refine the concept of audience, with regard to both its composition and role, in the securitization framework. Balzacq (2005) has suggested paying more attention to the audience (as well as to the context, more generally) in the securitization framework. He has argued that it would be more analytically beneficial to conceptualise securitization as a strategic or pragmatic practice – rather than a speech act – taking place in a specific set of circumstances, including a specific context and the existence of an audience having a particular 'psycho-cultural disposition' (Balzacq 2005: 172). From that viewpoint, securitization is understood as 'a sustained strategic practice aimed at convincing a target audience to accept, *based on what it knows about the world*, the claim that a specific development (oral threat or event) is threatening enough to deserve an immediate policy to alleviate it' (Balzacq 2005: 173). This has important consequences for the securitizing actor. Indeed, it means that a securitizing actor is more likely to be successful if (s)he can rightly perceive the feelings and needs of the audience and can use a language that will resonate well with the audience (Balzacq 2005: 184).

Another suggestion that has been put forward by several scholars is to conceptualise the audience as actually comprising different audiences (Balzacq 2005; Vuori 2008; Salter 2008). Vuori (2008: 72) argues that these 'audiences depend on the function the securitization act is intended to serve'. For example, the audience of some securitization acts can be quite general, whereas some acts in situations of crisis may be intended to an elite audience only. Given that the audience depends on each specific socio-historical situation, Vuori (2008: 72) considers that it would be impossible to define who constitutes the audience in securitization theory. However, he claims that '[what] could have been said within the model is that the audience has to be such that they have the ability to provide the securitizing actor with whatever s/he is seeking to accomplish with the securitization' (Vuori 2008: 72). In addition, although the issue of multiple audiences is not the focus of his article, Balzacq (2005) makes an important point regarding the potentially different roles of different audiences when he makes a distinction between formal support and moral support for the securitizing move. He observes that what matters for the development of policy is whether the securitizing move enjoys formal support (i.e. support by the institutions making decisions), since moral support is generally not sufficient (Balzacq 2005: 185). This point has been further developed by Roe (2008), who suggests breaking down the audience into the general public – who can offer 'moral' support regarding the 'securityness' of a given issue – and policy-makers, such as parliaments – who can offer the 'formal support' necessary for the adoption of the extraordinary measures aiming to tackle a security issue.

Finally, another important suggestion for reconceptualising the audience in securitization processes has been made by Salter (2008). In an article on securitization using the case of the Canadian Air Transport Security Authority (2008), he suggests reconceptualising securitization (including the role of the audience) by drawing upon insights from dramaturgical analysis, in particular Goffman's concept of 'setting'. Salter argues that, in line with the use of dramatic language by Buzan and Wæver themselves – 'the staging of existential issues in politics' or how 'an issue is dramatised' (Salter 2008: 328) – insights from dramaturgical analysis can add to the securitization model by offering a more nuanced understanding of the relationship between the audience and the securitizing actor and the reasons for which securitizing moves succeed (or fail). A dramaturgical approach does so by highlighting the existence of various 'settings', which are characterised by specific actors and debates, an audience with particular expectations, as well as specialised language, conventions and procedures – or, in other words, specific factors of success for particular securitizing moves. Indeed, 'a securitization act may be successful with a scientific or technocratic community, and yet fail in the elite and popular realm, such as the debate over global warming during the 1980s and 1990s' (Salter 2008: 325). Salter (2008: 328) identifies, without any specific justification for this choice, four types of settings: popular, elite, technocratic and scientific. He notes that there could be more settings in other contexts, but that considering four here allows for sufficient differentiation within this specific case.

According to Salter, the type of setting in which securitizing speech acts take place is important, because it influences their form, content and success:

In each of these different settings, the core rules for authority/knowledge (who can speak), the social context (what can be spoken), and the degree of success (what is heard) vary. This goes far beyond linguistic rules towards norms and conventions of discourse, as well as bureaucratic politics; group identity, collective memory and self-defined interest

(Salter 2008: 322)

Salter's contribution is significant, as it is the most elaborate and detailed attempt at identifying what the different audiences may be, which characteristics distinguish them (e.g. rules, norms, practices, languages) and what impact this has on securitizing moves. One of the main strengths of such a setting-centred approach is that it highlights the differences between settings and their impact on securitization, which is a very valuable point. Salter's conclusion that 'the process of successful securitization and desecuritization operates differently within different settings' (Salter 2008: 343) is an important contribution to the development of securitization studies. However, one is left with the impression that these settings are rather disjointed. It is not clear how they relate to one another or whether events in one setting can have an impact in another setting. One wonders how the overall direction of a policy gets decided in a context where there are different settings, which means that who speaks, what is said and what is accepted by the audience may vary. Also, which setting matters most in which context?

In conclusion to this section, it is evident that some attempts have been made to refine the concept of 'audience' in the securitization framework. The most interesting idea that has been put forward is the suggestion that we should re-think the audience as comprising different audiences, characterised by different logics of persuasion. However, what still needs to be addressed is the issue of the relationships between these different audiences and the overall impact that those various audiences have on policy-making. In other words, it is necessary to develop a general and unified framework that can account for the existence and the respective impact of various audiences on the securitization of an issue. In the next section, it is argued that some insights from public policy literature, in particular Kingdon's 'three streams model' are particularly helpful to refine the issues of the composition and the role of various audiences in the securitization framework.

Reconceptualising the role of the audience in securitization processes: the contribution from Kingdon's 'three streams model'

Agendas, Alternatives and Public Policy, which was written by Kingdon in 1984, has made a seminal contribution to public policy literature. Aiming to explain policy change, the intellectual puzzle leading Kingdon's research was 'what makes an idea's time come?' (Kingdon 1984: 1). His approach is informed by a broadly constructivist understanding of politics and international relations. The core of his model, described as a set of processes, includes the following categories: the setting of the agenda, the specification of alternatives from which a choice is made, and an authoritative choice among those alternatives in a legislative procedure (Kingdon 1984: 3). The agenda can be defined as 'the list of subjects or problems to which governments officials (. . .) are paying some serious attention at any given time' (Kingdon 1984: 3). The agenda-setting process narrows the set of alternatives for different policies due to the fact that only a certain number of issues can potentially be considered simultaneously. Thus, it becomes important to understand how and why the agenda changes over time. Kingdon highlights two factors that influence agenda-setting and the specification of alternatives. Those are the nature of the participants who are active and the process by which agenda items and alternatives come into prominence. Kingdon's model (1984: 92–93) suggests that there are three major process streams to explain 'policy change', i.e. (a) the problem stream,

(b) the policy stream, and (c) the politics stream. These three streams are thought to operate largely independently from one another.

When one examines Kingdon's 'three streams model', one can immediately identify points of convergence and possible cross-fertilisation between this model and the securitization framework. The two key-factors that he identifies in agenda-setting and the specification of alternatives – the participants and the process by which agenda items and alternatives become prominent – can be linked to the concepts of 'securitizing actors' and 'securitization processes'. The idea that there are three different streams – each characterised by specific participants – is reminiscent of Salter's idea that there are different possible settings for securitizing moves, each characterised by a different audience. As a consequence, this chapter argues that it would be very beneficial for scholars to draw upon certain insights from Kingdon's model to further refine some aspects of the securitization framework. In doing so, it is argued, a more robust and precise securitization framework would be developed, which would allow for (1) operationalising the concepts of 'securitizing actor' and 'audience' more precisely and for (2) conceptualising the audience as comprising different audiences, which respond to different logics of persuasion, but are all inter-linked as they are involved in a single policy-making process. This would address the problems affecting the existing versions of the securitization framework previously discussed and that can be summarised as follows: (1) the lack of clarity and pre-cision in the use of concepts, such as 'securitizing actor' and 'audience', which obstructs their operationalisation, (2) the over-simplification represented by the idea of one single audience (rather than several audiences characterised by different logics of persuasion), and (3) the lack of integration between these various audi-ences, which seem to be fragmented and whose respective impact on the overall policy-making process remains unclear.

The idea of integrating some insights from Kingdon's work into the securitiza-tion framework is actually not entirely new. The first scholar who suggested doing so was probably Eriksson in a conference paper written in 1999. The main aim of this paper was to address what Eriksson considered to be a major shortcoming of securitization theory at the time, namely the fact that '[it] fails to explain why some instances of securitization influence the agenda but not others' (Eriksson 1999b: 2). In his view, the securitization framework could be improved by drawing upon insights from agenda-setting theory, Kingdon's work in particular. Thus, Eriksson was mainly interested in Kingdon's work to tackle the issue of agenda-setting in the securitization framework, rather than that of the audience. Following on from Eriksson's paper, another scholar who attempted to integrate insights from Kingdon's work into securitization theory is Dunn Cavelty (2008). However, for all its strengths and the added value that it brings to the study of securitization, Dunn Cavelty's treatment of Kingdon's model may be seen as slightly problematic as it diverges from the original model in some respects without justifying these changes.[3] Furthermore, when one considers the main aim of this chapter, it can be argued that Dunn Cavelty did not go as far as it would have been possible in using insights from Kingdon's 'three streams model' to refine the concept of 'audience' and the relationship between the securitizing actor and the audience in securitization theory. It is therefore necessary to revisit Kingdon's 'three streams model' and examine the contribution that it can make to our understanding of securitization processes, in particular the role of the audience in such processes.

Thus, the attempts by Eriksson and Dunn Cavelty to integrate some insights from the 'three streams model' developed by Kingdon into the securitization framework have shown that there is a lot of potential for successful cross-fertilisation between these two frameworks. This chapter argues that this is also likely to be the case with regard to the issue at the heart of this chapter, that of the relationship between the securitizing actor and the audience. There is still a significant amount of untapped potential in Kingdon's work regarding this issue. Although both Eriksson (1999b: 1) and Dunn Cavelty (2008: 26) have criticised the vagueness of the idea of 'audience' in the Copenhagen School's securitization framework, neither of them has drawn upon Kingdon's model to specifically tackle this problem. The next section addresses this gap. It explores how the concept of 'audience' can be further developed in the securitization framework by drawing upon Kingdon's 'three streams model'.

Synthesising Kingdon's 'three streams model' and the securitization framework

Kingdon's framework (1984) of public policy change is based upon three 'streams', namely the problem, policy and politics streams, and the important role of 'policy entrepreneurs'. This section aims to synthesise Kingdon's insights and the securitization framework. It considers each of the three streams in turn and seeks to illuminate the specific composition and role of the audience in each of them. It then considers the related concepts of 'policy window' and 'policy entrepreneur' – which is very close to that of 'securitizing actor', as a securitizing actor can be seen as a specific type of policy entrepreneur.

The problem stream

In Kingdon's problem stream, an actor aims to construct a policy problem by using indicators and external events. Thus, the problem stream analyses in essence how conditions become policy problems by capturing the attention of decision-makers. Indeed, Kingdon (1984: 109) suggests that one should distinguish between a condition and a problem. Bad weather, illness and poverty are conditions, not political problems in themselves. They only become political problems once decision-makers perceive them as such and come to believe that they should be tackled. This process depends on the existence of dramatic events or crises, or on a variety of indicators of a problem, be they statistical or non-statistical (Kingdon 1984: 91). First of all, a crisis or a prominent event with extraordinary consequences may signal the emergence of a problem. In addition, indicators can draw the attention of decision-makers towards certain problems and therefore define the very essence of them. Kingdon states that these indicators are used in the political world by both governmental and non-governmental agencies to routinely monitor various activities and events. It is interesting to note here that not all activities are regularly monitored. As a consequence, the selection of monitoring activities already indicates that a certain number of assumptions are made by analysts.

This is evidently reminiscent of the securitization framework. One of its key-ideas is that there are no security issues in themselves, but only issues constructed as such by a securitizing actor and accepted as such by the audience (Buzan, Wæver and de Wilde 1998: 21). Security issues are intersubjective and socially constructed. Securitizing an issue (or a condition) is just a specific way of transforming it into a policy problem – a specific type of policy problem, namely a 'security problem'. As suggested by the Copenhagen School, 'uttering "security"' by the securitizing actor 'moves a particular development into a specific area' (Wæver 1995: 55). This means that, in this specific stream, the securitizing actor aims to construct a policy problem by using indicators and external events. In this case, the 'audience' mainly includes the other decision-makers involved in the policy-making process. They need to be convinced that a problem is indeed a 'problem'. They will operate according to their own logic, and constructions of problems will have to rely significantly on indicators and events. In the problem stream, decision-makers, even after the construction of a problem, continue to measure public approval or disapproval of policy problems, which in turn feeds into their own understanding of the 'problem'.

This insight from Kingdon's framework can significantly contribute to '[further unpacking] the dynamics of this acceptance [of the securitizing move by the audi-ence]', this resonance, this politics of consent' as called for by Salter (2008: 324). The politics stream is precisely conceptualising this politics of consent, which determines whether a policy problem becomes accepted as such. It highlights how a number of indicators or events are strategically used to construct a policy problem that is accepted as such by decision-makers.

The policy stream

The policy stream concerns the process of policy formation. As suggested before, policy alternatives are generated even in the absence of a policy problem. Even if no issue has been identified as a problem (or 'securitized' in the case of securitization processes), policy alternatives are being prepared. Kingdon suggests that the gener-ation of alternatives and proposals in a certain policy community of decision-mak-ers resembles a process of 'biological natural selection' (Kingdon 1984: 116). Only ideas that fulfil the following criteria tend to survive: technical feasibility, value acceptability for the policy community, and successful anticipation of future con-straints (such as budget constraints) (Kingdon 1984: 122–51). If there is a feasible, available proposal that is taken seriously, then the problem will feature high on the agenda and may survive the politics stream.

Interestingly, Kingdon argues that it is a futile exercise to concentrate on the ori-gins of ideas (or specific policy proposals) (Kingdon 1984: 75). Ideas can come from anywhere, implying that tracing the origins of a specific idea leads into infinite regress. Nobody really controls the information flow in the system; no source monopolises the flow of information and ideas (Kingdon 1984: 81). He argues that this makes rational decision-making behaviour almost impossible. If decision-makers were to operate rationally, they would first define their goals and define the level of achievement necessary for goal satisfaction. Alternatives would be compared systematically, assessing costs and benefits, and the most cost-efficient alternative would be chosen. However, this is not the case due to the human inability to canvass and compare many alternatives simultaneously.

In this stream, policy alternatives are generated in policy communities, which, in Kingdon's view, are composed of specialists in a given policy area and '[hum] along on [their] own' (Kingdon 1984: 117). Some of these specialists work in government positions, some in bureaucracy, some in think tanks, academia, etc. They relate to each other mostly through their common interest in the policy area. They often interact with one another and know each other's ideas, proposals and research. Through their frequent interactions, they develop shared debates and logics of persuasion. 'In some respects, the bulk of the specialists do eventually see the world in similar ways, and approve and disapprove of similar approaches to problems' (Kingdon 1984: 133). In this policy stream, the audience to be persuaded is therefore composed of specialists and technocrats. Such an audience tends to be convinced by arguments based upon knowledge, rationality and efficiency (Radaelli 1999). This implies that some problem constructions may persuade technocratic communities, but not the general public or decision-makers (and vice-versa).

The politics stream

The politics stream comprises elements such as public mood, pressure groups campaigns, election results, ideological distributions in the political institutions, and changes in the administration (Kingdon 1984: 152–72), which may have an important impact on whether policy proposals are adopted. The political mood is a particularly important aspect of the politics stream. Kingdon suggests that people in and around government 'sense' a political mood (1984: 146), which goes by different names – the national mood (or the different national moods in the EU), the climate in the country, changes in public opinion, or broad social movements. In his view, it is not important whether decision-makers perceive the political mood accurately, as what matters is that the perceptions that they collectively hold of the political mood are strong (Kingdon 1984: 147).

While the activity characteristic of the policy stream is persuasion, the main activity in the politics stream is bargaining, including building winning coalitions. Such coalitions can be built through the granting of concessions. The proposals in the politics stream have already been discussed in the policy streams; some people may have been convinced, whereas others have not. Therefore, the decision-makers that remain to be convinced will need to be given something in return for their support. Actors pay a heavy price in the politics stream if they do not pay sufficient attention to coalition building (Kingdon 1984: 160). The coalition building achieves a sort of bandwagon effect, where the more decision-makers join the coalition, the more other decision-makers want to be part of it.

In the politics stream, changes mainly occur because of either the shifts of important participants (e.g. administrations or legislators in parliament) or shifts in the political mood. As far as the audience in this stream is concerned, one can analyse it as comprising two different groups, namely the decision-makers involved in the decision-making process and the general public.

Policy windows and policy entrepreneurs

Having analytically examined each of the three streams, it is now important to go back to the crucial question of how policies get adopted in the end. One of the key arguments put forward by Kingdon (1984: 165) is that the three streams, i.e. problem, policy and politics streams, become coupled and form a *policy window*. Streams become coupled as they come together at critical times. As a problem is recognised and a solution has been developed and is available in the policy community, a change in the politics stream makes it the right time for overall policy change. This is the opening time for policy windows, which usually stay open for a short period only, thereby providing an opportunity for advocates to push for their solutions. As Kingdon describes them, these *policy entrepreneurs* already have prepared solutions in hand for problems that still need to emerge. Thus, they wait for policy windows to open in order to attach the former to the latter, which requires a specific development in the politics stream.

It is evident that there are close links between the ideas of 'policy entrepreneur' and 'securitizing actor'. In Kingdon's view, policy entrepreneurs play a crucial role in policy-making when the three streams become coupled. Having been waiting for a policy window to open, they seize the opportunity offered by the coupling of the streams to propose, lobby for, and sell a specific policy proposal. In Kingdon's definition (1984: 181), policy entrepreneurs need to possess resources which they are willing to invest, such as time, energy, reputation, money, and actively use those to promote a policy position in return for anticipated future gains. According to Kingdon, policy entrepreneurs have 'one of three sources: expertise, an ability to speak for others, or an authoritative decision-making position'. They are usually known for their persistence, '[their] political connections or negotiating skills' (Kingdon 1984: 180). This has clear connections with the securitization framework, where successful securitizing actors are said to have 'social capital' and 'be in a position of authority' (Buzan, Wæver and de Wilde 1998: 33).

According to Kingdon (1984: 168), the opening of policy windows is vital for the adoption of policies. These windows open due to a change in the politics stream (e.g. the political mood) or in the problem stream, but not in the policy stream of alternatives. The existence of policy windows mostly relies on the perceptions of participants (Kingdon 1984: 17). Kingdon (1984: 190) suggests that 'the appearance of a window for one subject often increases the probability that a window will open for a similar subject' (Kingdon 1984: 200). The reason for such a 'spill-over' is that, once political entrepreneurs realise the popularity of an issue, they are likely to pick up related issues. They will try and find as many related issues as possible in order to increase the probability of their success. From the point of view of the securitization framework, this is an interesting insight that contributes to our understanding of the emergence of 'security continuums', placing various partially related issues in the realm of security, such as drugs, organised crime, terrorism, and illegal migration in the European Union (Huysmans 2000).

In conclusion, several important points have been made in this section. It has been suggested that the securitization framework ought to include Kingdon's three streams in order to allow researchers to improve the conceptualisation of the audience (as well as the securitizing actor) in the securitization framework. This has the advantage of allowing for: (1) a more precise operationalisation of the concepts of 'securitizing actor' and 'audience' and (2) a more refined conceptualisation of 'the audience' as comprising different audiences, which respond to different logics of persuasion, but are all inter-linked as they are involved in a single policy-making process.

The next section presents a short case study examining an attempt by the British government to securitize asylum-seekers in the European Union in 2003. It cannot be extremely detailed because of the space restrictions inherent to this chapter. Nevertheless, it usefully illustrates how the amended version of the securitization framework, in particular with respect to the issue of the 'audience', can be applied to an empirical case and highlights some important issues that would otherwise remain unnoticed.

Illustrative case study

In this section, we use the British proposal for establishing transit processing centres for asylum-seekers outside the European Union (2003) to illustrate the aforementioned argument.

As Member States of the European Union (EU) were engaged in the long and complicated negotiations of several legislative instruments on asylum and migration as part of the so-called 'Tampere programme',[4] the British government made a controversial proposal on asylum that dominated the EU debates in this policy area for a few months in 2003. It suggested processing the claims of asylum-seekers having reached the EU – or on their way to the EU – outside the territory of its Member States, a policy known as the 'extra-territorial processing of asylum claims'. In this case study, the British government can be considered the securitizing actor (and policy entrepreneur). It constructed asylum-seekers as a security threat in the 'problem stream' using indicators and references to dramatic events and developed a proposal to tackle the high number of asylum-seekers in the 'policy stream'. However, the implementation of this proposal required the cooperation of the other EU Member States. The 'politics stream' was therefore to take place at the EU level, that is, it was to involve negotiations and bargaining with the governments of the other EU Member States.

Problem stream

The issue of asylum rose to the top of the political agenda in Britain early 2003. As suggested by Kingdon's model, statistical indicators played a particularly important role in the identification of asylum-seekers as a 'problem'. In February 2003, the final figures regarding the number of asylum applications made in the previous year were released. They showed that 2002 had seen an all-time record number of asylum applications, namely 85,865, meaning that there had been 110,700 new asylum-seekers in total (including dependants) (*Migration News Sheet*, 2003a). This was politically important because the number of asylum-seekers had passed the 100,000-symbolic threshold.

Moreover, asylum was not only presented as a 'problem', but more precisely as a 'security problem'. This was evident in some statements made by members of the British government in spring 2003. For example, Immigration Minister, Beverley Hughes, explained that the government aimed to tackle the issue of asylum and to separate it from migration because of 'warning bells that (. . .) had been sounding two years ago' (*The Guardian*, 2003). This was a reference to clashes between gangs of white and British Asian youngsters that took place in some towns of England between May and July 2001 and that led to considerable damage to property, hundreds of injuries and numerous arrests (Schuster 2003b: 514). It is noteworthy that, in 2003, the party in government, the Labour Party, was not the only party to present asylum-seekers as a security threat to Britain. Members of the Conservative Party also made statements to that effect. For example, in January 2003, the leader of the Conservatives, Ian Duncan Smith, stated that 'a significant number [of asylum-seekers are coming to Britain] for criminal or terrorist reasons' (*Migration News Sheet*, 2003 a). It is therefore evident that, in spring 2003, the view that asylum-seekers represented a problem, and more precisely a security problem, was widespread in Britain, in particular amongst the political elites.

Policy stream

The then Prime Minister Tony Blair's reaction to the publication of the asylum applications figures for 2002 was swift. In February 2003, he promised on national television to halve the number of asylum-seekers by September 2003 (*Migration News Sheet*, 2003b; Geddes 2005: 727). He was therefore expected to rapidly make a policy proposal to reach this objective. On 10 March 2003, Tony Blair sent a letter to Greek Prime Minister, Costas Simitis – the then President of the Council of the European Union – asking for a discussion at the upcoming Brussels European Council on an idea developed 'to help deal with the problems of refugees and migration'. Attached to the letter was a six-page document bearing the title 'New International Approaches to Asylum Processing and Protection' (UK Government, 2003), which had been developed over the previous months by a joint Cabinet Office/Home Office Committee. This policy document started by claiming that the 'current global [asylum] system [was] failing' for various reasons (UK Government 2003: 1). Several of those were economic in nature, such as the disproportionate amount of money spent on processing asylum applications compared to the amount of money spent in the regions of origin of the refugees and the high costs inherent to returning rejected asylum-seekers to their region of origin. Based on this assessment, the aim of the British proposal was to develop a 'better management of the asylum process globally' (UK Government 2003: 1) through a reduction in the number of unfounded applications and the improvement of the protection granted to genuine refugees. For this purpose, it proposed the establishment of a new asylum system, whereby asylum-seekers would no longer arrive illegally in Europe in order to claim asylum, but would rather arrive through legal channels, including refugee resettlement. More precisely, the proposal had two complementary components, namely (1) the adoption of measures to improve the regional management of migration flows, including the establishment of 'protected areas' for asylum processing and (2) the establishment of processing centres for asylum-seekers on transit routes to Europe. It is the latter that turned out to be particularly controversial. However, in order to increase the legitimacy of the proposal and make it more persuasive to the governments of the other EU Member States, the British government presented it as drawing upon the 'Convention Plus' initiative of the Office of the United Nations High Commissioner for Refugees (UNHCR) (UK Government 2003: 2).[5]

Thus, what is particularly noticeable about this proposal is that it mainly uses technocratic language and economic arguments to make its case. Its starting point is that the current asylum systems in Europe are costly and that money is not allocated in the most efficient way. In line with that assessment, the British proposal puts forward several measures to ensure a 'better management' of the claims of asylum-seekers. The specificity of this line of argumentation becomes even clearer when one contrasts this proposal with some of its previous versions, which were entitled 'A New Vision for Refugees'. Those were internal documents, which were evidently not intended for wide circulation.[6] Compared to the proposal sent by Blair to his EU counterparts, they have strong security undertones. First of all, they indicate how these plans aim to address security concerns in Britain, notably in relation to the use of the asylum channel by terrorists. In a section discussing potential changes to Article 3 of the European Convention on Human Rights – which prohibits the return of asylum-seekers to countries where they could be subjected to torture or to inhuman or degrading treatment or punishment–, it argues that such a change 'would assist with our security concerns' (UK Cabinet Office and Home Office 2003: 9). In addition, previous versions of the British proposal argue that the existence of large flows of asylum-seekers should be considered a 'legitimate trigger for international action in source countries', including diplomatic pressure, development aid, and even 'military action as a last resort' (UK Cabinet Office and Home Office 2003: 1). Such links between asylum-seekers and security concerns, terrorism in particular, were completely absent from the final version of the British proposal, which was circulated to the other EU Member States. Also, the threat of using coercive measures, including military means if necessary, to deal with countries generating large-flows of asylum-seekers was not included in the proposal sent by Blair to his EU counterparts. Thus, it is evident that the British government worked on the proposal in order to phrase it in a language that, according to their own perceptions, would persuade as many other EU Member States as possible.

Although the most controversial aspects of the initial proposals had been removed or toned down, the proposal to be discussed by the governments of the EU

Member States still represented a significant departure from the ways in which European states had been dealing with asylum-seekers since the adoption of the Geneva Convention in 1951. How and why, then, did such a controversial policy proposal emerge at that stage? This can be explained by the fact that a certain number of policy proposals to reduce the numbers of asylum-seekers had already been considered and implemented in Britain especially since the early 1990s. Those include measures on carriers' liabilities, the finger-printing of asylum-seekers, 'fast track' procedures for processing certain types of asylum claims, the detention of specific categories of asylum-seekers, and the dispersal of asylum-seekers across Britain (Schuster 2003a; 2005; Zetter *et al.* 2003: 91–98). However, the implementation of these measures did not lead to any durable reduction in the number of asylum-seekers; some of them even turned out to have undesired effects (Boswell 2003b; Betts 2004). This explains why the British government, considering that all other policy options had already been exhausted, came to formulate what many observers saw as a contentious policy proposal.

Finally, it is interesting to note that this case illustrates particularly well Kingdon's observation that the key-aspect of the policy stream is persuasion. In order to persuade its audience, i.e. primarily the governments of the other EU Member States, the British government produced a proposal that was mainly argued in economic terms. Rather than putting forward security arguments – which were likely to be persuasive in the British context as shown earlier, but may not have been persuasive in front of other audiences – it rephrased original drafts of its proposal in economic terms. Whilst security arguments may not convince the governments of countries where migration has not been constructed as a security threat, cost efficiency arguments seem more likely to persuade any government in the EU. Such arguments are also more in line with the technocratic arguments that are often at the heart of EU policy debates.

Politics stream

Having put forward a proposal for the establishment of transit processing centres for asylum-seekers outside the EU, the British government then tried to build a winning coalition in the EU in order to push it through. As described earlier, the proposal had been rewritten in a way that was supposed to be less controversial and appeal more to the governments of the other EU Member States, emphasising arguments of cost efficiency. Also, the proposal was presented as contributing to the realisation of the UNHCR's 'Convention Plus' initiative in a bid to appear more legitimate.

However, the British government found it difficult to find many allies during the debates about its proposal. The European Commission stated that the British proposal gave rise to several legal, budgetary and practical problems. In addition, the German and Swedish governments publicly voiced their opposition to the British proposal, whilst other governments were said to have reservations about the proposal (*Financial Times* 16 June 2003; *The Guardian* 20 June 2003). In addition, the UNHCR also disagreed with certain points of the proposal, in particular the idea that the transit processing centres would be located outside the EU's territory (*The Guardian* 5 Feburary 2003; The *Guardian* 1 March 2003). Faced with this mounting opposition, the British government announced that it was withdrawing its proposal on the eve of the Thessaloniki Council in June 2003, where it was due to be discussed again (*The Guardian* 16 June 2003b). According to several media reports, this change in the British government's strategy was mainly prompted by the 'strong opposition from Germany, Sweden and other EU partners' to the idea of transit processing centres (*The Guardian* 16 June 2003a; see also *EU Observer* 31 March 2003; *Financial Times* 16 June 2003). Thus, the British government, who is the securitizing actor in this case, did not manage to persuade its audience at the EU level (i.e. the governments of the other EU Member States and the European Commission) of the desirability of its specific 'problematisation' of asylum-seekers and its specific proposal on transit processing centres to tackle this issue. Sensing that the political mood was not in favour of its policy proposal, it decided to abandon it.

It is interesting to note that the opposition of the governments of some EU Member States was also reinforced by some media reports. Indeed, the media played a significant role in the case studied here by reporting regularly on the EU debates on the British proposal. Newspaper articles, in particular in the left-liberal press, went beyond the neutral language of the British government to speak about 'the camp proposal' and drew parallels with existing refugee camps, before explaining how refugee camps are often plagued with security issues and do not ensure the security of the asylum-seekers they host. They sometimes presented the proposal as having more support than it actually had, which heightened the concerns of its detractors and made it even more contentious. Some newspapers also echoed the concerns and criticisms of pro-migrant NGOs. In sum, the left-liberal media contributed to the heated character of the debates on the British proposal by highlighting its security dimension and presenting it in a more 'politicised' way than had been intended by the British government when it prepared the 'EU version' of its proposal. It appears that this media strategy of portraying the British proposal as being about the creation of 'camps' had some significant impact on the debates. According to the *Independent*, the British proposal on transit processing centres came to be known in 'Brussels' (i.e. in the EU circles) as the '"concentration camp" plan' (*The Independent*, 19 June 2003), and this is what led the UK to abandon it. This was indirectly confirmed by the Greek Presidency of the European Union, when Panos Beglitis, a spokesman for Greek Foreign Minister Papandreou, declared that 'Europe must remain a democratic area which provides asylum and does not have concentration camps' (*BBC News*, 19 June 2003; *Migration News Sheet*, 2003d). This demonstrates that, in the politics stream, the British government did not only fail to persuade its EU counterparts; it also failed to persuade the other part of the audience, i.e. significant segments of public opinion represented by the left-liberal media. As a consequence, the British government, the securitizing actor/policy entrepreneur in this case study, was not able to push through its specific proposal to tackle asylum. It withdrew it, once it saw that there was no policy window opening. Thus, this case study can be summarised as follows. Flows of asylum-seekers into

Britain came to be defined as a security threat in 2003, following a specific interpretation of statistical data on the number of asylum-seekers in 2002. The interpretation and representation of asylum-seekers as a security threat put forward by the Prime Minister, his Cabinet and the Home Office was accepted by most political elites, including beyond the Labour Party. Thus, the audience in the problem stream, i.e. the other members of government and political elites more generally, were persuaded by the representation of asylum-seekers as a security threat. A policy proposal was then elaborated, which aimed to tackle the 'security problem' of asylum-seekers by establishing transit processing centres where the claims of asylum-seekers would be processed outside the EU. This proposal received the support of the specialists and technocrats working on the issue of asylum in the British government circles. Thus, the audience agreed to the proposal in the policy stream. However, the British government did not manage to find enough allies during the negotiations to push its proposal through. Thus, in the politics stream, it failed to convince its two main audiences, i.e. the other governments and significant segments of the EU public opinion, represented here by some left-liberal media outlets. In other words, the British proposal ultimately failed because the British government did not manage to persuade the audience in all the three respective streams that are part of the policy-making process, only in two of them.

From a theoretical point of view, this case study illustrates the advantages of bringing some insights from Kingdon's work into the securitization framework. Kingdon's 'three streams model' allows researchers to make a useful analytical distinction between different audiences, which highlights their specific composition and role. At the same time, his model offers an integrated approach to the overall policy-making process, which also emphasises the specific impact of each audience (and the fact that it has been persuaded, or not, by the securitizing actor/policy entrepreneur) on the policy-making process.

Conclusion

This chapter has focused on what has been identified as one of the most problematic aspects of the Copenhagen School's securitization framework: the undertheorised conceptualisation of the audience and its role in securitization processes. It has examined how various scholars have attempted to reconceptualise the role of the audience. The main points emerging from this analysis have been that the audience should be conceptualised as comprising different audiences, which are characterised by different logics (i.e. they are persuaded by different types of arguments), but are all inter-linked as they are part of the same policy-making process.

The present chapter has argued that such a model could be developed by integrating some insights from Kingdon's work on public policy-making and his 'three streams model' in particular into the securitization framework. This new framework has the advantages of allowing for (1) a clearer operationalisation of key concepts such as 'securitizing actor' and 'audience', (2) an understanding of the audience as actually comprising different audiences, which are characterised by different logics of persuasion, and (3) a more systematic analysis of the linkages between the various audiences and their respective impact on the overall policy-making process. Thus, Kingdon's public policy model is very valuable as it allows for incorporating the political system as a whole into the securitization framework. It underlines the relative importance of individual actors, ideas, institutions, and external processes (John 1998: 173). His concept of 'policy entrepreneur' is particularly useful to the study of securitization processes, as it further develops and refines the concept of 'securitizing actor'.

In conclusion, this chapter has shown that drawing upon Kingdon's (1984) approach to public policy-making and integrating some of its insights into the securitization framework is beneficial for the continuous development and refinement of securitization theory. Kingdon's 'three streams model' can significantly contribute to our understanding of some inherently political processes, which have remained under-theorised so far – how do securitizing actors persuade an audience? Which audience do they need to persuade? Which type of argument is more likely to persuade which audience? What is the impact of each audience – and the fact that it is persuaded, or not – on the overall policy-making process? As a result, it can be argued that a framework integrating insights from Kingdon's 'three streams model' provides for a more comprehensive and integrated analytical framework for analysing securitization processes.

Notes

1 It is acknowledged that Wæver wrote a paper entitled 'Securitization: Taking stock of a research programme in Security Studies' in February 2003, in which he presented his latest thoughts on securitization framework and reflected upon some of its problems. However, although this paper was quite widely circulated, at the time of writing this chapter it had not been formally published. It was therefore not considered appropriate to choose it as the starting point for the discussion of the conceptualisation of the audience in securitization processes. Nevertheless, reference is made to some points made by Wæver in this paper later in this chapter.

2 This tension in the Copenhagen School's approach is actually related to a problem notably highlighted by Vultee in Chapter 4 of this book – 'How can the act of speaking security be performative if it relies on the consent of the audience?' By the same token, Balzacq (2009a) asks: "what power is left to the audience if the *word* security is the act?" In short, it seems difficult to reconcile these two ideas within one single analytical framework.

3 For example, Dunn Cavelty (2008: 34) writes that 'when [a policy window] opens, the three streams (problems, policies, and politics) are usually coupled together by *policy entrepreneurs* (...)'. Actually, in Kingdon's framework, policy entrepreneurs are not responsible for the coupling of the streams. The three streams may come together at some point, which is the moment at which a policy window opens for policy entrepreneurs.

4 The 'Tampere programme' was a five-year work plan for the development of various internal security policies in the EU, including asylum and migration, between 1999 and 2004. It was named after the city where the EU Council that approved it took place.

5 'Convention Plus' is an initiative that was launched by the UNHCR in 2002. Its main aims are to build on the Geneva Convention, by creating special agreements on the secondary movements of asylum-seekers (*i.e.* movements of asylum-seekers from a first

country of refuge to another country) and ensuring lasting solutions for refugees in regions of origin.

6 An early version of this document was leaked to the British daily newspaper *The Guardian* early in February 2003, which abundantly commented upon it. A later version, dated 07.03.2003, was also subsequently leaked to pro-human rights non-governmental organisations (NGOs), notably the German NGO *Pro Asyl*, which made it public on its website.

Framing of effects via
media.

4   Securitization as a media frame

What happens when the media 'speak security'

Fred Vultee

If securitization is not a speech act, why does it act like one? Or, put more formally: What makes some securitizing moves, toward some objects, under some circumstances, before some audiences, have the performative effect that the "philosophical" (i.e., the Copenhagen School view) approach to securitization suggests? Using the U.S. "war on terror" as a central example, this chapter examines contemporary approaches to framing as a theory of media content and media effects to illuminate the social and cultural conditions under which securitization is introduced, amplified or played down. A controlled experiment looks at how public opinion can be manipulated by securitizing or desecuritizing news accounts. The right securitizing move, made toward the right object in front of the right audience, has a significant impact on the elements that make up securitization.

The concept of securitization as a speech act is an elegant analogy, but as a theoretical proposition, it has faced an unresolved contradiction from the outset: How can the act of speaking security be performative if it relies on the consent of the audience? (Balzacq, 2005; Stritzel, 2007) Indeed, almost as soon as Buzan et al. (1998) offer the speech-act formulation, they qualify it:

It is important to note that the security speech act is not defined by uttering the word *security*. What is essential is the designation of an existential threat requiring emergency action or special measures and the acceptance of that designation by a significant audience.

(Buzan et al., 1998, p. 27; italics in the original)

Thus, securitization is better conceived as a process. "Who can 'do' or 'speak' security, successfully, on what issues, under what conditions, and with what effects?" (1998, p. 27). The parallels to Harold Lasswell's summary of communication – who says what to whom, through what channel, and to what effect (Briggs and Burke, 2002, p. 4) – and the centrality of media accounts in forming and shaping public opinions of distant events point to the relevance of media models in understanding the securitization process.

Critics of the speech-act formulation have sought to expand those contextual hints from other directions as well. Balzacq (2005, 2009a) suggests repurposing securitization as a pragmatic act: "a sustained argumentative practice aimed at convincing a target audience to accept, *based on what it knows about the world*, the claim that a specific development is threatening enough to deserve an immediate policy to curb it" (Balzacq 2009a, p. 60). This social-constructivist approach raises several elements to the level of the speech act – the "securitizing move" – itself: not just the actor who "speaks security," but the target audience of the move (underexplained in the Copenhagen approach, as Léonard and Kaunert suggest in Chapter 3 of this volume) and the context in which it is made. This contextualization is both sociolinguistic and sociopolitical (Balzacq, this volume; Stritzel, 2007).

This chapter seeks to advance that line of understanding by explaining securitization as a media frame. As such, it substantiates assumptions 2 and 3 of securitization theory laid out in "A Theory of Securitization." Drawing on a tradition of framing that blends sociological and psychological influences, it suggests that security is an organizing principle invoked by political actors – and, crucially, amplified or tamped down by the news media – in an effort to channel the ways in which issues are thought about. The workings of a securitization frame shed light on the conditions under which "the social content and meaning of security produces threats" (Balzacq, 2009a, p. 64). In line with contemporary approaches to media framing, securitization works as both an independent variable – an effect *in* media – as well as a dependent variable, or an effect *of* media. These effects are created in a multi-sided, often recursive interaction among political actors, the media, and the public that underscores the Copenhagen scholars' emphasis on identity as a centerpiece of security at the societal level.

Concerns that framing had become a theoretical flag of convenience for media studies, rather than a coherent body of assumptions and propositions, led to attempts to reorganize and respecify what framing meant. This process produced some occasionally surprising results; constructivist concepts, like frame valence and news judgment, found themselves measured through positivist methods. But it sometimes meant that the creation of frames as an effect in media was given short shrift – when considered at all, it was often as a deterministic outcome of market forces, rather than the complicated cultural process it is. Thus, the chapter will also look at the social routines of news work and their role in the framing process – the creation of the effect in content. Then, using a "process model" approach to framing, securitization is examined as an effect of content – the process by which, for a distinct portion of the audience, a bombing attributed to "the terrorists" is quantitatively different from an identical act, identically distant from personal or national interests, attributed to unspecified attackers. The "war on terror" is securitized not when "security" is spoken but when "terrorism" is spoken. First, though, conceptions of framing need to be untangled.

Literature

Framing

The study of framing in media has come to represent a robust tradition of its own, although it is rooted in two distinct disciplines. Cognitive psychology has looked at the differences that result when identical data are presented in "gain" and "loss" frames: what part of a population might live if a particular treatment was provided during an epidemic, vs. what part of the population would die (e.g. Heath and Tindale, 1994). A second conception arises from sociology, in which a frame is an element of media discourse that provides a "central organizing idea . . . for making sense of events" (Gamson and Modigliani, 1989, p. 3). Put another way, this sort of framing is "interactional" (Dewulf et al., 2009): participants give and get a series of cues with which they jointly build an interpretation for their exchange. Media learn from audiences even as audiences learn from media.

Rather than presenting identical data from different perspectives, social framing prioritizes the data that make an event into one kind of a story or another. Frames help make clear what kind of a problem a problem is, what sort of tools are used for dealing with it, and which actors are protagonists and antagonists (Entman, 2004). If the main function of framing is "to select some aspects of a perceived reality and make them more salient in a communicating text" (Entman, 1993, p. 52), securitization is a form of framing that highlights the existential threat of an issue — whether it arises at the interstate level or at the cultural level of a state's legitimacy, its linguistic and ethnic identities, or its customs (Buzan et al., 1998, pp. 22–23) — and diminishes the arguments for handling it as a matter of political routine.

The sociological approach to framing produced a rich literature illuminating the role of the media in the construction of reality, but it was not always a coherent one – to the point where Entman (1993) sought "clarification" for the "fractured paradigm" of framing. Indeed, Scheufele (1999) cautioned that there was little point in further attempts to identify particular frames in media accounts until more time was put into understanding framing as a theory. "Process models" of framing (Scheufele, 1999; De Vreese, 2005) offer a more specific organizational concept in which frames can be either causes or outcomes and can be located either in the audience or in the media: roughly, effects of media or effects in media. Increasingly, then, framing research has sought to combine the conceptual depth of the sociological side of framing with the organizational rigor of the psychological side. Often, these studies have investigated attitudinal responses (e.g. Coleman and Thorson, 2002; DeVreese, 2004; DeVreese and Elenbaas, 2008). Other studies have looked at cognitive responses: how frames affect the actual processing of news content. Price, Tewksbury, and Powers (1997) and De Vreese (2004) have used thought-listing as an index. Others have used memory to examine the impact of us-vs.-them terrorism frames (Dunn, Moore, and Nosek, 2005) or gender-related differences in processing positively or negatively framed news (Grabe and Kamhawi, 2006).

Those trends do not herald a return to the "big effects" or "hypodermic needle" days of media theory. Frames can make some thoughts more applicable and easier to use, but they do not act alone; rather, they compete for primacy with other current or long-held ideas (Price et al., 1997). Frames interact not only with attitudes (De Vreese and Elenbaas, 2008) but with other frames (Major, 2009). Nor are frames a linear-acting tool applied by elites to the opinion of the masses; framing's effects can be contingent on the credibility of source and channel as well as the audience's predispositions (Druckman, 2001). But the cognitive study of news framing adds yet another layer to the familiar summary of agenda-setting, in which media accounts tell audiences not "what to think" but "what to think about" (McCombs, 2004): Frames can tell people how (or how hard) to think about what they are told.

That distinction is pertinent because framing provides not just a set of cues for organizing data but a heuristic signal about the relative need to pay attention to text and context. Facing a torrent of information, people are "cognitive misers" (Pachur and Hertwig, 2006), constantly applying strategies that seek to maximize accuracy while minimizing complexity. Under dual-process approaches such as the heuristic-systematic model (Chen, Duckworth, and Chaiken, 2000; Eagly, Chen, Chaiken, and Shaw-Barnes, 1999), a heuristic cue signals a cognitive shortcut – a peripheral bypass route that takes the brain on an easy ride around the congested "systematic" zone of complex argument-building and comparison. Securitization, this chapter contends, can be signaled as just such a heuristic cue, and the peculiar role of terrorism in U.S. political and journalistic discourse makes the "war on terror" an ideal test case. Terrorism allows both journalists and audiences to render quick judgments on story types, actors, and appropriate solutions "without knowing much, if anything, about the particular people, groups, issues or even places involved" (Norris, Kern, and Just, 2003, p. 11). The actor who can successfully "call security" on an act of political violence is likely to gain significant advantages, but not without effort. Securitization is negotiated with multiple audiences: the political establishment and the public can provide "formal" and "moral" support respectively (Balzacq, 2005; Roe, 2008), but both audiences are addressed – and speak back – through the media. As this chapter suggests, the media's role can be significant, but its performance requires some explanation.

Media, terrorism, and identity

The "war on terror" is unquestionably a special example: "a rich current framing case, perhaps the most important of our time" (Reese, 2007, p. 152). For the purposes of understanding securitization, though, what makes it distinctive is the fusion of national security with national identity. The fight over how to name this phenomenon is reflected in an immediate consensus in the U.S. media about how the 9/11 attacks should be understood, but a steady divergence after that in where the "war on terror" is conducted, how frequently news organizations speak of it in their own voice, even how certainly it exists outside quotation marks (Vultee, 2010). Nor was the appropriate meaning settled after the decisive 2008 election. Indeed, tentative hints at desecuritizing the "war on terror" are derided by the neoconservative rear guard as a "War on the Word 'Terrorism'" (Safire, 2009).

Such disputes over lexical choices are hardly new, particularly in the context of political violence; the familiar trope that one person's terrorist is another's freedom fighter can be dated to the late 1940s at least. The choices themselves reflect conflicting norms within the media as well as pressures from outside the media. Journalists sometimes describe a legalistic, arbitrary procedure for determining the circumstances under which an act might or might not qualify as terrorism (Hoyt, 2008) – or even whether an attack linked to the India–Pakistan dispute over

Kashmir should be classed as "international terrorism" of the sort U.S. readers need to know about (Zeeck, 2006). There is no such ambiguity about the attacks of September 2001. When President Bush told the nation that "freedom itself was attacked this morning," he was naming "freedom" as a victim (Anker, 2005), but more importantly he was placing freedom at the core of the nation's identity. In the Copenhagen perspective, national identity can carry greater weight than national sovereignty "because it defines whether 'we' are still us" (Buzan and Wæver, 1997). Wæver puts identity at the core of distinguishing the security of a society from the traditional state-centered view of security:

> State security has *sovereignty* as its focus, and societal security has *identity*. Both usages imply survival. A state that loses its sovereignty does not survive as a state; a society that loses its identity fears that it will no longer be able to live *as itself*.
>
> (1995, p. 67; italics in the original)

Immigration, for example, can thus be painted as a threat beyond the reach of more effective diplomacy, stronger border controls, or other tools of politics. It brings forth calls to mandate the use of English in public business because it is not so much a threat to statehood as to nationhood: "the abilities to maintain and reproduce a language, a set of behavioural customs, or a conception of ethnic purity" (Buzan et al., 1998, pp. 22–23).

This centrality of identity emerges as early as 1983 in Buzan's suggestion that threats to political well-being emerge from "the great battle of ideas, information and traditions" that surrounds competition among ideologies (1983, p. 77). (As scholars have more recently turned to examining a media role in securitization,) O'Reilly has pointed to a U.S. "hyper-patriotism," under which "political dissent is seen by society as unpatriotic and/or treasonous" (2008, pp. 69–70), as an identity factor enabling the securitization of Iraq.

From the media's perspective, the September 11 attacks brought together three sets of circumstances under which journalists can freely abandon their objectivity: tragedy, public danger, and threats to national security (Schudson, 2002). Whether and how quickly things returned to normal is a matter of some debate. For important sectors of the media and the audience, any such return to politics as usual was conditional and tenuous – as was evident three years on in the 2004 presidential elections. To suggest that the contest with terrorism was anything short of war was, in the eyes of the Bush campaign and its media allies, not just quibbling but "naive and dangerous" (Bishop, 2004). To remove terrorism from its pedestal would be to deny its existential threat to the values embodied in "freedom."

To contend that security is a social construct is not to suggest that there are no corporeal threats to people, states, or cultures. It is to suggest that those threats can be securitized only when a securitizing move is enabled by a context – a frame – that "'selects' or activates certain properties of the concept, while others are concealed" (Balzacq, 2005, p. 182). Even military issues, the core of traditional security studies, are not presumptively securitized (Bynander, 2001) until they are created as such.

These concerns underscore the importance of media accounts in creating the picture of the world that the audience of a securitizing move sees.

The world outside

For even the most politically active audiences, the world of security is known secondhand. In Walter Lippmann's observation of nine decades ago, the world is seen through a media "pseudo-environment" (1922/1997, p. 10) interposed between people and their actual environment, such that people adjust to their environment through a series of fictions. These fictions are not necessarily fabrications, but representations that are "in greater or lesser degree made by man himself" (1922/1997, p. 10). What appears in news accounts about a war, an epidemic, or a fire is not necessarily the event itself but a careful, professionally structured reconstruction of what experts, authorities and victims have to say about the war, epidemic, or fire they have feared, observed, or endured. In a very real way, as much as the people they write for and about, journalists encounter the world through a pseudo-environment.

This sort of framing helps the machinery of journalism maintain the pace it needs. "Frames enable journalists to process large amounts of information quickly and routinely; recognize it as information, to assign it to cognitive categories, and to package it for efficient relay to their audiences" (Gitlin, 2003, p. 7). The skill and speed with which the world is reconstructed underscore another of Lippmann's points: "Without standardization, without stereotypes, without routine judgments, without a fairly ruthless disregard of subtlety, the editor would soon die of excitement" (1922/1997, p. 222).

News, like security, is a social construction. Some of the materials used in that construction reflect the industrial process that underlies any sort of mass production, whether of news or of automobiles; others reflect the culture in or for which news is produced. As cultural and social scholars of news (e.g., Carey, 1988; Schudson, 1978) suggest, news functions along parallel channels. One channel carries data, another a set of signals that put the data in social context: how the audience should feel about the data. That channel reflects the frame: whether a legislative vote is good news or bad news, what sort of epic saga a ballgame represents, whether "the terrorists" should be the first suspects in the latest marketplace bombing. The relevance of those frame choices puts the spotlight on the media.

The idea of journalism as "fourth estate" is, of course, fanciful rather than literal, but it does underscore the multiple roles of the news media: in addition to (or instead of) being an independent check on centers of authority, journalism is itself a center of authority. Thus, in Bennett's (1990) indexing theory, news is not necessarily an accurate barometer of public opinion or debate, but it does provide a reliable index of elite opinion and debate. Dissenting opinions are not necessarily shut out, but they have a better chance of being aired if they reflect a dissent that has already begun among elites (Entman, 2004). An out-group might not enjoy media legitimization on its own, but it can help direct attention toward its allies within the sphere perceived as legitimate (Gamson and Modigliani, 1989). Still, absent a known consensus for what sort of story something should be, news accounts are likely to put the parts of it that do fit established frames into those frames (Gitlin, 2002).

The industrial routines of news tend to reinforce a bias toward the status quo, though not the mechanistic influence suggested in some political-economic accounts. Legitimated news, whether it is from the Pentagon or the police department, is provided in regular places at regular times, in most cases by providers familiar with the needs and norms of journalism. Opposing or contradictory views are introduced through norms of balancing, but these views often represent an "official" opposition themselves (Gamson and Modigliani, 1989). Ideally, reliable sources provide reliable information; what makes them essential, though, is that they provide information reliably. Social routines are in play as well. Even if a newspaper is careful not to editorially conflate the "war on terrorism" with the war against Iraq, it is unlikely to challenge the citizen-on-the-street view that a loved one or relative in Iraq is fighting the "war on terror."

Those observations do not suggest that media frames are concocted in the publisher's office and ordered into the news wholesale. Such intervention is rare because it is rarely needed: newcomers to the newsroom learn what news should look like from seeing and hearing what is approved and how (Breed, 1955). And there are many reasons beyond direct influence for why news looks the way it does. The editing process works to make news sound more interesting, rather than less, often by making it more assertive and less hedged (e.g. Bell, 1991). News is oriented not only toward what officials think is news but toward how those close to power understand and explain news – particularly on the policy or international front (Schudson, 2003). And journalists do not work in a cultural vacuum; frames organize the world in a way that makes sense to the people who produce the news as well as those who read it. Through the lens of U.S. news magazines, the U.S. destruction of an Iranian airliner was a tragic outcome of technology gone awry in the heat of a military engagement, but the Soviet destruction of a Korean airliner was a callous reflection of Soviet morals (Entman, 1991). It is nearly impossible to imagine those two frames reversed; like an attack on freedom itself, they create the cultural resonance that makes a frame "appear natural and familiar" (Gamson and Modigliani, 1989).

Not all media securitize all things equally. It is entirely possible, if not commonplace, for one set of media actors to be pushing an issue toward the securitized end of the spectrum even as another is pushing it back toward the domain of normal politics. But securitization does not require the consent (formal or informal) of the entire audience, it only requires the consent of enough of the audience – the "critical mass" that O'Reilly (2008) explains as a combination of volume and quality. The importance of the media in securing this consent is underscored by the findings of Kull et al. (2003), in which misperceptions about motives for the U.S.–Iraq war (the presence of banned weapons or links with al-Qaida) were strongest among several overlapping categories of respondents: those who supported the Iraq war, supported President Bush, or got their news from Fox News (a corporate partner of the New York Post).

If that seems a far more complicated structure than a simple concept like the speech act, it remains one that strongly recalls Lasswell's model: who tries to speak security, to whom, through what channel, and with what impact. As with other political maneuvers, the speaker has several goals: persuading or daunting the opposition, ensuring the support of the base, winning the support of neutrals. Those are affective outcomes; they index how much the audiences likes or dislikes a messenger; trusts or distrusts a message, is frightened or reassured by a news event or a political figure's response. But they are complemented by cognitive processes as well. When the public has only limited knowledge about a topic, as with nanotechnology, opinions are especially susceptible to dramatic events and new information (Cobb, 2005) – the sort of volatile attitudes associated with hasty or heuristic processing, rather than the more stable, permanent ones produced by systematic processing (Griffin et al., 2002). Further, the sort of repetition that makes an issue salient is also likely to reinforce heuristic judgments: "The repeated activation and application of particular heuristics to particular judgments is likely to result in the development of strong associations between those heuristics and judgments" (Chen, Duckworth, and Chaiken, 2000, p. 48). A measure of how closely the audience reads, then, will supplement their attitudinal responses to what they read in the effort to isolate specific elements and outcomes of securitizing moves.

Securitization, in short, is conceptualized as a news frame that cues several results. When the right actor invokes the right threats under the right conditions to the right audience, the results should reflect a greater willingness to place authority, as well as civil liberties, in the hands of the government for the duration. As a cognitive cue, it should act as a heuristic signal to reduce the intensity of processing – though any such effects are expected to be contingent on the audience's readiness to accept the frame. Those propositions require a model for testing securitization in the laboratory.

Procedures

Reproducing securitization in the laboratory: it's alive!

A particular challenge in marrying a constructivist hypotheses like securitization to a positivist method like the controlled experiment is ecological validity; a statistically sound procedure is not necessarily one that reflects what a news audience might see in the wild. This study collected news articles from news agencies and newspaper and broadcast Internet sites over several months then narrowed the collection to eight articles that seemed likely to appear timely without reminding readers of a specific event toward which they might have already formed an opinion. (Thus, an article on North Korea's nuclear program was discarded because a very similar story became prominent again just before the experiment began.)

Articles were edited to a range of 200 to 250 words and manipulated between the second and fourth paragraphs to present the issue as a security threat or as an event handled through the routine functions of the state. The articles dealt with immigration or border security (3) and political violence (5), with the latter chosen to represent an array of conflicts, including the Philippines, the Middle East, the U.S. war in Iraq, and anti-U.S. attacks of the 1990s.

In an article about a rocket attack on southern Israel, for example, a manipulation at the third paragraph was created by using two quotations from the original 900-word news service article. One official said "Terror organizations will pay a heavy price" (the securitized condition); another said that Israel must bring about "a complete halt" to rocket attacks (nonsecuritized). For an article about a bombing in the Philippines, quotations were fabricated for a police official: "We are trying to trace the origins of the bomb now" (nonsecuritized) and "Nobody can do this except the terrorists" (securitized). A primacy effect was modeled in the following paragraph: similar bombs had been used by Qaida-linked groups, but extortionist gangs were also being considered (securitized), or similar bombs had been used by extortionist gangs, but the possible involvement of Qaida-linked groups was also being considered. Participants read all eight articles, four of them securitized and four nonsecuritized; the order in which the articles were presented was randomized.

Experimental studies using student populations are less commonly used to test hypotheses in international relations than in media studies or communications, but they do exist (e.g., Mintz and Geva, 1993; Beer *et al.*, 1995). Indeed, when students are standing in for the public at large, rather than for admirals or presidents, they do rather well (Mintz, Redd and Vedlitz, 2006). In the study described in this chapter, student participants are standing in for the news audiences before which political elites attempt to categorize security issues, sometimes working with and sometimes working against the news media that cover those issues. Participants (n = 151) were recruited from an undergraduate journalism survey class at a large university in the Midwestern United States.

Because of the contingent nature of framing effects and the flexibility of media frames used to organize security-related issues, two measures of attitude were hypothesized to influence the securitization frame: support for government (mostly for the incumbent Bush administration, but also including a strain of "government" in general) and orientation toward the news media (whether subjects saw the news media as politically to the left or right of themselves). These categories were similar but not identical.

These hypotheses and research questions were posed:

H1: News accounts employing the securitization frame will produce a higher level of trust in government than accounts that do not employ the frame, and this effect will be more pronounced among supporters of the government than among nonsupporters of the government.

Table 4.1 Orientation toward media

	Left of media	Similar to media	Right of media
Orientation toward govt			
Anti-government	36	29	8
Pro-government	11	31	36

H2:   Details of articles employing the securitization frame will be less well remembered than details of articles that do not employ the securitization frame. The effect will be more pronounced among supporters of the government than among nonsupporters.

H3:   News accounts employing the securitization frame will produce a greater sense of personal concern and anxiety than do accounts not employing the frame. This effect will be more pronounced among supporters of the government than among nonsupporters.

Two research questions address issues related to how audiences see themselves in relation to the news media and how closely they attend to news:

RQ1:   How does the securitization effect interact with participants' sense of their political alignment with the news media?

RQ2:   Is there a relationship between how closely participants follow news of security-related issues and the effect of the securitization frame?

Methods

The securitization frame is tested with a 2 (frame) × 2 (orientation toward government) mixed design. Frame was a within-subjects variable, operationalized as the presence or absence of the securitization frame. Orientation toward government was a between-subjects factor, operationalized as high support (favorable) and low support (unfavorable). It was measured by adding responses to four questions in the pretest. Each is measured on a 7-point scale:

How much do you trust the government to look after your interests?
Do you think the country is better or worse off than it was six years ago?
Do you think the country is safer or less safe than it was in 2003?
How good a job would you say the president is doing?

Participants were divided into two categories, high (n = 78) and low (n = 73) in orientation toward the government, at the whole number nearest the median split (17).

Orientation toward the news media was conceptualized as the degree to which participants considered their political stance aligned with that of the media. A scale was created by subtracting participants' rankings of the news media's politics on a 1-to-7 Likert-type scale (from "very liberal" to "very conservative") from their assessment of their own politics, then adding 7 to place the entire scale in nonnegative territory. A rating of 7 meant that participants saw themselves as exactly aligned with the media. Ratings less than 7 indicated participants who saw the media as being politically to their right; ratings greater than 7 indicated participants who saw the media as being politically to their left. For analysis, this was broken into three categories: Ratings of 6 or lower (n = 47) were considered left of the media; 7 or 8 (n = 60) were considered similar to the media; 9 and higher (n = 44) were considered right of the media.

Attention to security issues was measured by asking participants how closely they followed news about Iraq, terrorism, and civil liberties. The mean of these scores was taken and divided into three categories, low (n = 50), medium (n = 51), and high (n = 50).

Dependent variables

Recognition memory was measured by summing the number of correct responses to multiple-choice questions taken from the news articles. Each article had 4 questions, so each participant had a maximum score of 16 in the securitized and unsecuritized conditions.

Measures of the degree to which participants perceived events in the articles as threats to their personal safety and security and how much they trusted the government to deal with the situation described in each article were assembled from the questions measuring affective response presented after each news article. Factor analysis indicated that scales tapping orientation toward the government and personal threat formed two factors:

Trust, which represents the key dimensions of the securitization frame (Balzacq, 2009b). It comprises answers to these questions:

This sort of event represents a threat to our way of life.
The government needs to take extraordinary measures to deal with this situation.
I'm confident that our leaders will handle this properly.

Cronbach's alpha for these three questions was 0.75.
Safety measured the degree to which the participant deemed the situation a threat to his or her personal safety. It comprised answers to these questions (alpha: 0.91):

This story is personally important to me.
This story makes me worried.
This story makes me frustrated.
This story makes me anxious.
This story makes me concerned about the country's safety.

Answers were then separated into means for securitized articles and means for unsecuritized articles.

Experimental procedure

A pretest measured participants' political orientation and attitudes toward news media and current events. Each participant read all 8 articles on a laptop. For half the subjects (assigned at random), even-numbered stories were securitized; for the other half, odd-numbered stories were securitized. Order of presentation was randomized by the computer program.

Affective responses were measured after each article was presented. After a brief distractor task, recognition memory was measured with a set of 32 multiple-choice questions, four taken from each article, with question order randomized.

The experiment took an average of 30 to 35 minutes. Participants ranged in age from 18 to 26 (M = 18.81, SD = 0.995); 116 (76.8%) were women. On a scale of 1 (very liberal) to 7 (very conservative), participants rated their own politics to produce a mean of 3.62 (SD = 1.399), and the politics of the news media for a mean of 3.21 (SD = 1.111).

Results

The hypothesis that the securitization frame would produce a greater securitization effect – "trust in government" – was tested with a repeated measures analysis of variance (ANOVA), with the presence or absence of the securitization frame as a within-subjects condition and orientation toward government as a between-subjects condition. The interaction was significant, F(1, 149) = 5.016, p = .027, η²part = 0.033 (see Figure 4.1).[1] Securitized articles overall produced significantly more trust in the government, and the effect was significantly higher among supporters of the government; the impact among nonsupporters is negligible. H1 was supported.

H2, predicting that recognition memory would be lower for securitized articles than for nonsecuritized ones, was tested by the same procedure, with recognition memory for questions from the securitized vs. the nonsecuritized articles as a within-subjects condition. The interaction was significant, F(1, 149) = 4.856, p = 0.029, η²part = 0.032 (see Figure 4.2). Recognition memory in the two conditions is not different among supporters of the government, but memory for securitized articles is significantly lower among those low in orientation toward the government. H2 was partly supported. There is a main effect for the presence of the securitization frame, with the mean number of correct answers significantly lower for securitized articles than for nonsecuritized articles (F(1, 149) = 9.185, p = 0.003,

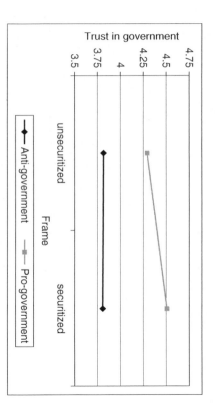

Figure 4.1 Effect of securitization frame and government orientation on trust in government

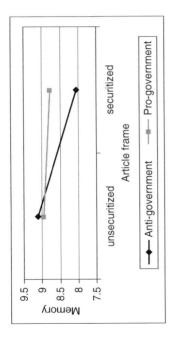

Figure 4.2 Effect of securitization frame and government orientation on recognition memory

η^2part = 0.058, but the interaction with support for government is in the opposite direction from the one hypothesized.

H3 predicted that the frame would be more closely associated with a sense of personal concern, with the effect stronger among those high in orientation toward the government. The interaction was not significant ($F(1, 149) = 2.076, p = .152, \eta^2$part = 0.014), and there was no main effect of the frame ($F(1, 149) = 0.906, p = 0.343, \eta^2$part = .006) or of orientation ($F(1, 149) = 0.089, p = .766, \eta^2$part = 0.001). H3 was not supported.

Research questions

RQ1 asks whether participants' political orientation with respect to their perceptions of media political orientation (whether they perceive the media as more liberal or conservative than they are) is associated with emotional or cognitive outcomes. This "media distance" is similar but not identical to support for government (see Table 4.1). RQ1 was tested with repeated-measures ANOVA, with the securitization frame as a within-subjects variable and media orientation – left of the media (n = 60), about the same (n = 47), and right of the media (n = 44) – as a between-subjects variable.

Although the overall interaction of the frame and media distance on recognition memory was not significant ($F(1, 148) = 1.337, p = 0.266, \eta^2$part = 0.018), there were several significant differences among the means (See Figure 4.1). Participants who considered themselves politically to the left of the news media showed no significant difference in recognition memory ($t(46) = -0.273, p = 0.786, d = 0.04$). Memory for securitized articles was significantly lower among those who saw themselves as similar to the media ($t(59) = -2.188, p = 0.033, d = 0.28$) or to the right of the media ($t(43) = -3.025, p = 0.004, d = 0.46$).

Similarly, the interaction of the frame and media distance on trust in government (see Figure 4.5) was not significant ($F(1, 148) = 1.616, p = 0.202, \eta^2$part = 0.021). But among participants who saw themselves as to the right of the media, securitized

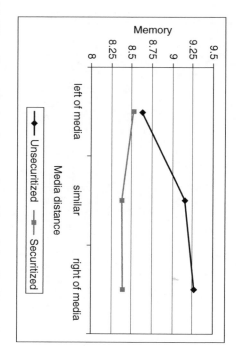

Figure 4.3 Effect of securization frame and participants' "media distance," or political orientation relative to the media, on recognition memory

articles produced significantly higher scores on trust in government than unsecuritized articles ($t(43) = 2.628$, $p = 0.012$, $d = 0.40$). There were no significant differences in trust for those who saw themselves as similar to the media ($t(59) = 1.467$, $p = 0.148$, $d = .17$) or to the left of the media ($t(46) = -0.008$, $p = 0.994$, $d < 0.01$).

RQ2 asks if the degree to which participants follow news about security-related issues is related to the effects of the securitization frame. There is a significant effect of securitization on trust in government ($F(1,148) = 4.95$, $p = 0.028$, η^2part $= 0.032$), such that securitized articles produce greater trust, but no effect from the degree to which participants follow news ($p = 0.23$).

There is a significant effect of the frame on recognition memory ($F(1,148) = 8.509$, $p = 0.004$, η^2part $= 0.054$), such that securitized articles are less well attended

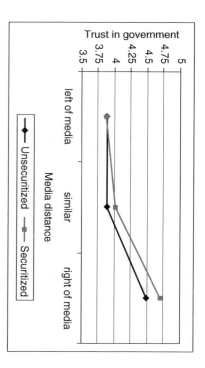

Figure 4.4 Effect of securitization frame and media distance on trust in government

Table 4.2 Effect of frame and how closely subjects follow security news on trust in government

Follow	Trust		Trust				
	unsec	SD	secure	SD	t	p	d
Low	4.05	0.803	4.19	0.908	1.701	0.095	0.16
Moderate	4.26	0.766	4.26	0.874	0.159	0.875	0.02
High	3.87	0.938	4.03	1.080	1.553	0.127	0.16

Table 4.3 Effect of frame and how closely subjects follow security news on recognition memory

Follow	Mem		Mem				
	unsec	SD	secure	SD	t	p	d
Low	9.00	2.119	8.38	2.089	−1.875	0.067	0.29
Mod	9.39	2.219	8.39	2.359	−2.763	0.008	0.42
High	8.66	2.219	8.50	1.982	−0.441	0.661	0.07

to. There is no overall effect of following the news ($p > 0.69$) but several group means show important differences. Among those low in following news, memory for securitized stories is lower than for unsecuritized stories, and the difference approaches significance ($p = 0.067$). In the moderate group, memory for securitized stories is significantly lower. Only in the group highest in its attention to security issues is the difference between frames conclusively insignificant.

Discussion

This chapter proposes that securitization works as an independent media frame – as a characteristic of some threats to security, rather than the presence of a threat itself, and of some ways of invoking those threats, rather that just an authoritative invocation of security. It has been widely, if not always accurately (Bynander, 2001) assumed that defense is a presumptive security call, but the results discussed here suggest otherwise. The defense-related threats raised by substate violence or border security issues are, on paper, effectively identical in both conditions. What appears to make a threat "existential" is not the presence or scale of armed violence, or the presence of such traditional news values as geographic or cultural proximity. Rather, it is the association of that threat with "the terrorists," whoever they might be.

A sense of personal risk does not appear to be affected by securitization. In line with the Copenhagen School's emphasis on the construction of threats to shared culture, securitization creates a sense of danger to "us," not to "me." A bomb in the Philippines or a missile in Sderot is not a proximate threat to a student in the U.S. Midwest, but if can be conceived as a threat to freedom itself, it is a step closer to threatening the community with which the student identifies. Securitization has the heuristic effect of an organizing frame in that it cues affective and cognitive responses. It is not a speech act, in that it is not performative by virtue of some agreed higher authority, but it has the effect of a speech act among a designated part of the audience: Those inclined to trust the government already are more inclined to do so when a securitization frame organizes distant events into a coherent picture. In practical terms, they are quicker to see a threat to "our way of life" and more ready to grant extraordinary powers to the government to mitigate that threat. To "speak security" on an issue will not invoke security for all, but it appears quite able to invoke a particular security for some.

Whether that "some" becomes "enough of the right people" – O'Reilly's (2008) description of "critical mass" – seems to depend in part on the cognitive impact of the frame. Securitization was expected to act as a cue that careful, systematic processing is not needed, and it appears to work as predicted among audiences that do not follow security issues closely – particularly those in the middle ground between the apathetic and the attentive. When "the terrorists" are involved, this audience appears to have received a clear signal that cognitive resources can be better spent elsewhere.

More intriguing is the response of those participants who were in the anti-government camp to begin with. Their processing is negatively affected by the securitization frame, while their pro-government counterparts show no appreciable difference. Here, the frame seems to be creating a "boy who cried wolf" effect: when "the terrorists" are invoked, the oppositional audience knows all it needs to know, and processing becomes less careful.

A very different effect arises when the audience's political relationship to the media is examined: there are no differences for the securitized stories, but when the frame is not present, those who see the media as similar to themselves and – especially – those who see the media as to their left are significantly more attentive in their reading. It is as if they are looking harder for an admission by the biased media that, indeed, this is the very sort of situation someone has been trying to securitize all along: a terrorist is a terrorist.

The relevance of securitization as an effect-of-media are underscored by the appearance of securitization as an effect-in-media. Securitization is not just an experimental fancy; it is a routine aspect of news framing. Two passengers on the same bus, or two employees in the same office, can see an issue through contradictory frames as easily as any two undergraduates at any midwestern university, depending on which choices are made at which stages of the construction of their news world. Securitization will seem like a better choice when it seems like the natural choice: the referential scheme that the right authorities (even, in many cases, the appropriately official opposition) are saying in a way that makes contextual sense in the newsroom and in the audience. The more closely they are bound by identity, the more readily is a perceived threat to that identity passed along.

It is worth remembering that this chapter represents a limited range of securitizable issues that are deeply bound up with a particular U.S. administration. Much remains to be done on which issues can be securitized, how much farther from the orthodox realm of state security they can be, and how different administrations will interact with different sets of supporters and opponents. Still, such investigations should start from the premise that securitization speaks more (and more effectively) to supporters of the actor who invokes it than to opponents. Indeed, those opponents appear likely to take themselves out of the discursive loop through inattention or dismissal – another advantage to the securitizing actor and another potential obstacle for the actor who would "speak normality" to an issue, rather than speaking security.

Whether the consequences of a securitization frame are intended or unintended, they appear to be quite real. Journalists who decline to choose an ostensible frame, or who think the frame that looks most like "news" is the only choice available under professional standards, are likely to end up with whatever the house is serving. However socially palatable that might seem at the time, it could produce consequences that run counter to the best professional intent of the practitioners.

Finally, an empirical laboratory test of securitization should not obscure the importance or normative or critical examinations. The political camp that deprecates English-only laws or restrictions on the provision of services to immigrants – clear indications that the immigration issue is being securitized – might welcome the securitization of energy or environmental issues. That is a process that can be measured by the aforementioned tools discussed; whether securitization is the best approach for furthering public understanding, or the proper way for news organizations to fulfill their roles in that understanding, is not the sort of question settled in the laboratory.

Note

1 The dependent variable "trust in government" was squared to improve normality of distribution for the ANOVA and t-test calculations. Means and standard deviations are reported in original units.

5 The limits of spoken words

From meta-narratives to experiences of security

C. Wilkinson

In sociological terms, reconceptualising security as a pragmatic act, rather than solely as a speech act, finally creates space for the issue of the context in which securitizations occur to be considered. This chapter takes as its starting point the premise that when used for empirical investigation, securitization theory results in an account of security that has effectively been decontextualized. I refer to these final, theoretically-compatible accounts as *abstractions of meta-narratives of security*, or *meta-securitizations*, in order to indicate that they are *abstractions of accounts of security* that conform to the theoretical model offered by securitization theory. As such, security meta-narratives are retrospective and, crucially, *selective* abstractions of all the different acts and narratives that contributed to a successful securitization, stripped of reference to any internal dynamics and local context that are not directly related to the final securitization. Problematically for empirical studies, meta-narratives often bear little resemblance to people's experiences of how securitizing moves developed and are understood within a particular context. The Copenhagen School's prioritisation of theoretical coherence has meant that consideration of *local understandings* have been largely ignored, despite the fact that such local knowledge offers the analyst a way to situate securitization specifically in relation to local conditions—i.e. as a pragmatic act — rather than in relation to potentially spurious theoretical assumptions.

In relation to context, two of the most problematic aspects of the Copenhagen School's concept of securitization are the privileging of speech and its outcome-dependent retrospective view of security. In its orthodox theoretical form, the only way to incorporate non-verbal expressions of security is by their subsequent or retrospective incorporation into a security narrative by a securitizing actor. Without this post-event "translation" of actions into words by actors, securitization is unable to accommodate non-verbal performances of "security" concerns such as protests and demonstrations or migration. The analytical consequences of this over-reliance on the medium of speech are considerable even for an orthodox retrospective application of securitization theory. Securitization presents a linear and stepwise dynamic of security construction, starting with a securitizing actor who constructs a referent object and threat narrative. This narrative of existential threat is then either accepted or rejected by an audience, thus determining the outcome of the securitizing move. In practice, however, the process may start at any point, with the component parts of a securitization – securitizing actor, referent object, threat narrative and audience – developing simultaneously and being mutually constitutive (Huysmans 1998; Wilkinson 2007). In addition, instances where physical action either precedes or replaces verbal expressions of security can only be accommodated if and when they are subsequently incorporated into a speech-act, that is, when they are interpreted as meaning "security". Conforming to this need for speech-act to have chronological precedence is only possible if a certain degree of 'editing' is carried out to present a logically and theoretically coherent account of how a situation developed (Wilkinson 2007: 20).

The Copenhagen School's traditional focus solely on successful, i.e. complete, securitizations is one of the key reasons that "editing" occurs during analysis. In practice the distinction between successful and unsuccessful is far less clear than the theory suggests, as Wagnsson explains:

it is helpful to be cautious when applying the notion of "successfully" securitised. A political leader may, for example, "speak security" primarily with an external audience in mind, with the aim of deterrence or to improve his/her state's position in a negotiation. If s/he then gains the ear of the public, securitization has been achieved more or less "by mistake", since the primary intention was not to convince the population that the problem amounted to an existential threat. Alternatively, if a president leads his/her country to war, but is widely criticised by the opposition and eventually ousted from office in a coup d'état, is this a case of successful securitization? In both cases, securitization has been reached, but not necessarily "successfully".

(2000: 18)

She goes on to suggest that in order to assess whether different actors view an issue in the same way, "we should always begin the analysis by asking *to whom* a securitizing move is directed and/or in the eyes of *whom* an issue is securitised" (Ibid; italics in the original). Salter extends this point, proposing that the success or failure of a securitizing move be measured "by ranking the degree to which policies, legislation, and opinion accords with the prescriptions of the speech act" (2008: 325). Both of these arguments are important steps towards creating space for the consideration of the processes involved in a securitizing move. Nevertheless, it is still necessary to address the issue of *how* such moves are constituted in terms of the mediums used in to invoke security. For this, securitization must be understood primarily as a *pragmatic act*, which necessitates the explicit and reflexive consideration of the context in which it occurs.

The need to pay greater attention to securitization's context has not gone unnoticed by scholars. Huysmans commented that a "cultural-historical interpretation of the rhetorical structure [of securitization] would reduce a tendency to universalise a specific logic of security" since how security is understood in different locations "is based on specific cultural and historical experiences" (1998: 501). More recently, building primarily upon Balzacq (2005), Stritzel has proposed extending the theoretical framework to elaborate securitization's "embeddedness", arguing that "security articulations need to be related to their broader discursive contexts from which both the securitizing actor and the performative force of the articulated speech act/text gain their power" (2007: 359–60). Salter, meanwhile, offers a methodological solution: the use of dramaturgical analysis to consider the "setting" of a securitization, since the process "reflects the complex constitution of social and political communities and may be successful and unsuccessful to different degrees in different settings within the same issue are and across issues" (2008: 324). Yet these proposals, though undoubtedly very welcome developments, have not addressed the charge that securitization universalises a particular "logic of security", focusing instead on ensuring theoretical coherence.

The consequence is that securitization theory is still far from unproblematic to use for empirical analysis of events, producing accounts that, although theoretically coherent, fail to illuminate local conditions and dynamics in any substantial way. Not only is the securitization framework likely to produce a version of events that has been "edited" to ensure chronological order and a linear and step-wise progression (from actor to speech-act to audience to outcome), but the final analysis is likely to erase the *local knowledge* that can be generated by fieldwork even if empirical detail is included. The result is an account that is informed not by reflexive consideration of local interpretations and understandings, but by the normative assumptions of the theoretical framework in the form of the so-called Westphalian straitjacket (Buzan and Little 2001: 19–35).[1] Specifically, the Westphalian straitjacket manifests itself in the assumption that the Euro-American model of the state and, perhaps more importantly, the accompanying political culture, is valid globally. Thus the use of words such as "state" and "society" take on a normative dimension, the assumption being that Western understandings — as opposed to local ones — can successfully "travel" to any locale.

This creates a considerable danger of misinterpretation, since local understandings and meanings will often remain unexplored and unarticulated in a securitization analysis: even when the analyst seeks to allow for local conditions and circumstances, in cases where there is significant divergence between theoretical normative expectations (e.g. that socio-political systems all over the world operate in a broadly European way) and empirical evidence, the precedence of theory over sociological insight means that the Copenhagen School's Westphalian straitjacket acts as an editor: similarities to European models and understandings are highlighted and if necessary reinterpreted to ensure congruence, while anomalies and specificities are excised or excluded on the grounds of irrelevance or merely cosmetic significance.

It is important to emphasise that the Westphalian straitjacket is not a phenomenon that only affects the Copenhagen School. Rather, the culture of IR (Valbjørn 2004) suggests that although new epistemologies are introduced, the underlying assumptions on which these are built have rarely been questioned, even in recent enterprises such as the CASE Collective's Manifesto (2006). Without explicitly addressing the normative assumptions of our theories, attempts to refine or extend theoretical frameworks can only go so far. In this chapter, I argue that there are potential benefits to be gained from taking what Kent has called an "anthropological approach to security" that interrogates, amongst other issues, "the inherent ethnocentricity of much security theory" (2006: 346). Such an approach is likely to be of particular utility in non-Western locales, where analysts and readers are unfamiliar with the socio-political culture. Central to this endeavor is going beyond the Copenhagen School's original framework, which focuses on *what* security means, to ask the question *how* security means. In addressing this latter question, we are able to extend the empirical utility of securitization theory, adding an explicitly sociological focus to security analysis. In doing so, it becomes possible to *recontextualise* and *situate* meta-narratives by explicitly interrogating how people experience and understand securitizing moves and securitizations in practice.

This chapter addresses two main questions: first, I discuss context as a level of analysis and the relationship between the *proximate* and *distal* contexts of securitization. I then consider when and in what ways it may be beneficial to focus on the distal context – the broader socio-cultural context – of a securitizing move or securitization, before outlining how an interpretive methodology can be used to explore the distal context. I demonstrate how this methodological approach can be utilised via a case study of a series of mass protests that occurred in Bishkek, the capital of Kyrgyzstan, in October 2005. Collectively, eight days of protests represented a series of interrelated securitizing moves. Yet they culminated in a protest that, despite being the direct result of the preceding protests, was presented as a distinct and separate securitization narrative. Working back from this final meta-securitization, I contextualize the events of the previous seven days, presenting two accounts of the protests. The first focuses on the internal, or proximate, context of the meta-securitization, while the second examines the external, or distal, context, exploring local understandings of what occurred and how this eventually resulted in a meta-securitization.

Via the case study I demonstrate how the retrospective analysis of events risks distorting the dynamics of a securitization by failing to take into account the distal context, resulting in a selective and edited account that has little empirical utility or relation to how people present locally, experienced the events. Reflecting on the contrasting accounts suggested by examinations of the proximate and distal contexts, I discuss how local interpretations are influenced by conditions such as the availability and perceived credibility of information at the time, illustrating how the consideration of context can affect our understandings of the processes of securitization and generate new insights. I conclude that in some circumstances the analyst's desire to consider local conditions may limit her to meta-securitization narratives unless she can decentre the theoretical framework's tendency to impose retrospective internal coherence and causality by using experiential knowledge to inform discussion of securitization's context.

Questions of context: proximate and distal context

Earlier in this volume Balzacq outlined two types of context: *proximate* context and *distal* context (2009a: 17). Proximate context refers to the "immediate features of interaction" (Hardy 2004: 417), or the setting of a securitizing move, which "includes the stage on which it is made, the genre in which it is made, the audience to which it is pitched, and the reception of the audience" (Salter 2008: 328). In effect, it is the micro-environment of the securitization. In contrast, distal context refers to the macro-environment of the securitizing move; that is, the broader socio-cultural context in which it is embedded: matters of social class and ethnicity, regional and cultural settings, and the sites of discourse, for example (Balzacq 2009a: 17; Neergaard and Ulhøi 2007: 196).

While this distinction is useful, the relationship between the two types of context is not unproblematic. Indeed, Schegloff, with whom the notion of proximate and distal context originated, argues that their relationship "must be taken as problematic for the purposes of disciplined analysis" (1992: 195) since

If there are indefinitely many potentially relevant aspects of context and personal or categorical identity which could have a bearing on some facet of, or occurrence in, interaction, and if the analyst must be concerned with what is relevant to the parties at the moment at which what is being analyzed occurred, and is procedurally consequential for what is being analyzed, then *the search for context properly begins with the talk or other conduct being analyzed.*

(Emphasis in original. Schegloff 1992: 197)

Thus while analysis begins with the securitization, we must then work out from that point to contextualize it and situate it in relation to other relevant events and actions. Schegloff explains the importance of this undertaking with reference to "modes of enquiry", including speech-act theory, which

commonly address their targets of inquiry – whether sentences, actions or stories – as if they were intrinsically autonomous objects, that is, objects designed to have integrity and coherence which are entirely "internal" to the object itself. In doing so, they systematically obscure the possibility that their objects of inquiry are designed not for splendid and isolated independence, but for coherence and integrity as part and parcel of the environment or context in which, and for which, they were produced by its participants. In response to such modes of analysis, it has seemed quite important to make clear how different a picture of the object of analysis emerges is one reengages it – sentence, story, gesture, and the like – to its context, and then reconfigures our understanding or its structure and character.

(1992: 193–94)

A further aim, therefore, of this chapter is to demonstrate how, utilising an interpretive methodology, we can reengage with the event or situation under investigation by making the focus of our enquiry the context itself as Schegloff proposes, rather than seeing it as "the 'given' relative to the object of analysis" (1992: 194). This process leads us through a series of concentric layers: from securitization, to proximate context and then on to distal context.

In contrast to Salter, who focuses solely on the proximate context, both Stritzel and Kent offer approaches to the consideration of distal context as well as proximate context. However, Stritzel's desire to consider context within an analytical framework around the relatedness of three forces (2007: 371–72), while arguably increasing the comparative analytical potential of securitization theory for empirical studies, limits the depth of insights that can be generated by exploration of context by more precisely defining what is and is not within securitization's theoretical reach. Anomalies and contradictions are likely to be either ignored or "edited" out of empirical analyses in the quest to ensure universality and comparability. This is particularly likely to affect distal context due to its more diffuse and wide-ranging influence on processes of securitization.

Proximate context is arguably more directly accessible for the analyst due to its focus on the immediate details of a securitizing move: it concerns the questions of who, what, when, where, to whom and with what effect. Distal context, in contrast, is far broader and potentially less accessible, especially in the case of cross-cultural research. At the same time, consideration of the distal context of securitizing moves is vital if we are to avoid simply replicating the normative understandings of security inherent in theoretical approaches and instead uncover local understandings of security and how they are created. This is largely the domain of "local knowledge" that is, in contrast to so-called "expert knowledge", *experiential, context-specific, tacit, everyday* and *practice-based* (Yanow 2004: S12; emphasis added). By focusing on such local knowledge, it is possible to explore both words and actions beyond the theoretical framework offered by securitization, revealing dynamics that would usually slip beneath securitization's radar. The aim is not, as Kent rightly points out, "about challenging scholars to choose between either unhesitatingly imposing their theories upon other people or utterly deconstructing them". Rather, local perspectives facilitate the consideration of "other cultural formulations as a corpus of knowledge and experience that might inform our own" (2006: 347).

Exploring contexts: an interpretive methodology

Building on Kent's argument for an "anthropological approach" to security but wishing to keep contact with the framework provided by the Copenhagen School, in this section I outline how an interpretive methodology can be used to extend the Copenhagen School's empirical utility by facilitating explicit consideration and comparison of the proximate and distal context of securitizations. It could be argued that for the Copenhagen School's purposes, consideration of the proximate context of securitization is sufficient insofar as their aim is to identify what security is, not how it is constructed. At the same time, as shall be discussed, there are instances in which understanding how security means may result in different analytical conclusions. However, if explorations lead to the re-evaluation of conclusions, this does not detract from previous analyses; rather, as Duranti and Goodwin note in their introduction to Schegloff's article, "multiple levels of sequential context mutually reinforce each other as they provide alternative types of organisation for the local production of action" (1992: 192).

An interpretive approach requires the analyst to assume a far more participatory role in her investigation, as Yanow explains:

the researcher draws on a basic commonality of human experience and processes of understanding, and that through learning the language of the setting and its customs, the researcher can acquire sufficient familiarity as to be able to understand events that transpire, while at the same time drawing on sufficient "stranger-ness" to make the accepted, unspoken, tacitly known, commonsensical, taken-for-granted, local "rules" of action and inaction stand out as, in some way, different, thereby opening them up for reflection and examination.

(Yanow 2006: 19)

This approach corresponds to the *externalist* understanding to the context of production described by earlier by Balzacq, whereby "the success of securitization is contingent upon a perceptive–external–environment pervaded by a sense of criticality" (2009a: 19). Through an interpretive methodology the researcher becomes part of this environment. Drawing on his pre-existing knowledge and experiences, he becomes a situated critical interpreter of events, rather than simply observing how others do things.[2] Central to this stance is that the researcher is attempting initially "to describe in great detail the interrelationships and intricacies of the context being studied" (Erlandson et al. 1993: 33), including multiple possible meanings of language, acts or physical artefacts, by accessing data from different sites and sources (Yanow 2003). The result of this process is the creation of a "thick" description of the research setting that can then be juxtaposed with the account offered by securitization theory to begin the process of loosening the Copenhagen School's Westphalian straitjacket.

Crucially, this approach is flexible enough to accommodate the inevitable "mess" of the social world, working on the principle that "multiple realities enhance each other's meanings" rather than being problematic (Erlandson et al. 1993: 14). In addition, it allows for a mixed methods approach that can accommodate both qualitative and quantitative data collection/generation methods such as surveys, various types of interview, discourse and textual analysis, participant observation and ethnographic methods. Regardless of what methods are employed, the aim is to build up a "thick" description of the situation under investigation, in contrast to the "thin" description provided by a basic factual account. While a thin description reports what people did, a thick description contextualizes it by explicitly considering the socio-cultural meaning of the actions as well to create a humanistic, detailed and inferential account. To illustrate the difference, Geertz uses the example of "two boys rapidly contracting the eyelids of their right eyes". For one boy, the action is "an involuntary twitch", while for the other it is "a conspiratorial signal to a friend". While the movement is the same in both cases, "the difference [. . .] between a twitch and a wink is vast, as anyone unfortunate to have had the first taken for the second knows" (1973: 5–6).

Although the Copenhagen School's original endeavor extended only to identifying *what* security is in different locations and situations, for empirical studies it is potentially important to consider *how* security is understood in order to start thinking "outside the Westphalian box" (Acharya and Buzan 2007: 286). I suggest that this is likely to be of particular benefit when undertaking cross-cultural studies of societal security, since it is in these circumstances that the researcher most needs to compare and contrast theoretically-informed interpretations with local understandings of security in order to avoid excluding of alternative interpretation(s) that may offer different conclusions to those of securitization theory.

In the case of the Copenhagen School, because of securitization theory's emphasis on outcome rather than process, the multiple and situated meanings of security are often excluded in favour of producing the definitive (i.e. internally coherent) retrospective meta-narratives described in the previous section of this chapter. Applying an interpretive methodology to the study of the proximate context of the securitization is unlikely to generate insights sufficient to potentially challenge a theory-driven meta-narrative due to the context being internal to the securitization. If, however, the analyst extends her investigation to consideration of the securitization's distal context, which may include previous securitizing moves that have recursively shaped the socio-cultural settings, it is possible (although not inevitable) that a more nuanced and multi-faceted understanding of security dynamics in that locale will be developed. In some cases, consideration of the distal context may generate understandings that challenge or even contradict those suggested by the original securitization meta-narrative.

Accessing and exploring the distal context of securitization is therefore of potential utility to reduce the danger that the researcher will find only what can be accommodated by the Copenhagen School's Westphalian normative assumptions. In fact, in contrast to the broadly neo-positivist ontology of the Copenhagen School, which presupposes an objective, step-wise, linear process of inquiry from hypothesis to testing to conclusions, interpretivism is founded on the "ontological and epistemological presuppositions" of phenomenology and hermeneutics, "which hold that knowledge and the knower are situated, rather than 'objective' (in interpretive philosophers' and researchers' understandings of the concept) and that researchers must, per force, interpret what they observe" (Schwartz-Shea and Yanow 2002: 461).[3] Yanow explains the implications of interpretivism for fieldwork-based research:

Phenomenology provides a constructionist (or constructivist) ontology centered on the primacy of context; such context-specificity is fundamental to case-based research, and it is completely antithetical to a positivist scientific insistence on universal, generalizable laws or principles. Hermeneutics provides an interpretive epistemology rooted in the potential for multiple possible meanings of language, acts or physical artefacts; also context-specific, such potential multiplicities and their possible incongruences are what lead field researchers to access data from a variety of sites (neighbourhoods, agency divisions, etc.) across a research setting.

(Yanow 2003)

As such, the researcher herself becomes an integral part of the construction of knowledge: using her a priori experience and knowledge – what she already knows and has experienced – in conjunction with "empathetic understanding" of others to create her findings.

Adopting an explicitly interpretivist approach does not, of course, directly address the shortcomings of securitization and societal security. What it can do, however, is offer the researcher an alternative way to engage with securitization theory. Rather than defining how the researcher should interpret a given phenomenon or situation – in this case protests in Kyrgyzstan – the securitization framework offers *one of many* possible interpretations. It is therefore a point of comparison, permitting the researcher to test her interpretations and those of others against it. Significantly, reinterpreting theory in this way creates space to consider the politics of knowledge production both empirically and within disciplines. However, it is important to be aware that interpretivist knowledge claims differ fundamentally from those made by positivist paradigms.

As previously noted, positivist science is predicated on the idea that the world is knowable via "rigorous, repeatable steps of discovery by a neutral observer making neutral, impartial observations following the rules of the scientific method" to create neutral observations that can be generalised to create universal laws (Yanow 1996: 5). Positivists assess truth claims against criteria of validity (representivity, repeatability, reliability) and objectivity, holding that there is a definite answer to be found. In contrast, the interpretivist paradigm holds that there are multiple realities with no "right" or "wrong" realities, and that there are differences amongst realities "that cannot be resolved through rational processes or increased data" (Erlandson et al. 1993: 14). As a result, validity is governed by inquiry being able to "demonstrate its truth value, provide the basis for applying it, and allow for external judgements to be made about the consistency of its procedures and the neutrality of its findings or decisions" (Erlandson et al. 1993: 29). All research, regardless of whether it is positivist or interpretivist, must demonstrate that it is rigorous and systematic, or, in other words, that it is *trustworthy*. However, as Table 5.1 demonstrates, the terms used to assess trustworthiness differ fundamentally between paradigms. Taken together, these criteria provide a way for the reader to evaluate interpretivist inquiry by establishing trustworthiness, and, by extension a reasonable claim to methodological soundness.

In adopting an interpretive approach to studying the October protests discussed in this chapter, rather than starting with the aim of reconstructing securitizations by matching suitable evidence to support the theoretical model, I draw on multiple sources to create a thick narrative account of events that is largely based in emic

Table 5.1 Establishing trustworthiness: positivist and interpretivist terms[a]

Criterion	Positivist term	Interpretivist term
Truth value	Internal validity	Credibility
Applicability	External validity	Transferability
Consistency	Reliability	Dependability
Neutrality	Objectivity	Confirmability

a Adapted from Erlandson 1993: 133.

perspectives as well as my own experiences of "eye-witnessing" the protests and living in Kyrgyzstan at that time. This creates an account of events and processes that can decentre theoretical assumptions, causing securitization theory to become a frame to facilitate one's exploration rather than as a tool to be directly applied. This process focuses on what *doesn't* "fit" with securitization or isn't accounted for and, most importantly, permits consideration by the researcher of *how* actions and words mean in addition to *what* they mean.

The accounts have been compiled using a range of materials and sources in order to ensure that multiple perspectives are considered: local Russian-language newspaper reports, editorials and commentaries, bulletins from a local non-governmental organisation's conflict prevention project, interviews and comments from people to whom I spoke, my own observations and photographs, as well as images published in local print and electronic media.[4] I have not sought to create one single definitive account of events, but rather focus on the disjunctures and contradictions of which I became increasingly aware as I, like many local people, tried to make sense of the protests. I argue that it is necessary to explicate these disjunctures and contradictions and their possible interpretations to better understand the context from which security gains meaning(s). As will be demonstrated, consideration of the distal context is vital in this process.

In the following section, I present a case study of a mass protest held on 29 October 2005 under the slogan "Peaceful Citizens for Kyrgyzstan Without Criminals" in Bishkek, the capital of the former Soviet Central Asian republic of Kyrgyzstan. Since the collapse of the Soviet Union in 1991, Central Asia[5] has frequently been portrayed as a region of instability, high conflict potential, danger and insecurity (MacFarlane and Torjesen 2005). Despite this, and in contrast to the other four republics, Kyrgyzstan initially seemed likely to make a successful transition to a democratic political system and free market economy under President Askar Akaev's leadership. However, by the early 2000s there was growing discontent with the Kyrgyzstani government, at time sparking mass protests, most notably in Aksy in 2002 when police shot dead six protesters and wounded a further twelve (cf. Radnitz 2005). Nevertheless, Akaev remained in power until 24 March 2005, when he was ousted by protesters storming the main government building in the culmination of three months of mass demonstrations over the conduct of parliamentary elections held in late February-early March of the same year.

Despite the change of political leadership and Kurmanbek Bakiev's election as President in July 2005, protests subsequently became a common feature of socio-political life in the small mountainous republic as the new government failed to carry out reforms to address socio-economic problems such as land distribution and corruption. Yet it was only in October of that year that protests became institutionally securitized – that is, in Kyrgyzstan *at that time* protests had become a "metaphorical security reference" in that "security and priority" was implicitly invoked when protests were being talked of and/or staged insofar as they indicated a matter that required urgent resolution (Buzan, Waever and de Wilde 1998: 27).

In the case of Kyrgyzstan in October 2005, protests came to mean security in two different ways. First, they served as a physical expression by demonstrators of a

LIVERPOOL JOHN MOORES UNIVERSITY LEARNING SERVICES

securitizing narrative. The protesters' common narrative centred on portraying Kyrgyzstan (the land, rather than the state) and/or its people as being subjected to an existential threat – from corruption, criminalisation, worsening economic conditions – and a demand for immediate action from the government to address the threats. Simultaneously, however, there was a counter-securitizing narrative being presented by other groups (such as the governments of neighboring republics) that portrayed protests themselves as a visible sign of Kyrgyzstan's continued instability and insecurity and therefore as a threat to the republic's existence as a state. Protests, therefore, in this context, meant security in at least two ways at the same time.

Consideration of the proximate context, which I describe first, provides a certain level of detail about the actors involved and their actions and narratives, but paradoxically it provides an account that is too comprehensive, thus editing out local socio-cultural dynamics and their recursive effects. I therefore then explore the distal context of the demonstration in the second part of this section using an interpretive methodology that draws heavily on *experiential* knowledge. A quite different understanding of the 29 October 2005 protest emerges from this exercise, supplementing and extending our understandings of security's construction in Bishkek at that time gained from securitization theory.

The 2005 Akmatbaev protests in Kyrgyzstan

As noted earlier, a protest held in Bishkek on 29 October 2005 marked the institutionalisation of protests as an implicit matter of security, urgency and priority in Kyrgyzstan. Described in securitization terms, the protest's instigators, a group of opposition politicians and civil society leaders, became a securitizing actor. Invoking Kyrgyzstan as a nation and homeland, they presented a narrative that claimed that the government had become criminalised and that President Bakiev's failure to take decisive measures to combat the influence of organised crime threatened Kyrgyzstan's very existence. In order to combat this threat, the protest's leaders demanded that the government take immediate action to crack down on crime, remove politicians with links to organised crime and ensure "order and security" in the republic (Malevanaya 2005b: 9).

Arguably the measures demanded were extraordinary not in themselves but because of the priority that was demanded for them via mass protests. Under other circumstances these measures would be classed as "normal" politics, but due to the urgency accorded to them and the physical way in which this was articulated, they came to represent "crisis" politics and therefore enter the realm of "security" issues and securitization. However, interpretations of how the protests were related to security in Kyrgyzstan varied considerably, as an exploration of the distal context demonstrates.

In order to assist readers unfamiliar with Kyrgyzstani politics in following the case study, before examining the contexts of the "Peaceful Citizens for Kyrgyzstan Without Crime" protest, an overview of the key actors and their roles in securitization dynamics at the two analytical levels (i.e. proximate and distal contexts) is provided in the Table 5.2.

Table 5.2 Actors involved in the "Peaceful Citizens for Kyrgyzstan Without Crime" protest

Analytical level	Actor	Role(s)
Proximate context	Protest leaders & protesters	Securitizing actor presenting Bakiev and organised crime as an existential threat to Kyrgyzstan.
	President Bakiev & Prime Minister Kulov	Desecuritizing actor refuting protesters' securitizing move and denying criminalisation of the government is a threat to Kyrgyzstan. Joint threat referent for protesters.
	Ryspek Akmatbaev/ Organised crime groups	Joint threat referent to Kyrgyzstan for protesters.
Distal context	Ryspek Akmatbaev & supporters	Securitizing actor presenting Kulov as a threat to the lives of his family and associates
	President Bakiev (on behalf of Kyrgyzstani government)	Threat referent to Kulov for Ar-Namys and Kulov supporters
	Prime Minister Kulov	Referent object in Ar-Namys' securitizing move; Threat referent in Akmatbaev's securitizing move Securitizing actor presenting Bakiev as a threat to Kulov Variously: Securitizing actor presenting Bakiev as a threat to Kulov and/or Kyrgyzstan's existence; Functional actor
	Ar-Namys & Kulov supporters	
	Local media	
	International community	Securitizing actor presenting Akmatbaev and Bakiev as threats to Kyrgyzstan's existence.

While the proximate context of the 29 October protest can be described relatively concisely with reference to the interactions of actors – questions of who, what and when – the distal context is far broader and multi-faceted, as suggested in Table 5.2 by the list of actors who were directly involved in events preceding the 29 October protest. Correspondingly, the researcher needs to make a decision about *how much* context to include. Duranti and Goodwin cite Schegloff's assertion that

an analyst is not free to invoke whatever variables he or she feels appropriate as dimensions of context, no matter how strongly grounded in traditional social theory – e.g. class, gender, etc. – but instead must demonstrate in the events being examined that the participants themselves are organising their behavior in terms of the features being described by the analyst.

(1992: 192)

The researcher is therefore looking for behavior or actions that are relevant to the event being investigated. Initially this is likely to be immediately prior events that are directly linked, but the recursive nature of context means that the range of "relevant" factors could expand almost infinitely, depending on how deeply one wanted to trace processes. Obviously this is neither desirable nor practicable in many cases, not least due to the challenge of managing the vast amounts of data generated and presenting an accessible analysis of the context.

In contrast to the Copenhagen School's intention to produce an internally coherent account of the event within the securitization framework, Schegloff's principle of relevance to the participants points to the importance of experiential knowledge. In other words, the guiding principle for exploring the distal context is how the *participants* interpreted the event *at the time*, rather than how the *analyst* interprets it *retrospectively* with the benefit of hindsight – the latter process giving a potentially more comprehensive view. The extent to which this is possible in practice is largely dependent upon the researcher and makes an interpretive approach particularly suitable for fieldwork-based studies where the researcher has been physically present and in the process has been able to develop her own "local" knowledge via her engagement with the locale. Thus, for example, my initial experiences of Kyrgyzstan were as an undergraduate student who had gone to Bishkek to study Russian for a year. Five years later, when I returned to carry out fieldwork for my doctoral thesis, my previous experience, combined with a high degree of competency in Russian, were invaluable as a basis on which to build up my interpretations of what was happening in circumstances of rapid and at times unpredictable change.

For the purposes of this chapter, I have by necessity imposed more stringent bounds on the scope of the proximate context than would be generally be the case for an analysis utilising thick description. In effect, the thickness of the account has been lessened by reducing the number of layers of context included; in contrast to the accounts presented in my thesis, I have sought to summarise rather than include quotations from specific sources where possible and have excluded visual materials entirely. While this may seem contradictory given that the supposed aim of an interpretive approach is often to build up as thick a description as possible, it highlights the fact that description should be as thick as necessary – a criterion determined by the aim of the investigation as well as the audience for whom one is writing. The aim in this chapter is primarily to demonstrate how an interpretive methodology can be deployed in order to access the distal context of a securitization, an exercise that can arguably be achieved with a lesser level of empirical detail than would be demanded by scholars focusing on the Central Asian region.

Consequently, when exploring both the proximate and then distal context in the following subsections, I have taken as my starting point the event that triggered the start of the protests that eventually led to the "Peaceful Citizens for Kyrgyzstan Without Crime" demonstration eight days later to provide a chronological limit. As such, there is minimal reference to the broader socio-political situation in Kyrgyzstan beyond the introduction provided at the start of this section. Within this timeframe, I have then focused on the protests, limiting my accounts to what is relevant to understanding the dynamics involved at both analytical levels. While the proximate context account provides a comprehensive overview of the settings involved (i.e. the who, what, and when of events), my exploration of the distal context considers factors that operate recursively, such as the public's perceptions of the actors involved, the impact of the media and the availability of information at the time.

The proximate context: who, what, when?

As previously noted, the proximate context concerns the setting or genre of the event or episode. It is about the internal structure of the event; "the sorts of sequences of talk or courses of conduct in which particular events may occur" and "the capacity in which participants act relative to the episode in progress" (Schegloff 1992: 195). A description of this level of context, therefore, is looking to trace or map who did or said what when in relation to the securitization. In the case of the Akmatbaev protests, the event that marked the beginning of the episode was the murder of parliamentary deputy Tynychbek Akmatbaev during a visit to a prison colony near to Bishkek on 20 October 2005. Coverage in the government newspaper *Slovo Kyrgyzstana* began the following day with a short article about the murders. It was reported that upon receiving news of the murders, Prime Minister, Feliks Kulov and other officials had travelled to the prison camp and that prisoners had asked to negotiate with Kulov, but no further details were given (*Slovo Kyrgyzstana* SK 106 [21867]: 2).

The day after the shooting, 21 October, Jogorku Kenesh deputies held a working meeting about the incident at which they heard information from "Prime Minister F. Kulov and representatives of the Ministry of Internal Affairs, the General Procurator's Office and the Special Procurator's Office" (Slashcheva 2005a: 3). Again, no further details were provided, nor was any comment made regarding how the government was intending to deal with the situation.

October 22 saw the start of a protest led by the deceased deputy's brother, Ryspek Akmatbaev, calling for the immediate resignation of the Prime Minister, who they claimed was responsible for the murders. The protestors initially congregated and set up yurts on Ala-Too Square, but moved to the old square opposite the parliament by 18.00. The same day Feliks Kulov held a press conference and gave his evaluation of events and claimed that he had been instructed by President Bakiev to take personal control of the situation (Turkmenov 2005: 2). Meanwhile *Moya stolitsa novosti* reported that "by the time of the press conference, 15.00 on Saturday [the 22nd], Bakiev had already discussed the situation three times with the Prime Minister and had held a session with the law enforcement agencies" (Orlova 2005a: 2).

A first attempt to hold an extraordinary session of parliament was held on 23 October, but was postponed due to quorum not being met. Ryspek Akmatbaev and his supporters remained in the old square, continuing to call for Kulov's resignation. A second attempt to hold an extraordinary session of parliament was made the following day, but once more quorum in the chamber was not reached, not least because around 500 protesters blocked entrances to the building. Deputy Speaker, Bolot Sherniyazov, "spoke with protesters for a long time" before entering the building (Slashcheva 2005a: 4–5). Rather than attend the extraordinary session, President Bakiev held a working meeting with high-ranking officials, including Prime Minister Kulov. *Slovo Kyrgyzstana* reported that "The head of the state demanded that all those present take measures to ensure public order. The President also demanded that the public and the media received information about the measures taken by the authorities on time" (SK 107: 1).

Also on 24 October, the Secretary of the State Security Council held a press conference for journalists, "where he gave his evaluation of the situation that had formed in the capital, talked about the measures taken by the authorities to diffuse and stabilise the situation" (Shepelenko 2005: 3). Feliks Kulov signed a government resolution, "On immediate measures for the stabilisation of the socio-political situation in the capital of the Kyrgyz Republic, the city of Bishkek". Tuesday 25 October, 2005 finally saw a parliamentary session to discuss the events take place, with 53 deputies attending. Proceedings were transmitted onto screens so that Akmatbaev's supporters could watch. Prior to the session, Speaker Omurbek Tekebaev met with an initiative group of protestors and reported their demands to deputies (Slashcheva 2005b: 6). President Bakiev also held a meeting with parliamentarians and government officials, including Prime Minister Kulov, that day. The President noted that he had not expressed any view about the murders, but did not say any more on the matter. He did, however, say that he would meet with a delegation of Akmatbaev's supporters on 27 October (SK 108 [21869]: 2).

In addition to the continuing protest led by Ryspek Akmatbaev on the Old Square opposite the Jogorku Kenesh on 25 October, an estimated 600 people joined a protest on the central Ala-Too Square until early afternoon led by the political party Ar-Namys in support of Feliks Kulov. The day's final development was the appearance of two open letters to the President and Prime Minister from civil society and political figures, calling for immediate action to "ensure the preservation of civil order and the safety/security of citizens of the Kyrgyz Republic" (MSN 123 [314]: 1).

The two protests continued in the same vein on 26 October. President Bakiev, meanwhile, finally held a press briefing, at which he noted that his duty as president was to uphold the Constitution and rule of law, and that a decision regarding Kulov's resignation would only be taken on the basis of the conclusions of the commission that had been founded to investigate. He assured journalists that "an adequate decision would be taken in relation to any person holding office, regardless of his position" (Vladimirova 2005: 3). The next morning, 27 October, Bakiev met with representatives of Akmatbaev's protesters, following which the anti-Kulov protest was "suspended until the completion of the investigation" and Akmatbaev's supporters dispersed.

Despite the situation seeming to have been resolved, one further protest – and securitization – took place on 29 October. Why this happened is not immediately clear from the above factual account. However, a closer examination of the distal context can provide insights into why events developed in this way.

The distal context: how, why?

The day following Tynychbek Akmatbaev's murder, newspaper coverage focused mainly on the circumstances of his death. *Vechernii Bishkek* led with the headline "Deputy Akmatbaev shot by prisoners", and recounted dramatically how two of the newspaper's journalists had accompanied the commission headed by Akmatbaev to three strict regime colonies (Khokhlova and Lokteva 2005: 1).

However, the initial reaction of the print media was muted, most probably due to the lack of information available at the time of going to press; for journalists and the public alike, it was simply too early to see how things would develop. Deputy Erkinbek Alymbekov was an exception, his initial reaction quoted in Friday's *Vechernii Bishkek*: "If we carry on like this then we will lose sovereignty and the country" (Temir 2005: 1).

Opinion about the danger posed by the incident gained resonance over the weekend as Ryspek and his supporters began protesting on Ala-Too Square. While none of the newspapers publish over the weekend, but *Gazeta.kg* provided extensive coverage for those with internet access. The site reported that 800 to 1,000 protestors had gathered on Ala-Too Square in front of the White House (Gazeta.kg 2005a). For many hearing such reports, or seeing the crowd for themselves on the Square, it is likely to have recalled the events of 24 March, leading to fears that "criminals" were about to attempt a direct seizure of power. A subsequent report that Akmatbaev "had declared jihad on Feliks Kulov" (Gazeta.kg 2005b) further heightened fears of impending disorder and insecurity due the implied extremism.

The weekend provided time for rumours both about what had happened and about Ryspek, who was widely acknowledged to be the leader of an organised criminal group or an *avtoritet* (VB 204: 1),[6] to be discussed, and for Bishkek's residents to experience the inconvenience and sense of uncertainty engendered by the protest. Ryspek's reputation meant that he was assumed to be capable of mobilising significant resources, both human and financial, to support his cause. As such, the potential threat that he was perceived to pose to the beleaguered Kyrgyzstani government was considered particularly grave. However, on Monday, 24 October *Vechernii Bishkek* observed that despite considerable TV coverage, there was uncertainty about the purpose of the protest (Khokhlova 2005: 1). What was known was that Ryspek claimed that Kulov was responsible for his brother's murder and was demanding his immediate resignation, promising to continue his protest until this was achieved.

On Tuesday, 25 October a pro-Kulov protest began on Ala-Too Square as the anti-Kulov protest led by Ryspek Akmatbaev continued on the Old Square. I decided to go and have a closer look at the protests. On Ala-Too Square banners had been erected and around one hundred people were milling around. The crowd was mixed by age, ethnicity and gender, and judging by their clothes and appearance I concluded that they were mainly from Bishkek. Shortly afterwards, a minibus bearing the logo of the Ar-Namys party pulled up and people congregated around it. The atmosphere seemed relaxed, though people were keen to take the microphone and speak support of Kulov, as well as ensuring that the media and those present could see their slogans as clearly as possible.

I fell into conversation with a student who had also come to see what was happening. She echoed my sense that the pro-Kulov protest was safe for bystanders, but felt that the atmosphere at the anti-Kulov protest could be less welcoming, adding that she had heard reports that weapons had been seen. Nevertheless, we were curious and decided to go and observe. Three things were immediately noticeable as we approached: there was a far greater police presence, although their behaviour suggested that they had little intention of interfering with the protest; the proportion of men and ethnic Kyrgyz was far greater than at the pro-Kulov protest and most of the protesters were not local – this last fact being unsurprising given that Tynychbek Akmatbaev was the deputy for the Balykchy electoral district some 110 miles east of Bishkek – and the atmosphere did indeed seem far tenser and hostile. The protesters had set up several yurts and portaloos and there was evidence of food being prepared. Some protesters stood on the steps of the parliament building, clustered around a TV that had been set up.

Most of Ryspek's supporters, however, sat in long rows opposite the parliament, flanked by groups of men dressed almost without exception in leather jackets or tracksuits – often called "sportsmen" collectively by locals with the implication that they are "heavies". The slogans displayed also appeared less temperate: for example, "Shame on Kulov, Kulov, you're guilty of Akmatbaev's death!", "Better death than the Kulov-Chechen mafia!", "Kulov + Batukaev = murderers" and "Kulov to resign!". It would have been quite an intimidating sight even without the rumours of people being armed and Ryspek's reputation; as it was, people's growing sense of concern and frustration with the apparent lack of government response to these "criminals" holding an unsanctioned protest appeared to be very understandable: why weren't the police doing anything?

The reportage in 25 October's newspapers reflected the sense of unease felt about the anti-Kulov protest. *MSN* reported Akmatbaev's demands and that his supporters were armed, concluding that "[t]he criminal world has declared war on the Prime Minister" (Malevanaya 2005a: 1). Another journalist echoed the sense of threat, suggesting that the danger posed was greater than many of Bishkek's residents, used to protests, thought (Orlova 2005a: 2). Meanwhile in reference to the absence of an official response from President Bakiev, *Vechernii Bishkek*'s headline asked the uncomfortable question "Will Bakiev back down to Akmatbaev?" and wrote bluntly that "Residents of Bishkek are concerned about a new wave of looting and outbreak of criminality". The sense of alarm and danger was added to by the publication of statements from NGO representatives and politicians addressed to the President and Prime Minister asserting that events "could lead to conflict in society" (MSN 123[3]4[:1).

The overall impression was that not only was the government being unacceptably slow to respond to the situation, it was perhaps unable to. Reports of heated exchanges during the second failed attempt to hold an extraordinary session of the parliament on 24 September and the unusual refusal by deputies to comment to the press did nothing to dispel this impression (Skorodumova 2005a: 4). Faced with the visible evidence of the ongoing protests and inactivity on the part of the police, reports in the same articles of the governmental meetings that had taken place in response to the murder compounded the impression of weak and indecisive leadership rather than demonstrate how seriously the situation was being taken. Media opinion was already massing behind Feliks Kulov, who in contrast to the President, was seen to have reacted satisfactorily to the incidence (Orlova 2005a: 2). Yet despite the article's heading – "Criminals will not dictate conditions to the President" – the only mention of Bakiev was a single sentence.

Wednesday 26 October saw the media's coverage focus on the danger of a "bandit revolution" and the ongoing crisis (Biyalinov 2005: 1). Even positive news was interpreted negatively. *Delo No* reported that contrary to public fears of an increase in crime, there had been a reduction. While officials attributed this to the intensified work of the police, popular opinion concurred with Meerim Beishenova's opinion that it was "due to the fact that they (criminals – one supposes) are protesting on the square" (Beishenova 2005: 3). In light of perceptions of the anti-Kulov protesters as "criminals", or at least being connected to organised crime, it was unsurprising that reports of Bakiev's intention to meet with a delegation of Ryspek's supporters was met with strong disapproval by many, further adding to opinions of Bakiev as a weak and inept head of state.

Support for Feliks Kulov was expressed strongly in the newspapers, including reports that the parliament had declined to consider his resignation (Avdeeva 2005: 1; Mukashev 2005: 1). At the same time, some commentators began to wonder whether the crisis was not being manipulated to the advantage of certain politicians and civil society leaders (Karimov and Satybekov 2005: 4). Yet others felt that the threat unleashed by Akmatbaev's murder and the resulting protests could not be underestimated, concluding that "there is a direct threat to both the state's security, to peace and order, and to the President's personal security" from "the corrupted elite" (Kojomkulov 2005: 7).

I returned to Ala-Too Square later that day and found fewer but evidently better organised pro-Kulov protesters. Most striking when surveying the scene was the increased prominence of a large yellow banner proclaiming "We're against civil war". Regardless of whether or not one felt that such slogans were overly dramatic – and I found myself undecided, on the one hand feeling that the level of threat was being exaggerated by the media and others with their own agenda, on the other aware that it was only a few months earlier that protests had led to the storming of the White House and two nights of widespread looting in Bishkek – it was difficult to feel sanguine about the state of affairs; like much of the public, I was waiting to see what happened next, fear of the unknown exacerbating my fears.

While nothing changed noticeably on the two squares on 27 October, dissatisfaction with President Bakiev was now voiced more stridently. He was increasingly being portrayed as a threat to the stability of the country and as a weak and prevarication-prone leader. One open letter described how, Bakiev's speech on 25 October had "shocked the entire people of Kyrgyzstan", explaining that:

The public expected from you a clear and unambiguous position. You should have said that you will not permit the criminal world to dictate terms to the state. You should have said that peaceful citizens can feel safe. You should have said that you firmly support the Government and its head, F. Sh. Kulov.

Instead of this, you said that you were waiting for the results of the investigation. You said that there is nothing awful about armed people, who are wanted for arrest, having gathered on the square.

(*Litsa* 2005: 1)

The strong condemnation of Bakiev could not be countered by the limited number of articles published about what actions the government and President were taking. *Delo No* reported in a single column article that "[t]he powers are starting to act", citing Kulov signing into force a decree on measures to stabilise the situation, and there were several other brief reports to be found on various pages – if people were actively looking for them, as I was. Many people did not feel inclined to give the government the benefit of the doubt once more; nor had time to comb through newspapers to find information that they instinctively disbelieved: Bakiev's assurance that Kulov had his complete support rang hollow to people already convinced by media accounts of discord between them.

Bakiev met with a delegation of Ryspek's supporters on the morning of the 27 October. Ryspek was not part of delegation, which subsequently halted their protest. Reactions to the curtailment were mixed: "Nothing's been solved yet. Things will get a lot worse" commented one *Gazeta.kg* reader. "The latest postponement of a solution to the conflict" concluded another. Coverage in Friday 28 October's newspapers echoed these sentiments: "Ryspekovites leave. But for how long?" asked *MSN* (Malevanaya 2005c: 2). The effect of such coverage, as well as commentary criticising the government and voicing fears that further conflict could threaten Kyrgyzstan's existence, was that even though the protest had ended, people felt more fearful about their future than ever: the speed at which Ryspek and his supporters left the Old Square following their private meeting with President Bakiev left many wondering if it was already too late to talk of the possible criminalisation of politics. The threat seemed more serious than ever, lending weight to a call for the public to unite: "Our ancestors always united and halted their infighting when a universal threat appeared. This time has come" (Skorodumova 2005b: 2). Two days later, people acted on this move, joining the "Peaceful Citizens for Kyrgyzstan Without Crime" demonstration on Ala-Too Square.

Conclusion: securitization in context(S)

Over eight days of protests, a series of securitizing and counter-securitizing moves were made that were closely intertwined and mutually constitutive. They were subsequently distilled into a distinct meta-securitization that was performed as a protest on 29 October 2005. Civil society, represented by the Coalition for Democracy and Civil Society and KelKel, acted as the securitization's initiator. Edil Baisalov, spoke explicitly of their motivation at the protest:

> We have gathered here because our civic conscience demanded it! We say 'no' to the criminals and bandits who are holding the whole country in a state of fear and threatening the first figures of the state. We are not just for the Bakiev-Kulov tandem; we are for order and security.
>
> (Malevanaya 2005b: 9)

They were also keen to highlight the damage done to Kyrgyzstan's reputation by Akmatbaev's protests at home and abroad. Their position built on the open letters and appeals issued by various NGOs earlier in the week calling for decisive action from the government. Organising a protest, rather than simply repeating their calls, strengthened their credibility considerably, since it demonstrated that they were able to *act* as well as *speak* – a distinction to which Kyrgyzstanis had become extremely sensitive in light of perceptions of government inaction and indecisiveness.

The narrative presented was already familiar to the public and the anecdotal evidence – most prominently Bakiev's meeting with a delegation of Akmatbaev's supporters – was extremely convincing to many who already felt that corruption was a major hindrance to their chances of living normally. The claim that the government was becoming criminalised and that if allowed to continue it would lead to the demise of Kyrgyzstan did not seem far fetched to many, especially six months after the "revolution" had started with no sign of life improving. To add insult to injury, the government's leaders – the tandem of Bakiev and Kulov – appeared oblivious to the seriousness of the situation and dismissive of people's fears. As Edil Baisalov argued:

They say that we're all very emotional, we're scared, and we've started demanding harsh measures. [. . .] They [the government] don't understand that as a result of the events of these two or three days there's been an irreparable blow to our international reputation. The authorities have been humiliated, sovereignty has been if not broken then severely shaken, and the people's spirits have fallen.

(Orlova 2005c: 7)

The potency of the narrative was highlighted by the fact that the securitization's third element – audience acceptance – was assured at the outset of the protest, i.e. when the securitizing move was launched. Moreover, people's endorsement of the threat narrative was not only expressed physically, by attending the protest, but also in word-based forms such as holding banners and placards, as well as shouting slogans. Many, if not the majority, of those who attended were already in agreement with the securitizing narrative presented and wished to demonstrate this; there was little need to try and convince them, making the progression from securitizing move to successful securitization seamless and almost instantaneous. The result was a meta-narrative that differed in key ways from the securitizing moves preceding it. Most crucially, criticism of President Bakiev was replaced with loud declarations of support for the Bakiev-Kulov tandem (Malevanaya 2005b: 9).

I have argued that in order to understand the significance of these protests as expressions of security it is not enough to focus on process instead of outcome. While this change of focus is necessary and does to a certain extent increase securitization's utility for empirical studies, it is still insufficient, for it does not necessarily challenge the normative assumptions inherent in the Copenhagen School's conceptualisation of security, nor permit the inclusion of non-verbal forms of expression. In order to address these shortcomings, I have extended the notion of *implied security* to directly include physical actions as well as verbal expressions, and, argued that the researcher should seek to actively decentre securitization's normative assumptions by explicitly considering multiple interpretations, both emic and etic, of the situation via consideration of the proximate and then distal contexts. In this way it is possible to look beyond, or perhaps more accurately, beneath, the meta-narratives that an orthodox application of securitization creates and explore specific local meanings and understandings that are inherently situated and often experiential.

As previously noted, in contrast to the first account of events (the proximate context), the public appeared to be unaware that the government had in fact responded to Akmatbaev's protest. This is likely to be partly because of the relative lack of popularity *Slovo Kyrgyzstana*, the government newspaper in which the decrees and orders were published, due to its perceived pro-government bias. As a result, few people would have read the decrees and simply not know that they have been issued, contributing to the perception of government inaction. This perception was exacerbated by articles in independently-owned newspapers that made frequent reference to Bakiev's failure to publicly condemn the protest. Similarly, the high levels of coverage given to Ryspek Akmatbaev in the media increased public anxiety about the threat (Orlova 2005b).

These two distal factors – the portrayal of events in the media and Ryspek's reputation – played a significant role in creating the threat narrative then fuelled the protests, yet there is little room for their explicit consideration within an orthodox application of securitization theory. In effect, the analyst remains at least one step removed from the contradictions and subjectivity of etic interpretations, striving for "balance" even as local perceptions reject it based on their local knowledge: which newspapers are to be trusted, who possesses social capital, what actions are deemed necessary? Truth, balance or objectivity are of limited relevance for those *living* and *experiencing* the events in question, as *Slovo Kyrgyzstana* concluded: "even if the truth is not spoken completely [about events], the enlightenedness, the observational powers of the public forces it to draw conclusions itself, to compare details, statements, actions'" (K.A. 2005).

Crucially, however, people's conclusions and perceptions of events and their meanings alter over time. We see this in the development of competing narratives over the course of the nine days of protests, particularly in relation to the pro-Kulov and then anti-crime protests: at the start the protests were concerned primarily with expressing support for Feliks Kulov and calling upon President Bakiev to express his personal support for his tandem partner (threat narrative 1). As the protests continued, this theme was incorporated into consecutive wider narratives; first, dissatisfaction with the government's handling of the protests and especially Bakiev's public silence (threat narrative 2), and subsequently demands for immediate action to counter the perceived criminalisation of the government (threat narrative 3), which was seen as posing an existential threat to Kyrgyzstan's future not only as a state, but more importantly as a people and homeland.

Securitization theory is in principle capable of analysing this final meta-narrative of threat, but in doing so it provides at best a largely decontextualized "snap-shot" of the dominant narrative at that point in time. Even if the analyst seeks to "embed" this narrative in its local context via more explicit consideration of facilitating conditions, as Stritzel proposes, or by analysing *setting* or the proximate context as Salter does, undertaking this task retrospectively is in danger of creating an account that bears little relation to how people experienced events as they took place due to the presumption that events are understood in the same way and have the same meaning in (for example) Kyrgyzstan and Copenhagen. Thus, in the case of the protests, it is possible to create a "comprehensive" chronological account that included government actions alongside with protests. That these actions and measures took place is not in question, yet the analyst's reading of the situation could be very different from the *locally situated* and *experientially-based interpretation* of the situation that is formed when the distal context in particular is explored in depth. Such differences of interpretation alter the apparent "security-ness" of a situation. In the case of Kyrgyzstan the events marked the start of a meta-securitization narrative of Kyrgyzstan in crisis that has proved extremely persistent to the detriment of alternative perspectives on the socio-political situation in the republic.

Schegloff observes that "at its worst, 'context' is deployed as a merely polemical, critical tool. In this usage, it is roughly equivalent to 'what I noticed about your topic that you didn't write about'" (Schegloff 1992: 214–15). However, when engaged with reflexively on the part of the researcher with the aim of generating insights that can complement and check theory-led approaches to securitization, the consideration of contexts is vital for the situating of security as a pragmatic act.

Notes

1 The "Westphalian straitjacket" phenomenon in IR is described as "the strong tendency to assume that the model established in seventeenth century Europe should define what the international system is for all times and places" (Buzan and Little 2001: 25).

2 Echoing Eriksson's (1999a) accusation that the Copenhagen School puts the analyst in a position of "observing how others advocate" without acknowledging his own role in securitization.

3 For a fuller account of interpretive philosophy, see Yanow (2006).

4 A more detailed account of the sources used is provided in Wilkinson, Claire (2009) *Interpreting Security: Grounding the Copenhagen School in Kyrgyzstan*. Unpublished PhD Thesis, University of Birmingham.

5 Central Asia here refers to the five former Soviet republics of Kazakhstan, Kyrgyzstan, Tajikistan, Turkmenistan and Uzbekistan.

6 Ryspek Akmatbaev was himself murdered in the village of Kok-Jar, Alamudunskii region, Chui oblast, on 10 May 2006.

6 When securitization fails

The hard case of counter-terrorism programs

Mark B. Salter[1]

Securitization theory has not provided a coherent model of failure. Because the Copenhagen School (CS) interprets all successful securitizing moves as a failure of normal politics, the null case – the dog that does not bark – has been under-studied. In the original formulation, securitizing moves can fail because of faults in the grammatical structure of the securitizing move, the inherent characteristics of the issue, or a rejection by the audience (Buzan, Wæver and de Wilde 1998: 25–27; Wæver 2000: 252–53). But, we must understand how the appeal of security is rejected or resisted. Huysmans concludes that politics must be understood both in terms of elite and public discourse and in terms of technocratic practices (2006: 153–55). Analysts and activists alike, regardless of their normative stance, must probe securitizing moves that do not receive audience acceptance. Balzacq speaks of a "confirmation bias" in securitization theory, which he persuasively argues must be overcome as securitization studies matures (Chapter 2, this volume).

Failed securitizing moves are not desecuritizing moves, which entails a reversal of a previous successful securitization. The linguistic focus of the Copenhagen School cannot account for the politics at stake in the securitizing move or promote a sociological model. In this comparison of several abandoned American counter-terrorism programs, this paper lays out a model of securitization failure. Two critical cases are then examined to test the model. The Total Information Awareness program, the Policy Analysis Market (also known as the Terrorist Futures Market), and Terrorist Information Protection System were all launched in 2003 within the wider war on terror. Each program sought to label particular issue areas as an existential threat, remove the policy from the scope of deliberative politics, and invoke the urgency of emergency. However, expert, political, and public actors rejected the attempted securitizing moves. This analysis of securitizing moves within the post-9/11 environment demonstrates that the appetite for securitization varies in direct relationship to the competing claims for desecuritization: the attention of the executive, the public imagination, the public purse, and bureaucratic windows of opportunity are all limited. This limited appetite or tolerance for security is a hidden premise of the CS: not everything can be pitched as security issue, not everything can be an existential threat. Obesity, heart disease, diabetes, even road accidents, for example, kill more Americans than the 9/11 attacks by several degrees of magnitude; however, these public health issues can not be successfully described as security issues. Furthermore, the contest for successful securitization takes place within a bureaucratic field in which many agencies, ministries, or actors are all seeking executive attention, public imagination, and the public purse. Within these bureaucratic contexts, governments try to be efficient and cost-effective – even in security matters – and so try to use risk management to make choices about what threats and dangers to prioritize.

The success or failure of securitizing moves depends on who can speak and what can be said. It is not simply a case of "he who spins, wins" – but rather that there are multiple discursive and technocratic fronts on which the competition for attention and resources is played out. Different actors are able to make competing claims, according to different narratives and social structures of authority, to identify the nature of threat, the appropriateness of the policy solutions, and the requirement for emergency action. A political sociological analysis of these different settings of securitizing moves needs to understand failure as much as success.

Sociological securitization

A solely linguistic model cannot account for the politics of the securitization process: the success or the failure of particular securitizing move is due to the "acceptance" of an audience. "I do (take this [person] as my lawfully wedded [partner]," to take Austin's example, requires a number of social, or meta-linguistic conditions: personhood of the speaker and the partner, the acceptance of that act by the audience (1975). I am not engaging in Austin *per se* (1962), but rather want to identify the social conditions that make the illocutionary act not simply "felicitous" or "infelicitous" but rather accepted or rejected. In order for the CS theorization of securitization to model actual moves, it must disaggregate the speaking/hearing/approval or rejection processes. This process is under-theorized in the original formulation of the Copenhagen School (Balzacq 2005). Securitization is a sociological and political process – manifest in language, but a complex effect of power, interest, inter-subjectivity, bureaucratic position, and process. Different securitizing moves have different effects in different settings, which provide different basic power dynamics, different linguistic rules, and different local knowledge structures (Salter 2008). It is over-simplistic to describe one securitizer and one audience – one message and one decision (and, indeed, none of the actual studies of securitization make this simple case – though one can see that that is a methodological appeal of the model). Securitizing moves in the popular setting use a unique language with a particular heritage, history, and heft – fundamentally different from securitizing moves within elite or technocratic settings (Roe 2008). This is one of the most powerful insights of Bigo (2001; 2002) and Balzacq (2005, 2008). Expert audiences within a particular field generate their own meanings of key signifiers like security – and these communities are not necessarily national. Indeed, in some cases, these expert audiences may conduct effective securitizing moves with no external audience. This has been applied by Salter (2008) with regard to the Canadian Air Transport Security Authority: a similar securitizing motive was expressed in different securitizing moves in different contexts, according to audience. Securitizing moves to technocratic audiences were radically different than those made in the elite, scientific, or popular realms.[2] Security measures and emergency powers that were accepted within elite or technocratic discussions were rejected in the popular scene. This adds a vital supplement to the method of discursive analysis prevalent in some areas of securitization studies.

Method

Hansen provides an inspirationally clear research design template for discourse analysis of political events (2006). She suggests that researchers must make a series of four basic choices for the object of study: number of selves, events, or issues; intertextual model; temporal perspectives; and number of events. The majority of empirically-minded securitization studies focus on official discourse and the wider political debate (not cultural representations or marginal political discourses). There is a large movement to include other forms of media in this discursive analysis (Williams 2003; Hansen 2007). Williams argues that at root the ability of the state to declare an emergency is the fundamental political process that the CS identifies as securitization, which stems from Schmitt's reduction of politics to the friend/enemy binary. For Schmitt, Agamben, and Williams, the key lies in the phrase "sovereign is he who decides the exception. As a consequence, CS analysis inherits the statist, decisionist, and rather monolithic view of speech acts. This bias is engaged by the analysis of Stritzel (2007) and Balzacq (2005), in particular, who argue that political context, audience, and history must play a larger role in understanding the meaning of speech acts. These studies rightly point our attention to a disaggregated state apparatus. Doty goes further to argue that other, non-state actors may also declare states of exception: "What if 'the state' is not the only site of the 'sovereign decision' on the exception, the enemy, and the political? What if securitization is a widely dispersed and at times amorphous phenomenon not controlled or even initiated by elites?" (2007: 116). In this reading, securitization must take account of multiple actors, social forces, and audiences – and indeed, may not ever crystallize into one statement or speech act (McDonald 2008: 564). Process of securitization must be taken as dispersed, iterative, and interactive. This raises, for me and others, the question of audience – a condition of success or failure for the securitizing move will be how the move or message is made, how it is received, how the prime mover then changes the messages, etc. It is a dialogical or relational process, but one that takes place within already existing bureaucratic, social, economic, and political structures. If we accept that there is not a single decision, nor a single speaker, nor a single audience – then we need a much more complex, sociological method of analyzing the processes of securitization.

We must analyze different particular cultures that set the linguistic, historical, and affective contexts that facilitate or impede securitizing moves. A mid-range theory is needed to frame the insights of national political cultural theorists, neoliberal institutionalists and organizational sociologists. It is not enough to say that the EU and US have different political cultures that structure what securitizing moves are possible or felicitous in those contexts, but the organizational and bureaucratic cultures can also differ widely within one nation, to say nothing of differing opinions within national publics.

Goffman's dramaturgical analysis provides an important depth to this model by drawing our attention to the difference between "front-stage" and "back-stage": while all roles are performed for audiences, the sociological *setting* determines the mode, language, tropes, figures, and structure of the particular act (Goffman 1959; Hajer 2005). Vaughn discusses this in terms of genre – but arrives at essentially the same conclusion:

The same actors will behave and speak differently in different settings, according to the expectations and norms of different audiences. securitizers shape their discourse to reflect and respond to the perceived needs and priorities of each group by drawing on different linkages, responsibilities and social understandings.

(2009: 275)

Each factor can operate independently, the setting of a budgetary meeting will set the rules for particular speech acts, even if the audience changes; similarly, the same audience, such as a government minister, can change the tone, substance, and language of meeting by her mere presence. The settings of press conference, testimony before the legislature, internal meetings, interdepartmental meetings, budgetary negotiations, etc. have a fundamental effect on what is said. And, in all of these different settings, discourse is not monolithic: small decisions accumulate and mundane security practices build-up to yield a securitizing move. Let us use the concepts of distal and proximate contexts: the setting is a distal context that sets the epistemological grounds for kind of knowledge and language what counts as true; the audience is a proximate context that further refines what is politically-sayable. It is not the grammatical or historical context that matters most, but the social setting that co-constitutes the role and the audience within a particular relation and sets the limits of the sayable. Thus, I want to suggest that – as there are four primary settings for securitizing moves (elite, popular, technocratic, and scientific), we reconceptualise successful/failed securitization as a threshold, rather than a binary.[3]

Process

We cannot accept a simply binary result of "accepted" or "failed" securitizing moves: in other words, a single snapshot or coup de grace. Rather, there are several steps in the acceptance or failure of a securitizing move. Abrahamsen's model of a continuum of normalcy, risk, threat approaches this process, which relates only to the status of the issue, but does not distinguish enough between different kinds of political actors or the settings in which they operate (2005). I suggest a matrix of success/failure that better captures the process of the failure/acceptance of a securitizing move (Salter 2008). This matrix also helps us distinguish which actors can make the appropriate knowledge claims about an issue and the status of those claims within different settings. This is based on the component parts of the securitizing moves, guided by four questions:

1) To what degree is the issue-area discussed as a part of a wider political debate?
2) Is the description of the threat as existential accepted or rejected?
3) Is the solution to the threat accepted or rejected?
4) Are new or emergency powers accorded to the securitizing agent?

The threshold is approached through all of these vectors. Abrahamsen's identification of the discourse is useful here: but in addition to a general theme of normalcy, risk, and threat, I argue that there must be specific linguistic, discursive connections between the issue area and the substance of these four questions: politics, existential threat, solution, new or emergency powers. Perhaps because Roe focuses on the popular setting, he asserts that there are only two characteristics of an audience's acceptance of a particular securitizing move: "securityness" and "extraordinariness" (2008: 616). However, I would argue that the more fundamental question of politics – is this an issue for explicit, democratic politics – and the specific solution to extraordinary circumstance are also in play, in both popular and other settings. Like Abrahamsen and others, the concept of the threshold puts the analytical focus firmly on the process of the shift, the process of changing the meaning of, an issue into and out of the realm of security.

First, the issue-area must be within the universe of possible political discussion. The possible space of the system of "politics" will, of course, vary with each community, hence the need for more empirical case studies. The role of government and the sphere of potential political debate vary between states. The first claim that any securitizer must make is that the object of the securitizing move is a proper concern with the subject (be it the nation, the state, the society, the bureaucracy, or the individual) (McDonald 2008). Huysmans makes this point clear: "security rhetoric defines existential challenges, which endanger the survival of the political order. As a result it alters the premises for all other questions; they become subjugated to the security question" (2006: 25). The definition of security both prioritizes the policies within the realm of the possible, but also depends on the limits of the politics. Thus, every securitization requires a prior politicization, even if the consequence of securitization is depoliticization. Security issues must be brought into the realm of the political before it is redefined as outside normal politics.

Second, the threat to the community may be accepted, but the existential nature of threat also has to be accepted. Security panics, like moral panics, are cyclical – perhaps because every political, communicative space is limited. Agamben's key insight in *State of Exception*, in this sense, could not be more banal, even having borrowed it from Benjamin: every situation becomes "normal" (2005). The human psyche is a normalization machine, as any attempt to understand trauma, life under totalitarian conditions, or "the camp" will demonstrate (Todorov 1996).[4] The political imagination suffers from entropy: every security issue tends towards politicization over time. We know this of all primary political structures. Campbell argues "states are never finished as entities; the tension between the demands of identity and the practices that constitute it can never fully be resolved, because the performative nature of identity can never fully be revealed" (1993: 12). In order for a threat or a danger to remain present in political discourse, resources must be spent to counter this entropy.

Third, the solution to the existential threat must be accepted. While the CS presents the acceptance of a securitizing move as removing the security from public debate, many moves already include the proposed solution and these solutions can be debated. The American public, for example, accepted the existential threat of Al-Qaeda to the US and in particular the US way of life after the 9/11 attacks. However, even with the successful securitization of many sectors of American public life, the actual counter-terror policies were frequently challenged. Honig makes a strong case for the resistance of courts against the efforts by the Bush administration, even if in the past "courts have explicitly deferred on such matters to executive branch claims of national security needs" (Honig 2005: 210). A clear example of this in the public realm is the Transportation Security Administration and aviation security. The issue of pre-board screening occupied the public and officials, and a new federal agency was created to implement tighter security at airports – but this did not stop wide-scale outcry by the travelling public, airport and airline officials, civil libertarians and privacy experts, and even government officials themselves: the existential threat was acknowledged as was an emergency role for government, but the measures to mitigate the risk were robustly debated.

Finally, the policy solution to the existential threat must be new or emergency powers accorded to the securitizing agent. It is not enough for governments or agencies to propose that policies be continued – new executive powers are evidence of securitization, even if it is the dispersion or deputization of previously-centralized powers of decision-making. This is a distinct move away from the Copenhagen School, which argues

we do not push the demand so high as to say that an emergency measure has to be adopted, only that the existential threat has to be argued and gain enough resonance for a platform to be made from which is it is possible to legitimize emergency measures.

(Buzan, Wæver and de Wilde 1998: 25)

There must be some public policy change, either in discourse, budget, or in actual policy: resonance is simply too unstable a category to really evaluate, and can lead to analysis by counter-factual (though no measure was taken, there might have been, would have been, could have been). For example, setting aside the vigorous debate about the exact legal status of Guantanamo Bay, the US government claimed publicly that in response to a new threat, new powers were needed to interrogate criminals. There had been public and terrorist threats to the US before (the Weathermen, Animal Liberation Front [ALF] and the Earth Liberation Front [ELF], etc.) – but it had not expressed a need or right to water-board (whether or not this practice legally constitutes torture) to deal with the other threats. There were new legal opinions provided that argued the new measures were already inherent in the law, but the fact remains that they were new opinions that were newly adopted. An actual change occurred, not simply the resonance of an audience that might make a policy change possible. The policy solution must be accepted as much as the securitizing move – and this acceptance takes place in both the public and technocratic registers.

This is to say that we must disaggregate the process of securitization, and analyze these processes within various settings, expecting and explaining how social, bureaucratic, and political games influence how these different discourses and practices come to be accepted or rejected – and eventually, explaining how these different processes relate to one another, which must be done in an empirically-driven way.

I take seriously Balzacq's analysis of securitization "without the explicit assent of an audience" (2008: 76), but wish to modify it slightly. Rather than suggest that following Huysmans there are two audiences (popular and technocratic), I would suggest that there are four settings: elite, technocratic, scientific, popular. The adoption of security measures must be made to someone somewhere – if only to approve a budget, amend regulations, pass legislation, adopt a particular technology, or set best practices. These different settings operate on different logics of persuasion, different epistemologies and power/knowledge networks: in short, the threshold for securitization varies according to the setting. This will be demonstrated later. For example, securitization of "total information" was successful in the technocratic field – it was supported by scientists, technologists, and bureaucrats within the Pentagon, Defense Advanced Research Projects Agency (DARPA), and the National Security Agency (NSA). However, when the issue moved to the popular setting, the threshold of securitization was different and the move to conduct counter-terrorist data-mining on all public and private information was rejected. The process of securitization is iterative, dynamic and multi-layered. How, then, might it fail?

Theories of failure

The threshold model of securitization specifically does not address the counter-factual question of whether particular securitizations were necessary; i.e. that some moves should be or should have been rejected.[5] Failure of securitizing moves may be politically-desirable, following Wæver's normative commitment to desecuritization. Or at a minimum, securitization is always 'for someone and for something' – it grants powers, privileges and positions to some and excludes others. Epistemic-realists – of both the pragmatic and idealist varieties – would each be interested in the success/failure of securitization, either because of a realist belief that there are some existential threats that must be countered with emergency policies or because of a liberal belief that democratic discussion and openness are always better. However, this paper is not concerned with intelligence, strategic, tactical, market or policy failures as such – only in the failed attempt to securitize a particular sector or issue as part of the political process.

We can locate three possible kinds of failure: normal failures are non-purposive results of complex, interdependent systems; internal failures are securitizing moves that do not meet the grammatical conditions (i.e. Questions 1 + 2: is the threat accepted as political? is the threat existential?); external failures are securitizing moves that meet the grammatical elements but are not accepted by the audience (Questions 3 + 4: is the solution accepted/rejected? Are new/emergency powers granted?)

Normal accidents

Framed initially by Perrow, Normal Accident Theory (NAT) argues that accidents are an inherent result of a complex, technologically-interdependent society (1984, 1999). An organizational sociologist, Perrow makes an argument familiar to sociologist Beck that modern, technological, industrial societies embrace risk (1992). There is a new sensitivity to the accident as a test or a diagnosis of the society. Der Derian insists that the accident has become a primary driver of international politics (2001). The unexpected reveals what we have already expected as normal. Virilio makes a similar point: "the accident is diagnostic of technology. To invent the train is to invent derailment; to invent the ship is to invent the shipwreck. The ship that sinks says much more to me about technology than the ship that floats!" (1998: 20). The citizenship regime solidified after the First World War created refugees, and the system for their management. The abuse of the passport and visa system in the Millennium, Shoe-bomber and 9/11 attacks put pressure on the international travel system and national systems of identity documentation. Nyers argues that those citizens who gain or lose their citizenship accidentally reveal important dynamics of inclusion/exclusion within the political community (2006): by describing the limits of "normal" and "accidental," we can chart the contours of identity, belonging, nation, and the excluded. Ellhefnawy makes the point about accidents in economic language: the neoliberal drive towards efficiency eliminates the slack and redundancy so necessary for resiliency in the face of normal accidents (2004). These authors argue that, at root, complexity exceeds risk management: ignorance or uncertainties, vulnerabilities, weakness, gaps, or inflexibilities mean that failures and disasters are inevitable. It is important that these failures are understood as inevitable and not purposive.

If we accept that securitization is a political process that takes place within that complex society, often involving multiple and competing bureaucracies, then we would expect that NAT explain some failed securitizing moves. The ghost of intentionality haunts the original formulation of securitization theory: if the internal and external conditions are met, then securitization *should* occur. However, NAT suggests that accidents are inevitable. The Bush administration convinced Congress that the threat was existential. But, as wider political debate continued on this point – a wider securitizing move from the elite to the popular setting – the existential nature of the Iraqi threat was debated openly. There is a wider point here that, even in the absence of an effective popular securitizing move, securitization of the Iraqi regime was still possible. Aradau and Munster make the argument that within the political, popular, and technocratic settings, the war on terror has acted as a kind of general facilitating condition, wherein threats are more easily accepted as existential (2007). While agreeing with this completely, the cases where threats are not accepted are equally interesting.

Part of this public story about the infamous intelligence dossier is a narrative of NAT. The original intelligence reports contained nuance and uncertainty that was subsequently simplified and made less ambiguous as they ascended from the bureaucratic/expert setting to the elite political setting and finally into the popular setting. An independent assessment of the Institute for Strategic Studies by the former head of UNSCOM concludes:

> the Strategic Dossier appears to be a sober and balanced account, in no way discreditable to its authors. Some clearly mistaken statements as to the likelihood of a ballistic missile force and of a chemical weapons stockpile do disfigure the overall impression, and even these incorrect assessments are qualified with some balancing reservations.
>
> (Ekeus 2004: 86)

Thus, the transmission of subtlety and nuance, which provided a more robust and ambiguous image of the threat, does not need to be explained through a conspiracy theory of evil geniuses or the banality of evil, but through the regular, complex process of the production of knowledge within the government.

Internal failures

A securitizing move may fail because a particular audience rejects the issue as a matter of politics, or a matter germane to that setting. Critical theorists, in particular, are predisposed to say that at root all decisions are political – but I think that we can identify that some issues are considered appropriate to political debate, not on the basis of facts vs. values, but on the basis of whether the issue involves justice or survival. Recent popular debates regarding the financial sector bail-out demonstrate the former. As Best argues, the economy has often been set as an exception from politics as normal (2007). In the current debate, the need for emergency state action to shore-up the financial sector, national economies, or the international economic system is hotly debated as "necessary." The Washington Consensus, and neoliberalism in general, made the case that the market capitalism functioned most smoothly and efficiently when political discussion was subservient to technical accuracy. But, the crisis reinjected that discussion into the political realm: what was the best, most effective, most just solution. On the other hand, the attempts by members of the US Congress and President G.W. Bush to intervene in the Terri Schiavo case, the removal of a feeding tube from a patient in a persistent vegetative state, is an example of the limits of political discussion – as legislators later regretted their interference in a legal proceeding.[6] To take a frivolous example, the US would have a difficult time mobilizing the National Guard to monitor the Golden Globes voting process: the Hollywood Foreign Press Association is simply not political, and the threat of subversion of democratic processes in that venue does not concern justice or survival. The National Guard is deployed to Iraq and

Afghanistan to oversee elections there because these elections are understood to be political, and the threat to America of continuing its imperial occupation of Iraq and Afghanistan is seen as existential (at least in terms of American values if not American hegemony). The first iteration of the Total Information Awareness program sought to data-mine library records to create profiles of potential terror suspects. However, this limitation on the freedom of speech and invasion of privacy was rejected by librarians, civil libertarians, and others as outside the authority of the state. The existential threat of terrorism to the US was accepted by the protestors, but the colonization of this sector of private life was rejected as being outside of the security purview of the state.

Also, as an internal condition of securitization, the threat must be existential. The REAL ID act, for example, is a clear example of elite and popular audiences rejecting the existential description of identity fraud/theft. Bush administration security officials have long argued that having hundreds of kinds of acceptable personal identification documents makes law enforcement, screening, and counter-terror operations more difficult. Driver's licenses, which act for a large proportion of the American popular as their primary form of ID, are the responsibility of state governments, rather than the Federal government. The REAL ID act would harmonize all state driver's licenses, and make their databases interoperable. While initial proposals had touted the knock-on benefits this would have for identity-theft, fraud, and other economic drivers, its passage through the Congress was facilitated only when national security was invoked – and Federal funding for highway infrastructure was made dependent on the adherence to national standards. The 9/11 Report had argued that travel documents were an essential tool of the terrorist, but had focused on passports and visas rather than state issued ID. Popular and state resistance to the scheme came on legal grounds (state's rights within a federal system), but also a rejection that identity theft was an existential threat. Identity certification was seen as a legitimate area of security concern, but it did not pass the acceptance threshold and this particular securitization of identity documents failed.

These two kinds of internal failure are about the conditions of possibility: the issue must be considered a matter of politics and an existential threat for the audience to consider accepting the securitizing move. Without these two conditions, the securitizing move cannot make grammatical or sociological sense. The limits of the political define what threats may be considered, but a successful securitization also requires that the target audience accept the threat is not simply serious, but existential. These are internal failures of the securitizing move.

External failures

Even if the structural, internal or grammatical conditions for securitization are accepted by the audience, the securitizing move may fail on two external grounds: either the specific solution is rejected or the potential for new emergency powers is rejected. This is a new addition to the securitization theory: we can point, particularly in the case of the global war on terror, where the Bush administration's securitizing moves were rejected not because of the nature of the threat, but the proposed solutions. This, I would argue, is a reassertion of debate, discussion, and politics.

Solution rejected. The global war on terror, embodied by the Al-Qaeda terrorist network, was accepted by the vast majority of American audiences as an existential threat to the American way of life. We can see two clear cases where subsidiary or minor securitizing moves were made, in part to exempt the Bush administration from the strictures of its own laws, that were rejected – by the courts and in the populace (if not always the Congress). First, as suggested earlier, the invasion of Iraq was rejected as a solution to the problem of Al-Qaeda. While the intelligence dossier in particular can be seen as a "normal" failure, whereby the bureaucratic process of creating an intelligence dossier readable and actionable by the President entailed the simplification of complex issues and the erasure of doubts and uncertainties – it was not after all a "slam dunk." But, in the public view by a significant portion of the American populace, in the elite (Obama, for example), and in the technocracy (military-intelligence establishment and the network of think-tanks that surround and permeate Washington), there was a rejection of the invasion. At the very least, this should indicate that "acceptance or failure" is complex and multifaceted, and that different audiences may have different thresholds for securitization – but it also indicates that part of the acceptance of a securitizing move is a judgment that the prospective response meets the existential threat. Second, the courts and the populace rejected the use of torture for interrogation – even if it was accepted by some part of the military and bureaucratic establishment.[7]

I want to add a final category of external failure, and that is an acceptance of the issue, the existential nature of the threat, and the solution – but not emergency powers. If no new powers are granted, if there is not invocation of an emergency or an exception, then the securitizing move is rejected. The effort by the Bush administration to bring water-boarding into the legal domain was because the public had rejected granting new powers to torture, as suggested by Dershowitz. Again, supported by McDonald, this leads us away from thinking of securitization as a bell that can be rung, and more of a consideration of political debate – even about specific security measures – as an on-going discussion. These categories of failure will be analyzed using two critical cases: Total Information Awareness and the Policy Analysis Markets.

Securitization and US counter-terrorism policies

A prima facie application for the concept of the "setting" and the importance of failure can be seen in an evaluation of the American war on terror. The United States is clearly a critical case for securitization in the contemporary period: the 9/11 attacks and the subsequent war on terror have generated a great deal of political capital that the Bush executive has (over)spent in an expansion of its power. If there is anywhere that the move towards securitization has been made easily and often, it is the post-9/11 US (Agamben 2005: 22). But, the attacks of 9/11 did not allow for a whole-scale securitization of American public life and foreign policy, which highlights also the structural limit of an economy of attention. So, if there are cases of failed securitization, then they will illuminate something important about that process. And, there is clear evidence of selective desecuritization in post-9/11 American discourse, even the desecuritization of particular aspects of a generally popular legislative agenda, the USA PATRIOT Act.

Total information awareness

The 'Total Information Awareness' (TIA) quickly renamed Terrorist Information Awareness, aimed to create a virtual database of all government documents and commercially or publicly available literature one all individuals: "Every purchase you make with a credit card, every magazine subscription you buy and medical prescription you fill, every website you visit and e-mail you send or receive, every academic grade you receive, every bank deposit you make, every trip you book and every event you attend . . . passport application, driver's license and bridge toll records, judicial and divorce records, complaints from nosy neighbors to the F.B.I., your lifetime paper trail plus the latest hidden camera surveillance" (Safire 2003). TIA was known within the Intelligence community – and indeed amongst technology journalists. John Poindexter of Iran-Contra fame had touted the need for joining intelligence gathering and modern data-mining for some time in public and amongst Pentagon officials (US Department of Defense 2003). He became Director of the Information Awareness Office at DARPA, and presented the program in a number of government and public venues (Poindexter, Popp and Sharkey 2003). Terrorists, it was argued, "conduct quasi-military operations using instruments of legitimate activity found in any open or modern society, making extensive use of the Internet, cell phones, the press, schools, houses of worship, prisons, hospitals, commercial vehicles, and financial systems" (Popp and Poindexter 2006). As a result, the vast amount of data available in government databases, private data warehouses, and on the internet, was a resource that was untapped. The original TIA program aimed to integrate "automated subject face identification, automatic language translation, audio and text processing, text summarization, and document filtering, clustering and categorization. Automated analysis and assessment developed through the Genoa project, allow[ed] for model selection, building, and updating; structured argumentation; and automated risk analysis" (Maxwell 2005: 3). Even though the underlying algorithms were suspect, the fundamental case that this public data should be mined for counter-terrorism purposes was not questioned in the Pentagon (Amoore 2009). The project received funding and support from DARPA under the aegis of the Information Awareness Office in January 2002,[8] in a clear, successful attempt to securitize personal data that had previously been considered private and to argue that privacy was a privilege of peacetime and that emergency measures were needed. Markoff recounts how Poindexter and then Secretary of Defense Donald Rumsfeld met over lunch to discuss the project, which was approved by Rumsfeld despite the reservations made by scientists and civil libertarians who sat on a review committee (2002). This suggests divisions between the elite (Rumsfeld), the technocratic (DARPA), and the scientific (review committee). Within the military-bureaucratic setting of DARPA, the case for new measures and emergency powers was easy to make. However, spearheaded by efforts by library, privacy, and libertarian groups, funding for the TIA program whether terrorist or total) was halted by the US Senate in July 2003 (Levy and Wall 2004).

A similar program to monitor library records was defeated by the mobilization of the American Library Association (ALA) (Monahan 2006). TIPS was aimed at a "Citizen Corps" of postal workers, gas meter readers, cable TV technicians, truckers, and public officials "to serve as extra eyes and ears for law enforcement . . . to look out for suspicious and potentially terrorist-related activity and in how to report that information through a toll free number" (White House Press Office 2004). Passage, approval, and amendments to the USA PATRIOT Act were equally random in their public discussion, often generated by the complaints by "banks, libraries, and universities" about the law (Abdolian and Takooshian, 2003).

What prompted action by the Congress to shut down funding for TIA was the move of the program into the public setting. The securitizing move failed – the issue was seen as a political issue, the threat was seen as existential, but the specific powers plus policies that the securitizing actors said that they needed was rejected. This is an example of a process failure: the grammatical elements were there, but the failure to "accept" the securitizing move was in the political-sociological realm – and more precisely the popular political setting.

Equally, some notable securitizations of similar issues have been successful. The REAL ID Act makes all US states' driver's licenses functionally interconnected – with similar data, a common format, and the ability to be mutually searchable. However, while there has been some pressure by states due to funding requirements, there has been little push-back in terms of public resistance (Garcia et al. 2005). Furthermore, the de-citizenship processes engaged against Jose Pedilla and others has received little critical public attention (Nyers 2006).[9] The conclusion of the kind of failure is structured by the setting in which securitization was attempted, and accepted or rejected. Consequently, even though the war in Iraq was debated publicly, and one could make a similar argument that the Iraqi invasion was rejected in a popular setting, this particular example focuses exclusively on the internal use of intelligence within the Bush administration in the run-up to the war. However, the RealID act and decitizenship proceedings have not gained much public attention, and so the possible setting is limited to technocratic and/or scientific (in this case, scientific refers to legal spheres). Consequently, if we accept that desecuritization is re-politicization[10] – the repatriation of a security issue back to the realm of deliberative politics, then these brief examples from different settings of the American of the war on terror suggest that the appetite for securitization varies greatly according to the rhetorical or discursive appeal made in direct relationship to the competing claims for desecuritization. Thus, different actors were able to make competing claims to the nature of threat, the appropriateness of the policy solutions, and the requirement for new powers that were not based exclusively on their democratic or elite legitimacy, but on other grounds such as technocratic or scientific legitimacy. The ALA and ACLU were able to marshal different desecuritization strategies based not on the total number of votes they could muster (in the legislature or general election) but on an appeal to a wider narrative of civil liberties and privacy. Conversely, there were no actors who successfully desecuritized the RealID Act, which creates a nationally-searchable database of identity documents, despite the grave concerns of privacy advocates.

Policy analysis market

In 2003, a proposal by the Pentagon for a "Policy Analysis Market" (PAM) – in which a crowd of experts would bet, or place a value, on particular targets, tactics, and groups – also failed. In PAM, experts from across government (intelligence, military, diplomacy, and other 'interested' parties) would buy and sell stock in particular scenarios – and the market value of these scenarios would reflect their likelihood. The system was not designed to focus on individual acts of terror, but on more abstract measures of stability within the Middle East: "markets were to be created in more mundane events like "How fast will Saudi Arabia's non-oil gross domestic product grow next year?" or "What chance does Prince so and so have by the end of the year in ascending to the throne in Country X? (Looney 2004: 415). The self-described architect of the PAM, Hanson said that the system was "intended to forecast aggregate measures of geopolitical stability in the Middle East. PAM would have used speculative markets to estimate economic growth, political stability, and military activity four times a year in each of eight nations, and how those measures would depend on each other and on various U.S. policy choices" (2006: 257). Again, different settings saw different degrees of securitization, and in particular different levels of acceptance of the new measures (i.e. betting on terror futures). Amongst behavioral economists and some technologists, the idea was greeted with support (Surowiecki 2004: 79–83; Seife 2003). While the program had been a success within the intelligence community, DARPA, and the Pentagon more widely, it failed in spectacular fashion, once made public by *The New York Times* and Sens. Wyden and Dorgan on July 28, 2004 and was shut-down by the end of the same day. Within one day of the public announcement of this DARPA program, "newspapers responded by denouncing this 'unbelievably stupid' and 'grotesque' market. Later that day, the program was officially cancelled" (Meirowitz and Tucker, 2004: 331). Hanson, argues that the cancellation of the program was due to entirely the public and elite perception that betting on terror attacks "crossed a moral boundary," completely independent of expert analysis of the futures market (2006: 260). There is some scientific evidence that this kind of ideas futures market can have some real predictive capacity, which often exceeds the best guess of any individual or sub-group of experts (Wolfers and Zitzewitz 2004). However, and this is crucial for understanding the importance of difference settings, the experts used politically-sensational examples (the assassination of Arafat and the collapse of the Jordanian monarchy) as their samples to gain funding from the technocrats. The general public and political elite reacted to these examples, and the program was terminated with extreme prejudice within a day of publicity (Abdolian and Takooshian, 2003; Clifton 2003). The theory of behind betting on terror futures and the emergency property of the "wisdom of crowds" essentially tried to securitize economic theory: the terror threat was an emergency and required government action to generate knowledge about the future. PAM failed on the popular scene, while scientific experts were completely unable to mount a defence – in part because of how they had presented their expertise. By couching the defense of PAM in terms of abstract economic principles, it was represented in the media as a morally bankrupt "bloodless betting shop" at best. In other words, the very same discourse by the economists of the advantages of value-free, market-generated assessments that gained them support within the bureaucracy of DARPA became the source of a majority of criticism.

The difference between scenes is also important: the REAL ID Act makes all US states' driver's licenses functionally interconnected – with similar data, a common format, and the ability to be mutually searchable, putatively for policing and counter-terrorism purposes. There has been little push-back in terms of popular resistance, even from the same libertarians who protested other national ID card proposal. But 17 states are rejecting this attempted securitization by the Department of Homeland Security (Garcia et al. 2005). This speculative analysis of securitizing moves within the post-9/11 environment demonstrates that the appetite for securitization varies in direct relationship to the competing claims for desecuritization. The success or failure of securitizing moves depends on who can speak and what can be said. Thus, different actors are able to make competing claims, according to different narratives and social structures of authority, to identify the nature of threat, the appropriateness of the policy solutions, and the requirement for emergency action.

Conclusion: value-based securitization

To identify the threshold of securitization, we must evaluate the values that the securitizing move will supersede. The economic value of airline travel superseded the concerns about comprehensive and inefficient screening. The values of privacy and freedom of speech, epitomized by library records, superseded the questionable value of data-mining. The value of "good taste" or rather disgust for betting on terrorist acts superseded the forecasting value of the PAM. But, in the cases of the invasion of Iraq or water-boarding the securitizing move was successful, at least in some settings. Thus, securitization theory needs a sociological approach to understanding how audiences understand security as one value in a set of other values and how settings structure the way that securitizing moves are made.

What both of these critical cases demonstrate is that securitization is complex, multiplicitous, overlapping, and heterogeneous. The very grounding, the justification, the explanation for both TIA and PAM that supported the securitization in the elite, scientific or technocratic setting were precisely the grounds that were rejected when the issue moved to the public setting. Social capital is field-dependent and does not necessarily translate between settings. The scientific econometric justification for marketizing terrorist futures was seen as morally grotesque, patriotically insensitive, and politically stupid. The wide scope of automated digital surveillance that would allow for better profiling was seen to lack the discretion of human operators or respect privacy. As issues moved from one setting to another, the definition of the threat, the justification of new/emergency powers, and the legitimacy of particular policy instruments all became subjects of contention.

To emulate Hansen, I would propose that future studies of securitization and securitizing moves must take in account of the following questions for future analysis. How is the referent object constructed as a matter of politics, security, and within a particular field? How do the different settings in which the securitizing move is attempted interaction? Within the interplay of success and failures, which setting becomes dominant? What kind of data can measure the acceleration, deceleration, entropy, or maintenance of the "security-ness" of a particular issue? How can we account for null-cases (failures or disjunctures between what discursive or sociological factors we would expect to be salient that are not)?

Notes

1 This project was support by the Centre for Research in the Arts, Social Sciences and Humanities and the Centre of International Studies at the University of Cambridge, and through funding by the Social Sciences and Humanities Research Council of Canada. I would like to thank Thierry Balzacq, Sarah Léonard, and the other reviewers for their comments, including those posed at the initial presentation of this paper at the International Studies Association in New York, 2009.

2 For a thoughtful, friendly critique, see Balzacq and Léonard (2009) mimeo.

3 Although I take issue with significant parts of the original formulation of the CS model of securitization, Buzan, Wæver, and de Wilde do use the language of threshold, although the process is under-theorized.

4 How has this criticism of Agamben gone so long unregistered. "It is not true that life in the camps obeyed only the law of the jungle. The rules of camp society may have been different but they still existed . . . This law functioned as rigorously in the gulags as it did in the camps" (Todorov 1996: 36) – which at a minimum must push back against Agamben's bleak view of the camp.

5 This is the normative argument engaged by Aradau, Floyd, Behnke, etc. I am relatively agnostic.

6 Then democratic leadership candidate said in a debate with Hilary Clinton on February 26, 2008 that the intervention by the Senate was his chief regret in his short career in the Senate: "I think that was a mistake, and I think the American people understood that it was a mistake. And as a constitutional law professor, I knew better."

7 "Only 5% (of the total sample) found physical torture acceptable, 16% found mental torture acceptable, 19% found humiliating and degrading treatment acceptable, and only 16% found threatening physical torture acceptable" (Program on International Policy Attitudes/Knowledge Networks Poll 2004: 6). *Americans on detention, torture, and the war on terrorism*. Program on International Policy Attitudes. College Park, MD: The University of Maryland. Available at: http://www.pipa.org/OnlineReports/Terrorism/Torture_Jul04/Torture_Jul04_rpt.pdf(Accessed on August 4, 2009).

8 Poindexter's presentation at DARPATech 2002, titled "Transforming Fantasy," has since been removed from DARPA's website, although it was available until 2004. http://www.darpa.mil/DARPATech2002/presentation.html

9 Jose Pedilla is an American citizen who was declared an unlawful combatant by the Bush administration, and consequently lost the ability to claim rights as a citizen.

10 This I take to be the core of the original formulation of the CS, and subsequent discussion by Aradau, Huysmans, Taurek, and others.

Part II

Securitization and de-securitization in practice

7 Rethinking the securitization of the environment

Old beliefs, new insights

Maria Julia Trombetta

Other chapters in this book have pointed at the limits of a formalistic and de-contextualized approach to securitization. They have shown, in different ways, that the social construction of a security issue is a more dynamic, nuanced and complex process than the one described by the Copenhagen School (CS). This chapter deals with the implications of adopting a narrow, textual approach to securitization when analyzing the social construction of global environmental problems as security issues. It thus amplifies the third assumption developed in Chapter 1, while taking seriously some of the methodological precepts offered thereof. The chapter does this by reconsidering some of the debates surrounding environmental security. The first one is related with the opportunity of speaking environmental security: What are the consequences of evoking security? Are they always as problematic as the CS assumes? The case of the environment is a relevant one because the debate is divided between those supporting the term environmental security, suggesting that is a good way to promote action and those who warn against its implications. The second debate is about the practices brought about by securitization: Are they fixed and unchangeable or can they be transformed by securitizing non traditional issues?

The environmental sector is relevant because several appeals to environmental security have been made with the intent of challenging existing security practices and provisions and yet many contemporary security discourses – mentioning precaution and resilience – seem to have been influenced by the environmental debate and concepts. An approach, like securitization, which considers the discursive formation of security issues, provides a new perspective to analyze the environmental security discourse, its potential to transform what counts as security and the ways to provide it. It allows, for instance, an investigation of the political process behind the selection of threats, exploring why some of them are considered more relevant and urgent than others. In this way, the focus shifts from supposedly objective threats to the collectivities, identities and interests that deserve to be protected and the means to be employed.

In this chapter, however, it will be shown that the possibility of understanding the transformation of security practices and provisions is precluded because, by focusing on the textual, formal aspect of speech acts, the CS imposes a problematic fixity on security as a form of social practice. For the School the label security brings with it a specific mindset and a set of problematic practices associated with the logic of war and emergency. For the CS, these practices are not open to negotiation or political debate. Accordingly, transforming an issue into a security issue is not always desirable. In the case of the environment, the warning seems clear: "When considering securitizing moves such as 'environmental security' . . . one has to weigh the always problematic side effects of applying a mind-set of security against the possible advantages of focus, attention, and mobilization" (Buzan, Wæver and de Wilde 1998: 29). The solution suggested by the CS is to avoid the transformation of an issue into a security issue or to "desecuritize" as many issues as possible. This however cannot always be possible or desirable, as the debate about environmental security has shown. First, the performative, constitutive approach suggested by the speech act theory implies that even talking and researching about security can contribute to the securitization of an issue, even if that (and above all the practices allegedly associated with it) is not the desired result (see Huysmans 2002: 43). Second, attempts to show that something is not a security issue can lead to the marginalization and the minimization of urgent threats, especially when several attempts to transform environmental issues into security issues seem to have mobilized actions and produced forms of cooperation rather than conflict.

The second reason that makes the environment a relevant case to investigate is that the CS has dealt specifically with it. For the School the environment sector is one that need to be considered to analyze contemporary security dynamics. In this way several tensions emerges between an empirically driven approach adopted by the CS, which is attentive to the peculiarities of the environmental sector and the attempts to identify the quality that makes an issue a security issue or the "security-ness" of security. Amongst the peculiarities of the environmental sector the CS observes that few attempts to evoke security within the environmental sector have not passed the border of ordinary politics or brought about exceptional measures and the logic of confrontation. The School has dismissed those appeals as failed securitization moves that are appeals to security that did not lead to securitization. Against this perspective, or old beliefs, this chapter argues that the securitizations of the environment were indeed successful since they brought about measures and policies that probably would not otherwise have been undertaken, and yet they contributed to transform the logic and the practices of security.

The chapter is in three parts. The first part deals with the limits that a textual approach to security creates in the case of the environment. It introduces the key elements of the theory of securitization and their relevance for the analysis of environmental security discourses and their implications. This part shows that a discursive approach like securitization can potentially capture several aspects of the transformative intent that characterizes many appeals to include environmental issues in security analysis, and yet, it points out that the fixity imposed on security practices by the CS creates an impasse that leads to the problematic suggestion of keeping the label security away from as many issues as possible, including the environment. The necessity of this fixity is challenged by the second part, which outlines a tension between the empirically driven analysis of the environmental sector and the conceptualization of the "securityness of security" and suggests that the securitization of the environment has contributed to bring about a transformation of security practices. The final part provides some examples from the environmental sector. It argues for a more contextualized approach, which suggests that in a process of securitization not only are issues transformed into security issues, but also the practices associated with security are challenged and sometimes transformed (Balzacq, 2009a; Balzacq, this volume). More specifically, the chapter deals with two cases of securitization of environmental issues. They are the hole in the ozone layer and environmental conflict.

Securitization and the environment: potential and limits

In order to explore the potential and limits of securitization theory in dealing with the social construction of environmental problems as security issues, it is necessary to briefly review the key elements of securitization theory: the performative power of evoking security, its inter-subjective nature, and the "specific rhetorical structure" (Buzan, Wæver and de Wilde 1998: 26), and analyze them in relation with the environmental problem.

Wæver, drawing on Austin's work, considers "security" as a speech act. "In this usage, security is not of interest as a sign that refers to something more real; the utterance *itself* is the act. By saying it, something is done (as in betting, giving a promise, naming a ship)" (Wæver 1995: 55). While this is not the place to discuss whether Wæver's understanding of speech act is appropriate (see Balzacq in this volume), it is relevant to emphasize that Wæver is interested in Austin's theory because it captures the power of language in transforming situations and provides a perspective in which the problematic distinctions between "true" and "false" or objective and subjective threats become irrelevant. Accordingly, to say: "global warming is a security issue" is not considered as a constative (that can be true or false – the point, in this perspective, is not to decide whether global warming is a real threat or not), but a performative (that can be felicitous/successful or not). What matters for the School is whether saying that global warming is a threat transforms the way of dealing with it. In this way, the CS does not focus on the truth of a statement but on the "truth effect" of it. Considering the performative power of speaking security opens a new perspective to analyze the development of environmental security discourses and their consequences. Many environmental problems are uncertain and will fully manifest their consequences in a more or less distant future; this makes the political process of constructing insecurities crucial to understanding why some problems are considered as more relevant and urgent than others or why some issues mobilize action while others are largely ignored.

However, focusing on the security utterance only can be problematic because this could suggest that everything can become a security issue when someone names it that way. Indeed not all the appeals to security transform an issue into a security issue. To avoid this problem the CS distinguish between securitizing moves (Buzan, Wæver and de Wilde 1998: 25), which are appeals to security that can be successful or not, and proper securitization. The School then qualifies securitization in two ways: first, securitization is a collective phenomenon, "a specific form of social

Conclusion

praxis" (Buzan, Wæver and de Wilde 1998: 204); and second, it has a specific rhetoric structure and follows specific rules.

Securitization, for the CS, is a collective phenomenon in two respects. First, it is an inter-subjective practice. One actor can try and say that something vital is at risk and can point at a threat, but a successful securitization is not decided by the speaker alone, but by the audience as well: "[S]ecurity . . . ultimately rests neither with the objects nor with the subjects but *among* the subjects" (Buzan, Wæver and de Wilde 1998: 31). Securitization in this way reflects the values and interests of a political community. In the case of the environment, its securitization suggests a growing relevance and awareness of environmental problems and a shared aspiration to do something about them. Second, security is about collectivities not individuals. For the School, this is relevant because it allows scholars to "historicize security, to study transformation in the units of security affairs," an opportunity that for the School is precluded both to traditionalists, who focus only on the state, and Critical Security Studies that focuses on the individual (Buzan, Wæver and de Wilde 1998: 206–7). This is quite relevant for the environmental debate since it opens up the possibility of transforming political community through the social construction of common threats, and several attempts to link security and the environment embody cosmopolitan intents. As Beck suggests "threats create society and global threats create global society" (Beck 2000: 38). The CS, however, is sceptical about the possibility of a security unity as large as humankind,[1] and the reasons have to do not with historical or sociological analyses that could outline the enduring relevance of the state as a security actor, but with other assumptions of the theory. These aspects are those related to an antagonistic logic of security and are the same as those that determine the problematic fixity of security practices, which precludes the possibility of analyzing the transformations of security units, at least in universalistic terms.

In order to clarify why it is difficult to imagine a security unity as large as humankind, it is necessary to explore the other qualification of securitization provided by the CS, namely that security is a specific kind of speech act; it has a specific rhetoric structure and brings into existence a specific set of practices. Security is about "the staging of existential issues in politics to lift them above politics. In security discourse, an issue is dramatized and presented as an issue of supreme priority; Thus, by labeling it as *security*, an agent claims a need for and a right to treat it by extraordinary means" (Buzan, Wæver and de Wilde 1998: 26, emphasis in the original). For the CS this appeal to survival carries with it a set of connotations that invokes the logic of "threat-defence," the identification of an enemy and eventually the logic of war (Wæver 1995: 54). The mechanism that identifies the "securityness of security," the "quality . . . that makes a security issue in international relations" (Buzan 1997: 13), recalls the understanding of the political provided by Schmitt, for whom "the political is the most intense and extreme antagonism, . . . that of the friend-enemy grouping" (1996: 29). Securitization is identified with the exceptional decision that constitutes enemies and brings into existence the logic of war. Even if the School does not share this vision of the political, it suggests that this logic characterizes the security mindset. Accordingly the problem with the broadening of the security agenda is that this mindset is spread as well.

In this way, the problems with securitization, when the environment is involved, starts to appear. On the one hand, an approach that considers the discursive formation of security issues provides a new perspective to analyze the environmental security discourse and its transformative potential. It allows, for instance, an analysis of the political process that leads to prioritizing some issues instead of others, the transformation of the political communities that are supposed to be protected, the legitimizing of security practices and the empowerment of the actors that can contrast specific threats. On the other hand, securitization is problematic for the set of practices it is supposed to bring about, which are supposed to be fixed and based on a very narrow understanding of what security is about, which is identified as the inscription of enemies in a context. While the securitization of an issue is open to negotiation and political debate, the practices it brings about are not, and they will necessarily come into existence once an issue has been successfully securitized, and, moreover, are those practices themselves that allow us to decide whether an issue has been securitized or not.

This tension is evident in the long term debate about environmental security, which opposes those who suggest considering the environment as a security issue in order to promote action, to focus on the issues that really matter and to adopt a cooperative rather than a confrontational approach to security, and those who argue that security has a tradition it cannot escape and thus appeals to security should be avoided. The latter argument has been reinforced by securitization theory and the sense of necessity it seems to impose.

Several commentators have tried to bridge this divide and avoid what Dalby (2001), talking about environmental security, has described as "the dangers in a good idea." Floyd (2007) has suggested that there are positive and negative securitizations and that this can be decided on the basis of their results. This is largely based on the consideration that within the environmental sector not all the appeals to security have introduced a confrontational logic, identified enemies or allowed exceptional measures against them; on the contrary, some of them have promoted quick and effective actions. However, without challenging the logic of security suggested by the CS, the solution proposed by Floyd seems to imply that, in some circumstances, the logic of creating enemies can be the most appropriate. However, this seems to contradict the attempt to overcome the divisions between the CS and Critical Security Studies since the latter adopts a positive understanding of security (see Booth 1991, 2007).

Another example is provided by Jon Barnett. He first argued that the securitization of the environment can have perverse effects and shown that several attempts to transform environmental problems into security issues have resulted in a spreading of the national security paradigm and the enemy logic, even if the intentions behind them were different. Then, to avoid these problematic developments, Barnett has suggested promoting a "human centered" understanding of security. However, if one accepts the ineluctability of the security mindset and logic evoked by securitization: "environmental security is not about the environment, it is about security; as a concept, it is at its most meaningless and malign" (Barnett 2001: 83) one cannot expect that an appeal to a human centered security will provide different outcomes. If the practices evoked by speaking security are fixed and unchangeable, why should the sort of claim made by Barnett be different from similar ones? Why should his appeal to a "human centered security" be different from the appeals to environmental security, if the intentions of the speakers or the context are irrelevant? These dilemmas, however, are based on the idea that security practices are inescapable and unchangeable and the theory of securitization, as elaborated by the CS, has contributed to suggest so.

Failed securitization or changing security practices?

The CS has contributed to making a specific, negative understanding of security – which has characterized the dominant Realist discourse within IR – appear as 'natural' and unchangeable since all the attempts to transform it appear to reinforce its logic as the examples from the environmental security debate have shown.[2] This perverse mechanism, however, can be challenged by showing that the social construction of a security issue does not necessarily follow the formal mechanism described by the CS, and the environmental sector provides relevant examples. More specifically, it will be shown that the attempts by the CS to combine an empirically driven approach, which is attentive to the actual processes of securitization and the specificities of different sectors with a de-contextualized "securityness of security" create several tensions and inconsistencies. These tensions will be analyzed by considering the peculiarities of the environmental sector as described by the CS itself.

The CS explores the specificity of the environmental sector in *Security: A Framework for Analysis* (Buzan, Wæver and de Wilde 1998), the theoretical book in which the CS illustrates the theory of securitization and analyses the dynamics of securitization within five relevant sectors. For each sector the School identifies the actors or objects (referent objects) that are threatened, specifies the relevant threats and the agents that promote or facilitate securitization. The environmental sector is rather different from the others. Amongst the peculiarities of the environmental sector described by the School, two deserve a specific analysis for their implications: first, the presence of two agendas – a scientific and a political one; second, the multiplicity of actors. They both stress the relevance of a contextualized analysis and the importance of factors which suggest that the social construction of security issues is more complex than the successful performance of a speech act. This will lead to the final characteristic of the environmental sector, namely the consideration that several securitization moves lead to politicization, rather than to securitization, since they do not exceed the "normal bounds of political procedure" (Buzan, Wæver and de Wilde 1998: 25). Against this problematic compromise it will be argued that the securitization of non traditional issues like environmental problems is challenging and transforming existing security practices, but the focus on the fixity of security practices does not allow the CS to account for this process. The three aspects are analyzed in turn.

"One of the most striking features of the environmental sector," it is argued in *Security*, "is the existence of two different agendas: a scientific agenda and a political agenda" (Buzan, Wæver and de Wilde 1998: 71). They explain that the scientific agenda refers mainly to natural science and non-governmental activities and it "is about the authoritative assessment of threat" (Buzan, Wæver and de Wilde 1998: 72). In the case of the environment the relevance of the scientific agenda is evident in the attempts to legitimize different competing claims with the authority of science, but it is often present in other sectors, such as health issues related with the spread of pandemic or other diseases. Buzan, Wæver and de Wilde argue that "the extent to which scientific argument structures environmental security debates strikes us as exceptional" (Buzan, Wæver and de Wilde 1998: 72), but, quoting Rosenau, they admit that "the demand for scientific proof is a broader emerging characteristic in the international system" (Buzan, Wæver and de Wilde 1998: 72).

This, however, has two implications. First, it seems to challenge the possibility of transforming the way of dealing with an issue by appealing to security and focusing on the "truth effect" of a statement. In other words it questions the "self referential-ity" of the speech act security (Balzacq 2005). That is, if one starts to admit that a successful securitization within the environmental sector requires specific condi-tions, namely the presence of authoritative knowledge, or scientific proof, one has also to admit that the specific nature of an issue, an environmental problem, for instance, requires a context and issue-specific analysis. This calls for a more con-textualized approach that considers the peculiarities of each case and challenges the possibility of translating the dynamics of securitization from one sector to another. Second, the existence of two agendas has implications for the suggestion of desecuritizing as many issues as possible. Is it possible and what does it mean to "desecuritize" an issue which is on the scientific agenda? If scientific research out-lines the dangerousness of an environmental problem, how is it possible to provide security? This suggests the importance of an epistemic community and experts in a process of securitization, and shows that some actors are in privileged positions to perform a successful securitization, an argument suggested by Bigo (1994, 2002) to outline the importance of security experts and argue against a de-contextualized approach. This leads to the second peculiarity of the environmental sector: the presence of a multiplicity of actors.

The environmental sector is characterized by securitizing actors, supporting actors and veto actors. This suggests the political struggle and the complexity of the social construction of threats. This contrasts with Wæver's suggestion that "security is articulated only from a specific place, in an institutional voice, by elites" (Wæver 1995: 57). In the environmental case the multiplicity of actors is largely justified by the School with the relative novelty of the securitization of the environment. "The discourses, power struggles, and securitizing moves in the other sectors are reflected by and have sedimented over time in concrete types of organizations – notably states . . . nations (identity configurations), and the UN system" (Buzan, Wæver and de Wilde 1998: 71). However, this is not the case with the environment: "It is as yet undetermined what kinds of political structures environmental concerns will gener-ate" (Buzan, Wæver and de Wilde 1998: 71). This suggests that the logic of security described by the CS refers to a specific one that has developed with and contributed to the development of specific institutions and, with them, of the actors, practices and means that are supposed to provide security. The presence of several actors is not only a prerogative of the environmental sector, but it also characterizes other new sectors in which no institutional arrangements are in place.

These considerations lead to the final peculiarity, which can also be considered as the solution adopted by the CS to deal with the problem that, within the environmental sector, several appeals to security have not brought about the logic of security and the practices associated with it. The third peculiarity is that many securitizing moves result in politicization. This is problematic for the School, which argues that "transcending a security problem by politicizing it cannot happen *through* thematization in security terms, only *away* from such terms" (Wæver 1995: 56). For the School, once the enemy logic has been inscribed in a context, it is very difficult to return to an open debate. Nevertheless, the various politicizations of environmental issues that followed the appeal to security – those the CS dismissed as failed securitizations – seem to suggest that there is a tendency to politicize issues through their securitization.

Securitization theory, for the CS, is meant to be descriptive; however, the environmental sector suggests that the focus on the formal aspect of the speech act security prevents it from providing an adequate instrument for analysis. A decontextualized, self-referential approach to security underestimates two aspects: first, different contexts can have different logics and practices of security, and they can influence and challenge each other; this process is not one way only or from the military to the other sectors. A lot of work has been done on the implications of applying the (realist) logic of security to environmental issues, while little has been done on how the environmental logic (and which one) influences security practice. This transformation is likely to occur through securitizing moves – that is, through appeals to security in different contexts and for different needs – rather than away from them. Second, the logic of security itself can change, as new principles, actors, capabilities and threats gain relevance and different security discourses emerge (Huysmans 2002: 58).

Environmental security is about transformation and this is the reason why the environmental sector is so problematic. In order to provide an account of the discursive formation of security issues and of the process of transformation that securitization implies, it is necessary to move away from the emphasis on the self-referential character of the speech act security to move into the realm of communicative action (Williams 2003: 512) and social change. This is in line with the suggestion proposed by de Wilde that securitization "triggers two debates: one about the underlying risk assessment, one about the strategic answer to it" (de Wilde 2008: 596).

Two cases from the environmental security debate

This section describes two securitizations within the environmental sector, namely that of the hole in the ozone layer and that of environmental conflicts. It emphasizes the relevance of a more contextualized analysis and – contrary to the conclusion reached by the CS, which considers environmental securitization as failed securitization moves – suggests that these securitizations have challenged and somehow transformed some of the practices associated with securitization.

For each one the threats, the securitizing actors and the causal mechanisms invoked are explored to show how the social construction of a threat is a more complex matter that relies on different actors, shared understanding and symbolic references. The emphasis, however, will not be on showing that securitization does not rely on formal, linguistic aspects only, but on the implications of this for security provisions and the transformation of the practices of security. In this respect, the choice of the cases is relevant. In the case of the ozone, appeals to security have determined the first international agreement based on the precautionary principle. In the case of the environmental conflict, the debate has contributed to promoting preventive approaches. They both suggest the relevance of security practices based on prevention, risk management and resilience, which have recently gained relevance in the climate security discourse. They somehow contrast with the logic of emergency and exception which characterizes the speech act security as described by the CS. In this sense, the logic of security captured by the CS represents a very specific case. An empirically driven, sociological approach can outline when it occurs and why, avoiding subsuming all the construction of threats to this logic.

The securitization of the depletion of the stratospheric ozone

The depletion of the stratospheric ozone is one of the global environmental problems often mentioned as a threat to security (Prins and Stamp 1991; Mathews 1989; Barnett 2001). Waever Buzan and de Wilde mention it in *Security* and Clinton in the National Security Strategy considers it as a direct threat to the health of US citizens (1998: 13). This prompts several questions: how was it conceptualized as a threat, which actors were involved in the process, which measures resulted from that conceptualization?

The earth is protected from dangerous high energy radiations by a layer of ozone in the stratosphere. Ozone is a molecule constituted by three atoms of oxygen; it adsorbs the energy of the radiation by splitting into two compounds – a molecule of oxygen and a radical – and then recombining again. In the 1970s, concerns emerged that, in the high atmosphere, exhaust gases could destroy ozone by preventing its recombination. The initial debate was prompted by environmental concerns related to the construction of a fleet of supersonic airplanes by the US, the UK and France and heated by the dispute on landing permits and accusations – on both side of the Atlantic – of trying to export environmental standards. The issue was largely framed as an environmental problem which might have implications for the national economy, and was not considered as a security issue. This initial framing (Litfin 1994: 62) contributed to the selection of the actor who became the legitimate scientific authority in the field of atmospheric research. Since space expeditions were also suspected of interfering with the stratospheric ozone, NASA convinced Congress it was the best agency to study the stratospheric ozone's depletion and it soon became a major authority in the field, providing about 70 per cent of spending on stratospheric research (Litfin 1994: 63).

In 1974 Rowland and Molina, two chemists at the University of California Irvine, suggested that CFC gases, widely used in industry for their inertia in the lower atmosphere, can release chlorine into the stratosphere, thus acting as a catalyst in a set of reactions that have the final result of impeding the recombination of the ozone molecules. They forecasted the depletion of between 7 and 13 per cent of the ozone layer. At that time, CFCs had an impressive diffusion, both as aerosol propellants for deodorants and as coolers in refrigerators and air conditioners. They were also used for blowing polyurethane foams, sterilizing medical equipment and for a variety of other uses. They were considered wonderful chemicals, very useful in a variety of settings and with no side-effects.

Ozone depletion started to become one of the emerging global environmental problems. The problem was first discussed by UNEP (United Nations Environment Programme) in 1976. The following year a meeting of experts on the ozone layer was convened and UNEP and WMO (World Meteorological Organization) created a committee to periodically assess ozone depletion (Litfin 1994: 73–5).

While research on the atmospheric dynamics was still in its infancy, there was a relevant body of research on the impact of ultraviolet radiation on life. Ultraviolet radiations is dangerous for people and for various forms of life, causing cancer and blindness. It was the possibility of an impact on human health that heated the debate on CFCs and shaped states' actions in the international arena, even before consensus emerged on the relevance of the thinning of the ozone layer and it causes. The debate within UNEP and WMO was characterized by the creation of two committees. The choice of two committees (one discussing the economic dimension and the other the health issues) suggested how two contrasting constructions of threats were emerging: the first one considered the threat to human life posed by the production of CFC production, the second the threat to human health and in promoting international efforts. In this sense the issue these chemicals. Securitizing actors were NGOs and environmental groups, which tried to mobilize states to act collectively. Scientific research on the health impact of high energy radiation played a relevant role in transforming ozone depletion into a threat to human health and in promoting international efforts. In this sense the issue was securitized in the scientific agenda.

Despite the lack of consensus on the extent of the problem and its causes, in 1981 inter-governmental negotiations to phase out ozone-depleting substances started. Their result was the signature of the Vienna Convention for the Protection of the Ozone Layer in March 1985. The Vienna Convention was a framework convention; it did not set up specific targets or incentives but called for common research. For several states involved in the negotiation the main concern was the protection of their industries rather than that of the ozone layer, which appeared to be a distant, uncertain threat. In this respect this was a failed securitization that did not mobilize exceptional measures.

In May 1985, a British research team discovered what was immediately labeled as the "ozone hole." The term hole is actually a metaphor since it refers to a depletion of about 30 per cent of the ozone in the Antarctic region, something rather unexpected and not forecast by any scientific model. Despite the initial scepticism, the alarming results were verified by NASA. The authority of science was somehow challenged since it had not been able to predict such a dramatic development and the relevance of acting on the precautionary principle gained relevance. The broadcasting of NASA images of a computer model representing the polar zone characterized by 30 per cent depletion in a bright, alarming colour contributed to the visualization of the "hole" and the perception of a threat (see Litfin 1994: 96–9).

This led to a process of securitization of a new kind of threat. While in the negotiation of the Vienna Convention what was supposed to be protected, at least by a number of states, was the industry producing ozone depleting substances, the symbolic representation of a hole in humanity's stratospheric protecting blanket mobilized action. The ozone layer was considered as a fragile asset to be protected (Litfin 1994: 97). This created a sense of crisis and the transformation of the depletion of the stratospheric ozone into an existential threat to the whole of humankind. Several securitizing actors were involved, from states to civil society and the scientific community. Boycotting of spray cans and food packages followed. Nevertheless no measures outside the borders of normal politics were taken.

Even if scientists cautioned against basing international negotiations on the discovery of the ozone hole because there were other plausible causes for this occurrence, it is difficult to imagine that it did not play a role in the subsequent agreements. The representation of ozone depleting substances as a threat to human life contributed to the quick signature of the Montreal Protocol, in which 50 countries agreed on a gradual phase-down of CFC production and consumption and set a target of 50 per cent of their 1986 levels by 1998–99, with a ten-year grace period for developing nations. A few months later new scientific evidence confirmed that the Antarctic phenomenon was likely related with CFCs and consensus mounted for a total phase-out. The Protocol was amended and strengthened at Conferences of the Parties in London (1990), Copenhagen (1992), and Vienna (1995). The number of controlled substances was increased from the original eight to over eighty. By 1995 most of them were phased out by the industrialized countries while substantial steps were taken by several developing countries. As Kofi Annan stated: "Perhaps the single most successful international agreement to date has been the Montreal Protocol."

The case of the Montreal Protocol seems to represent a case in which the politicization of an issue occurred through its securitization and not outside it. The representation of the threat was the result of a social process in which different interests were shaped and transformed. The process was characterized by the interplay between the scientific and the political agenda and outlined the dialogical rather than formal nature of the process of constructing an issue as a security issue. Symbols and images played a determinant role but they had to be framed in a context characterized by the production of cumulative knowledge suggesting a causal link between CFCs and ozone depletion. Decisions however were taken without the legitimizing authority of scientific research and ozone negotiations are the first case of international agreements based on the precautionary principle. And yet the security measures and provisions were based on cooperation rather than confrontation and included economic sanctions and incentives.

Environmental conflict

In the aftermath of the Cold War, the number of environmental problems which were argued to have security implications was quite large, including problems like climate change, pollution and depletion of natural resources (Mathews 1989). In the 1980s the emergence of global environmental problems, like global warming and ozone depletion, determined one of the first attempts to broaden the international security agenda. The Brandt Report (1980) suggested that "few threats to peace and survival of the human community are greater than those posed by the prospects of cumulative and irreversible degradation of the biosphere on which human life depends" (quoted in Brauch 2003: 81) and the Brundtland report (1987) used the expression "environmental security." In the 1980s the tendency to frame environmental problem in security terms was encouraged by peace movements interested in mobilizing action on the issues that really matter and by the attempts to promote a non confrontational approach to the non military dimensions of security. However, it was with the end of the Cold War that the debate on environmental security gained relevance.

Even if the initial interest for environmental issues was quite broad, ranging from pollution to global warming it narrowed down in a few years. An example is provided by the negotiation of the United Nation Conference on Environment and Development; while security was an issue broadly discussed in the preparatory work, by the time of the Conference, held in Rio in 1992, it was no longer on the agenda and the term security was carefully avoided in the official documents. Several reasons lie behind these de-securitizing moves, such as the concerns of developing countries about green imperialism and interference in their security agendas, the diminishing concern for environmental security in the former communist countries where the slogan was used to mobilize political action against the Soviet Union. There is, however, an exception, which is the debate about environmentally induced conflict. In this perspective environmental degradation is a security issue since it may contribute to triggering and sustaining violent conflicts. The argument was rather persuasive in the post Cold War environment. It resonated with the more familiar understanding of national security and opened up a new role for the military.

The academic discussion was largely shaped by the work of Thomas Homer-Dixon, who chaired a series of research projects which aimed to study the relationships between environmental degradation and violent conflicts (Homer-Dixon 1991, 1994). Even if Homer-Dixon was cautious in suggesting a straightforward connection between environmental degradation and conflict, his argument was spread and amplified by Kaplan's article "The Coming Anarchy" (1994), which forecast massive population displacement and violent conflict, and baldly labeled the environment as the "national-security issue of the early twenty-first century" (Kaplan 1994: 58). The argument was quite influential within the Clinton administration. As Matthew reports the then US Undersecretary of State for Global Affairs, Timothy Wirth, sent a copy of Kaplan's article to every US embassy and the alarming picture it provided seemed to give an account of the crises the US had to face in Somalia and was struggling to address in Haiti (Matthew 2002: 111). This contributed to the securitization of environmental conflict within defence and political circles, at least in the US. This has promoted further research and political initiatives, in both the US and Europe.

This further research suggested that conflicts are likely to be sub-national and low-intensity (Homer-Dixon and Blitt 1998; Homer-Dixon 1999). These results have been reinforced by the projects undertaken by Spillmann and Bächler. (Bächler 1998, 1999; Bächler, Böge *et al.* 1996), whose results have been largely influential on the study "Environment & Security in an International Context," launched in 1995 by the NATO Committee on the Challenges of Modern Society (CCMS) and carried out by research teams in Germany and at the Pentagon (Lietzmann and Vest 2001). The project identified a number of "syndromes," which are sets of complex, abnormal and problematic relationships between environmental and other social, demographical and political factors that might help monitor and provide early warning systems for potential conflicts.

Research on environmental conflicts has determined an intense academic debate concerning the empirical validity of the claim that environmental degradation causes conflicts, the methodology of various research projects and the normative implications of their results. The argument that environmental scarcity induces conflicts has been challenged by empirical research showing how environmental degradation often provides the opportunity for cooperation (Hauge and Ellingsen, 2001) demonstrating that it is resource abundance rather than scarcity that determines conflicts (Berdal and Malone 2000). Nevertheless this debate is more relevant for the security provisions it has determined. During the Clinton administration, Homer-Dixon's research was used to promote a more proactive foreign policy (Harris 2001: 121–22) while the EU commission, largely influenced by the NATO project, has promoted actions to include environmental consideration into its development programmes and has used environmental concerns to develop and legitimize security capabilities and competencies at European level. Once again, the relevance of the appeals to security rested on the truth effect they produced, and on the groups securitization was accepted by, in this case the political and defence elites. However, even in this case the security practices adopted do not seem to reflect the antagonistic logic of war but suggest a process of transformation.

One of the aspects of this transformation is the growing interest in human security. As Duffield and Waddell explained: "[h]ow conflict has been understood in the post-Cold War period is central to understanding the concept of 'security' within human security" (Duffield and Waddell 2006: 43). Human security shifted the focus of security from the state to the individual and the UNDP 1994 annual report, which provides one of the definitions of the concept, identified environmental security, together with economic, food, health, personal, community and political security as a relevant component of human security (UNDP 1994: 22) and stressed the "all-encompassing" and "integrative" qualities of the concept (UNDP 1994: 24). A second aspect of the transformation is that the debate on environmental conflict has challenged a set of security practices, which focused on military threats and reactive measures and outlined how military responses and preparation are inadequate to deal with environmental issues. And yet it has contributed to shifting the attention to different kinds of vulnerability, suggesting that the instruments to provide stability require effort to promote both mitigation and adaptation to environmental impact and change and that the best results are associated with early intervention and preventive measures (Duffield and Waddell 2006: 10).

The debate on environmental conflict has been criticized on normative grounds (Dalby 1999; Barnett 2001) because it shifted the focus of research on developing countries and represented people in the Third World as "barbaric Southern Others" (Barnett 2001: 67); erased the responsibility of developed countries for causing environmental change; and tried to frame environmental problem in terms of national security. Nevertheless one has to consider that this debate and the policies it has determined have achieved two things: first, they have legitimized new actors and instruments to develop forms of security governance, which play down the role of the state and of traditional reactive responses; second they have promoted the development of human security and of a new paradigm of preventive measures which are often legitimized by the use of the concept. This does not mean denying the relationships of power or even domination that are behind the environmental conflict discourse or even the human security one. Duffield and Waddell have considered that discourse as an attempt to broaden the neo-liberal governmentality on a global scale. This, however, suggests that the security practices are different from those identified by the CS as are the means to resist or challenge them.

Conclusion

Securitization theory has the great merit of conceptualizing the power of discourses, and, more specifically, of the word security, in transforming a situation, but the CS's focus on self referential speech act and the emphasis on the de-contextualized "securityness" of security, while providing an elegant theory which captures the structural and social dimensions embedded in language and the problematic persistence of a set of practices which associate security with the identification of an enemy and the confrontational logic of war, does not allow us to explore the complexity of the social construction of security issues and explore the potential of a discursive approach. This tension is evident in the analysis of the environmental sector provided by the School itself in *Security: a New Framework for Analysis*. In that case, the empirically driven analysis which characterized the original approach of the School and which pays attention to the multiplicity of actors involved in the process of securitization, their different rules and capabilities, and emphasizes the importance of a scientific and a political agenda, contrasts with the self referential understanding of security suggested by considering securitization as a speech act.

The point however is not only about providing a more accurate picture of the social process of the social construction of a threat and of its implications. The problem is that the approach suggested by the CS tends to essentialize a specific logic of security and the practices associated with it. This is problematic because the possibility of exploring any transformation in the logic and practices of security is precluded, and this is particularly problematic within the environmental sector. Moreover, the CS, in questioning the opportunity of inscribing enemies in a context, suggests the desecuritization of as many issues as possible, leaving unchallenged problematic sets of practices associated with national security and opening up the space for governing through them, every time the word security is successfully evoked.

Suggesting that different security logics interact and coexist does not mean that they can be freely chosen or that other logics, like those based on risk management are without problems. One can always imagine air strikes against factories producing ozone depleting substances (Dabelko and Simmons 1997) or warning against the depoliticization determined by risk management (Aradau and van Munster 2007).

Adopting a sociological approach to the political construction of security issues can outline the transformation in the form and content of securitization and of the practices of security. However, rather than opposing a pragmatic (or sociological) to a philosophical approach to securitization (Balzacq 2009a), it is worth considering the latter as an analysis of a very specific construction of security and revaluing the original approach of the CS, based on an empirically driven approach. This is how I read *A Theory of Securitization* (Balzacq, this volume). By fixing the securityness of security and identifying it with a specific understanding of security, and of the political, the CS has limited its analysis to one logic of security only and it has essentialized it. The philosophical approach to securitization has thus explored the possible implications of that logic, taking for granted that it subsumes all the other logics. A greater attention to the various practices of security provides more nuanced results than those which are often associated with securitization and above all with some applications, generalization and simplifications of the insights the theory provides.

Notes

1 See Waever 1997; 'Concepts of Security', PhD thesis, University of Copenhagen. 355–357.
2 See Trombetta, M.J. *The Securitization of the Environment and the Transformation of Security, paper presented at the* SGIR, Sixth Pan-European Conference on International Relations, Turin 12–15 September 2007.

8 Health issues and securitization

The construction of HIV/AIDS as a US national security threat

Roxanna Sjöstedt

In April 2000, the Clinton administration formally declared AIDS to be a major threat to the national security of the United States. This was the first time a disease was viewed in terms of having security implications such as being able to "topple foreign governments, touch off ethnic wars and undo decades of work in building free-market democracies abroad" (The Washington Post, 2000). In addition, President Clinton designated the National Security Council to be the main agency for drafting policy solutions to fight the threat, the first time this agency would handle an epidemic. Finally, the requested funding from Congress for the AIDS issue was doubled compared to previous years and was now set at $254 million (Ibid.). Through these actions, AIDS was transferred from the sphere of health politics to the national security agenda, receiving great attention from the media and other actors. The implications of the disease were no longer the concern of individuals or healthcare organizations; now AIDS was viewed as something that could endanger the very foundation of the United States. In other words, Clinton performed a *securitizing move*, that is, he constructed HIV/AIDS as a threat to national security.

Linked to this move is the event that took place four months earlier on January 10, 2000. Vice-president Al Gore then chaired the first UN Security Council session of the new Millennium, a session that was seminal in the sense that it was the first time the Security Council spent an entire meeting discussing the implications of an epidemic on peace and security (United Nations Security Council, 2000b). These two events are directly connected and can be viewed as two entities of the same securitization, as the initiation of the UN meeting was the result of an intense American political campaign. In sum, the two seminal events during the first months of 2000 not only came to reshape the international understanding of the security implications of the AIDS epidemic; they also constructed the United States to be one of the most important international and transnational policy entrepreneurs in designing and diffusing the idea that HIV/AIDS threatens national and international security. This securitizing move was followed by other important occurrences, reconfirming that HIV/AIDS had been transformed from the health sector to the realms of both national and international security.[1]

This recount of events brings up one immediate question: What caused the Clinton administration to place HIV/AIDS at the national security agenda – rather than viewing it as a health issue – despite a fairly low domestic prevalence of

HIV, and the seemingly little risk of that the disease would in any way directly endanger the United States? Although HIV/AIDS had reached pandemic proportions in Africa, why was it seen as a threat to the US?

This chapter attempts to shed light on this question by tracing different political and societal processes leading up to the securitization of HIV/AIDS. It argues that the temporal dynamics regarding the actual framing act of the epidemic as well as the actors involved in this process served to promote certain hegemonic ideas which facilitated a general internalization of AIDS as national security. This opened a window of opportunity for the Clinton administration to instigate a securitizing move which reflected this general internalization.

The act and the actors: analyzing the securitization of HIV/AIDS

As discussed in the first part of this book, the pragmatic view of securitization moves away from many of the assumptions associated with the Copenhagen school, arguing that "it is not possible to examine and understand the complexity of the process of securitization simply by treating it as a speech act" (Balzacq, 2009a). Instead, the pragmatic act of security attempts to explain why an issue is securitized by analyzing the interaction between the power and identity of the *actors* – being both the securitizer and the audience – involved in the securitization process, the *contexts* within which these actors function, and the discursive construction of the *act* itself – i.e. the linguistic and argumentative techniques (Balzacq, Chapter 1 of this volume). Using these assumptions as a point of departure, focus in this chapter concerns the circumstances under which a *securitizing move* in relation to a specific issue becomes possible, i.e. why the US decision-makers initiated a securitization process concerning HIV/AIDS. A securitizing move is here defined "as the public framing of an issue as a national threat, accompanied by a strategy to act" (Sjöstedt, 2008:10). I thus argue that only speaking of an issue in terms of a threat does not meet the criteria of a securitizing move, instead policy action is also required.

The concept of securitization has previously been employed in relation to HIV/AIDS (see for instance Elbe, 2006). To link a disease to the concept of security, particularly national security, is, however, not uncontroversial, and two diametrically opposing discourses can be discerned (Sjöstedt, forthcoming). In short, some argue that the particularities of AIDS, and the severe effects it has on a state's society, economy, and military, qualifies it as a security matter (Heymann, 2003; e.g. Price-Smith, 2002; Singer, 2002; Coupland, 2007; Ostergard, 2007), while the opposite camp claims that however horrible consequences AIDS may have it should be viewed as a health issue (McInnes, 2006; Peterson, 2002; Whiteside, de Waal, and Gebre-Tensae, 2006). In this chapter the AIDS – security nexus becomes an empirical question and is not discussed further as focus is on tracing the processes and discourses constructing the idea of viewing an epidemic as security.

In order to explain how this idea was established we need to adopt a broad approach since "public policy is not one single actor's brainchild" (Kingdon, 2003: 71). To draw a comprehensive picture of how HIV/AIDS came to be constructed as a security issue, a process-tracing of three separate contexts – the international, the domestic political, and the domestic societal – is performed. It is important to cover all of these three dimensions, although the distinction between them often is blurred. The international level needs to be included since the decision making elite in charge of the securitization of an issue does not work in a vacuum but is affected by norms and ideas produced by international institutions (e.g. Finnemore and Sikkink, 1998; Checkel, 1999). These institutions may function as norm entrepreneurs that help to influence domestic actors and shape their ideas and interests concerning a particular issue area. The domestic societal context is important as the elite is both a member of and accountable to its domestic society, and what is being said there can be highly influential (cf. Hopf, 2002). The views of society can be described as "the national mood" or "the climate in the country", and implies

that a rather large number of people out in the country are thinking along certain common lines, that this national mood changes from one time to another in discernable ways, and that these changes in mood or climate have important impacts on policy agendas.

(Kingdon, 2003: 146)

The link between the national mood and the decision making elite are societal actors such as different organizations and pressure groups and the media. The domestic political context, finally, covers not only the immediate decision-making circles close to the president, but also other political actors who work as policy entrepreneurs, helping to promote ideas and create interest.

These three contexts are analyzed through a combination of a traditional within-case processes tracing and a structured form of discourse analysis. This method serves to trace the chain of events that led up to my analytical endpoint, the securitizing move. It also helps to capture the discursive environment in which the AIDS issue was constructed by different key actors and the particularities of their framing act. This analytical structure serves to build the argument that securitization was made possible because a number of different actors pushed the HIV/AIDS issue into the public eye and reinvented the conception of AIDS. The narrative begins in the 1980s when HIV/AIDS was first discovered, though the analytical focus concerns the time period starting at the early 1990s, leading up to President Clinton's securitizing move in 2000.

A number of texts have been analyzed – ranging from secondary sources, to newspaper articles, to political statements and debates.[2] Although discourse analysis by tradition favors an approach colored by induction and phenomenology, I argue that the transparency of the investigation, and thereby the persuasiveness of the argument, improves when allowing a certain degree of pre-set assumptions, or "extant theoretical categories" (Balzacq, 2009a: 14), to direct the inquiry and analysis (cf. Sjöstedt, 2007; 2008). Therefore, the discourse analysis performed here is structured in the sense that in each selected text I ask *how* HIV/AIDS is framed; *who* is doing the framing; and *what* linguistic tools are being employed in the framing process. The analysis is focused in the sense that the investigated texts are delimited to the AIDS issue (cf. George and Bennett, 2005).

From health to security: the case of HIV/AIDS in the United States

The 1980s: AIDS as a domestic health issue

There has been a significant change of discourse over the twenty years time frame that includes the AIDS epidemic in the American context. Over time, AIDS has been re-framed from being a homosexual problem, to a societal outcast problem, to a general American problem, to a problem of foreign policy. Along with these different frames, different policies have followed. However, an important distinction between the 1980s and the 1990s becomes apparent, as in the initial decade AIDS was not linked to security; instead morality and sexuality was in focus. The 1980s can be summarized as a lengthy policy struggle in which various lobby groups, health care organizations, politicians, religious groups, pharmaceutical companies, and – stuck in the midst of it all – the HIV infected, attempted to advance various interests. Since these interests have been very disparate depending on who has been pursuing them – ranging from economic gains, to political influence, to moral considerations, to staying alive – the overall process of handling HIV in the US has met vast obstacles, making the policy struggle "particularly contentious" (Siplon, 2002: 4). These different actors used various frames for the epidemic – frames which clearly had implications for the way it was handled.

Initially, AIDS was mainly viewed as a problem of the gay community. As homosexual relations were found to threaten traditional American family values, several voices of both the political and the societal discourse argued against spending federal funds on AIDS education as it could indirectly promote "homosexual activities". AIDS was associated with lack of morality; those affected by the disease constituted a sub-identity which stood in stark contrast to the more mainstream US identity. The acquired immunodeficiency syndrome was however not confined to homosexuals, already in 1983 health officials had identified four groups at particular risk: "the 4-H Club", or homosexuals, heroin users, Haitians, and hemophiliacs (Siplon, 2002: 6). The media then created a "two-tier structure of victims", consisting of "innocent victims", i.e. those who contracted the disease by accident, for instance hemophiliacs, children, spouses; and "guilty victims", i.e. homosexuals and drug-addicts (Ostergard, 2002: 338–39).

As the view on AIDS transformed over the 1980s, owing to a combination of "gay activism, scientific breakthroughs such as antiretroviral therapy, and the increasing heterosexual transmission of HIV / . . . / a more medicalized discussion [was created]" (Johnson, 2002: 86). AIDS was no longer solely associated with societal subgroups; instead anyone could be affected by it. This realization became embodied by Ryan White, a hemophiliac who had contracted the HIV virus through a blood transfusion at the age of 13 and died of an AIDS related illness just before turning 18. Although initially facing stigmatization – for instance, when his condition was made public he was barred from his local middle school – Ryan White eventually came to symbolize the "average" person with AIDS. Neither a drug addict nor a homosexual, White's fate appealed to America at large, and in commemoration of him a piece of legislation passed by US Congress in 1990 was named the *Ryan White CARE* (*Comprehensive AIDS Resources Emergency*) *Act*. This act has been reauthorized three times, 1996, 2000, and 2006 (Health Resources and Services Administration, 2008), and is central to the financing of AIDS treatment in the United States. The initial passing of the act also came to represent a seminal event for the first time ever Congress passed a health care act that supported funding to people with a specific disease. Although President George Herbert Bush was somewhat reluctant towards this narrow focus — fearing that lobbyists for other diseases would demand similar treatment — the act was passed "by overwhelming votes: 95:4 in the Senate and 408:14 in the House" (Siplon, 2002: 94). Although it has met a great deal of criticism and dispute — for instance, how the money should be spent and who should get to spend it — the Ryan White CARE Act still is an important milestone in the politicization of HIV/AIDS in the American decision-making context.

To sum up the first decade of AIDS in the US setting, it becomes evident that a number of important political actors were involved in the framing of the issue, and that the frames employed by these actors to a large extent determined subsequent policy actions. When AIDS was discursively transferred from being an immorality problem of stigmatized sub-identities to a general American health problem, it was also brought onto the broader political agenda. Still, it was not viewed as anything but a health problem, and was far from being seen as a security threat. This discourse would, however, eventually change when focus moved from the domestic to the international.

The 1990s: AIDS as an international security issue

From the mid-1990s and onwards, the AIDS epidemic "altered demonstrably / . . . / now [being] disproportionably lodged among African Americans" (UNAIDS, 2004). The demographic change of AIDS led to a weakened impact on the American discourse. In all, minorities living with AIDS did not, particularly compared to the often well-educated, well-organized and outspoken gay community, have the same power and resources to voice its grievances. In addition, the Ryan White CARE Act, and the new efficient therapies that caused a sharp decrease in the AIDS mortality rate in 1997 (US Department of Health and Human Services, 2000), resulted in that AIDS in the United States was far from being a central issue in the domestic discourse. Also, since the mid-1990s people living with HIV/AIDS have constituted less than half percent of the population (HIV/AIDS Policy Fact Sheet, The Henry J. Kaiser Family Foundation, 2007), indicating that the epidemic is not an imminent domestic threat.

Instead, a more notable milestone in the history of HIV/AIDS in the United States was the linking of the epidemic to foreign affairs. Although the first case of AIDS on the African continent was reported already in late 1982 (Sepkowitz, 2006), followed by a rapid rate of infection, it was not until mid-1990s that the implications of AIDS in Africa began to be recognized in the US political and societal discourse. The analysis that follows traces the actors who were dominant in these discourses, as well as the construction and evolvement of the actual framing act. Several differences between the 1980s and 1990s are revealed, concerning both actors and act, clearly demonstrating how certain hegemonic ideas formed within the dominant discourses, eventually making the securitization of AIDS possible.

The major discursive actors are spread into three rough clusters or *contexts*; the international, the domestic societal, and the domestic political. When tracing the framing processes of HIV/AIDS it is thus essential to examine all three as they all contribute to the dynamics of the American discourse.

The international context

Beginning with the international setting, there are in particular three international actors who from the early 1990s were central in the response against AIDS. Still, they all faced organizational shortcomings that delimited their powers and abilities to both act and influence.

The World Health Organization (WHO) initiated its Global Programme on AIDS in 1987, which attempted to raise awareness of the epidemic, support affected countries, and instigate research. This program viewed AIDS largely as a health issue and did not connect it to matters of security. Rather quickly the Global Program came to face serious obstacles concerning its ability to influence "the political will in donor and affected countries" (Merson, 2006: 2415). Also, the program suffered greatly from internal clashes on how to handle the AIDS epidemic. Jonathan Mann, the program's first director, made several attempts to restructure the organization in order to increase its efficiency. However, Mann's unorthodox style, operating "on passion, commitment, an almost manic energy / . . . / disregarding hierarchy" was not appreciated by all, and after irreconcilable differences with the Director General, Hiroshi Nakajima, Mann was forced to resign in 1990 (Fee and Parry, 2008: 65). According to Mann, the leadership of WHO was to blame for obstructing and paralyzing the global fight against AIDS (Ibid.). Also, the effectiveness of the organization "was comprised by rivalries with other United Nations (UN) organizations" (Merson, 2006: 2415), further undermining its ability to act against the AIDS epidemic.

In 1996, the WHO program was replaced by UNAIDS, i.e. the Joint United Nations Programme on HIV/AIDS, which came to be headed by AIDS activist and researcher Peter Piot until 2008 (UNAIDS, 2008). Although co-sponsored by several UN agencies and with a "mandate to lead an expanded, better-coordinated multisectoral global response", UNAIDS initially had limited success, and was not able to resolve conflicts between various UN partners or engaging wealthy nations in the struggle to fight the AIDS epidemic in the developing world (Merson, 2006: 2415). These organizational difficulties occurred simultaneously with the dramatic global expansion of AIDS, causing an unfortunate delay in the international response towards the demands of handling the epidemic. Also, UNAIDS failed on the subject of HIV prevention, and Piot admits that he "should have pushed prevention efforts sooner", although "in the early days thousands of deaths a day where so overwhelming and needed immediate action that treatment had to take precedence" (Das and Samarasekera, 2008: 2101). Nevertheless, over time, UNAIDS became a successful policy entrepreneur, much owing to the "rock star persona" of Piot (Ibid.: 2100). Piot has relentlessly argued that "[t]he case for AIDS exceptionalism – prioritizing HIV/AIDS over other health problems" (Ibid), something which eventually helped to push the AIDS issue onto the political agendas.[3]

The effects of Piot's campaigning on the framing act of AIDS become evident when comparing two resolutions from the United Nations Economic and Social Council. In the 1994 resolution, which establishes the "joint and co-sponsored United Nations programme on HIV/AIDS" – i.e. UNAIDS – the disease is framed as a "global concern" and the objective is among other things to "[a]dvocate greater political commitment in responding to the epidemic" (United Nations Economic and Social Council, 1994). Two years later, the same council declares in a second resolution that "HIV/AIDS has devastating social, economic and other related impacts . . ." and it also

Invites the Secretary-General to play an active advocacy role in regard to the *serious threat* posed by the spread of human immunodeficiency virus/acquired immunodeficiency syndrome (HIV/AIDS) / . . . / [and] urges the United Nations Secretariat to be fully and effectively involved in the *fight* against HIV/AIDS.

(United Nations Economic and Social Council, 1996; author's emphasis)

The change of language here is obvious. From an emphasis on "advocacy" and "political commitment", the Council in the subsequent document uses expressions like "threat" and "fight", a terminology inevitably linked to the language of security. It can thus be assumed that there was a gradual change of understanding of the international implications of HIV/AIDS.

Finally, the World Bank, under director James Wolfensohn, is another central international actor in the fight against AIDS, but whose initial accomplishments were restricted. Wolfensohn became president of the World Bank on 1 July 1995 after a nomination by President Clinton. Although the Bank since the turn of the Millennium has been recognized as one of the most important actors in relation to fighting HIV/AIDS, Wolfensohn nevertheless admits that its involvement began too late. He has also declared that the wishes he could have influenced political elites and organizations to "act faster in the early days" (Wolfensohn, 2005), and says that

I think that we recognized early the problem of AIDS but that we could not get governments in many cases to respond quickly. My judgment is that we could have done better in trying to make more of a noise.

(Australian Broadcasting Cooperation, 2005)

The problem with the international organizations working on the AIDS issue during the 1990s was in other words not lack of commitment and most organizations tried to make a difference, particularly by pushing the international aspect of the epidemic and transferring it from the individual/local sphere to international politics. For instance, the XI International Conference on AIDS in Vancouver, July

7–12, 1996, had the theme "One World, One Hope", and strived towards a global move against the disease. However, many activists in 1996 argued that this was far from being the case, and that things like the pharmaceutical companies' excessive pricing and the lack of any coordinated international political action, prevented all attempts of global action. Jonathan Mann, then professor of epidemiology and international health at Harvard University, stressed that

[t]oday, there is NOT "one world" against AIDS, and this reality of separatism and isolation threatens progress against AIDS and is the central reason why real leadership and coherent global action against AIDS has become virtually impossible.

(ACTUP, 1996)

To sum up the discussion on the international level, there were incremental changes regarding the way HIV/AIDS was framed as well as the involvement of the actors. Still, the direct effects on the US decision-makers are not self evident, and the overall impact of the international setting will be further discussed in the final section.

The domestic societal context

Turning to the next context of analysis, the domestic setting, focus is on how HIV/AIDS was framed by the US national media, and how the American society viewed the epidemic in the decade prior to Clinton's securitizing move. When scrutinizing the societal discourse for the period 1991–1999 it can be concluded that at least during the first half of the investigation period AIDS was linked to domestic issues and was far from being viewed as any form of security issue. It was nonetheless threatening in the sense that it appeared to be more dangerous than any other disease; the risk of being infected was highly exaggerated, and those infected were viewed as dangerous. Despite that AIDS had been a known illness in the United States since the beginning of the 1980s, a number of misconceptions nevertheless existed a decade after, resulting in a continued stigmatization of people living with AIDS. Surveys conducted in 1991, 1997, and 1999 indicated that 34 percent in 1991 and 20 percent of the respondents the following years were "afraid" of people with AIDS. It was noted that 27 percent; 20 percent; and 14 percent were "angry". As these figures indicate, the negative views did decrease over time, as did opinions of punitive or coercive nature such as the belief that the AIDS infected should be separated from the rest of the population (Herek, Capitanio, and Widaman, 2002).

An analysis of one of the central societal *actors*, the domestic media, demonstrates that these views were apparent at several aspects of society, and that the framing *act* constructing AIDS linked it to various conceptions of threat. The media discourse, however, reveals a greater temporal dynamic regarding what AIDS was being associated to than what was indicated by the aforementioned population surveys. In the first years of investigation, i.e. the early 1990s, references to AIDS in the news media mainly occurred in stories on two other topics, gays in the military and immigration. Through a somewhat fuzzy chain of association, these two groups were, at least indirectly, framed as threats to the United States.

The first group of articles concerned President Clinton's promise to lift a ban against homosexuals serving in the US military. This became a highly debated issue which was viewed as a question of "morale and discipline / . . . / and even the spread of AIDS" (The New York Times, 1993). A related issue appeared in 1995 concerning a provision which aimed at discharging 1,214 HIV-positive soldiers from the US military (Pittsburgh Post-Gazette/The Associated Press, 1995). This proposal was rejected and re-proposed by different congressional committees, but was eventually passed by Congress in 1996 as part of a larger defense legislation which was seen as critical to the national security of the United States. President Clinton declared the provision to be "unconstitutional, completely abhorrent and offensive" (The New York Times, 1996), and it was eventually repealed. The framing of these two related stories differs somewhat. In relation to homosexuals in the military opposing voices were often quoted, interviewed, or published in the news media. The HIV infected soldiers were more framed as victims, receiving less opposition, and appeared to be seen less as a threat to the security of the United States.

In 1993, one third of the media texts on HIV/AIDS concerned the internment of 270 Haitian political refugees at Guantanamo.[4] As almost the entire asylum seeking group was HIV positive, it was prohibited from entering the United States, while it at the same time could not be sent back to the political turmoil at Haiti. This issue received great media attention and the immigration policy barring foreigners with communicable diseases caused extensive political and societal debate (e.g. USA Today, 1993). Some argued that "more HIV-infected people admitted to the country are not a possible threat of more fatal AIDS infections – they are a certain threat" (Chicago Sun-Times, 1993), while representatives from the medical community stressed that there was a "lack of a public health threat" (Osborn in Time, 1993b). Civil rights leader, Jesse Jackson, began a fast in support of the refugees at Guantanamo (Time, 1993b), a move also taken by a number of college students at Yale and Harvard (The Boston Herald, 1993). Eventually, in June 1993, a federal judge ordered that the Haitians to be immediately allowed entry to the US, arguing that their detainment was "outrageous, callous, and reprehensible" as they were "neither criminals nor national security risks" (Times-Picayune/Associated Press, 1993). This ended the Haitians 20-month detention at the US military camp. With regard to the general immigration ban, both the Senate and the House nevertheless voted to uphold it, although a particular "INS waiver for athletes with HIV or AIDS" was given to participants of the 1994 Gay Games (The Washington Post, 1994).

In sum, the societal discourse in the early 1990s mainly viewed HIV/AIDS in an American context, concerning the effects of AIDS on the military's ability to defend the homeland, or whether immigrants posed a threat to the American nation.

However, this fairly one-dimensioned focus started, to change by mid-1990s. A search for texts on HIV and Africa generated for instance 66 documents in 1993; 122 in 1996; 216 in 1998; and 270 in 1999.[5] These figures indicate that the media space given to cover the situation on the African continent continuously increased during the second half of the 1990s (Milwaukee Journal Sentinel/New York Times/Associated Press, 1996; Pittsburgh Post-Gazette/Reuters News Service, 1997). Along with the increased attention came an increased US involvement abroad, although the latter was not always applauded. In 1997 several different media sources told the story about, and strongly criticized, an American AIDS research project that conducted experiments in developing countries. The effects of the drug AZT was assessed by giving it to some HIV infected pregnant women while others in a control group received placebo. The critique from the media was harsh:

The United States has a moral obligation to refrain from conducting experiments on human subjects abroad that it would not allow here / . . . / one cannot discount the humanity of another without diminishing one's own.

(The Houston Chronicle, 1997; The Denver Post/ The New York Times, 1997)

These experiments were discussed by a number of other societal actors as well and various organizations and scientists raise the issue of ethics. The executive editor of New England Journal of Medicine called the research project a "retreat from ethical principles" (The Denver Post/The New York Times, 1997), comparing it to the infamous Tuskegee experiments.[6]

By the end of the 1990s different news media also began to report on AIDS as a "epidemic of color", both with regard to the situation in sub-Saharan Africa, and in the United States (The Houston Chronicle/The New York Times, 1998; The Columbus Dispatch, 1998), highlighting the demographic changes of the epidemic. Now the discourse definitely began moving away from framing AIDS in terms of a health problem. Reports from southern Africa viewed AIDS as a threat to social order (Buffalo News/Los Angeles Times, 1998), highlighting the number of deaths caused by AIDS and other diseases. The construction act of AIDS changed vocabulary; now there was a much greater sense of alarm, employing phrases like "the war on disease" (The Washington Post, 1999b). Viewing AIDS and other diseases as something with greater implications than only human health has led to an increased linkage to other societal factors. This implied that the very idea of security incorporated also non-military issues:

Think of what the world would be like if we could shift a fraction of the money, energy, ingenuity and talent that went to the Cold War to a campaign to eradicate the six most deadly infectious diseases. This may well be the key to world stability in the 21st century.

(The Washington Post, 1999b)

The AIDS situation was now labeled a "State of Emergency" and focus was on the global aspect of AIDS and its devastating effects on communities in the third world. Collective work against AIDS was now stressed and "we must get beyond seeing this as a moral issue" (The Houston Chronicle, 1999).

Analyzing societal actors other than the media, it becomes apparent that during the initial years of investigation AIDS abroad, or the implications of the epidemic in Africa on the international community, was hardly mentioned. "What is the global health community doing to help prevent HIV and AIDS in Africa?" asked the deputy director of the International Health Program Office of the Centers for Disease Control and Prevention (The Atlanta Journal and Constitution, 1993). Judging by the amount of attention given to the international AIDS issue, perhaps not enough – although even less was done outside the health policy field of expertise. When asked to assess the US government's past record concerning different aspects of AIDS – for instance research, treatment, and prevention – a board of AIDS activists gave a very low score with regard to the US' involvement in the "world arena" (San Antonio Express-News, 1998). By mid-1990s this, however, began to change. In 1995, USAID organized a three-day conference on fighting the global spread of the disease, and it was stressed that

The United States will continue to exercise leadership – in word and deed on the issue of HIV/AIDS. The United States will not run away from its responsibilities on this issue. The stakes are too high.

(Deutsche Presse-Agentur, 1995)

By late 1990s also other important societal actors started to take active measures against AIDS. In 1998 Bill Gates, for instance, donated $100 million dollars to improve access to vaccines among third world children, followed by $25 million in spring 1999 for the development of an AIDS vaccine (The Boston Globe, 1999a). That was the largest charitable AIDS gift to date (USA Today, 1999b) and was the initiation of Gates' continued work to fight AIDS through the Bill and Melinda Gates Foundation. Also domestic AIDS activists became involved in the international sphere of the epidemic. The organization AIDS Action, which by tradition had mostly been concerned with issues at home, visited the Capitol Hill in April 1999 "to lobby for funds to fight the global epidemic" (USA Today, 1999a).

The African American community also started to get involved. This societal group had received much criticism from members within its own camp for being slow to respond to the domestic AIDS issue. David Satcher, the surgeon general appointed by President Clinton, claimed that civil rights groups and black preachers had not acted against AIDS, despite the changing domestic demographics of those infected with HIV:

I grew up in the black church. I think the church had problems with the lifestyle of homosexuality. A real problem has been getting ministers that are even willing to talk about it in their pulpits.

(The Houston Chronicle/The New York Times, 1998)

Different actions indicate, however, an increased involvement by the black community to work against AIDS in the United States. This led to a call for international involvement, as pointed out by Julian Bond, chairman of the board of the NAACP:

African-Americans, too, must no longer sit idly by as African die by the millions / . . . / African-American leadership, finally waking up to AIDS at home, must rally its political might to open the nation's eyes – and pocketbooks – to this growing tragedy.

(The Boston Globe, 1999d)

The changing demography of AIDS also moved focus away from morality as the epidemic in Africa had nothing to do with any "life style issues" of the victims. Church representatives now had a new platform for approaching AIDS, as stated by Rev. Eugene Rivers III, co-chairman of the National Ten-Point Coalition, a church based anti-crime network.

Promiscuity and rape now function as weapons of mass destruction. We need a post-civil rights freedom movement to free the women of the world from rape and sexual exploitation.

(The Boston Globe, 1999c)

To sum up the investigation of the US societal discourse the analysis indicates fairly great changes over time – both with regard to the way HIV/AIDS was framed, and the actors involved in the issue. From mainly linking AIDS to homosexuality, AIDS was by the mid-1990s seen as a human security issue. These framing changes, and especially the increased involvement by a number of actors, certainly formed a national mood which certainly facilitated the eventual securitization of AIDS.

The domestic political context

Tracing the statements and actions of the American political elite, a discursive change over time regarding the framing of HIV/AIDS and the parties involved – i.e. act and actors – can be discerned. At the beginning of the 1990s, the AIDS issue was mainly the concern of the Department of Health as well as various organizations devoted to public health. AIDS as a domestic issue was less controversial than it had been in the previous decade, although the policy struggle between various interest groups indeed continued. AIDS as an international issue was not viewed as any major concern to the United States, and "[u]ntil the late 1990s the African epidemic received little direct US attention outside of health-based organizations such as the National Institutes of Health (NIH) and development organizations such as US Agency of International Development (USAID)" (Gow 2002: 66).

Some members of US Congress were, however, continuously engaged in the fight against AIDS, both home and abroad. For instance, US Congressman, Ron Dellums was one key figure in the political sphere. In 1993, with regard to the ban against gays in the US military, Dellums, then chair of the House Armed Services Committee, spoke out against the ban, saying that "I think we ought to move beyond our ignorance, beyond our fears, beyond our prejudices, beyond our discrimination" (The Virginian-Pilot/The Ledger-Star, 1993). Also regarding the aforementioned military HIV discharge provision, Dellums was a strong opponent.

As regards AIDS in Africa, Dellums, who later became the head of an AIDS awareness advocacy group, became an important force in creating recognition of the problem among the African-American community. At the end of the 1990s Dellums devoted his time to inform church leaders and other key figures in the black community.

People have been slow to recognize the changing face of AIDS, and therefore the changing politics of AIDS / . . . / What this issue has lacked is people prepared to talk loud enough to take it to the political level.

(The Boston Globe, 1999d)

Also Congressman Jesse Jackson Jr. supported the fight against AIDS both through his Congressional voting record and verbally. In a statement on the floor of the House Jackson stressed the gravity of the AIDS epidemic in Africa and strongly criticized the United States for being "more responsive to the narrow commercial interests of the pharmaceutical industry than to the public health and humanitarian interest", with regard to the issue of allowing cheap manufacturing of drugs in developing nations (Jackson, 1999a). Jackson also introduced a Hope for Africa Act, an economic plan that strived among other things toward sustainable economic development, food security, and "strengthening health care, particularly for AIDS prevention and treatment" (Jackson, 1999b).

US Senator Russ Feingold was another member of the political elite who worked actively in lifting the AIDS issue up on the agenda. Being the ranking Democrat on the Senate Foreign Relations Committee's Subcommittee on African Affairs, Feingold consistently attempted to raise the issue in Congress, arguing that "the Senate should support legislation that works with the countries of Sub-Saharan Africa to diversify and strengthen African economies and fight the real enemies of economic progress on the continent: the overwhelming debt burden and the devastating AIDS epidemic" (Feingold, 1999a). In accordance with this, Feingold introduced the HOPE for Africa Act, a legislation that similar to Jackson's legislation attempted to promote US–African trade relations and which would take "crucial steps to support the fight against the crushing HIV/AIDS epidemic" (Feingold, 1999b). After visiting a number of countries in Africa together with Richard Holbrooke in December 1999, Feingold declared that he "found the specter of AIDS in Africa to be terrifying", concluding that

not only from the point of view of the people there and international dangers of AIDS we need to be more aggressive in helping those countries attack this problem Feingold urges more attention on AIDS.

(Milwaukee Journal Sentinel, 1999a)

Another actor in the political sphere that is a key figure in shaping the discursive act on HIV/AIDS is Sandra Thurman, often nick-named 'the AIDS czar', who was appointed director of the White House Office of National AIDS policy by President Clinton in 1997. Having been an AIDS activist for 15 years, Thurman became an important political figure in terms of "giving AIDS a strong voice at the White House" (The Atlanta Journal and Constitution, 1997). In November 1997, Thurman went on her first fact finding mission to Africa and declared after the trip that

> I think we knew that the epidemic was moving faster than we could capture, but I had no idea that the numbers would be as large as they are in fact.
>
> (The Atlanta Journal and Constitution, 1997)

During Easter 1999, US Congress went on another fact-finding delegation to sub-Saharan Africa. Also this trip was led by Sandra Thurman, and included several Congressmen and their staff. The report that summarized the findings of the delegation came to form "the basis of much of the government's response" (Siplon, 2002: 126) with regard to how to handle the international HIV/AIDS issue. Thurman was persistent in urging on the fight against the epidemic and to support the struggle to African countries and stressed that "we need to be united in our efforts to stop the disease here and throughout the world" (The Denver Post, 1999).

Perhaps the most central figure at the political setting besides President Bill Clinton and Vice-President Al Gore when it comes to the construction act of HIV/AIDS is the Clinton administration's ambassador to the UN, Richard Holbrooke. In December 1999, Holbrooke undertook a 10-nation trip to Africa with Senator Russ Feingold. The three main aims of the journey was to review a potentially explosive situation in the Democratic Republic of the Congo; to discuss UN's role in Africa; and to strengthen aspects of President Clinton's and Secretary of State Albright's agenda for Africa (Milwaukee Journal Sentinel, 1999b). Having been a US diplomat for over thirty years, Holbrooke had been involved in several different issue areas in several different parts of the world – most notably the restoration of peace in Bosnia. He had, however, never been to southern Africa, and never worked on the AIDS issue, thus having "much in common with other Americans who have taken decades to recognize the global AIDS threat" (USA Today, 2002). While traveling around Africa the implications of the epidemic became painfully clear, and after meeting a number of AIDS orphans in Lusaka "Holbrooke was galvanized to act" (Barnett and Prins, 2006: 360). According to Feingold, "what Richard Holbrooke did on that trip has to be one of the seminal events that led to an increased focus on AIDS in Africa" (USA Today, 2002). Deciding that the situation demanded a quick response from the world community, Holbrooke, Feingold says,

> started doing what Dick Holbrooke does. I watched him call up the Secretary General [Kofi Annan] and tell him that we had to have a Security Council meeting on AIDS. The Secretary General said, "We cannot do that. AIDS isn't a security issue".
>
> (USA Today, 2002; also Prins, 2004)

Also some of the permanent members of the UN Security Council were skeptical "France and China relented, and eventually Russia agreed, but only because everyone else wanted it; not on positive grounds" (Prins, 2004: 941). The Secretary General also rather quickly changed his mind, and as mentioned in the introduction of this chapter, the Security Council meeting took place one month after this phone conversation. Holbrooke explained his reasons for pushing for this meeting taking place:

> Some people wonder, why hold a Security Council meeting on a health issue? There has never been a Security Council meeting on a health issue. The reason is simple. In Africa, in southern Africa, in countries like Namibia and South Africa, Zimbabwe and other countries, AIDS is far more than a health issue. It is jeopardizing the advances that these countries have made.
>
> (The New York Times, 1999)

Finally, turning to the two central actors in this securitization process, President Bill Clinton and Vice-President Al Gore, we find that already in his inaugural speech in January 1993, Clinton demonstrated an awareness of the implications of HIV/AIDS by declaring that

> we must meet challenges abroad as well as at home. There is no longer division between what is foreign and what is domestic – the world economy, the world environment, the world AIDS crisis, the world arms race – they affect us all
>
> (Clinton, 1993)

Clinton continued to place HIV/AIDS on the agenda by pursuing the removal of the aforementioned controversial policies concerning the ban on AIDS-infected immigrants and the ban on gays in the military. Although Clinton's interest in these two issues clearly indicates his belief in the importance of AIDS, it actually can be viewed as a form of desecuritization of the issue – at least that is what the political opposition argued when voting for the maintaining the bans. That was probably not the case, but rather being an attempt to alter two highly discriminatory policies that had been criticized by the international community as well as domestically. However, in the immigration case, Clinton did not waive the HIV ban on humanitarian grounds until a federal judge ordered the immediate release of the refugees (Pittsburgh Post-Gazette/Miami Herald, 1993).

By mid-1990s, the attention to the AIDS issue by the Clinton administration intensified. At the USAID's conference on AIDS in 1995 a representative from the State Department claimed that it was "a recognition on the part of the US government that such medical problems are a major national security concern in the post-Cold War world" (Deutsche Presse-Agentur, 1995). A government-supported council committee, CISET, also concluded in a study that diseases such as AIDS constitute a global threat (Heymann, 2003: 197), and in December the first-ever White House Conference on HIV and AIDS took place (US Department of Health and Human Services, 2000).

In February 1996, the Clinton administration released its national security strategy, appropriately called "A National Security Strategy of Engagement and

Enlargement" as it included several issues beyond traditional military arms races and deterrence strategies. Instead, US national security also incorporated

assisting developing nations who are fighting overpopulation, AIDS, drug smuggling and environmental degradation [to] ensure that future generations of Americans will not have to contend with the consequences of neglecting these threats to our security.

(The White House, 1996)

These ideas were further developed during 1996. In a speech on June 12, Vice President Al Gore declared that "emerging infections threaten national and global security", and went on saying that

we cannot sit by and wait for the next AIDS or Ebola virus to come knocking at our door. We can never rest on our laurels or let down our guard. There will be no victory parades, but there must be unyielding vigilance.

(Gore, 1996)

The same day as Gore's speech the White House released the information that President Clinton had issued *Presidential Decision Directive NSTC-7* a decree designed to establish "national policy and implementing actions to address the threat of emerging infectious diseases" (Clinton, 1996). Clinton declared that "I have determined that the national and international system of infectious disease surveillance, prevention, and response is inadequate to protect the health of United States citizens", and called for a number of actions which "[w]here relevant / . . . / will be coordinated with Presidential Decision Directive (PDD)39/United States Policy on Counterterrorism". Particularly interesting about this document is that Clinton views disease as a possible threat, and calls on a number of different governmental departments and agencies to implement a number of actions against infectious diseases, among them the National Security Council (NSC) and the Department of Defense (DoD). The mission of the Department of Defense was expanded, establishing a special disease surveillance system, the DoD-GEIS. Among other things this system includes "support of global surveillance / . . . / and response to emerging infectious disease threats", as they "are a threat to US military personnel and families" and "present a risk to US national security" (GEIS, 2009).

In 1997, Clinton appointed, as mentioned earlier, a special AIDS policy advisor, Sandra Thurman, and later announced a $150 million federal initiative for AIDS research. In 1998, on World AIDS day, the Clinton administration further increased its work against AIDS by pledging a $10 million assistance package to help AIDS orphans and $200 million to AIDS vaccine research. A US Congress fact-finding delegation to sub-Saharan Africa was also announced (Buffalo News/ Associated Press, 1998). On July 19, 1999, Al Gore revealed the administration's new health plan, the Leadership in Fighting and Epidemic (LIFE) Initiative. The United States would spend $200 million on AIDS prevention and treatment the following year, two thirds of which would be earmarked for sub-Saharan Africa

(Gow, 2002). At the same time, however, the administration was criticized by AIDS activists for running the errands of the large pharmaceutical companies and not promoting the cheap manufacturing of AIDS drugs (ACTUP, 1999; The Washington Post, 1999a). Heavy protesting by activists clearly shook the administration and in December Clinton announced that American trade rules would be relaxed in order to increase access to HIV drugs.

When HIV and AIDS epidemics are involved / . . . / the United States will henceforward implement its health care policies and trade policies in a manner that ensures people in the poorest countries won't have to go without medicine they so desperately need.

(American Health Line, 1999)

On World AIDS Day, December 1, Hilary Rodham Clinton appeared at the United Nations imploring leaders to "step up the war against AIDS", and called it a "plague of biblical proportions" (Daily News, 1999). The reports from Holbrooke's and Feingold's ten-day trip to Africa in December also made great impact on the President and Vice-president, and Gore was to chair the debate at the Security Council meeting on January 10, 2000, the first time a US vice-president sat the chair for a council debate as well as spoke at the Council.

These actions aside, the Clinton administration was criticized by activists for not "dedicating enough attention to Africa generally and AIDS in particular" (CNN, 2000). About the UN meeting Peter Piot said:

the good news is that the US government is mobilizing. The bad news is that it took so long. This is not a catastrophe that came out of the blue. It has been clearly coming for at least 10 years.

(The Washington Post, 2000)

Gore agreed to this: "The (AIDS) activists are right that this was ignored for far too long" he said (King *et al.*, 2000).

In sum, the process-tracing of the US political context indicates that a number of different political actors over time became involved in the HIV/AIDS issue and helped to bring it into the political spotlight. The framing act also changed, becoming increasingly linked to international issues and security.

Concluding discussion

The in-depth process-tracing of the events taking place during the 1990s and the reconstruction of the major discourses with regard to HIV/AIDS demonstrate a shift over time with regard to both the framing of the epidemic and the actors involved in this framing process. In all three contexts — the international, the domestic societal, and the domestic political — AIDS increasingly became viewed as an international problem and a security issue.

At the international context it is evident that in particular three important actors attempted to transform the HIV/AIDS issue from its initial public health oriented focus to a major international concern. Interestingly, the relevance of the actor becomes even more evident when taken down to the individual level. All three of these major international organizations, WHO, UNAIDS, and the World Bank were headed by individuals – Mann, Piot, and Wolfensohn – who recognized the scope and the implications of the epidemic, and who strived to diffuse the idea that AIDS was exceptional and thereby needing an exceptional and unified global response. In line with the literature on the diffusion of international norms it can be argued that these central actors – meaning both the organizations per se, and these three individuals in particular – form a necessary foundation to the securitization process. However, the empirical record, as discussed earlier, indicates that the direct discursive powers of these actors were limited – several of the international actors admitted in retrospect that they were unable to convey the ominous global consequences of the epidemic to the political decision-makers of states.

Nevertheless, although it is difficult to establish any direct ideational causal chain between the international level and the US decision-making elite (cf., Finnemore and Sikkink, 1998), it can be argued that the gradual discursive change by the international community played some part in the creation of a new security discourse that began to form in the mid-1990s.

Looking at the societal context a clear temporal change of discourse is also found. Various societal actors were involved in the reconstruction of the AIDS issue during the 1990s. The US media perhaps being the most powerful actor when it comes to determining what was being said and how the stories were told, but also other actors such as AIDS activist groups and other societal organizations played important roles in the framing of the epidemic. All these actors began simultaneously from mid-1990s to pursue a different framing act compared to previous years, and the main difference concerned the international connotation. Although the situation in Africa had been extremely serious since the beginning of the decade, it took until 1996 before it was recognized by a greater societal collective. After that, the media focus shifted almost exclusively towards the pandemic on the African continent, and the linkage of AIDS to US national security became indirect, as opposed to the direct threat posed by the Haitian refugees in 1993. Indirect or not, the African pandemic would be viewed as a much greater danger to the security of the United States than any other situation concerning AIDS.

These changes in the societal setting clearly constituted a new "national mood" (Kingdon, 2003) concerning the outlook on AIDS, as well as facilitated the construction of the AIDS-security nexus proposed by the decision-making elite. Also here it is naturally difficult to establish the direction of any causal chain – was it the societal context that influenced the political or vice-versa? – since they time-wise occurred concurrently. Nevertheless, as with the international setting, it can be claimed that the societal discourse constituted one important part in a broader process.

The political context, finally, mirrors the aforementioned processes. Regardless if the reaction to AIDS by the Clinton administration was too slow or not – a number of political actors nevertheless continuously pushed for at least a politicization of HIV/AIDS during the 1990s, both domestically and abroad. These actors used different policy tools to alter the United States' political and economic policies towards AIDS. In all, it can be concluded that in the political context both the discourse and the policy actions concerning AIDS certainly intensified during the mid-1990s, when the framing act changed and AIDS as an international issue, and more importantly the implications of AIDS on security, started to dominate the discourse.

Although some might claim that the changes in the political setting were the main determinants for the subsequent securitization of AIDS, the three-level analysis performed here nevertheless indicates that the process leading up to the securitizing move was not exclusively a political one. Instead, similar processes occurred both internationally and domestically, in the political sphere and in society at large. Although one cannot claim for certain that the Clinton administration was influenced by the other two discursive settings, it can be argued that the existence of three parallel processes certainly increased the likelihood of a securitizing move. As suggested by Léonard and Kaunert in this volume, and building on the works by Kingdon, a broader focus that incorporates different aspects of a policy process is necessary when studying securitization (Léonard and Kaunert, Chapter 3 this volume). By focusing on how the framing act of HIV/AIDS was constructed over time, and on the actors of different contexts involved in this framing act, we are able to get a more comprehensive understanding of why President Clinton securitized HIV/AIDS in 2000. The three simultaneous discursive processes together opened a window of opportunity that not only made a securitization possible but actually viewed as something necessary. Had, for instance, the US domestic societal setting not undergone the change of opinion with regard to AIDS, and instead continued to view the epidemic as a problem of a domestic sub-culture, it might have been much more difficult for the President to manage to frame it as a national security problem. Had not the international community recognized the implications of AIDS it would probably have been more difficult to dedicate a Security Council meeting to this epidemic. As the framing act of AIDS now was remarkably similar in all three discourses by the end of the 1990s, it can be argued that AIDS was internalized as a security threat which both shaped the ideas and interests of the US administration as well as helped to realize these ideas and interests.

Notes

1 For instance, on July 17, 2000 the Security Council passed resolution 1308 in which the Council stressed that "the HIV/AIDS pandemic, if unchecked, may pose a risk to stability and security" (United Nations Security Council, 2000a). Less than a year later, in June 2001, the important United Nations General Assembly Special Session (UNGASS) took place, being the first time the UN convened in a special session to discuss a disease. The HIV/AIDS has also continued to be a topic for discussion at a number of other international gatherings, for instance the G8. During the presidency of George W. Bush, the United States sustained the policies set by the Clinton administration. Although criticized for attempting to include a conservative Christian morality aspect into the PEPFAR program of foreign aid, the US government is regardless the single largest contributor to funding AIDS prevention and therapy programs in developing countries (Vieira, 2007).

2 To reconstruct the international context documents from international organizations such as the UN, WHO, NATO, and the World Bank have been gathered, as well as secondary source texts on this topic. The US societal and political discourses were investigated by searches in the Lexis-Nexis Academic database. Searches were delimited to the 50 most circulated US newspapers ("major US newspapers"), using different search terms such as 'HIV' or 'AIDS' followed by *w / 15 United States*, *w / 15 national security*, or *w / 15 Africa* to ensure that only documents containing these two terms no more than 15 words apart, i.e. in the same sentence, would be gathered. US Library of Congress database and search engine *Thomas* www.thomas.gov / was also used for the congressional records and debates.

3 This stance has, however, also generated critique from many in the field of public health who argue that the AIDS threat is exaggerated and that the "single issue advocacy is harming health systems and diverting resources from mover effective interventions against other diseases" (Das and Samarasekera, 2008: 2102).

4 Lexis-Nexis database, using search terms HIV/15 United States

5 Lexis-Nexis search: Major US newspapers, 'HIV w/15 Africa'

6 In those the US government withheld treatment from poor black syphilis patients.

9 Securitization, culture and power

Rogue states in US and German discourse

Holger Stritzel and Dirk Schmittchen

The portrayal of rogue states as a serious threat to global security remains part of a unique US security discourse. While the rogue states image is a central continuity in US strategic discourse after the end of the Cold War characterising states supporting terrorism and seeking the acquisition of Weapons of Mass Destruction (WMD), the reception of rogue states in Germany could not be more different within the transatlantic security community. After having been largely ignored, its late reception has been marked by scepticism, irony and open hostility towards the US, criticising the United States of stigmatising other nations and separating the world into dichotomous spheres of good and evil. German politicians, academics and political lobbyists talking about rogue states can hardly be found.

In recent years explanations of US or German foreign policy and differences between the two countries have stressed the importance of identity, culture and social role (see e.g. Berger 1998; Dalgaard-Nielsen 2006; Duffield 1998; Harnisch and Maull 2001; Longhurst 2004; Szabo 2004; Williams 2005). Scholars who have examined both countries with regards to the perception of rogue states (see e.g. Rudolf 1999; Ponemann 1998) follow a similar line of argument, claiming that Germany has developed the identity of a 'trading state' and 'civilian power' with strong economic interests so that it prefers soft measures such as diplomacy; positive economic incentives and multilateralism. In contrast the US has developed the identity of a 'security state' and military superpower which has the willingness and capacity to act if it comes to believe that there is an important security problem at stake.[1] A similar argument has also been provided by Robert Kagan who describes cleavages between Europe and the US with the opposing cultures of Mars and Venus which are derived from different positions of power in the current international system (see Kagan 2003). Since Europe is not able to act unilaterally and militarily, European states attempt to solve international problems by diplomatic and economic means. Furthermore, as Europeans made disastrous experiences with power politics in the twentieth century and found a path to a lasting inner-European peace by integration and cooperation, they now regard the positive example of the European Integration as a worthwhile archetype to solve conflicts worldwide. In contrast to Europe, the US never had negative experiences with power politics and therefore shows no negative attitudes towards what Kagan calls a 'policy of strength'.

There is certainly a grain of truth in these readings. As one will see, the security discourses on rogue states in both countries are indeed marked by excessive references to 'US leadership' in the US and non-military and multilateralist lines of argument in Germany. Also, Germany's outlook after the end of the Cold War has indeed been much more regional than the US outlook, trying to stabilise its immediate environment through economic cooperation and diplomacy in an attempt to 'export' stability to Eastern Europe and Russia.

Yet, while we agree that cultural discourse traditions of 'US internationalism' and 'German civilian foreign policy' play an important role in understanding US–German differences, we argue that traditional explanations suffer from two sets of conceptual problems. The first problem is the diversity of the discourse. A reconstruction of the actual threat discourses on rogue states in both countries reveals that the discourses are much more heterogeneous, with different positions competing with one another. For example, in the case of Germany's rogue state reception, conservative security experts such as Joachim Krause have launched several initiatives to promote the threat image of rogue states for Germany. In the US, the evolution of the rogue states doctrine has been controversial from the very beginning with scholars such as Michael Klare or Robert Litwak and politicians such as Colin Powell or Madeleine Albright expressing their scepticism about the rogue states metaphor (see Schmitchen and Stritzel 2008). The threat perceptions in Germany and the US are thus far from homogeneous. Acknowledging this heterogeneity in the threat discourses is particularly rare in the academic literature on German foreign policy, creating the false impression of monolithic threat perceptions and neglecting the role of actors for the genesis of threat images (see in particular Berger 1998; Duffield 1998).

Second, a related problem of the existing explanations is that they leave unexplored the black-box of what precisely maintains the different outlooks and dominant perceptions in both countries. Is it indeed the culturally determined *mindsets* of German and US elites as many cultural and identity-based explanations at least implicitly suggest? Taken on its own, orthodox explanations based on identity, culture and social role tend to provide a too structural and too static perspective which ignores discourse dynamics, social power struggles and political decisions which lie behind threat perceptions.[2] Threat images and security discourses are always constructed by certain actors struggling against other actors from specific positions of power. Structural dispositions always need to be sustained and translated into action. Therefore, threat images such as the rogue states metaphor result from sociolinguistic and socio-political processes that are embedded in but not determined by its respective cultural context.

We argue that the existing culturalist literature on differences between US and German security policy would therefore gain from an engagement with a contextualist reading of securitization as elaborated by Stritzel (2007; forthcoming). We begin with an analysis of the origins of the rogue states image before we reconstruct the threat discourse on rogue states in the US and Germany which we then relate to its sociolinguistic and socio-political dimensions.

Origins of the rogue states image

In a general sense, the rogue states image gives a name to the decades-old structural problem of isolation, revisionism and revolutionism in international society. There have always been more or less radical challengers to the international status quo, to its fundamental values, its main powers and/or its existing geographical demarcations. The rogue states image frames these general structural problems in a distinctly American language and gives a great variety of perceived security problems a unitary frame ('the' rogue states problematic).

In the US the usage of the rogue states image or similar expressions can be traced back to the 1970s, especially in academic circles. In 1971, Yehezkel Dror analysed the threats originating from *crazy states*: irregular actors not abiding by international norms which according to Dror must not under any circumstances be allowed to acquire WMD (see Dror 1971). At the end of the 1970s it was Robert Harkavy dealing with the similar concept of *pariah states* who warned against the potential proliferation of WMD to internationally isolated states trying to deter their neighbours from invasion (see Harkavy 1977; 1981). In 1985, US President Ronald Reagan characterised Iran, Libya, North Korea, Cuba and Nicaragua as *outlaw states* supporting terrorist groups and forming a 'new, international version of Murder, Incorporated' (Reagan 1985).[3]

In the broader context of these academic and political traditions the term rogue states itself was a media creation in the late 1970s before the expression entered into the official language of US administrations, criticising mainly Pol Pot's Cambodia and Idi Amin's Uganda for massive human rights violations, genocides and brutal dictatorships. In this example, the label 'rogue regime' gives illegitimate political representation and repressive leadership practices a distinctly moral connotation of acting as a 'criminal against one's own people' which is portrayed to stand in contrast to the Western/liberal notion of democracy (see Litwak 2000: 50). Henriksen (2001: 358) and Tanter (1999: 19) also argue that a semantic parallel to the notion of the 'rogue elephant' can be drawn. The term is based on research by zoologist Rob Slotow (see Slotow and van Dyk 2004) on African elephants in Kenya and describes unfounded aggressions of male animals due to an exorbitant production of testosterone. As a result of their 'abnormal behaviour', they are isolated or attacked by other elephants. In the early 1980s, this notion of 'rogue elephant behaviour' entered the US media discourse as well, first to describe the involvement of the US Central Intelligence Agency in acts of sabotage, contract murder and civil war abroad, later on increasingly to characterise state behaviour. For this latter group, the term 'rogue elephant state' was occasionally used.

The post Cold War discourse on rogue states in the US

The threat image of rogue states was thus first used by a US president in the political speech by Reagan in 1985. Yet, although the spirit and semantic of the early speech by Reagan was kept in the years that followed, at that time the invocation of the rogue states spirit remained cursory, structurally fragmented and not in any substantive way related to a new overall strategic doctrine. Therefore, it also did not manage to construct a broader coalition of supporters who promoted its usage in the strategic discourse. In the second half of the 1980s, it was mainly used to comment on single events such as Gaddafis' involvement in the attack against US soldiers at the German discotheque La Belle in West Berlin on 5 April 1986 or Iraq's first attack against its Kurdish population in Halabja in March 1988 using poison gas (see Reagan 1986; 1988). This situation changed under George H. W. Bush. Entering the post Cold War constellation, the threat image became semantically more consolidated and was now actively promoted by a powerful discourse coalition of internationalists in the US strategic community.

As Michael Klare (1995: 3–7) has stressed, the end of the Cold War came as a shock for the security establishments in the US and world-wide. Previously, the entire field was structured in relation to the Soviet threat. The military force structure and weaponry, the defence industry as well as a comprehensive Washington think tank machinery have been concerned for decades with how to defend against the Soviet enemy and win the Cold War. With the Soviet threat rapidly disappearing towards the end of the 1980s, the field was in a severe identity crisis.

The early 1990s were thus marked by several strategic ideas and assessments (see e.g. Bowen and Dunn 1995; Melanson 1996) underneath which struggles took place on new directions for US security policy and their institutional and budgetary consequences. George H. W. Bush's own famous vision of a 'new world order' was initially intensively discussed in the field and soon severely challenged. The peace movement saw prospects for a comprehensive nuclear disarmament and a debate on prospects for a post Cold War 'peace dividend' started. Other actors identified 'instability', 'fragmentation' and 'unpredictability' as the new structure of security challenges. Under the heading of a 'new world disorder', they provided a pessimistic antithesis to both Bush's 'new world order' and the optimism conveyed in the peace dividend discourse. At the same time inter-bureaucratic rivalries over available and future funds intensified, as did debates about the future shape of the military force structure and prospects for severe cuts in the military budget.

These ideas and agendas appeared in the public realm at a time when the US economy was weak and fears arose that the US may decline as a leading economic power relative to its main international competitors (see e.g. Kennedy 1988). The general public was described as apathetic with regards to foreign policy issues and as increasingly inward-looking (see e.g. Rielly 1995; Lindsay 2003). This did not only redirect the attention to domestic policy issues such as health, education, social security and economic growth. It also stirred up fears in the strategic community of a 'new isolationism' in US foreign policy. With the economy perceived to be in need of fundamental reconstruction and the general public disinterested in foreign policy, the traditional lines of conflict in US strategic discourse of 'internationalism' versus 'isolationism' seemed to gain a very urgent momentum. The prospect that the US may retreat from international engagement was alarming news for a heterogeneous group of 'internationalists' who – for several reasons – were in favour of maintaining a strong US power position in the world.

The combination of a concern for US power projection capacity and international engagement is clearly evident in early speeches by Bush and others, reflecting the concerns of US internationalists in a context of fears about isolationist tendencies:

America must possess forces able to respond to threats in whatever corner of the globe they may occur. Even in a world where democracy and freedom have made great gains, threats remain. Terrorism, hostagetaking, renegade regimes and unpredictable rulers, new sources of instability – all require a strong and an engaged America.

(Bush 1990: 3)

It is this threat scenario that would justify, Bush argues, the maintenance of a strong military:

The budget constraints we face are very real; but so, too, is the need to protect the gains that 40 years of peace through strength have earned us. The simple fact is this: When it comes to national security, America can never afford to fail or fall short.

(Bush 1990: 5)

Under Clinton the rogue states image continued to dominate the US strategic discourse and became fully developed and firmly consolidated. The political dynamic at that time had three central characteristics. First, a lack of political leadership by Clinton in foreign policy issues (see e.g. Cimbala 1996) and clear preferences for focusing on economic issues and domestic reform (see Clinton and Gore 1992). As a result, other actors in the US foreign policy complex such as early security advisor Anthony Lake and Martin Indyk, at that time senior director for Near East and South Asian Affairs at the National Security Council, could play a stronger role in giving the rogue states doctrine shape and direction. Second, there was an attempt to embed the rogue states image in a broader strategic doctrine for the post Cold War period (see Lake 1993; 1994; The White House 1996), initially as an internationalist vision for a future 'world of democracies' and then increasingly as a doctrine for regime change in the Middle East. Finally, its genesis at this stage was marked by a fierce political and ideological struggle between Clinton and the Republican-led Congress, with the Congress receiving support from conservative think tanks and ethnic and religious lobby groups, promoting the threat image and pressuring Clinton.

The security policy of the early Clinton administration set itself three major tasks. First, actors felt obliged to address the question of engagement versus retreat, to justify their position in this respect and to reach agreement on a respective military force structure. Second, with the war in Iraq, the question of the future policy towards Iran and Iraq became again more virulent. And finally, the US security community of 1993 was still in search for an overall strategic vision and vocabulary to make sense of the post Cold War world, a search which also stemmed from the

US self-perception of having to provide vision and mission for its own policy and those of the world.

Anthony Lake tried to define all three aspects in one stroke. His reflections are laid down in three main documents: first, in the speech *From Containment to Enlargement* (see Lake 1993) which is his first attempt to pin down a strategic vision for the post Cold War world; second, the article *Confronting Backlash States* (see Lake 1994) in which he elaborates these thoughts by turning the rogue image into a leading doctrine for future US security policy; and, finally, the US strategic doctrine of *Enlargement and Engagement* (see The White House 1996) which translates Lake's visions into the official language of the US National Security Strategy under Clinton. Lake's elaboration of the rogue states image appears as a move to amalgamate the several previous discourses, concerns and immediate policy requirements of that time into a single overarching threat metaphor:

As suggested at the outset, in many ways, we are returning to the divisions and debates about our role in the world that are as old as our Republic. On one side is protectionism and limited foreign engagement; on the other is active American engagement abroad on behalf of democracy and expanded trade. [. .] The internationalists won those debates, in part because they could point to a unitary threat to America's interests and because the nation was entering a period of economic security. Today's supporters of engagement abroad have neither of those advantages. The threats and opportunities are diffuse and our people are deeply anxious about their economic fate. Rallying Americans to bear the costs and burdens of international engagement is no less important. But it is much more difficult. [. .] It is time for those who see the value of American engagement to steady our ranks; to define our purpose; and to rally the American people. In particular, at a time of high deficits and pressing domestic needs, we need to make a convincing case for our engagement or else see drastic reductions in our military, intelligence, peacekeeping and other foreign policy accounts.

(Lake 1993: 11–12)

Against this background, Lake's article *Confronting Backlash States* which popularised the rogue states image reads as providing exactly this kind of *unitary threat* Lake thought to be needed to maintain an internationalist agenda with respective resources for the military.

With the mid-term elections of 1994 the then Republican-led Congress turned into the main player and advocate of the rogue states image in increasingly fierce opposition to Clinton. At the same time ethnic and religious lobby groups gained more ground to articulate their position through the Congress. With that the threat image received more repressive connotations and was mainly used (i) as a political instrument for the deployment of a missile defence shield against traditional/liberal arms control strategies, (ii) for more repressive policies against states in the Middle East and against a policy of engagement with these states and (iii) against the belief in the logic of deterrence in the non-proliferation discourse.

A major policy effect of the rogue states image at that time was the establishment of the Cuban Liberty and Democratic Solidarity Act of March 1996 and the Iran-Libya Sanctions Act of July 1996 against Iran, Libya, Syria and Cuba. The two sanction regimes were mainly achievements of the American Israel Public Affairs Committee (AIPAC) and the Cuban American National Foundation (CANF) who managed to get support from Congress against economic interests and a fragmented early economic counter-lobbying coalition (see Tanter 1999: 45–86). Yet, with the election of Khatami in Iran – and hopes for substantive reform in Iran – as well as perceived improvements in negotiating with North Korea on giving up efforts to acquire sensitive nuclear technology, the Clinton administration attempted to switch the threat lexicon from 'rogue states' to 'states of concern' towards the end of his presidency (see Boucher 2000) which was soon criticised in Congress as a flawed policy of 'appeasement' towards rogues.

With the election of George W. Bush in 2000 one may think that the Republican agenda which already took shape and had indeed penetrated the policy of the Clinton administration was now ready to reach fruition. However, Bush only marginally won the elections against his Democratic opponent Al Gore and possessed a very fragile majority in Congress (see Hils and Wilzewski 2004). In the House of Representatives the Republican majority was shrunk to only 9 seats and in the Senate 50 Republicans stood against an equal number of Democrats. This situation got worse in August 2001 when the Republican Senator James M. Jeffords of Vermont left the Republican Party. With the new political constellation in the Senate, the Democrats soon began to strengthen their foreign and security profile to separate their approach from the policy of the Bush administration. They criticised harshly Bush's 'single-minded approach' and his unilateral foreign policy.

Yet, the terrorist attacks of 9/11 had a strong 'rally around the flag' effect on both the Congress and the general public as a result of which this situation got reversed. According to some opinion polls immediately after 9/11 Bush received support of almost 90 percent (see e.g. Jones 2002). A high degree of support for presidential leadership is also true for the Congress: On 14 September 2001, Bush was authorised to take military action against those responsible for the terrorist attacks, the Patriot Act of October 2001 attributed far-reaching powers of domestic surveillance to the US executive and the Department of Homeland Security with 170,000 employees was established with overwhelming support; in addition, a substantial increase in military spending of more than $400 billion for 2003 was agreed and in October 2002 Bush was empowered by the Congress to take military action against Iraq.

It was in this context that Bush could bring about a substantial change in the further development of the new post Cold War US security doctrine under the heading of the rogue states image that had started in the early 1990s. This so-called 'Bush doctrine' of military pre-emption of which the rogue states image is part and parcel stands in the tradition of earlier initiatives such as the Defense Counterproliferation Initiative (see Aspin 1993) whilst at the same time radicalising and prioritising military elements of it. Whilst the attention of the Bush administration was initially directed against terrorist networks, Bush soon started to link terrorism and rogue states, giving the diffuse terrorist problematic a more clearly identifiable and state-centric frame. This also increased the perceived threat potential of both rogue states and terrorists with the threat henceforth appearing as a relational three-tier structure of nuclear proliferation, rogue state support and (nuclear) terrorism. As Bush pointed out in 2002: 'Terror cells and outlaw regimes building weapons of mass destruction are different faces of the same evil' (Bush 2002b: 2).

The post Cold War discourse on rogue states in Germany

The reception of the rogue states image in Germany was largely negative and much more cursory and passive than the process of securitization in the US, often simply reacting to US moves and/or discussing the issue implicitly in the context of specific US policy initiatives. One can hardly find any public enunciations at all which use the rogue states metaphor to frame problems of horizontal proliferation. This is particularly true for the first half of the 1990s when the issue of rogue states was almost ignored in German discourse (but see e.g. Vogel 1992; Müller 1995a; 1995b). Whilst in the US media and policy circles the discourse on rogue states was already intense in the first half of the 1990s the German reception occurred only in the second half of the 1990s when newspapers and policy experts began to pay attention to the concept.

Searching for the first usage of the term *Schurkenstaat* – the German translation of rogue state – in five major German newspapers and magazines shows that the term was not used before 1996 and its use only slightly increased in the following years.[4] A usage that would be comparable to the intensity that occurred in the US has never taken place. Moreover, the connotations of the German term *Schurkenstaat* differed completely from the US term rogue state. Whilst US policy actors regularly referred to North Korea or Iran directly when mentioning rogue states, actors in Germany used the term to describe US policy towards these nations. Furthermore, German journalists tended to distance themselves from US foreign policy and criticised the US when using the term *Schurkenstaat*. In other words, the term was not used neutrally but rather to express criticism and disaffirmation of US policy towards 'so called' rogue states. This process was brought about either implicitly by using the term in inverted commas – thereby signalling that a foreign threat text was quoted that was not meant to be incorporated into the journalists' own vocabulary or into German discourse – or explicitly by criticising the term as a '*Beschimpfung*' (bashing) (e.g. Amirpur 1998; Zand 1999) or '*Brandmarkung*' (denunciation) (e.g. Buhl 1998). Others went further and defined rogue states polemically as the '*Lieblingsfeinde*' (favourite enemies) of the US (e.g. SPIEGEL 1997) or as 'states that have a bad relationship with the US' (e.g. Chauvistre 1998).

Apart from analysing the media discourse in Germany we have also conducted interviews with leading foreign and security professionals from all major German parties represented in the *Bundestag* – the German parliament – from November 2005 to April 2006.[5] The result was unambiguous. All politicians interviewed felt uncomfortable with the usage of the term rogue state and preferred the expression *problem state* when asked if they could agree on a term. The view on the US usage of the term rogue state varied between complete rejection and slight understanding while in the latter context the interviewees emphasised that rogue states would merely make sense within the peculiar US context which could not be translated into the German or wider European discourse.

Specifically, the reaction of the German elites in these interviews shows that to a large extent they follow traditional lines of German foreign policy discourse. In terms of policies towards 'rogue states' they stress diplomacy, negotiations and dialogue. Behavioural changes are only perceived to be possible through positive incentives as well as economic, cultural and technological cooperation. Over time this can help to initiate a process of democratisation within these countries, a process, however, which would have to come from inside. In other words, German elites still stress a policy of integration and engagement that dominated former Foreign Minister Klaus Kinkel's policy of a 'critical dialogue' with Iran. Furthermore, parallels are striking with the rationale of German *Ostpolitik* and the CSCE process which is usually considered in Germany as a milestone of successful German foreign policy. In contrast, any kind of containment, isolation and punishment as well as military force and pressure is ruled out. Military pressure would not open space for negotiations but it would rather make diplomatic solutions more difficult. According to German political elites this foreign policy stance starts with the very language of diplomacy because they consider the term rogue state as a means to legitimise military action. They criticise the rogue states image for having too ideological, too moralising and too dichotomous connotations. Because of European secularisation the use of quasi-religious terms in politics could no longer be legitimated. To admit errors and doubts would be part of German political culture and often the only possibility to mobilise resources. Because of the disruptions and fissures in German history and society, there would be no sense of a mission in the world. Germany would instead now define its foreign and security policy and its very identity in strong opposition to the militarism of the nineteenth and twentieth century.

These reactions resonate with much German expert discourse. The only comprehensive reflection on the rogue states image by a German mainstream security expert is an article by Peter Rudolf from the major German think tank Stiftung Wissenschaft und Politik (SWP). His main argument is already present in the heading: 'Stigmatisierung bestimmter Staaten – Europa bevorzugt den Dialog' (stigmatising certain states – Europe prefers political dialogue) (Rudolf 1999). More radical framings can be found among left-wing politicians and German peace-researchers. For example, Lutz Schrader understands the rogue states image as a 'means to establish a *pax americana*' (Schrader 2002: 211), for Peter Strutynski the rogue states image characterises 'countries which currently lie at the centre of US expansionism' (Strutynski 2004: 33) and left-wing politician Wolfgang Gehrcke argued in the German parliament at a time the official US lexicon had switched from 'rogue states' to 'states of concern': 'If US politicians allocate certificates for states in the world and classify countries as worrying – in the past they even used the term rogue states – then I can only label the US itself as worrying [. .] The US is worrying to me [. .] [NMD] isn't a defence system but part of an aggressive policy. In other words: the US is striving for world domination' (Gehrcke in BT 2001: 15372–73). Even German transatlanticists expressed their scepticism towards the rogue states image in an attempt to mitigate the negative effects of the threat image in the German context as the 'Transatlantic Joint Memorandum' by the Konrad Adenauer Foundation (KAS)[6] and the Bundesverband der Deutschen Industrie (BDI) (Federation of German Industries)[7] on 'the future of transatlantic relations' made clear: 'Successful non-proliferation policy needs containment as well as diplomatic integration of possible proliferators [. . .] The US have already turned down the unhelpful term rogue states to characterise problem states' (Memorandum 2001: 65).

Nevertheless some actors in favour of a German rogue states *policy* can still be found in German discourse. Among the small group of supporters for central aspects of the threat image, Joachim Krause has perhaps most vividly and most often openly pledged for the substance of the rogue states image.[8] With respect to the notion of rogue states itself Krause prefers a switch to the term problem states or states of concern (other German actors have switched the name to 'risk states' or 'high risk states'; see e.g. Schwarz 2003: 27) although he is not entirely consistent with his usage of the term, referring to the issue as 'states the US calls rogue states' (Krause 2000: 37; 1998: 380), 'highly armed problem states' (2000: 37), 'rogue states' (2000: 38), 'radical islamic states' (2000: 40), 'adventurer, criminal family clans, religious zealots and eccentrics' (2006: 10), 'rentier states' (2006: 10), 'states which massively challenge world order' (2006: 12) or 'states which the majority of the international community considers to be problematic due to the radicality and ruthlessness of their political leaders' (1998: 343). However, Krause also expresses his uneasiness with the US rogue states terminology which would give a new nonproliferation doctrine he supports an overtly military connotation (in other words, a connotation that does not resonate with German discourse): 'With regards to the use of military means this implies that it has to be built on a broader basis than the US concept of rogue states at first seems to suggest' (Krause 1998: 343).

Whilst the reconstruction of US and German discourse has shown that different cultural framings and identity narratives indeed play a role for understanding US and German discourses and their differences, a more comprehensive analysis reveals that the discourse results from an interplay of the sociolinguistics and sociopolitics for the threat image. Cultural framings and identity narratives are not static but result from the dynamic of threat texts embedded in discourse and the positional power of the coalitions of support for the threat image.

The sociolinguistics of the rogue states metaphor

The socio-linguistics of the rogue states metaphor mainly concerns the embeddedness of the threat image of rogue states in the discourse tradition of American exceptionalism (see e.g. Madsen 1998; Lipset 1997). In the US context the threat image could therefore be effective as a linguistic reservoir, was emotionally potent and convincing, and enabled to construct a strong and heterogeneous coalition of support. In the German context it had the reverse effect: for securitizing actors it was highly ineffective as a linguistic reservoir and weakened an already weak coalition of support. On the contrary, in the German context it was rather effective as a linguistic reservoir to mobilise resistance.

In US foreign policy discourse American exceptionalism leads to 'Manichaean' framings as a result of which enemies of the US have often been demonised as representatives of an evil system which is antagonistic to the values the US stands for. The 'savages' in the French and Indian War, the British King George III during the War of Independence, the Mexicans and the Spanish in the Wars of 1846/47 and 1898, the German Kaiser in World War I, totalitarian Germany and Japan in World War II and finally the Soviet Union during the Cold War all sat in this 'Manichean trap' (see Junker 2003), now followed by rogue states accused of seeking WMD and harbouring fundamentalist terrorists (see Litwak 2000).

Apart from the term itself, American exceptionalism is also strongly evident in the major speeches that have put forward the rogues' image in the US. The move to use American exceptionalism as a linguistic resource for mobilising support is clearest in Reagan's speech in 1985:

Now, for the benefit of these outlaw governments who are sponsoring international terrorism against our nation, I'm prepared to offer a brief lesson in American history. A number of times in America's past, foreign tyrants, warlords, and totalitarian dictators have misinterpreted the well-known likeability, patience, and generosity of the American people as signs of weakness or even decadence. Well, it's true; we are an easygoing people, slow to wrath, hesitant to see danger looming over every horizon. But it's also true that when the emotions of the American people are aroused, when their patriotism and their anger are triggered, there are no limits to their national valor nor their consuming passion to protect this nation's cherished tradition of freedom. [..] Freedom itself is the issue — our own and the entire world's. Yes, America is still a symbol to a few, a symbol that is loved, a country that remains a shining city on a hill. Teddy Roosevelt [..] put it so well: 'We, here in America, hold in our hands the hope of the world, the fate of the coming years; and shame and disgrace will be ours if in our eyes the light of high resolve is dimmed, if we trail in the dust the golden hopes of man.' And that light of high resolve, those golden hopes, are now ours to preserve and protect and, with God's help, to pass on to generations to come.

(Reagan 1985: 4–7)

Reagan here clearly and excessively makes use of the existing reservoir of distinctly US cultural values and icons to steer the emotions of his audience: e.g. 'patriotism', 'freedom', 'American history'. He frames the security threat of terrorists as a fight of us, 'the American peoples', against them, evil outlaws: 'foreign tyrants, warlords, totalitarian dictators'. It is part of the founding myth of the US that the grass-root uprising of the people and their striving for freedom prevails over despotism. Reagan then goes on to portray the fight against rogues as not only a fight to protect the US but to the same extent as a fight for the world, their values and their very destiny ('We, here in America, hold in our hands the hope of the world'). Reagan develops these thoughts in a highly metaphorical, symbolic and in its tone and rhythm religious language (e.g. 'and shame and disgrace will be ours if in our eyes the light of high resolve is dimmed').

No one else made so extreme – and culturally rich – enunciations in the context of promoting the rogue states image. Still, Anthony Lake stands in this tradition in promoting the rogues image accusing rogue states of being 'on the wrong side of history' (Lake 1994: 54) or stating that 'such states tend to rot from within both economically and spiritually' (Lake 1993: 8). This aspect became again stronger in enunciations of George W. Bush: 'We are in a conflict between good and evil, and America will call evil by its name. By confronting evil and lawless regimes, we do not create a problem, we reveal a problem. And we will lead the world in opposing it' (Bush 2002a: 3).

However, this language was successful only in the US context while in Germany it was not only highly unsuccessful but rather helpful in mobilising resistance. As one could see, this aspect of using the rogue states image as a linguistic reservoir against the US is clearly expressed in the enunciations of left-wing politician Wolfgang Gehrke and German peace researchers Lutz Schrader and Peter Strutynski.

The socio-politics of the rogue states metaphor

The socio-politics of the rogue states metaphor in the US and Germany concerns different patterns of social power in the two contexts which is equally important to understand US–German differences. In a nutshell, for the American Israel Public Affairs Committee and Evangelical groups the threat image was attractive because of its implications for the Middle East and Israel. The Cuban American National Foundation supported the issue because Cuba was on the list of rogue states. For several Republicans, supported by like-minded think tanks, the linkage of the image with ballistic missile defence was a viable foreign policy alternative in their mainly domestic and moral political campaign in the elections. The increase in military spending was in the interest of the Pentagon and the defence industry. Finally, for proliferation experts it was useful to promote a new rationale for non-proliferation away from a focus on regimes and treaties towards 'pro-active' strategies against seemingly irrational 'new enemies'. In what follows these actors will be analysed more closely and compared to patterns of positional power in Germany.

The first group of supporters for the threat image in the US, who played a particularly strong role in the early promotion of the rogue states image, have been referred to in this article as 'internationalists'. Their internationalism is usually the result of a conglomerate of ideology, professional concerns and egoistic interests which are difficult to separate. All three elements constitute a particular 'outlook' and have to be read in conjuncture. In the early 1990s, their outlook led to fears that the US may retreat from an internationalist foreign policy agenda.

Within this broader group the Pentagon and the US security bureaucracy is worth to be analysed more closely. The power of this actor is to a large extent based on its ability to strike alliances with industrial lobby groups and like-minded members in the US Congress and goes back to the National Security Act of 1947 which established the National Security Council, the Central Intelligence Agency and the Pentagon with a civilian leader for Army, Navy and Air Force. These institutions were originally supposed to strengthen the institutional role of the US President in relation to the State Department as a strong force of early US foreign policy. The National Security Council, and in particular the National Security Advisor, gained in importance over the years and the decision making process of the executive branch increasingly shifted to processes within the White House (see Rosati and Twing 1998: 47–52).

With regard to the Pentagon, the CIA and the State Department, scholars have observed a dramatic increase in the power of the Pentagon and the CIA and a concomitant decline in the role of the State Department in shaping US foreign policy (see e.g. Wiarda 1996: 200–205). This has several reasons among which are the outsourcing of foreign policy planning capacities to think tanks, the centralisation of the foreign policy decision making process and the recruitment culture of hiring 'generalists' in the State Department. While the budget of the State Department has turned into the smallest of all ministerial agencies (see Kegley and Wittkopf 1996: 386; Wiarda 1996: 206), the Pentagon and the CIA could steadily grow in importance under the conditions of the Cold War and establish themselves as the providers of national security (Sarkesian, Williams and Cimbala 1995: 96–97).

Second, due to the rather strong permeability of the US institutional system and the Congress, other domestic actors such as think tanks or lobby groups can have a rather strong influence on US foreign policy. As one could see, powerful lobby groups such as the American Israel Public Affairs Committee (AIPAC) or the Cuban American National Foundation (CANF) influenced the US foreign policy process from the societal sphere. AIPAC, which represents the conservative wing of Jewish organisations in the US, is considered to be the most important actor behind the Iran-Libya Sanctions Act, an initiative AIPAC mainly brought about with the help of Republican Senator D'Amato (see Alikhani 2000: 177). Interestingly for the rogue states genesis in the US, AIPAC have a very close relationship with Martin Indyk who was a major actor of drafting the rogues image as a dual containment strategy against Iran and Iraq: before Indyk worked as senior director for the Near East at the National Security Council, he was employee of AIPAC in Washington and founded the *Washington Institute for Near East Policy* with financial support from AIPAC (see Alikhani 2000: 166).

Curiously, AIPAC's strictly pro-Israeli policy, favouring hard measures against Arab states hostile to Israel, resonates with the ideology and the interests of another actor in US politics: the Evangelicals, a group of conservative and right-wing Christians who have grown in importance in recent years. They are professionally organised in Congress as the *Republican Study Committee* (RSC) (Branl 2004: 17) and have close links to several Republican politicians such as Elliott Abrams, senior director for the Near East at the National Security Council and former director of the religious think tank *Center for Ethics and Public Policy* whose mission is to bring together conservative Christian and Jewish ideologies and interests. The Evangelical lobby was a strong supporter of the Bush doctrine, they are in favour of a hard policy in the 'war on terror' and against the states hostile to Israel, including 'rogues', and the war in Iraq (see Judis 2005: 6). Interestingly also, George W. Bush's former speech writer David Frum who invented the 'axis of evil' metaphor is a member of the right-wing Evangelicals.

In contrast, to assess the positional power of the German coalition in support of the threat image it is interesting to have a closer look at the German Ministry of Defence (BMVg) and the German armed forces in general which are much weaker than the Pentagon and the US security complex. As Schlör argues: 'Because of German history, the *Bundeswehr* has always been less a manifestation of statehood than a means of defending against the Soviet threat' (Schlör 1993: 18). It thus only received 'borrowed' and momentous legitimacy to fulfil a specific task that could not be avoided for Germany as the frontline state of the Cold War. This general ideological disadvantage has become sedimented in Germany's domestic structures and practices of security policy. For example, many important security policy decisions have been made without even consulting the military leadership such as the creation of a joint Franco-German corps or the deployment of German military staff during the humanitarian mission for Kurdish refugees in Iraq. Also, major public announcements on the closing of bases and the dismantling of units were made without prior briefing of the commanders (Schlör 1993: 18). The reputation and status of the military leadership is not much better in German society. According to a 1992 public opinion poll, a majority of Germans believed that military officers were not important or superfluous and 57 percent believed that military careers have a low or rather low reputation (Schlör 1993: 18). Furthermore, Germany does not have a senior military commander and General Staff in command of the three military services. The highest-ranking officer, the *Generalinspekteur*, only serves in an advisory capacity and lacks direct access to the Federal Chancellor. Finally, the military is also counter-balanced by a sceptical media and a rather pacifist public opinion. When asked at the end of 1990 about a role model Germany should follow after the end of the Cold War a majority of Germans chose Switzerland (Schlör 1993: 14). The pacifism in public opinion often leads to a high sensitivity and an emotional concern for a non-military 'logic' and 'semantic'. Although German politicians have on several occasions, such as the deployment of medium-range ballistic missiles in the 1980s, taken decisions against public opinion, pacifist public sentiments provide a reservoir that can be exploited by political leaders or opposition parties – as it was the case in the 2002 elections by the Schröder government. And while in the US a massive think tank machinery is publically engaged in security policy discussions, in Germany only very few institutions can be found which are often faced with public indifference.[9]

Conclusion

Differences between German and US security policy do not only result from different strategic or political cultures, different identities or different foreign policy norms. US–German differences also, and at least as importantly, result from the power politics of domestic discourse coalitions in both countries who interpret cultural dispositions, mobilise support or resistance, legitimise perceptions and actions and this way (re-)direct the policies in both countries. They do so through the medium of language and culture.

Evidently, language and culture are interrelated. A US politician using the metaphor rogue state is able to activate high degrees of resonance when addressing a US audience by resorting to an inherent culturally based value system, while a German politician would only irritate his domestic audience when referring to rogue states. To this extent culture has an influence on the choice of language by actors in the security discourses, meaning that a German politician seeking to gain high degrees of resonance is likely to fail if he used the term rogue states without any reservations when addressing a German audience. Since securitizing actors in Germany face the difficulty of having to argue against a contrastive mainstream, they have to 'sell' the perceived threat differently than US actors and the language that is used, either in the US or in Germany, has an impact on the patterns of support and resistance for a threat.

Such a more complex and dynamic perspective on discourse dynamics with regards to threat images results from a merger of the dominant culturalist perspective on US–German differences with the recent wave of contextualist securitization theory. While the culturalist literature elaborates the sedimented sociolinguistic contexts of securitizing moves, the securitization literature adds a more dynamic, language- and power-based element to these perspectives. Specifically, we have applied the generic securitization framework developed by Stritzel (2007; forthcoming) to illustrate that securitizations and counter-securitizations result from an interplay of the sociolinguistics and socio-politicals for a threat image in different cultural and political contexts.

Notes

1 An alternative (realist) explanation could stress the strategic character of the threat of rogue states to the US and Germany with regards to the positional power of both states in the international system. Following this line of argument one could argue that rogue states are much more a threat to the US than to Germany. The US is a global superpower which poses a challenge to the ambitions of rogue states, it has a history of hostilities with many 'rogues', in particular Iran, and it is a close ally of their enemies, mainly Israel but to a lesser extent also South Korea. In contrast, Germany does not have a bad history with most 'rogue states' and it even has trade relations with some. As a weak military power it does not pose a challenge to these states.

2 For an exception, see Dalgaard-Nielsen 2006; see also Longhurst 2004.

3 This latter understanding stood in the continuity of an annual listing of states that were supposed to protect or sponsor international terrorism. Since the late 1970s, the US administration had to deal with several terrorist attacks against US citizens abroad. This led to the Export Administration Act of 1979 with which the US government enabled sanctions against states sponsoring terrorism. In this context, an annual overview, entitled 'Patterns of Global Terrorism', was published which explicitly named and listed such states. For example, in 1979 it mentioned Cuba, Iran, Iraq, Libya, North Korea, Syria and Yemen, accusing these states of accommodating and protecting terrorist organisations on

their territory (Henriksen 2001: 357–58). In the 1980s, the general perception of the terrorist problematic then shifted more strongly away from the terrorist organisations themselves towards its supposed state sponsors (Klare 1995: 26).

4 Our analysis included *Frankfurter Allgemeine Zeitung, Frankfurter Rundschau, Der SPIEGEL, Süddeutsche Zeitung* and *Die ZEIT*.

5 The interviews included Ruprecht Polenz (CDU/CSU), Karsten D. Voigt (SPD/former Coordinator for Transatlantic Cooperation at the German Foreign Office), Reinhard Weißhuhn (Bündnis 90/Die Grünen), Werner Hoyer (FDP), Wolfgang Gehrke (Die Linke) and Bernd Mützelburg (at that time Head of Foreign and Security Policy at the German Chancellery).

6 The KAS is an institute close to the CDU which combines political education, think tank consultancy and research support to young scholars.

7 The BDI is the most important representative of the German industry.

8 Krause is the most prominent conservative proliferation expert in Germany. He was research fellow and divisional director at the major think tank SWP before he became co-director at the research institute of the DGAP. Currently, he is director at the Institute for Security Policy at the University of Kiel (ISUK) and chairman of the academic directorate at the DGAP.

9 With a much stronger party bureaucracy incorporating scientific expertise, the think tank culture in Germany is much less developed than in the US where think tanks compensate a relatively weak party infrastructure.

10 Religion bites

Falungong, securitization/
desecuritization in the People's
Republic of China

Juha A. Vuori

In this chapter I argue that securitization theory can be a useful entry-point in a variety of studies dealing with broader fields of human action. The question is what the study of securitization can bring to various debates on political theory or the study of persuasion, legitimization, and social mobilization, for example. Here, I relate securitization theory with research on social mobilization and its suppression, and thereby argue that securitization theory has something to offer for this broader field of study.

I focus here on an aspect of real securitization processes that has not received much attention: the interaction between securitizing actors and the 'targets' of securitization. How do securitization moves affect the inter-unit relations of securitizing actors and the claimed threats present in securitization moves? How do securitization moves become part of the context of the subsequent stages of the process of securitization and its possible contestation? How are securitization and desecuritization moves used to suppress social mobilization or to resist its suppression? I deal with these questions here by studying the Chinese campaign against Falungong (FLG),[1] a sectarian organization[2] based on a semi-religious system of qigong. I show how various identity frames,[3] which both the practitioners of FLG and the authorities produce in their interactions, can be seen as attempts both to legitimize social mobilization and make it illegitimate through security discourse in the People's Republic of China (PRC). The combination of securitization and identity frame theory (Palemaa and Vuori 2006) can be used to analyze and conceptualize the interaction between social movements and authorities that has been lacking in studies on Chinese social mobilization and its repression, even though there is extensive research on the subject.

In addition to its interactive features, resistance to securitization has thus far not been one of the major focuses of securitization studies, although some of the earliest articles on securitization by Ole Wæver (1989 and 1995) precisely discussed the possibility and possible effects of failed securitization.[4] The focus has been more on who can securitize, rather than who can resist securitization. The 'targets' of securitization, the claimed threats presented in the performatives, have been left out of most analysis.[5] This is one of the things this chapter aims at remedying. Examining securitization processes as an interaction between the securitizing actor(s) and the target(s) of securitization(s) may bring us forward in understanding who can securitize, which issues (threats), for whom (referent objects), why, with what kinds of effects, and under which conditions (what explains when securitization has been successful) (Buzan, Wæver, and de Wilde 1998). I will now present the kinds of research methods that I have used in increasing our understanding of these issues here.

On methods and levels of securitization analysis

By departing from cross-cultural pragmatics (Wierzbicka 1991), I argue in this chapter that a linguistic or a sociological approach to the study of actual acts of securitization cannot replace each other. These approaches should be seen as complimentary instead. Norman Fairclough (1992: 72–73) has made a similar argument with his three dimensional, textually oriented approach to discourse analysis. His goal was to bring together textual and linguistic analysis, analysis of social practices and structures, and the analysis of commonsense social procedures. For Fairclough, all of these traditions are indispensable for textually oriented discourse analysis. For securitization analysis, the most relevant social practices, structures, and procedures are socio-political by nature.

Moving to both distal and proximate (see Balzacq's Chapter 1 in the present volume) historical, social, and political contexts beyond the original application of securitization theory means that we have to be careful not to 'stretch' our concepts (cf. Sartori 1970). In order to avoid the distorting effect of assuming that our concepts are culture-free analytical tools, we have to look for a near universal perspective from within our own culture and to develop a framework of near universal human concepts that are accessible to most specific languages (Wierzbicka 1991). I have elsewhere (Vuori 2008) shown how a broader categorization of securitization allows us to move beyond the European and liberal democratic political context in our studies of securitization: it is not only about legitimating future acts of the speaker that break the rules of liberal democracy, securitization can have political functions beyond legitimacy, such as deterrence and control, and securitization can happen 'after the fact' (cf. Wilkinson's Chapter 5 in the present volume).

In terms of levels (see Balzacq's Chapter 2 in the present volume), the starting-point for securitization analysis here is the level of 'acts', or the constitution of securitization moves, the analysis of which is based on illocutionary logic (Searle and Vanderveken 1985; Vuori 2008).[6] This however does not imply that the linguistic rules of speech acts are entirely deterministic, or that the study of securitization should only focus on linguistic analysis: models based on illocutionary logic are used here to identify relevant samples of discourse for further analysis. From the level of acts we can focus our attention to the levels of both agents and contexts: the research methods applied here combine both linguistic and socio-political analysis that are necessary for understanding the performative of securitization in real situations and contexts.

While illocutionary logic provides the 'grammar', or necessary culture-independent meta-language for the cross-cultural study of securitization processes, identity frame theory is used here for deciphering the specific 'vocabulary', the situated pools of resonant values (cf. Stritzel 2007), or the heuristic artefacts

(Balzacq's Chapter 1 in the present volume) of the empirical case under investigation. In a way, while illocutionary logic is used to study the '*langue*' of securitization, frame theory helps us to study the '*parole*' of the case investigated here (cf. Culler 1986). The 'grammatical' models of securitization (Vuori 2008) are used to identify relevant texts and discourse samples for analysis. Once the relevant discourse samples have been identified, collected, and analysed with speech act analysis we can determine whether or not we are dealing with a securitization discourse or not. We can then move on to analyse the discourse samples with further sociolinguistic means, as well as broaden our analysis beyond the discourse samples to the historically situated socio-political contexts beyond the specific samples of discourse.

Due to the way Chinese politics and the construction of political realities in China work, authoritative texts are most relevant here. The discourse samples studied can be categorized into several 'genres', e.g. editorials, party circulars, speeches, and open letters. As Fairclough (1992: 232–33), we can view the samples from a variety of angles: How are the samples connected to other texts, and how does this facilitate or impede the possible aspect of securitization evident in them? How do the samples draw on culturally resonant ideas, cognitive maps, or precontracts? What kinds of signs are there of the assumed audience(s)? Is it possible to determine 'who' consumed the samples, and 'who' is speaking in them? What kinds of systems of knowledge and belief are evident in the samples? What types of social relations and social identities (selves and others) do the samples contain?

Securitization is an aspect of a sample of discourse or text: even texts identified as constituting securitization moves have other relevant aspects to them and there are many methods for analysing text and discourse. What securitization theory brings to this analysis are the means of identifying something as a securitization move or as the maintenance of a security discourse. The textual analysis of securitization has to then be related to the political context, where theories of politics and models of political orders become relevant as well as the capabilities and capacities of both agents and structures. Securitization moves can have various political functions and effects that may depend on the political order they are performed in. Similarly, securitization is only one tactic among others vis-à-vis social mobilization and its suppression, and accordingly, I will now discuss how securitization theory relates to the study of identity frames and social mobilization.

Identity frames and social mobilization

The interactive nature of suppression and resistance is already evident in how contestation and resistance can be influenced by the forms of suppression authorities aim at them. Indeed, comparative study of social movements has shown how various forms of policing influence protest behavior (Porta 1996). The securitization of social movements or activities is also a form of suppression: using soft forms of repression, e.g. labelling, increases the likelihood of subsequent hard repression, as it lowers its costs both by intimidating protestors and justifying violence, and may thus eventually up the ante on both sides of the struggle.[7]

Securitization arguments can for example be used for deterrence (Vuori 2008): they can suggest that acquiescence would be preferable to the continuation of the securitized activity. Once these types of securitization moves appear in the media for example, they often become the natural focus of refutation and thereby also protest legitimization. This forces the people engaged in the securitized activities to talk about their own protest/movement and its goals among themselves and to their audiences in terms that will, it is hoped to render the suppression ineffective as well as mobilize popular support and give the protest a sense of common cause. Indeed, in non-democratic states most of this kind of 'identity talk'[8] by protest movements is produced under soft or hard forms of repression. Which words and symbols are used for characterizing an issue have great importance for how it is understood, how it should be regarded, and how it should be responded to. Meaning does not only imply what is at issue, but also what is to be done about the issue in question (Schön and Rein 1994: 29).

The frames through which social movements are presented can have significant effects, and the frame of national security is a powerful one in China. Being labeled a revisionist, a running dog of capitalism, or a counterrevolutionary has had drastic consequences for the bearers of these labels. But if social activities are framed according to the set goals of the authorities, the likelihood of their suppression diminishes. Even criticism against the authorities may be tolerable, when presented through the correct frame. For example, criticism of Chinese authorities through a patriotic or nationalist frame is tolerated to a greater extent by state authorities than many other frames of critique.

The empirical case studied here exemplifies how the use of security frames has influenced the identity talk of Li Hongzhi, the master of FLG: he has tried to refute and deflect the suppression of FLG by presenting his doctrine in a favorable way vis-à-vis the stated goals of the CCP. It is indeed well established in studies on Chinese social mobilization that the way the CCP legitimizes its rule is important for the ways protestors legitimize their collective actions in Mainland China. However, most studies of social mobilization and securitization of social movements have biases to them. Securitization studies focus on legitimization from the side of the authorities, while protest studies focus on legitimization by the movements. Both literatures often overlook the *interaction* between the authorities and protestors: both sides of the struggle may take the other's moves into account, the moves of the other side may become part of the proximate context in these contentious social processes. I argue here that the theory of securitization provides a single framework for studying both sides of this struggle.

The need to see protest legitimization as a result of an interaction is apparent when one remembers that in post-totalitarian[9] states such as China, social movements and protracted protests generally operate under some degree of repression, which is often also the primary motive for the activists to produce protective identity framings. As such, there is nothing new in the notion that social movements and authorities interact with each other on the level of identities that play a key role in mobilization and repression. Indeed, the idea that the success or failure of social movements is largely dependent on the interaction between activists and authorities (the state) was already clear in the 'political opportunity structure' approach to social movements of Charles Tilly (1978).[10] It has also been noted that this interaction holds true on the level of identities. As Sidney Tarrow (1998: 22) argues, the state always engages in a 'struggle over meanings' with the movements, and this struggle includes identity avowals and imputations on both sides (Hunt *et al.* 1994: 185–86).

Furthermore, it has been noted that framings are not built from scratch but usually employ 'resonant ideas' or the vernacular of 'cognitive maps' of societies. According to Doug McAdam (1994: 37–38), the central task in framing is to advocate a view that both legitimizes and motivates protest activity, and its success is partly determined by the 'cultural resonance' of the frames the activists draw on.[11] The audience of protests is therefore seldom offered new, and perhaps alien, ideas. Instead, mobilization draws on existing ideas which are applied creatively to the situation, something which is called 'frame alignment' (Snow and Benford 1988).[12] Alternatively, Chaim Perelman (1988) termed this phenomenon the 'precontracts or premises' that form the self-evident beginning-point for the argument a political speaker is making to the audience. The speaker attempts to fuse the obviousness of the shared undercurrent with the argument s/he is presenting. Precontracts have cultural resonance, which makes the movement and its identities appear natural and its message familiar (Gamson 1988: 227). They can also help to evoke emotions that are needed to get collective action going (Tarrow 1998: 111).[13]

Ideologies are an especially salient source of frames and resonant ideas in totalitarian settings, and they can therefore guide both individual and collective identities and actions. Ideologies also provide a ready value base upon which social movements and their activists can construct their identities and legitimization (Rokeach 1979; Warren 1990). Both the Chinese Democracy Wall Movement of the late 1970s and the student movement of 1989 relied on socialist morals and attempted to align their identity talk accordingly (Paltemaa and Vuori 2006). While the identity talk of FLG in the 2000s draws and relies more on values that predate both the CCP and the PRC, in the 1990s FLG's identity talk was much more in line with socialist morals. In the 1990s, Li and his followers tried to operate within the boundaries of the 'allowed' in the Chinese political order.

Countermoves to securitization and the legitimization of resistance

While the construction of security issues is a very useful political tool for powerholders, this political move can also be resisted. It is indeed important to keep in mind that neither the linguistic nor the social felicity conditions of securitization are entirely determining: no-one can be guaranteed the success of their utterances of securitization, as this is up to the audience. Both the linguistic and social felicity conditions are necessary, but neither are sufficient conditions for successful securitization. As an open social process, securitization can always fail (Wæver 1995; cf. Derrida 1988). The success or failure of the political aims sought by the means of securitization is an even wider and more contingent social issue than the success or failure of achieving a security status for an issue.

Here I view processes of securitization as a type of political game constituted by moves and countermoves. Just as securitization is one specific type of media-frame among many (Vultee's Chapter 4 in the present volume), securitization/desecuritization moves are a specific set of tactics among a larger group of tactics in a suppressor's or resister's 'playbook'. It is possible to suppress and to resist without securitization/desecuritization, but this would entail different costs than action with successful securitization/desecuritization. From this point of view, processes of securitization are a much smaller group of phenomena than processes of social mobilization and its suppression in general. Social mobilization and its suppression can be based and achieved by a variety of tactics, yet the logic of security is one of the strongest among these moves.

Accordingly, I view desecuritization here as a counter-strategy or-move to securitization. Desecuritization has largely been understood in terms of deconstructing collective identities in situations where relations between 'friends' and 'enemies' are constituted by existential threats; i.e., they are securitized. For Wæver, desecuritization is a process by which security issues lose their 'securityness', and are no longer restrictive by nature.[14] Andreas Behnke (2006: 65) sees desecuritization as a 'withering away': explicit debate on whether something no longer is a security issue retains the logic and possibility of securitization. For him, desecuritization can only happen through lack of speech. I argue here however that explicit speech acts can at times be desecuritization moves: whether or not something is successfully desecuritized may perhaps depend on a withering away, but this withering may begin with active moves.[15]

The question whether desecuritization is withering away dependant on silence, or whether desecuritization can or even has to be an active performative is an issue, in Searle's (1995: 106) terms, of the termination of institutional facts: here desecuritization is seen as terminating the institutional fact of a securitized issue. In Searle's view, when a conventional power is destroyed, the negation operates on the collective acceptance and not on the content of the acceptance. In terms of securitization, this means that an 'act of desecuritization' would translate as 'we no longer accept (X is an existential threat to Y)'. Josef Moural (2002: 283–84) however argues that Searle's formula would not allow the distinction between a formal termination of a social institution and a collapse of a social institution (e.g. the difference between a divorce and the collapse of marriage acceptance). 'An act of desecuritization' would therefore be perhaps better phrased as 'we accept (X is no longer an existential threat to Y).'[16]

The question is about whether security is an institutional fact that needs maintenance:[17] is securitization like a wedding (once it is done you do not have to care about it) or is it like a marriage that needs maintenance? In the case of desecuritization: is it a divorce, or is it a collapse of a marriage (a formal procedure, a shared disbelief in the continued existence of the marriage, or a lack of belief in a wedding having taken place)?[18]

I argue here that especially in non-democratic settings such as the PRC, securitization and desecuritization provide one possible logic for legitimizing repression and resistance respectively, while the vocabulary of both of these is drawn from the resonant values, myths, laws, and proclamations of the authorities. As an attempt to raise the cost of resistance, authorities resort to framing activists with identities that make them appear as a threat to certain referent objects which are usually some valuable goals of the regime. Activists then attempt to desecuritize their movement by invoking identities that are aligned with these same values and framing their activities as conducive to them, not as threats. Although constructing identities for a movement serves other important functions as well (such as the mobilization of popular support and providing the participants with a sense of belonging, commitment, and legitimacy of collective action) (Gecas 2000: 95–100; Polletta and Jasper 2001, these functions are not mutually exclusive. A good frame satisfies all of them. However, the necessity of responding to the issue of security is forced on activists and becomes a prime constraint on their identity framings.

The question of social capital (Bourdieu 1991) is also related to identity framings. It would seem that, almost by definition, social movements lack the social capital needed for achieving desecuritization, capital which the authorities have stored in their formal positions. Desecuritizing the movement is nevertheless something that movements must try to bring about if they are faced with soft repression (denial of their identity frames by the authorities) in the form of securitization (imputations of negative identities on them). This is made possible by direct appeals to various audiences through the use of resonant collective and activist identities that carry moral authority and therefore endow their carriers with social capital, such as popular support and approval. Furthermore, movements can also engage in the persuasion of leading authority figures in the authoritarian polity in order to make them declare the movement acceptable. Through the use of resonant collective and individual identities the activists can also try to utilize possible fissures among the authorities and make those they deem responsive use their social capital to desecuritize the movement and thereby grant its activists the right of social activism.

Should this desecuritization strategy fail to remedy the situation, and as the costs of resisting increase, activists may turn to tactics which can be termed reverse-securitization and counter-securitization. In a reverse-securitization discourse, the activists reflect the security arguments of the authorities back at them in the same terms, i.e. they frame the adversaries' identities in exactly the same terms as they frame the movement. In a way, they try to present themselves as a 'matched pair' (Buzan and Wæver 2009) with the authorities, a status which could increase their social capital if their move were to succeed. This kind of reverse-securitization was apparent in both the Democracy Wall Movement and the 1989 Student Democracy Movement in China (Paltemaa and Vuori 2006). Activists could however discard the vocabulary of the authorities, and instead turn to counter-securitization, where the authorities are still securitized, but the identity frames are not the same as the ones the authorities use. Activists could turn to other reservoirs of cultural resonance prevalent in the wider society, or they could turn to their own inner discourses.

In the contest for rightful social mobilization and the repression of mobilization in Mainland China, the authorities have securitized **FLG** as an 'evil cult' that jeopardizes Chinese national security, while Li Hongzhi and his disciples have used a mixture of desecuritization, reverse-securitization, and counter-securitization as their moves. Let us now turn our attention to how this contest has played out.

The Falungong's rise to the security agenda in China

The 1980s was a decade of a crisis of faith vis-à-vis Chinese socialism. The last decades of the Mao era had reduced the authority of party administrators, and the loosening of socialist morals along with Deng Xiaoping's economic reforms increased cynicism towards the party. The dissatisfaction with incessant corruption and nepotism culminated in the mass-protests of 1989 and their eventual violent suppression.

The crisis of faith and increased cynicism towards the party led many people in China to search for new spirituality from qigong, especially as the party had to an extent loosened its control on religious practice in the 1980s (Lai 2006). Other sources of appeal qigong had included, first the failure of the health-care system, which left poor elderly people looking for alternative ways of maintaining their health,[19] second the negative effects of modernizing society, which lead to resistance against modern ideas and modernity, and third new opportunities to build solidarity networks, when for example those of the work-unit were lost. The majority of FLG practitioners were middle-aged or retired women (Tong 2002). This correlates with the disproportionate laying off of middle-aged women in reforming state owned enterprises (Perry and Selden 2003; Lee 2003).

In the early 1990s, even the party supported the practice of qigong, which was seen as apolitical activity together with other traditional folk-beliefs like fengshui. The Chinese origin of qigong fit well with the calls for patriotism and nationalism that the party emphasised. As a result, qigong-masters rose to celebrity status during the 'qigong-fever' gripping China. Li Hongzhi[20] who introduced a new qigong-system called Falungong or Falun Dafa in 1992 was the master of the qigong-group which claimed to be the largest in China.

Li's system differs from most qigong-systems in that it also contains religious beliefs and an ethical code.[21] These combine Buddhism, Daoism and traditional Chinese folk-beliefs with millenniarianism[22] and supernatural beliefs (Chang 2004). It has proven to be very difficult to classify FLG as it is not a splinter group from any world religion (Wong and Liu 1999).[23]

In the early 1990s FLG was known only for its qigong while the religious beliefs and ethical code that are an integral part of the system were mostly unknown (Hua and Xia 1999). This meant that FLG was not considered a direct threat to the party and it had a legal status. The party's control apparatus closed its proverbial eyes from practices like qigong and fengshui. As the popularity of FLG began to rise, its religious and ethical aspect also received more attention. Li's main work, Zhuan Falun (Turning the Law-Wheel) was banned in 1996. There was also a gradual increase in campaigning against the sectarian group, but it remained uncoordinated.

Although Li and his followers have denied having any worldly political goals (Li 1999a), the practitioners did not view the banning of Li's works favourably, and they organised protests against the defaming of Falungong (Renmin Ribao August 5 1999d). Initially these protests were successful, for example some local TV-stations recanted critical reports on the practitioners' activities.

The protestors seemed to be following the script of 'rightful resistance'. For example, they were seeking the attention of political elites by protesting near the leadership compound of the CCP on April 25 1999 by behaving orderly and presenting a petition for officially recognizing the FLG as a benefit for society to the authorities, in line with ancient Chinese traditions and practices of the CCP. FLG practitioners were protesting the banning of FLG literature, the treatment of protestors imprisoned after a previous protest in Tianjin and a critical article on FLG by He Zuoxiu, a researcher at the National Academy of Sciences. But as has been noted by O'Brien (1996), even rightful resistance has its limits.

The authorities utilised a range of tactics in its anti-FLG campaign. These included securitizing FLG as a threat to socialism, the ridiculing of Li[24] and separating the majority of hapless followers from a 'small group of evildoers', portraying the practicing of FLG as unpatriotic, and setting FLG into a security continuum[25] with the international anti-cult campaign and even the 'war on terror'.

The authorities' tactics of delegitimizing Falungong

Jiang Zemin increased the anti-FLG campaign to the level of a crackdown three months after the Zhongnanhai protests of 1999. This happened in the proximate context of national and international crises: massive floods and the tenth anniversary of the violent suppression of the student movement of 1989 created internal pressure, while the bombing of the Chinese embassy in Belgrade by NATO forces and Taiwanese President Lee Teng-hui's move towards 'state-to-state' relations in the Taiwan question provided a sense of international crisis.

The propaganda campaign[26] employed cadres for millions of hours during the two-year active phase of the campaign.[27] Anti-FLG activities took charge of the political agenda. Even television news broadcasts were extended to an hour to present this new threat to the state and the Chinese. It could not be unclear to anyone that FLG was considered dangerous by the party, and thus also dangerous to anyone who continued to practice it. FLG publications and tapes were confiscated and destroyed on a massive scale and websites related to the practice were closed down or blocked.

Falungong as a threat to socialism

The regime approached the problem of FLG from an ideological point of view. Li Hongzhi had introduced a belief system that was in complete contradiction with communist ideology. In addition to this, FLG requires that its followers give up their old beliefs and only follow the preaching of FLG. These elements of FLG were a serious concern 'involving the fundamental beliefs of the communists, the fundamental ideological foundation of the entire nation, and the fate of our party and state' (Renmin Ribao July 23 1999b), while the activities and teachings of FLG had 'seriously endangered the general mood of society, endangered social stability, and endangered the overall political situation' (Ibid.). FLG has also been said to be a 'plot to overthrow China's socialist system by hostile foreign powers' (Renmin Ribao January 1 2001). This was in line with the long tradition of party campaigns against 'counterrevolutionaries' and 'rightists' who were pawns in the 'international conspiracy to topple socialist rule in China'.[28]

Adding FLG to this tradition facilitated its appearance as a threat to the party. The threat of FLG was also facilitated by other historical experiences. The party was keenly aware of the role of religious movements in the collapse of socialist systems in Europe, especially that of Poland (Lam 2000). China also has an impressive amount of quasi-religious popular uprisings in its own history: in the eighteenth and nineteenth centuries almost every popular uprising was somehow connected to religious movements (Yang 1961).[29] As with FLG, these movements did not have a clear ideological or political doctrine, but they were formed around one or more charismatic figures and fuelled by a general discontent with the current state of society and the religious euphoria generated by the religious leader-cum-savior. Li Hongzhi could be perceived as the next in line of these self-appointed mouths of truth who had arrived to save the Chinese people from governmental oppression.[30]

The sudden appearance of such a massive group[31] of semi-religious protestors without prior warning from security intelligence signalled a lapse in control. The vagueness of the FLG doctrine and its 'organization without organization' was also a cause for concern. FLG had organized itself into a national network, developing, in the eyes of the regime, into a strong political power that could challenge the party and government. FLG was a form of system-crisis as it provided an alternative system of social organization for socially alienated people, for the ones who had not reaped the benefits of reform and consequently did not recognise modernity and economic prosperity as a source of legitimacy. FLG also represented a genuinely Chinese alternative for moral leadership in China. This combined with the mass support (estimates of the amount of people involved in this spiritual group exceeded those belonging to the party), organizational prowess (FLG had succeeded in organizing concerted protest activities all around China), and rumours of even top-level cadres involved in FLG made it seem like a secret society, the likes of which have toppled rulers in Chinese history.[32] In the distal context of Chinese politics, FLG seemed to have a great threat potential for the CCP, even though the majority of practitioners were 'grannies in the park'.

The leadership justified the crackdown on FLG and other 'evil cults' on its laws and regulations on the registration and management of mass organizations, on assembly, parades, and demonstrations, on the administration of public security, and on the criminal law (Fazhi Ribao July 25 1999), turning the issue into a legal one. To gain further legitimacy for its campaign, the government passed a law prohibiting heretical cults. Since FLG did not have official recognition, and it had failed to follow regulations relating to the registration of mass organizations for example, it and all its activities were illegal.

The law on heretical cults, and the judicial interpretation of the Supreme People's Court, define a cult as any unauthorized group that 'disturbs social order and jeopardizes people's lives or property' or 'endangers society by fabricating and spreading superstitious heresies'. Particularly serious transgressions are listed in the law as: 'setting up transprovincial, transregional, and transmunicipal organizations', 'collaborating with overseas organizations and individuals', and publishing 'large amounts of materials'.[33] A cult could thus be any autonomous social group that is capable of large-scale concerted action. It is clear that the law is aimed at the organizational structure of cults at least as much as at their religious beliefs. This illustrates that the regime is actually more concerned with the organizational potential of social groups than with their ideology or religious beliefs. This threat is obviously considered severe, as after the legislation banning heretical cults, it has been possible to classify religious crimes as crimes endangering national security.[34] These crimes can carry a sentence of life imprisonment or even the death penalty. Even though new legislation was passed the old method of sending 'class-enemies' to labor re-education camps with local administrative decisions without trial was the preferred means of detaining FLG practitioners for longer periods (Seymor 2005).

Because the regime denies it opposes qigong practice or the freedom of religion,[35] it was not obvious that the spread of FLG was a political struggle. This is why FLG had to be presented as directly opposing Marxist ideology and science, and contending the position of the party, which legitimate, patriotic qigong and religion do not do. FLG was a matter of national security as 'the generation and spread of Falun Gong is a political struggle launched by hostile forces both in and outside the country to contend with our party for the masses and for battle positions' (Renmin Ribao July 24 1999c). Marxist ideology was claimed to be under threat from these hostile forces:

> we are exposing and castigating Li Hongzhi and his Falun Gong precisely for the purpose of adhering to Marxist materialism and science, opposing idealism and theism, and for the purpose of upholding the political beliefs of Communists and the ideological basis for united struggle by the people of the whole country.
>
> (Ibid.)

From the point of view of the party, the use of force or any other means at its disposal is justified in repelling these kinds of political threats. 'Stability and unity' require drastic measures against threats to them. The authoritative securitization of FLG already on its own constituted a form of soft repression. It also formed the basis of legitimacy for the subsequent forms of hard repression that were used as the securitization of FLG was not sufficient in suppressing its activities.

Defaming Li Hongzhi and separating him from his followers

One of the lines of attack against FLG was the defaming of Li Hongzhi. This was also evident in the beginning circulars of the anti-FLG campaign, as the 'The life and times of Li Hongzhi' (Renmin Ribao July 23 1999a) presented a biography that challenged the supernatural claims presented in FLG's biographies[36] of Li, disputes his birthday coinciding with that of Sakuyamuni, and listed various nefarious deeds by Li.

Putting major emphasis on refuting Li's claims about his life and supernatural abilities underlines the interactive nature of resistance and repression. Even the initial acts of soft-repression by the authorities exhibited this tendency, which was also to become apparent in Li's resistance to the authorities' securitization arguments.

In the CCP's biography of Li, he was portrayed as being nothing special, dishonest, and merely a swindler who was deceiving trustworthy Chinese out of their fortunes and endangering even their lives through his superstitions (Renmin Ribao July 23 1999a). In accordance with these claims an arrest warrant was issued for Li, which was also pursued through Interpol.

Part of this tactic was to separate the masses from the 'small group of people behind the deceived masses' – the usual way to portray protest as the work of a small minority in China. It was these trouble-makers that threatened the internal stability of the PRC, not the average practitioners deceived by Li's dangerous superstitions. This tactic allowed the dismissal of the importance of the large numbers of FLG practitioners; the masses were not dismissing CCP authority or reality, it was merely the anti-China forces behind Li and FLG. This tactic also allowed the qualification of the securitization: loyal Chinese should be compelled by this act of 'securitization for control' (Vuori 2008). If practitioners would recant their beliefs, they could be allowed to join the ranks of obedient citizens. The perhaps paradoxical tactic of emphasizing the dangers of FLG and talking its leader down underlined that the real danger emanated from the anti-China forces behind the charlatanic figure of Li.

'Practicing Falungong is unpatriotic'

FLG's social function was problematic for the party, as the justification of party rule in the post-Mao era has rested on symbolic order and social unity, which have been seen as requirements for China's rise. The party labelled FLG as a threat to social stability, and by extension to China's rise and prosperity. The 'evil cult' was branded unpatriotic while the party could rekindle its patriotic struggle against hostile foreign powers that would see China subjugated.

The campaign provided the authorities with another vessel of self-description and positive identity framing. The use of identity frames has the same function for the authorities who try to suppress movements they deem undesirable, as it has for social movements that try to frame their identities as positive; authorities also want to garnet support and legitimize their policies. Non-democratic leaderships, like the one in China, often frame themselves as the savior and guarantor of the nation, which excludes alternative representation of the state and alternative political or social orders and actors within it (Holm 2004). In this vein, the legitimization of CCP rule has rested on its claim to be the sole guardian of 'benevolence, truth, and glory' (Shue 1994). The nation is built on a narrative or myth of struggle, with a pantheon of national heroes ranging from glorious workers to the fathers of ideology. For example, the preamble of the Constitution of the People's Republic of China emphasizes the struggle against imperialism and feudalism, and the role of the CCP in this arduous struggle. In China, the unification of the country and the hostility of foreign powers, as well as some 'bad elements' of Chinese society, are the building blocks of national history writing, and much of official popular culture. Such reification of an encircled 'us' by the regime renews discipline, legitimizes the use of repression, and maintains a crucial link between the leadership and the people (Bourdieu 1991). This also informs the images and labels the regime is likely to give those it deems its enemies.[37]

In addition to affirming the patriotic tie between party and people, the continued struggle also legitimated and called for renewed discipline. Claimed threats to public order and security, like FLG, provide the party with arguments for maintaining the most enduring means of protecting its rule, like the possibility of sending people to labour re-education camps through local administrative decisions, without trial.

Security continuums

From very early on, FLG was portrayed as part of the international struggle against cults. Chinese authorities often listed FLG together with the Solar Temple cult, the movement of the restoration of God's Ten Commandments, and Aum Shinrikyo. These types of 'cults' are claimed to 'wantonly preach the fallacy of "the end of the world", destroy social stability and jeopardize the lives and property of the public' (People's Daily October 9 2007).[38]

The anti-cult aspect of the campaign became especially prevalent after the self-immolation event on Tiananmen Square in January 23 2001. A video of seven people trying to burn themselves on Tiananmen Square was widely broadcast in China, and it seemed to turn the tide in favor of the authorities' campaign, as it appeared to validate the dangers of following Li's doctrines.[39]

The CCP also constructed another security continuum linking the legitimacy of fighting terrorism to FLG after the worldwide attention to terrorism in 2001. Although mainly aimed against China's insurgency and political separatist movements in Xinjiang, the campaign against the 'three evils', namely separatism, religious extremism, and terrorism, linked the FLG to separatist and terrorist groups through this continuum.[40]

Although not presented as terrorists or separatists, this security continuum framed FLG practitioners' identities in the same canvas as the gravest threats to national security. The self-immolation event in 2001 facilitated this framing, as self-immolation was viewed as 'religious extremism'. The framing was also useful in the international campaign, as FLG was not only tied to the struggle against (death) cults, but now also terrorism.

Still in the run-up to the Seventeenth Party Congress in 2007 this security continuum was quite evident. Zhou Yongkang, the minister of public security and a member of the politburo at the time, is quoted by the BBC as saying: 'All police should . . . strike hard on overseas and domestic hostile forces, ethnic splittists, religious extremists, violent terrorists and the Falun Gong cult so as to safeguard national security and social stability.'[41]

Together these tactics framed the issue of FLG as an issue of 'contradictions between the people and their enemies', one of the most influential doctrines of Mao Zedong defining the correct handling of contradictions among the people. This framing defined FLG as an enemy, as a threat to national security, although this status was qualified: those who chose to refute their beliefs could be accepted back into the 'people'. Those who would remain outside, would not only be the target of labeling, but also methods of hard repression remaining from the Mao era.

Falungong's 'Rightful Resistance' – desecuritization moves by Li Hongzhi

Unlike the Chinese democracy movements (e.g. Democracy Wall and the 1989 student movement) Li did not embed the legitimacy and rightfulness of his doctrine and practice in socialist dogma, although his doctrines are also influenced by socialist morality. Li was mostly drawing on a much older reservoir of resonance, 'traditional Chinese values'.

In FLG's identity talk, FLG is presented as a cultivation practice that promotes good health and moral living. According to Li, his teachings are non-political and non-violent. By cultivating their bodies and morality, FLG will save the world: 'We are cultivators, people walking the road to godhood, we transcend the human world, and we neither seek nor covet the fame and profit found in this world' (Li 2005).

In the FLG biographies of Li, he is presented in a very similar way to Maoist model comrades like Lei Feng. The definitions for the three-part moral code of FLG – truth, benevolence, and forbearance (*zhen*, *shan*, *ren*), are very similar to socialist moral instructions: one should tell the truth and help the weak. Li also stressed his duty towards the people and his social rather than individual goals. He claims to be improving the morality and health of people, and as a result, stabilizing society, in accordance with party doctrines:[42] 'I, Li Hongzhi, unconditionally help practitioners improve human morality and keep people healthy, which stabilizes society; and with their healthy bodies, people can better serve society. Isn't this bringing good fortune to the people in power?' (Li 1999b). 'I have always though the government and the leaders would want to see every Chinese become a person with lofty morals' (Li 1999a).

This type of identity talk aligns the 'nature' of FLG in accordance with the goals of the CCP, thus denying the possibility of being a threat to it. Similarly, as the anti-FLG campaign has gone on, Li has directly refuted both the party's self-descriptions and the representations of FLG as unpatriotic. This illustrates the interactive nature of the struggle, but may also indicate that the party's tactics and campaigns have been successful (see for example Li 2005).

In the FLG biography of Li, he is presented as having a lack of interest in politics or social organizations. As a youth Li did not join the Red Guards during the Cultural Revolution, although according to the biography he was asked to join many times. Li's lack of organizational interests was a positive attribute[43] in 1992 for qigong practitioners (Penny 2003: 659), and also a means of deflecting the attention of authorities.

Once the soft-repression of FLG began, Li responded by repeating the self-representations already constructed in his previous writings, but emphasized aspects of them as desecuritization arguments. He continued the line of not having any worldly political goals, and of definitely not being anti-party in his open letter to the Central Committee of the party:

> Falun Gong is merely a popular activity for practicing gong. It has no organization, and even less does it have any political objectives. Nor has it ever participated in any antigovernmental activity. I am a [gong] practitioner and have never had anything to do with political power.
>
> (Li 1999a)

The question of 'getting political' has remained an important aspect of Li's desecuritization moves:

> The crux of the matter, it would seem, is that a cultivator's motive is to stop the persecution, and not to 'get political' for the sake of gaining human political power. Cultivators have no desire for power among men: just the opposite, cultivators are to let go of any attachment to power.
>
> (Li 2007)

In accordance with his claims of 'not having gone political', Li separates himself from *The Epoch Times*,[44] which have published the *Nine Commentaries on the Communist Party* (The Epoch Times 2004), although he has endorsed the publication at times. The Commentaries lay out a history of CCP oppression, portray the CCP as an 'evil cult' and Jiang Zemin as a 'tool of evil', and posit the FLG with the most oppressed groups in world history undergoing a 'genocide' at the hands of the CCP. In tandem with the Commentaries, *The Epoch Times* claims that over 27 million Chinese have resigned from the CCP.[45] The Commentaries is a clear anti-party document,[46] which is perhaps why Li does not attribute it to himself (see e.g. Li 2005).

In the 1990s, the majority of FLG practitioners' desecuritization moves were identity framings, which aimed at refuting the securitization moves of the authorities. These acts focused on self-description and criticized the CCP only implicitly. In the 2000s this however has changed.

Upping the ante: counter-securitization of the CCP and Jiang Zemin

When FLG practitioners continued to defy the rituals of conformity by publicly performing FLG and protesting the campaign against it – FLG practitioners still continue their resistance a decade after the launching of the anti-Falungong campaign – the government began to use stronger measures against the group. The campaign led to the most extensive series of arrests since 1989. Hundreds of torture and dozens of death in incarceration cases have been reported outside of China.[47]

Self-representation is still a major part of FLG activists' struggle with the CCP. However, as these desecuritization moves have proven unsuccessful, and as the campaign against FLG became more intense, starting from late 2000 Li, FLG practitioners and other groups sympathetic to FLG began to express the struggle in terms of defining the opponent, the CCP and especially Jiang Zemin. Li declared that FLG disciples were undergoing the period of 'Fa-rectification':[48]

> Dafa disciples amidst Fa-rectification have a different situation from when personal cultivation was done in the past. In the face of the groundless harming, in the face of Dafa's persecution, and in the face of the injustice forced upon us, we cannot handle things or categorically accept things the way it was done before in personal cultivation, because Dafa disciples are now in the Fa-rectification period.
>
> (Li 2001b)

Just as heterodox religious organizations were harassed and driven underground in Confucian China, leading to a self-fulfilling prophecy of them 'going political', the party is driving the 'evil cults' of today underground. Whether or not it had been on the agenda of these organizations, the campaign against them has led to them engaging in politics and explicitly resisting party rule, which can be seen outside of China in protests at the gates of Chinese embassies, during Chinese state visits, and in publications supporting FLG. The battle is also waged online,[49] as FLG spreads its message while FLG is one of the major targets of China's as vast Internet-censorship and control operation.

After denying having 'gone political' for many years, in 2007 even Li admits that 'going political' could be what FLG is and should be doing:

> If when the world's media are kept silent by incentives and disincentives from the CCP, Dafa disciples' forming their own media to counter the persecution and save the world's people is labeled 'political', then let's go ahead and confidently make use of 'politics' to expose the persecution and save sentient beings!
>
> (Li 2007)

In the counter-securitization discourse among FLG practitioners Jiang Zemin is portrayed as 'the highest representative of the evil force in the human world' who is being used by higher beings to persecute FLG.[50] Only by eliminating the evil can FLG practitioners return home through consummation of the Falun Dafa paradise; if disciples fail and recant the Fa, they cannot reach consummation. As a result Jiang Zemin is an existential threat to the Falun Dafa paradise and the salvation of the practitioners. As Li Hongzhi's task is to save humanity during this period of the 'end of times' by restoring humanity's morality, Jiang becomes an existential threat to the entire world: 'The moment the party and that evil ringleader [i.e. Jiang Zemin] exclaimed that they wanted to "defeat Falun Gong," the gods gave the verdict that the party must be dissolved and destroyed' (Li 2005).

This counter-securitization discourse comes close to Barend ter Haar's 'demonological paradigm' (Haar 2002). According to him, the demonological paradigm has been used in China to form a dyad of us (*tianxia*, all under heaven) and them (*yaoguai*, demons). During political strife, for example during the Taiping rebellion, real people could be defined in demonic terms, and become the target of the most severe violent acts.[51] In Chinese traditional beliefs, demons are believed to reside in liminal spaces (e.g. doorways, bridges, cross-sections of roads) and liminal times (e.g. the fifteenth day of the seventh month is the period of the ghost festival). Li's declaration of the era of fa-rectification coincides with this belief, as during fa-rectification the whole world is in a liminal state, and thus demons are widely abound: 'China's Labor Re-education Camps are dark dens of evil forces. Most of the disciplinary guards there are reincarnated minor ghosts from hell' (Li 2000a). '[T]he way the evil beings are currently performing shows that they are now completely without human nature and without righteous thoughts' (Li 2001c).

The exorcism of demons has been used to legitimize the use of violence in China. This tradition may also explain Mao's use of quasi-religious language like 'ox-demons', 'snake-demons', 'evil spirits', and 'poisonous weeds' in his political rhetoric and practices like 'loyalty dances' that were prevalent in Maoist politics (Perry and Selden 2003). These concepts and practices[52] have long traditions and there was widespread awareness of demonic folklore in China,[53] and thus cultural resonance that could be used to guide popular traditions in support of the CCP.[54] During the Mao era, demons were replaced with 'struggle' and 'counterrevolution', which retained the grammatical relationships of the demonological paradigm: counterrevolution was a violent threat that had to be answered with equal counterviolence (Haar 2002: 54).[55]

While the CCP securitizes FLG as a threat to socialism, FLG practitioners engaged in counter-securitization demonize Jiang Zemin. Li has also used demonization against other forms of qigong by labeling them as *xiejiao* (heterodox teachings, evil religion, evil cult), which is the label used by the CCP in describing FLG, and demonized even practitioners claiming to be cultivating FLG.[56]

The counter-securitization of the CCP and Jiang Zemin has legitimated – if not breaking – at least altering the rules of FLG. In the early teachings of Li, disciples were told to give up their worldly attachments while cultivating among humans. Still in 1999, as response to the anti-FLG campaign, Li stated: 'We do not oppose the government now, nor will we do so in the future. Other people may treat us badly, but we cannot treat other people badly. We cannot regard people as enemies' (Li 1999c).

In the period of Fa-rectification, i.e. under an existential threat to faith itself (Laustsen and Wæver 2000), it is allowed to 'go beyond forbearance': 'If the evil has already reached the point where it is unsavable and unkeepable, then various measures at different levels can be used to stop it and eradicate it. Going beyond the limits of Forbearance is included in the Fa's principles' (Li 2001c).

During Fa-rectification, Li calls all disciples to 'step forward' and actively engage the 'evil'. So far, 'stepping forward' has meant going to Tiananmen Square, spreading the 'truth', and other activities that express true faith and challenge the CCP. Even these can entail high costs for individuals engaged in such activities. Li claims that should a disciple be captured and be 'persecuted', 'sending righteous thoughts' will protect true believers from all acts of violence, as these will be turned against the torturers themselves. 'Sending righteous thoughts' is told by Li to also help him eradicate the evil he is in battle with almost constantly. Only by eradicating this evil can consummation be reached, as Li will not allow his disciples to 'leave' until the campaign is over.

The interactive nature of counter-securitization is also apparent when Li legitimizes 'stepping forward':

> We haven't been involved in political struggles, whether it be our going to Tiananmen Square, going to Zhongnanhai, or clarifying the truth to people in all sorts of situations. This is because if the evil hadn't persecuted us, we wouldn't need to explain the truth to people whatsoever.
>
> (Li 2000c)

The 'evil' that Li is fighting is still in other dimensions. Patsy Rahn (2002) however sees the potential of the demonizing paradigm in legitimizing not only acts against 'demons' in 'other dimensions', but even the use of violence in this world.[57] Thus far, Li is limiting the measures against the oppressors to 'sending righteous thoughts' and 'stepping forward':

> [Y]ou may stop them [human beings doing acts against gods] by taking all kinds of approaches, such as exposing the evil acts, clarifying the truth, and directly telephoning those people. [. . .] [Y]ou can stop them with righteous thoughts. [. . .] When [. . .] the wicked policemen are using electric batons or when bad people are injecting drugs to persecute you, you can use your righteous thoughts to redirect the electric current or the drugs back to the person doing violence to you.
>
> (Li 2004a)

> [M]obilize your greater abilities, disintegrate all of the dark minions and rotten demons, and eliminate the final disruptions that are in other dimensions.
>
> (Li 2004b)

While Li has engaged in counter-securitization of the evil that is the CCP, his disciples in *The Epoch Times* have portrayed features of reverse-securitization in their securitization of the CCP and Jiang Zemin. In the *Nine Commentaries on the Communist Party*, the CCP is portrayed as the largest cult in history (The Epoch Times 2004: xix), reversing the authorities accusations of FLG being an 'evil cult': 'The Communist Party is essentially an evil cult that harms mankind' (Ibid.: 236), and placed the CCP as the worst case on an anti-cult continuum with death cults like Aum shinrikyo and the Solar Temple cult (Ibid.: 246). Similarly, Jiang Zemin's

LIVERPOOL JOHN MOORES UNIVERSITY LEARNING SERVICES

family, background is claimed to be fabricated, mirroring what the CCP claims about Li Hongzhi's biographies (Ibid.: 118–19, 126). As the CCP portrays FLG as being totally opposite to Marxist science, the CCP is argued to directly contradict traditional Chinese culture and undermine the cohesiveness of the Chinese nationality (Ibid.: 156, 185).

Li and his followers have used a mixture of desecuritization moves, reverse-securitization, and counter-securitization as tactics in their resistance. In the beginning FLG activities conformed with 'rightful resistance' but after the soft repression by the authorities began in earnest, Li was forced into engaging in desecuritization moves in his identity framings. As the desecuritization failed and the authorities turned to hard repression, Li began his counter-securitization moves, identifying the CCP as the tool of evil that is threatening the entire world and the FLG paradise of his disciples.

Conclusions

While focusing on European and 'Western' contexts, the majority of studies of securitization have not focused on either the 'targets' (i.e. the identified threats) of securitization, or on the interaction between the claims of securitizing actors and the claims by the 'targets'. I however argued in the present chapter that some processes of rhetorical struggle between authorities and social movements utilize security discourse to either legitimize social mobilization or to block it from the political arena. I used the combination of securitization/desecuritization theory and identity frame theory here to show how both protest legitimization and repression can be conceptualized within the same framework, and how their underlying logic can be deciphered.

In the **PRC**, especially with regard to social mobilization and repression, the stakes of applied identity frames are high as they are about the right to take part in social activism and/or the survival of the regime, and in the case of FLG, even the 'fate of the world'. It does not matter whether the activists or the authorities really believe or are sincere in their identity framings of themselves or their adversaries, or whether they are merely engaged in a political game of cynical manipulation. The approach I presented here does not deal with the sincerity of the actors or their 'real' motives. Regardless of the motives or sincerity of the proponents and opponents, the approach explains why certain types of frames are more likely to be used than others in justifying soft or hard repression and resistance to repression.

Although FLG, with its stated goals of bettering the health and morals of Chinese was tolerated at first, the FLG was a problem for Chinese authorities in that it provided an alternative world-view and social system for people who had not benefited from the economic reforms and thus did not view the increased material prosperity of the Chinese as a source of legitimacy for CCP rule. FLG overstepped the thresholds of allowed autonomous social mobilization and rightful resistance. In addition to curbing a potential political adversary, the anti-FLG campaign provided the CCP with an opportunity to reproduce its own positive identity-frames and to call for renewed discipline, in a period when Jiang Zemin was preparing to canonize his political legacy.

In the anti-FLG campaign FLG has been portrayed as an 'evil cult' in the service of hostile forces within and outside China that endangered individual people, social stability, and eventually even the sovereignty of the People's Republic. In response, Li Hongzhi tried to refute this label by referring to the lofty morals and the non-political aims of FLG. When this has not proven to be successful, Li has upped the ante of resistance by resorting to counter-securitization, and his disciples to reverse-securitization of the regime.

The campaign against the FLG has been portrayed for the practitioners of FLG as a persecution of FLG ordained in history, and perpetrated by evil forces. Most of the identity framings aimed at non-anointed-ones however do not focus on the supernatural evil of the CCP, but on the party's campaign violating human rights. Li has for example emphasized that the *Nine Commentaries on the CCP* should not be part of the material that explains FLG.[58] FLG should be framed as a pacifist meditation exercise, the practitioners of which are being persecuted by the CCP in violation of their human rights. This frame resonates with Western media, and accordingly the actual teachings of FLG often do not appear in Western media beyond repeating the three-part moral code of FLG, namely truth, benevolence, and forbearance. The story about FLG is Chinese human rights violations.

The findings presented here are generally useful in social movement research for revealing the centrality of security discourse in repression and protest legitimization in non-democratic political orders. Authorities in liberal systems can also resort to securitization of their opponents, as examples in Western history of the repression of radical left- or right-wing oppositions, or more recently fundamental Islamists, have shown. However, the exclusionary nature of non-democratic political systems makes it more likely that they will utilize security discourse, as the need to legitimize the possible use of extraordinary means (e.g. hard repression) to prevent other political actors from emerging in society arises at a much lower threshold than in liberal democratic contexts. Although there is no automatic or deterministic mechanism for deploying hard forms of repression after softer forms have been used, the use of soft forms of repression increases the likelihood of hard repression, as it lowers its costs both by intimidating or provoking activists engaged in resistance and justifying violence. Soft repression quite likely may end up upping the ante on both sides of the struggle. This has also been the case with Li Hongzhi and his disciples.

Notes

1   Falungong (法輪功) literally means law-wheel cultivation, or law-wheel qigong, while Falun Dafa, the other name used by FLG means the great law of the law-wheel. Falungong is usually written Falun Gong in English, but the direct pinyin transliteration of fǎlúngōng is used here. Qigong means the cultivation of qi- or cosmic energy, and is a general label for various styles of breathing exercises that often contain esoteric beliefs.

2   Chinese sectarianism has contained a wide spectrum of dissenting religious groups functioning outside the mainstream of clerical traditions. These groups have often been informed by an acute sense of eschatology and been preoccupied with hopes of salvation

in the impending doom of the essentially corrupt world of the present. They have often developed a salvational scheme that has not relied on temples and priests of either folk religion or state-recognized Daoism and Buddhism. These groups have often also created an alternative community that has provided identity, solidarity, and sustenance to its members, thus making families, lineage, and village communities obsolete (Shek 1990: 87–88).

3   Frames are here understood as interpretive schemata that simplify and condense 'the world out there by selectively punctuating and encoding objects, situations, events, experiences, and sequences of actions in one's past' (Snow and Benford 1992: 137). For security analysis utilising frame theory, see Eriksson (2001) and Bendrath *et al.* (2007).

4   Failed securitization has recently received more attention, see for example Salter (2008) and Vuori (2005).

5   As security is relational, claimed threats may also be relevant targets of study on the level of agents (cf. Balzacq's Chapter 2 in the present volume).

6   The logical theory of illocutionary acts is called illocutionary logic. John R. Searle and Daniel Vanderveken's (1985) objective was the formalization of the logical properties of illocutionary forces. Illocutionary logic can be used to study the entire range of possible illocutionary forces however they may be realised in particular natural languages and utterances of them. It is thus interested in all possible illocutionary forces and not just the actual realizations of these possibilities in actual speech and in actual languages. Searle and Vanderveken propose that speech acts are the basic form of human communication, and that speech acts can be divided into five elementary types (assertives, directives, commissives, expressives, and declarations).

7   Repression is understood here as 'any action by another group which raises the contender's cost of collective action' (Tilly 1978: 100). These actions of raising the contenders' costs can further be divided into hard and soft forms. Myra Marx Ferree (2005) argues that states engage in hard repression through use of force, and in soft repression when they try to limit and 'exclude ideas and identities from the public forum' in nonviolent ways. Soft repression is specifically directed against movements' collective identities and ideas that support 'cognitive liberation' or 'oppositional consciousness.' In non-democratic systems like China, the use of soft repression (e.g., labeling) is an integral part of hard repression (e.g., sending dissidents to labor camps). Both are used in unison, so that soft repression precedes hard repression.

8   'Identity talk' refers to processes whereby social movements' identities are constructed and expressed through communication among the movement's participants and with non-participants. It occurs, for example, when the activists explain the movement to others, recruit new members, proselytize their message by making public pronouncements, and engage in disputes and debates. Identities are also expressed in cultural materials, namely, names, narratives, symbols, verbal styles, rituals, clothing, and so on. See for example Snow and McAdam (2000) and Polletta and Jasper (2001: 285).

9   For post-totalitarianism, see Havel (1992). For applications to analysis of Chinese politics, see Lai (2006) and Paltemaa and Vuori (2009).

10 That movements' identity frames depend also on the way outsiders frame movements is noted in new social movement research, by Einwohner (2002). That identities are constructed also with strategic goals in mind is noted by Westby (2002).

11 Holger Strizel (2007: 369–70) separates the socio-linguistic reservoir of analogies and contracts from the socio-political context of more sedimented structures and positions of power. If securitizing actors are able to frame their discourse compatibly with existing linguistic reservoirs and they have positional power, they are more likely to succeed in getting their 'texts' as the dominant narrative.

12 Frank Pieke (1994) refers to what is basically the same phenomenon through the concept of 'recontextualization.'

13 In China this has been observed, for example, in the way the CCP mobilized its revolutionary movement through highly emotional frames deliberately designed for this purpose (Perry 2000; Snow and Benford 1988: 198–99).

14 Wæver has outlined three options for this: (1) simply not to talk about issues in terms of security, (2) to keep responses to securitized issues in forms that do not create security dilemmas and other vicious spirals, and (3) to move security issues back to 'normal politics.' See Wæver (1995; 2000: 253).

15 Jef Huysmans (1995: 65–67) has proposed three approaches for desecuritization strategies: 1) the objectivist strategy, 2) the constructivist strategy, and 3) the deconstructivist strategy. The objectivist strategy is premised on a traditional objective-subjective understanding of security: security has an objective content while subjective notions of this are either real or illusory. Someone intent on desecuritizing something with an objectivist argument would thus claim that something is not really a security problem. I argue that just as with securitization, this type of desecuritization strategy can be considered a speech act, and it also has felicity conditions related to the social capital of the enunciator of the argument, conditions related to the threat, and conditions related to the audience.

16 A good practical example of these two different understandings of desecuritization as a termination of institutional facts from an eroding totalitarian socialist setting are the failed securitization moves of the Socialistische Einheitspartie Deutschland (SED) in the German Democratic Republic (GDR). As Steven Pfaff (1996) has shown, the revolution in the GDR was conducted under the slogan, 'We Are the People,' which the protestors framed as their collective identity to thwart the prospect of a 'Chinese solution' to the demonstrations. The ruling party, the SED, attempted to frame the demonstrators as counterrevolutionaries, but failed and finally had to cede power. Ole Wæver (1989 and 1995) has emphasized that the fall of the SED was, *inter alia*, due to the failure of the securitization moves of the ruling party.

In a way, by stating 'We Are The People' and resisting the securitization of the 'West' by the authorities, the protestors were making the statement 'we no longer accept (X is an existential threat to Y)', i.e. the protestors no longer accepted that the 'West' was an existential threat to the people of the GDR. As the authorities gave way, and ceded to the slogans on the streets, they in a way made the statement 'we accept (X is no longer an existential threat to Y)', i.e. the SED authorities accepted that the 'West' was no longer an existential threat to the people of the GDR. The protestors made explicit moves towards dismantling the social institution of a securitized 'West', which the authorities eventually accepted. The authorities no longer maintained the securitization of the 'West' and the threat label withered away, it was desecuritized.

17 Searle (1995: 43): as long as people continue to recognise the X as having the status function of Y, the institutional fact is maintained.

18 This is in a way what the Barack Obama administration is debating regarding the question of whether 'waterboarding' and other 'harsh' interrogation methods were legal or illegal. CIA interrogators using these methods were under the belief that they had the right to use 'extraordinary measures', that the securitization of terrorism was in effect in legitimating these procedures. The Obama administration seems to be retracting the right to use torture as an 'extraordinary measure', they are in a way not recognizing that these methods would be justified even when terrorism in general is securitized. For the Obama administration, the marriage did not actually take place even though everyone present at the reception thought it did. For how the breadth of practical applications of securitizations can fluctuate, see Bendrath *et al.* (2007) and Salter (2008).

19 Patricia Thornton emphasises that the non-traditional, and non-medical methods of healing through the cultivation of paranormal capabilities is implicitly critical of 'scientific Marxism'. By claiming the body of the practitioner a private realm or 'open space', and by presenting a set of radically different values and doctrines, FLG departs from the CCP's prerogative of control. The somatization of personal social, moral and economic distress into bodily problems translates into a metonymical criticism of the Chinese 'body

politic'. Claiming to alter the body of the practitioner is a subversive act against Marxist doctrines (Thornton, 2002). Attaining 'consummation' in the FLG paradise would amount to the negation of the CCP and defection from the system of state control. Although Li Hongzhi may not have viewed his doctrine as a metaphysical escape from the Chinese political order, by claiming an alternative truth about the world, Li challenges the CCP on a cosmological level.

20 The most authoritative work by Li (1996) is Zhuan Falun. Li's writings can be downloaded from the FLG website, www.falundafa.org.

21 Also Zhonggong displays religious beliefs, and it too has been banned (Thornton 2003).

22 Millenarian communities generally consist of ethnocentric people, who perceive themselves as being disrupted by an evil power of seemingly demonic dimensions that upsets and menaces traditional ways of life. In the presence of such a danger, the community perceives itself as the chosen elect, whose task is to defend the community so that righteousness overcomes the evil. The most receptive audiences for millenarianism have been found in areas undergoing rapid social and economic change, which bring about cultural shocks and disorientation, disrupt existing socioeconomic orders, and have powerful impacts on ways of life (Rinehart 2006: 23). The rise in popularity of qigong in general and FLG in particular coincides with rapid socioeconomic changes of 1980–90s China. Ways of living and understandings of the world that predate the CCP have been preserved in China, and the socioeconomic tumults of the reform period combined with the loosening of socialist morals may explain the popularity of FLG's millenarian beliefs.

23 FLG has not always been viewed favourably even outside China, largely due to some of the doctrines of Li Hongzhi. Li is claimed to possess supernatural skills, like levitation and the ability to know the thoughts and doings of all his disciples (Li 2001a. Li (1997) also claims that aliens are among us, and trying to take over humanity through destroying human morality with empirical science and computers. As Li claims to cure his disciples, and as cultivation will keep practitioners healthy and illness free, going to hospital would betray their faith. He also discourages his followers from reading 'evil texts' that lie about FLG, meaning that only his teachings and writings are proper. Some of Li's views on homosexuals and modern society have also raised controversy. Li's system forms an antiscience, conservative critique of current morals, aesthetics, and the way of modern life, spiced up with supernatural beliefs, and presented in a strongly manichean way. For Li's claims see Li (1997 and 2001a).

24 This took many forms. One example is describing Li as an 'ex-army trumpet player' in the Party's official exposé of him (Renmin Ribao July 23 1999a).

25 The concept of security continuums comes form Didier Bigo's (e.g. 1994) studies of the internal security field in Europe. In a security continuum a general feeling of unease or insecurity is linked to a group of issues, e.g. terrorism, organized crime, and immigration as they are often listed together in official European documents without overarching justification for doing this. As a field effect, the fear of terrorism is grafted on to issues of migration. Security continuums can also be found in the Asian context, for example in Singapore where piracy and terrorism have been conflated in public official statements (Young and Valencia 2003), and in Australia where illegal migration has been connected to terrorism (Emmers 2004). In China the issue of North Korean immigration has also been framed in terms of security by the PLA (Curley 2004: 18), but the 'Strike Hard' and the campaign against the 'three evils' are the cases in point when discussing security continuums in contemporary China. The 'three evils' are also the Shanghai Cooperation Organization's main 'threat package' which has been used to securitize human trafficking by linking it with terrorism (Jackson 2006: 310).

26 Alan Kluver (1996: 130–34) lists three types of audiences for Chinese propaganda: I) officials for whom official language is a game and a tool for social impact, II) intellectuals for whom official language is a tool of aggression and defense, and III) the masses for whom official language is transformatory, it legitimates and delegitimates different forms of action. The Chinese propaganda system (renamed into Public Relations in the 2000s)

also has an international dimension and function, and it is divided into three sections: internal party propaganda, domestic propaganda, and foreign propaganda (Shambaugh 2007).

27 The active phase, followed by active silencing is apparent in FLG disappearing completely from the pages of Renmin Ribao after 2001 when between 1999 and 2001 it was mentioned in more than 1700 separate pieces in the paper, while before 1999 it had not appeared once. After the active phase, FLG still at times comes up in security continuums of the 'three evils', namely 'separatism, terrorism, and religious extremism.'

28 For a history of these campaigns, see Dutton (2005).

29 Patsy Rahn (2002) sees this as forming a historical 'ruler-sectarian paradigm' in China, and that the anti-FLG campaign and resistance to it follows this historical paradigm.

30 The CCP had also waged a campaign against sects in the 1980s (Munro 1989: 10–11).

31 The number of protestors in the April 25 protest has been estimated at 10 000.

32 Religious sectarians, espousing beliefs and practicing rituals the authorities have deemed heterodox were a major governmental concern in imperial China (Shek 1990: 87).

33 These are seen by Perry and Selden (2003) as the gravest dangers perceived by CCP leaders, cross-regional or-group organization cannot be allowed. These aspects were also evident in the 1980s campaign against cults (Munro 1989).

34 The criminal law on counterrevolutionary crimes was changed to that of jeopardizing national security in 1997.

35 '[B]anning cult organizations and punishing their activities is to go hand-in-hand with protecting normal religious activities and people's freedom of belief' (ChinaOnline 1999).

36 The FLG biographies have not been available since may 2001. They present Li as an extraordinary youth, who received special training from various masters, possessed supernatural skills, and describe how Li decided to publish his doctrine. The biographies follow the form of traditional Chinese religious and dynastic biographies. For a discussion, see Penny (2003).

37 Some see the defining of enemies as *the* form of politics in Mao's China; see Dutton (2005) for a narrative of the Mao era of Chinese politics presented through a Schmittian enemy-friend dyad.

38 This continuum of 'evil religions' (xiejiao) has also been used against the fourteenth Dalai Lama.

39 Li and his disciples have vehemently denied any connection to the immolators, and provided a deconstruction of the video that undermines many of the claims made by the authorities: 'Recently the CCP's lies and propaganda have again been pushing fabrications such as the "self-immolation" and been spreading fake versions of the Nine Commentaries so as to further poison the minds of the world's people' (Li 2005). For a version of the self-immolation video that contains commentary and editing by FLG-supporters, see http://www.faluninfo.net/tiananmen/immolation.asp; For the official original video, see CCTV (2001). Whether the event or videos of it were hoaxes or not does not matter here; that the videos and the event were perceived as legitimating the authorities' campaign has more relevance from a performative point of view. Truth and accuracy are less poignant for performative acts.

40 Whereas violent incidents in Xinjiang during the 1990s were termed 'splittism', after 2001 these have been framed as 'terrorism', which shows the practical effects of the 'Global War on Terror' macrosecuritization (Buzan and Wæver 2009) in China.

41 Quoted in Bristow (2007).

42 Perhaps ironically, the current dogma of the CCP also emphasizes harmony in society, and espouses similar morals of truthfulness and working hard for the motherland. For Hu Jintao's criteria of honor and disgrace, see Mille (2007). Quoting Mao Zedong, Jiang Zemin similarly stressed that the task of the party is to serve the masses. Given that Li's appearance in public life was accredited to Deng Xiaoping's 'imperial tour of the South'

and the deepening of reform in one of his biographies (Penny 2003: 658), had things gone differently, Li would quite likely have picked up Jiang's and Hu's line as well.

43 See Lu (2005) for an analysis of entrepreneurial logics in FLG activities.

44 According to *The Epoch Times* self-description, it is a privately owned, general purpose newspaper founded in New York 2000 in response to the arrest of Chinese journalists. It favours FLG and opposes the CCP and is a major outlet for the FLG securitization of the CCP. According to Li Hongzhi, *The Epoch Times* was founded by FLG disciples, but 'it's Dafa disciples who are initiating things themselves and organizing to do it, and it's not Dafa itself that's doing that' (Li 2003). FLG disciples have also established their own radio and televisions stations.

45 See http://en.epochtimes.com/211,95,1.html(Accessed October 29 2007). The number of resigned people comes from a web-service *The Epoch Times* provides (http://tuidang.epochtimes.com/, Accessed March 17 2010), which cannot be accessed from the Mainland. This decreases the credibility of the numbers claimed. CCP statistics show that the CCP has more members than ever.

46 E.g: 'the Chinese need to help themselves; they need to reflect, and they need to shake off the CCP' (The Epoch Times 2004: 268); 'the CCP is the real source of turmoil' (The Epoch Times 2004: 275).

47 It is difficult to estimate the validity and numbers of claims of torture, as most of the evidence is from FLG practitioners, while the Chinese authorities dispute most claims and do not provide information on misconduct of detainees, not to mention condoning torture. The credibility of FLG sources is in question as their numbers of incidences varies from just over 1400 to more than 10 000 in a single source, see for example The Epoch Times (2004: 81, 205, 211). For reports on torture in incarceration, see www.amnesty.org.

48 The period of Fa-rectification seems to parallel the idea of kalpa-disasters marking the end of a world (Li claims that the world has already been destroyed several times, and that the aliens are beings that have survived the previous destructions of the world) for Li, the current world seems to have moved from the period of the 'true doctrine' (*zheng fa*) to the 'counterfeit doctrine' (*xiang fa*) and now to the 'end of the doctrine' (*mo fa*). The belief in the cosmic crisis and Li's role in saving his disciples and even humanity are typical features of a Chinese sectarian group (cf. Shek 1990: 88–98).

49 See for example www.falundafa.org, www.faluninfo.net, www.clearharmony.net, and www.epochtimes.com.

50 Quoted in Rahn (2002: 44).

51 For example, 1850 onwards the Taipings referred to both external conflict and internal strife in demonic terms; the Taipings were the divine army needed to combat the demons, while real people ranging from local opponents to the Manchus were represented as demons (Haar 2002: 47). Li's writings after 2000 seem to follow the same pattern: Li's true followers are divine in nature, while the persecutors of FLG are demons from the netherworld. While Chinese sectarian scriptures often portray apocalyptic destruction as a cosmic happening principally carried out by spirits and demons, some sectarians, like the Taipings have felt compelled to take it upon themselves to do violent acts in order to expedite the arrival of the millennium (Shek 1990: 103). Not all Chinese sectarian groups have rebelled or become violent. Similarly, not all millenarian religious groups have used violence but have remained non-violent (Rinehart 2006: 26). Yet, the urgent and immediate eschatology of sectarian groups makes their potential for subversion greater than orthodox forms of religion (Ibid.: 108).

52 For example, the ox-demon (*niugui*) appearing in many folk tales was used to dehumanise people; in the CCP's usage it labelled its targets as threats to society as well as backward, in a time when there was a call to 'smash the old and build the new' (Haar 2002: 56).

53 The popularity of FLG's beliefs in the 'end of times' shows how millenarian ideas have been carried on even in socialist China as elsewhere in the world (see Rinehart 2006).

54 Political legitimacy in some other Asian societies also depends on exercising political power in ways that resonate with religious notions of righteousness and world order, for example in Cambodia (Kent 2006: 350–51).

55 Similar practices have been deployed in Indonesia where 'subversive forces' from 'certain quarters of society' served an important political function in legitimating a rationalist form of 'political paranoia'. The fear that the New Order maintained was a subversive (i.e. communist) force from within that would destroy the harmony of the 'people-state' and bring about the dreaded 'mad disorder' (Bubandt 2005: 282, 284). Supplanting communism with Islamist extremism has not been successful as a securitization strategy in Indonesia in the 2000s.

56 For example: 'Recently, a wretch in Hong Kong who lost her senses has been severely interfering with Dafa by saying absurd things, having bred demons in her mind, about how a Law Body of mine was telling her what to do. She even caused damage by using a telephone call I made to her, and has been constantly doing bad things' (Li 2000b).

57 While consistent with typical features of millenarianism, Li's preachings do not concur with James F. Rinehart's (2006: 30) definitional criteria for millenarian terrorism. While many millenarian groups that resort to the use of violence believe that the world has to be destroyed, Li claims to be trying to save the world from destruction.

58 'In order to prevent misunderstandings by those who have lost their way in the Party's culture, I told Dafa disciples in Mainland China not to incorporate the Nine Commentaries as they clarify the truth' (Li 2005).

11 The continuing evolution of securitization theory

Michael C. Williams

In the decade and a half since its initial formulation and development, securitization theory has evolved into a remarkably broad and vibrant area of research. Indeed, it is difficult to think of another perspective in security studies that could embrace (and virtually none that has embraced) the analysis of military affairs, the environment, gender, migration, and communications theory, to mention but a few, under a single theoretical orientation. Nor is it easy to think of another perspective in security studies that has generated such diverse and yet focused debates over its theoretical structure and empirical application.[1] This book demonstrates that unity and diversity. Its contributors are united by need for a more sociological or pragmatic view of securitization. They share the view that if securitization theory is to reach its full potential, the formulations of the Copenhagen School are in need of further development and – in some cases – substantial redirection. Broadly speaking, it seems to me that these arguments run along two related lines. The first is that in its original form the idea of security as a speech act is constrained by a version of social theory that is too thin and too formal to capture the concrete dynamics, strategies, and forms that securitizing acts can take. The second, is that while the Copenhagen School stresses that securitization is an interactive process, where the relationship between securitizing actors and audiences is crucial, the theory leaves this dimension radically underdeveloped, with a resulting inability to see the different forms the securitizing acts take depending on the context and audience.

Combined with previous work, including that by many of the authors represented here, these claims represent important developments in securitization theory, both methodologically and empirically, and my purpose in this chapter is not to review them in detail, or to evaluate systematically their relationship to the Copenhagen School, which remains the largely silent partner in this emerging dialogue. Instead, I would like to take some of these themes as an inspiration and opportunity to open up key issues that they touch upon, and that point in directions for future research in this vibrant and still developing area of security studies.

Method

At the heart of a contextual approach to securitization is a critique of the Copenhagen School's initial theorization of security as a speech act. In contrast to what is seen as the formal and rather abstract structure of the initial formulation, a 'pragmatic' approach stresses the variety of symbolic technologies through which securitization can take place. Different forms of technical, bureaucratic language, for example, as well as a vast repertoire of gestures and images, and the diverse audiences to whom they are addressed, or whom they effect, means that the form and content of speech acts need to be seen in the context of their production and potential effectiveness. These arguments build on a key ambiguity within the original formulation, whereby although security is seen as a speech act, the Copenhagen School stressed that it is not the *word* 'security' that necessarily matters, but the effects that it produces – the recognition of an existential threat and the mobilization of extraordinary measures (the 'breaking free of rules') to respond to it. In this sense, a contextual approach calls for deeper and more detailed analysis of securitizing acts as pragmatic accomplishments.

In a second move, a pragmatic approach holds that these diverse securitizing acts and their effectiveness (or lack thereof) cannot be understood without a much more sustained analysis of the audience, something the Copenhagen School leaves radically underdeveloped. Here, we need to see context in order to understand what threat representations and rhetorics resonate with specific audiences; to see how different speech acts function in different institutional or bureaucratic settings; and to differentiate between proximate or distal audiences. In short, the audience is not a passive category, and a contextual theory of securitization pushes the claim of the Copenhagen School that security takes place as an interactive process – 'between the subjects' of a securitizing move and its reception – in new directions and much greater depth.

These are important insights, and as the chapters in this volume demonstrate, they provide the basis for developing finely-grained and empirically rich studies of securitization processes. Whether this marks an evolution in securitization theory so fundamental that it amounts to a change in the theory itself is not a question that I want to engage here; nor do I want to set out to defend the Copenhagen School from its critics. However, there are a number of questions about the formal nature of the initial formulation that are worth highlighting since they pose key issues for future theoretical development.

The first of these issues involves what precisely we mean by a formal speech act. A pragmatic approach finds this wanting; it is too abstract to allow detailed empirical analysis of concrete practices. Yet is important to note that the formal nature of the securitizing act in the Copenhagen School has two possible meanings. One, accurately diagnosed here, is a methodological or linguistic formalism. This is at best a methodological ambiguity in the Copenhagen School, and at worst a considerable shortcoming. But formalism can have a second meaning. This has less to do with speech act theory, and more to do with the specific understanding of security proposed by Buzan, Waever, and their collaborators. In the Copenhagen School's formulation, what is formal, abstract, and universal is the definition of security as extremity – its identification with existential threat. It is extremity that allows security to be identified *as* security.

Here, interesting divergences emerge between contextualist approaches. Some of the authors in this collection, for instance, advance a pragmatic approach that continues to adhere to the view of security as extremity, suggesting that explicit policy change within its logic needs to be seen as a defining feature of successful or failed securitization. Others stress that in local or particular contexts equating security with extremity may be misleading, leading to a failure to see how security logics can have effects even if they do not conform to the criteria of existential threat and emergency measures. This position is illustrated, for example, in Trombetta's analysis of environmental security, and perhaps in Wilkinson's stress on the importance of local understandings that may not be captured by 'meta-narratives'.

This raises at least two sets of questions directly related to the explicitly the formal approach found in the Copenhagen School. If security is articulated contextually and can mean many things to many audiences (including, for example, a sense of riskiness or unease that uses the language of security but does not invoke an explicit logic of extremity) and policy change is just that – change, then does it become impossible to define a 'security' issue in a way that is not determined wholly *by* these contextually-delimited relationships of securitizing agent and audience? In other words, does a fully contextualized understanding of securitizing lead back to the very 'widening' debates the surrounded the concept of security in the early 1990s, where it was either subjectively defined according to relative values, determined contextually by specific communities, or 'objectively' defined by analytic fiat? Since it was precisely this situation that securitization theory initially claimed to circumvent, it is certainly worth asking whether a contextual approach does not end up pushing security studies (for better or worse) back toward the analytic and normative debates that it was designed in part to overcome.

Seen in this light, the question is not just whether context matters – clearly it does in any proper account of specific securitization processes, and it matters that we have the appropriate theoretical tools to understand this. The question is also, however, whether the abstract, formal designation of what security *is*, provides an orienting device for understanding what is happening within specific contexts. If security is not extremity, for the Copenhagen School we are left in a world of multiple interpretations at lower levels. Moreover, if policy shifts are not defined by the threshold of extremity, it becomes difficult to disentangle any number of policy changes and dynamics from specifically *security*-related ones. Formalism is here designed in part to solve a methodological dilemma that arises from looking at security in less extreme terms and as substantively defined by local contexts. The Copenhagen School (or my interpretation of it) may be mistaken in this regard – this is not an issue that can be unpacked in this setting; but its importance to securitization theory and its challenge for contextualist theories and methodology are worthy of further examination. When viewed in this light, the formalism of the Copenhagen School is not transcended by a contextual approach, its importance, and its contestability is foregrounded.

The methodological issues at stake here also go well beyond the debates over positivism and explanation/understanding that have characterised much of IR theory and security studies. The Copenhagen School is sceptical toward interpretivism within the tradition of hermeneutics. In my eyes, this stems not from a residual positivism traced to modern science, but is a different part of its debt to post-structuralism. The critique of hermeneutics developed by Derrida and Foucault, for instance, and the latter's famous characterization of himself as a 'happy positivist' was not a reflection of their unfamiliarity with interpretive methods, but of their views on the limits of the hermeneutic tradition.[2] The idea of judging by 'effects' and the importance of the 'limit case' in demonstrating social processes and phenomena is thus part of a well-developed vision of social science, albeit one that has had relatively little exposure in IR. The Copenhagen School has to the best of my knowledge never developed these ideas fully, and it is difficult to discern precisely how big a role they play in its claims. Certainly, however the centrality of Derrida in Waever's early thinking seems to me indicative of more than just a narrow concern with language, or a privileging of discourse over social structure. And if this is the case then the methodological and philosophical issues at stake go much deeper than a contrast between explanation and understanding, positivism and interpretivism, or most other oppositions that continue to dominate much of IR theory.

A final question concerns the creative dimension of securitization. Contextualism is certainly correct to stress the need to theorize the audience, and to highlight the need to locate securitizations against the backdrop of what Balzacq nicely captures as "what the audience already knows" (Balzacq 2009b: 60). However, there is also something important that needs to be emphasized and perhaps retained in the formalism of the initial formulation: its basic creativity. Securitization theory in all its forms stresses the importance of audiences. But this audience does not necessarily exist prior to securitization: it is also possible that securitization can *create a receptive audience*, by bringing it to consciousness of itself as a unified audience. This process, which Bourdieu analyzed as the "mystery of the Ministry", may well be particularly important in the domain of security with its explicit connections to one of the most socially volatile emotions, fear. Fear may appeal beyond something we know; it also evokes Donald Rumsfeld's famous trilogy of "known knowns, known unknowns, and unknown unknowns", and the much less easy to quantify – and perhaps less cognitive and more emotional – domains, affects, and effects of politics that operate at the limits of knowledge. In an important sense, security appeals to what we don't know: to fears of the unknown, the unforeseen, and the perhaps unforeseeable – to dire possibilities that might be realized even if we don't (and maybe even can't) know exactly what they are. Here, it is useful to recall another element of Copenhagen School's vision of the logic of security: its 'if-then' character. 'If we don't deal with this, then . . .' can point to knowledge and context (tanks on the border, or the deeper forms of contextual knowledge explored by many of the authors here), but it can also mobilize a more radical fear of an unforeseeable future and the limits of knowledge, a domain that Hans Blits once perceptively identified as "Hobbesian fear" (Blits 1989).

I will return to this latter point in a moment. At this juncture, what is important is that an appreciation of the importance of context does not lead to analytic conventionalism. Securitizations surely do not occur *de novo*, yet some of their most intriguing and important characteristics are how they can challenge (again, for better or worse) existing social and political orders, as well as reproducing them. Their creativity can be tied as much to uncertainty as to knowledge, and here contextual analysis of precisely what fears are available to be mobilized in a given setting, through which logics and rhetorics, while essential, cannot fully circumscribe the indeterminacy of the act and its potential appeal to an audience. Methodologically, this means that the analyst cannot forecast definitively the success of an attempted securitization, though a finely-grained assessment of specific fields of practice can certainly provide powerful insights into those strategies, mobilizations, and counter-strategies that are most likely to succeed or fail in specific settings. To some degree, however, securitization analysis – like all social theory cogent of its limits – must remain a post-facto analysis, something that is a consequence of the complexity and creativity that remains a characteristic of even the most powerfully structured social settings.

Intensification

If the formalized nature of security as a speech act contains two separable, if related, components – a sociological claim about speech and discourse, and a substantive claim about security as extremity – then research into this second dimension has involved the question of whether and to what degree an 'exceptional' view of security can capture the way that security actually functions within concrete settings, and how to recognize it when it occurs. Here again, contextual approaches provide important contributions and clarifications, while at the same time opening up complex further questions.

The focus on institutional settings and differentiation fruitfully suggested by Bigo (2002), and insightfully explored and developed by a number of the contributions in this book, shows the weakness of focusing only on exceptional acts and logics of emergency. As Léonard and Kaunert, and Salter argue in detail, securitizing acts must often conform to appropriate institutional logics in order to succeed, and in differentiated social and decision-making structures, these logics often take different forms: what succeeds in one setting may not in another. This, they suggest, opens up connections to other theoretical traditions, from public policy to dramaturgical analysis, while at the same time providing a richer explanation of the processes (and failures) of securitization than is possible while remaining tied to the single, authoritative institutional voice and declaration of emergency that they see in the Copenhagen School's view – a position that is echoed although differently developed in Wilkinson's stress on the need to shift the focus "from what security means to how security means", and in Vulee's examination of communicative structures. Different discourses and symbolic technologies dominate different political domains and institutions. Whereas technical expertise may hold sway and foster effective securitization within certain institutions – as, for instance, in both Salter's analysis of anti-terrorism policies and Trombetta's account of the role of scientific expertise in environmental security – it is perhaps less likely to do so in mass political communication. The interaction of context and strategy, as Balzacq, Stritzel and Schmitchen, and Vuori all also stress, are key parts of securitization processes.

These represent important advances toward a robustly sociological understanding of securitization. However, as noted earlier, a key issue then becomes how we can recognize a securitization if it does not use either the overt language of security or manifest a logic of extremity. Salter addresses this question by making policy change the criteria of successful securitizations, as does Sjostedt. But this raises the crucial question of when a policy change constitutes a securitization: when do the rules broken (or when are enough rules broken, or what kinds of rules need to be broken) comprise a securitization rather than simply a policy evolution? At what levels of decision-making, and across what thresholds of practical impact do policy changes have to occur to fit within a security logic? Do minor regulatory changes (or a series of them) even if they are made within an explicit language of 'security' constitute a successful securitization, or is this to be reserved for more spectacular decisions within traditional elite structures and security institutions? Not all changes in policy and practice are exceptional, even if they partake explicitly of the language of security – and this raises difficult questions about what it means to 'break free of rules', and the threshold via which such events might be identified.

My suspicion is that it is partly in response to such dilemmas that the Copenhagen School sets the bar as high as it does in terms of exceptionality, and that its apparent commitment to security as issuing from a 'sovereign voice' arises as much from an attempt to circumvent these kinds of questions as it does from any residual Westphalianism. Here, the paradox is that while the language of emergency can appear an obstacle to more theoretically nuanced and empirically grounded understandings of concrete practices, it may at the same time provide an anchoring device through which 'security' dynamics can be discerned and distinguished from 'normal' change within the policy process.

One way to address this paradox might be to link the idea of thresholds suggested by Salter to the concept of intensification, and thereby to develop in a different direction the controversial question of the relationship between securitization theory and political realism. This connection has often been made through the figure of Carl Schmitt, whose concept of the political and stress on emergencies and exceptionality resonates powerfully with certain parts of the Copenhagen School. Schmitt, of course, was hardly alone in theorizing the exception, and nor was he beyond the influence of other thinkers. One of the most interesting of these influences may well have been the young Hans Morgenthau, whose theory of intensification was designed to address what he saw as fundamental shortcomings in Schmitt's thinking.[3] To make a (very) long story short, the core of Morgenthau's argument with Schmitt's vision of politics revolved around the claim that 'the political' (like 'security' in the Copenhagen School) was a distinct sphere of action. In contrast to Schmitt's original vision of the political as defined by the division between friend and enemy, and with – to use Schmitt's language – 'the real possibility of killing', Morgenthau argued that the political was marked by a *process of intensification*. The 'political' was thus not a distinct sphere or a boundary between two dramatically different spheres of activity. It was instead a particular orientation towards an issue – any issue – that involved an intensity of importance with the possibility of mortal violence at its apogee. For Morgenthau, any issue can be made political in Schmitt's sense if the requisite degree of intensity is attached to it. Nor are all issues equally susceptible to intensification in given contexts. It is a question for concrete analysis to determine what issues are regarded in this way, and why. And issues are in principle as subject to a diminishment of intensification as they are to its opposite.

The concept of intensification may hold some promise as a means of moving beyond the division between exceptional and normal politics that pragmatic approaches see as a key problem in securitization theory. Through it, the relationship between forms of 'unease', thresholds, cascades, and strategies of policy entrepreneurship and security, might be brought into view by seeing them as forms of intensification below extremity. For however far in a pragmatist direction securitization theory moves, and even if the languages, discourses, or symbolic technologies are not explicitly those of extremity, the effect of emergency in the sense of a fundamental breaking of rules remains central for security analysis, since it provides the limit condition, or perhaps even an ideal-type, that allows the identification of processes within and/or below its ultimate expression.

For those who wish to expand the sociology of securitization, as formulated throughout this book, and even in my own cursory suggestion here, such a move involves complex methodological problems that cannot be swept away by assuming that sociology as a discipline has the answers – it doesn't; or perhaps more charitably, it has many (not always compatible) answers, whose connections to the concern with violence and extremity at the core of securitization are by no means clear. Yet there is little doubt that a more sustained engagement between securitization theory and various strands of sociology can only be beneficial, and that a pragmatic understanding of strategies, structures, and contexts – in short, an engagement with theories of practice[4] – can be an important dimension of this emerging agenda.

The politics of fear

If securitization cannot be tied exclusively to extremity and emergency; but comprises a wider spectrum of intensification, including unease and risk, and a variety of institutional settings and practices for its enactment, this leaves open the crucial question of precisely what unifies these apparently disparate practices under the rubric of 'security'? If it is not the word, 'security', nor the breaking free of rules in a spectacular sense, what defines a 'security' act, and what makes a securitization different from any of the myriad tactics, logics, rhetorics, strategies, that actors use in attempts to change or break 'the rules' in governments or in societies at large? Does such a broadening simply leave us back in debates over widening the security agenda, debates that the Copenhagen School sought expressly to leave behind?

One possible answer to this question is to focus on fear. Unease and risk, like emergencies and threats, play within a register of fear. Even the most technical (or risk-calculating, or governmentalizing, or whatever) of discourses and practices, if they are related to security, take on their special resonance as a result of their connection to fear – indeed this is what in tends to make them recognizable as 'security' practices in the first place. To place fear at the center of securitization doubtless raises a series of difficult issues and questions. Talking about fear is not particularly politically attractive. It is obviously a challenging theme to research, and encompasses such a variety of registers and resonances that it risks becoming as amorphous as security has often seemed to be. But I would like to suggest that it is in part because of its many registers and manifestations that fear provides an important trajectory worthy of further exploration and investigation in the study of securitization.

Fear has generally had a bad name in modernity. It has been seen as something to be banished – freedom from it was the target of one of Franklin Roosevelt's 'four freedoms', and it is today one of the unifying elements of the Human Security agenda and, in certain forms at least, of Critical Security Studies. From a different but equally hostile perspective, some philosophic accounts see modernity as based in fear, and its (generally destructive) preoccupation with security as a consequence of this more basic foundation. To still others, fear is an instrument which, far from being part of the existential condition of modernity, has been made more powerful and effective by the structures of modern politics.[5]

Each of these three views, despite their apparent (and by no means insubstantial) differences, are united in their basic vision of fear as negative. And there is no doubt that their assault on the politics of fear and its negative effects is an indispensable element of any serious analysis of security. Yet it is also the case that to reject fear completely, or to see it as wholly antithetical to security is both analytically and politically blinding. In contrast to these modern views of fear, many older traditions of thought exhibit a rather different sensibility, and provided a more nuanced and potentially more productive view of the politics of fear. To take one example, in the eyes of perhaps the greatest political philosopher of fear, Thomas Hobbes, the human condition was dominated by multiple and often contradictory and competing forms of fear: the fear of death itself; the fear of violent death at the hands of others, which marked a fear of dishonour (of Pride and the sense of self) more than it did of mere mortality;[6] fear of the unknown and unknowable future and its potential hazards (Blits 1989).[7] Fear, in short, was everywhere, and while Hobbes freely admitted that he might have felt its effects more acutely than many people, he was convinced nonetheless that it dominated the human condition, and that a complete escape from fear was possible only temporarily in sleep, and ultimately, in death.

Yet Hobbes did not view fear wholly negatively. Indeed, he believed that the absence of fear could be as dangerous as its over-abundance. Disregard of the fear of death as a result of vanity and the search for glory or honour, he believed, could lead to the worst forms of conflict, while misplaced certainly (belief in the security of knowledge) could result in dogmatism, intolerance and violence in the name of universal truths. Recognizing these dangerous beliefs and fearing their consequences, however, could act as a positive constraint on human excesses, and foster peace. Fear arising from the absence of specific forms of fear (of, for instance, conflicts arising from Vain-glory or religious zealotry that overwhelmed the fear of death, or that arose from a failure to acknowledge the limits human knowledge and an unwillingness to live with the fear presented by the inability to control an essentially uncertain future) could lead to a politics that restrained these beliefs and behaviours. In other words, the fear of fear (and of the practices likely to lead to extreme fear) could act as a check upon the politics of fear. However difficult it might be to achieve, fear was in principle capable of supporting forms of positive, pacific action.

What does all this have to do with securitization theory? Potentially, quite a lot, I think. In the form initially suggested by the Copenhagen School, securitization theory posits a clear distinction between the norm and the exception, between "security" and "normal" politics, between – if I am correct in linking security and fear – a politics of fear and a politics free from fear. Yet if we take inspiration from Hobbes, this dichotomy provides at best limited guidance. In the political vision sketched by Hobbes, fear and normality, security and politics are not divided: they are necessarily (and practically) related, and any attempt to draw an absolute divide between them is misleading. The key question is not whether fear can be expunged from social and political life, the question is how fear functions. In Hobbes' vision, normal politics is in important respects based on fear – not only the famous fear of a Leviathan that can impose order, but also on the fears of ideas and identities that lead to conflict and that need self-consciously to be marginalized if social life (and, indeed, sovereign power) is to be secure.[8]

Despite his deeply ambivalent relationship to liberal politics, Hobbes' thinking provides important insights into the politics of security within liberal societies. In Judith Shklar's account of democratic politics, for instance, the fear of fear provides a key component of liberal-democratic politics. As she puts it,

Where the instruments of coercion are at hand, whether it be through the use of economic power, chiefly to hire, pay, fire and determine prices, or military might in its various manifestations, it is the task of a liberal citizenry to see that not one official or unofficial agent can intimidate anyone, save through the use of well-understood and accepted legal procedures. And that even then the agents of coercion should always be on the defensive and limited to proportionate and necessary actions that can be excused only as a response to threats of more severe cruelly and fear from private criminals.

(Shklar 2004: 58–59)

What Shklar is describing here is, of course, an idea of liberal politics, not an account of its actuality. But as she notes, it is an ideal with more than a little resonance in the practices of many liberal societies.

An illustration of this potential significance of this point for securitization theory can be seen in Salter's incisive analysis in this volume of failed securitizations in U.S. counter-terrorism policies. In this case, the fear of terrorism, and its successful securitization within the technified language and logic of certain specialist institutions, was outweighed by the fear of the threat that such policies could pose to liberal-democratic politics. Fear is here a productive and countervailing power (a desecuritizing element) within normal politics, and a means of defending it against an intensifying and intrusive politics of fear.[9] Whether one finds this a comforting element of liberal-democratic politics, a part of 'governmental' practices, or the symbol of a debilitating weakness or a worryingly conservative power within it (as both the traditional Right and Left have argued), its underlying fear of the politics of fear is an important constitutive dimension of liberal-democratic societies – and a key component of some de-securitizing dynamics within them. Securitization theory, seen in its contextual mode, and in concrete studies such as Salter's, can illustrate these dynamics, as well as illustrating their institutional dimensions and their limits.

As Balzacq and many of the authors in this volume show, themes such as these can be mobilized in explicit strategies surrounding securitization. Exceptions and emergencies can call these strategies into clear view – this, after all, is part of the analytic appeal of the exceptional for Schmitt and others. But they can also function in less spectacular ways, as things that remain unsaid in order to produce the effects – the dialectic of fear and the fear of fear – that they do. Arguably, religious fundamentalism has long played such a role in liberal societies, and these kinds of practices are important parts of the politics of security.

These 'deep' securitizations, fears of fears that may be called up in extremity, or that may not rise to the level of explicit articulation but still exercise important effects, may take securitization theory in interesting if by no means unproblematic directions. They open up questions such as the social mythologies embedded in what Bourdieu called the habitus and bodily 'hexis', in structures and strategies of 'deep play', or in symbols, images, and other forms of non-verbal representation that can occupy important roles in security politics. They also allows us to appreciate the unsaid meanings in securitizing or desecuritizing acts by looking not only at discursive absences or silenced voices, but also at social location and locution. As Bourdieu used to stress, statements like "He's not stand-offish" almost always carry an important social corollary ("for a Duke") that give them their meaning and effect. Entire practical structures and social mythologies are expressed in such performances and pragmatics. In security, too, the politics of fear – and particularly the potentially desecuritizing fear of fear – can take a similar structure. These acts do not necessarily have to adopt the form or the language of security and fear to be about security and fear, and to have real impacts on whether securitizations can be attempted, the forms they take, their chances of success. They can also be crucial in grasping the forms of resistance these strategies may encounter, strategies that are effective precisely because they play upon a different politics of fear. Thus, as the accounts of strategies of resistance to securitization highlighted by Vuori and other contributors to this volume show, we need to map these less effable structures and the strategies (conscious or not) through which they may take effect.

Conclusion

In an early review of securitization theory, Jef Huysmans (1998) cast securitization theory as marking the development of a new and vibrant research agenda in Europe. Over the last decade, this judgement has been borne out – though it must be admitted that (thus far at least) the qualifier "in Europe" remains an important reminder of the agenda's still-limited appeal in many parts of the world, particularly in the United States. As the studies in this book amply demonstrate, the development of contextual or pragmatic approaches mark important and welcome new trajectories within this agenda. Yet as I have tried to suggest in this chapter, this evolution also raises key theoretical questions and methodological challenges, both within broadly contextual approaches and in their relationship to securitization theory more widely. These debates seem likely to ensure that securitization theory will remain a vibrant area of research and insight well into the future.

Notes

1 For a sweeping recent survey of the field, see Buzan and Hansen 2009.

2 For a still valuable account, see Rabinow and Dreyfus 1982.

3 For a detailed study of Morgenthau, and to some extent Schmitt, within their wider intellectual contexts, see Oliver Jütersonke (forthcoming); the first significant analysis of the relationship was William Scheuerman 1999.

4 A broad-ranging exploration of practice as concept in International Relations can be found in Emmanuel Adler and Vincent Pouliot, eds, *International Practices*, forthcoming.

5 For an account of both, with a critique of the former and advocacy of the latter position, see Robin 2005.

6 This fear was fundamental in Hobbes vision of the state of nature, something that advocates of a 'Hobbesian analogy' as a foundation for thinking about IR would do well to consider. For developments of it, see Strauss 1952 and Oakeshott 1975. I have attempted to develop some of these themes in Michael C Williams, 'Recasting the Hobbesian legacy in international political theory' in Gabriella Slomp and Raia Prokhovnic, eds, *International Political Theory After Hobbes* (London: Palgrave, forthcoming).

7 For a rare, and perceptive, exploration of some of these trajectories in terms of security, see Der Derian 1995.

8 To an extent, studies of governmentality and security have explored these themes; by returning to older traditions of political philosophy, this could be developed in interestingly different directions as well.

9 For a revealing wider analysis with connections to this theme, see Huysmans 2004.

References

Abdolian, L. F. and Takooshian, H. (2003) The USA PATRIOT Act: Civil Liberties, the Media, and Public Opinion, *Fordham Urban Law Journal* 30: 1438.

Abdelal, W., Herrera, Y. M., Johnston, A. I., and McDermott, R. (eds) (2009) *Measuring identity: A guide for social scientists*, Cambridge: Cambridge University Press.

Abrahamsen, R. (2005) 'Blair's Africa: The politics of securitization and fear', *Alternatives*, 30(1): 55–80.

Acharya, A. and Buzan, B. (2007) 'Preface: Why there is no non-Western International Relations theory: reflections on and from Asia', *International Relations of the Asia-Pacific*, 7(3): 285–86.

ACTUP (1999) *AIDS Activists Hit Al Gore Three Times in Two Days. Vice President Dumfounded, Confused, Unable to Respond*. Online. Available HTTP: www.healthgap.org/pressreleases/99/061899AUPRGORE.html (accessed 22 September 2008).

—— (1996) *XI International Conference on AIDS, 7–12 July*. Online. Available HTTP: http://www.actupny.org/Vancouver/Vanindex.html (accessed 22 October 2008).

Adler, E., and Pouliot, V. (eds) (forthcoming), *International Practices*.

Agamben, G. (2005) *State of exception*, Chicago: University of Chicago Press.

Alikhani, H. (2000) *Sanctioning Iran: Anatomy of a failed policy*, London: IB Tauris.

American Health Line (1999) *HIV/AIDS drugs: Clinton says relax trade rules*. Online. Available HTTP: http://www.americanhealthline.com/archives/1999/12/m991203. 10.html (accessed 3 December 1999).

Aminzade, R. (1993) 'Class analysis, politics, and French labor history', in L. Berlanstein (ed.) *Rethinking labor history*, Chicago: University of Chicago Press.

Amirpur, K. (1998) Iran spielt fair. *Süddeutsche Zeitung*, 20 June.

Amoore, L. (2009) 'Algorithmic war: Everyday geographies of the war on terror', *Antipode*, 41(1): 49–69.

Anker, E. (2005) ' Villains, victims, and heroes: Melodrama, media, and September 11', *Journal of Communication*, 55(1): 22–37.

Aradau, C. and Van Munster, R. (2007) 'Governing terrorism through risk: Taking precautions, (un)knowing the future', *European Journal of International Relations*, 13(1): 89–115.

Aras, B. and Polat, R. K. (2008) 'From conflict to cooperation: Desecuritization of Turkey's relations with Syria and Iran', *Security Dialogue*, 39(5): 495–535.

Aristotle (1992) *Physics*, books I and II, trans. by W. Charlton, Oxford: Clarendon Press.

Aspin, L. (1993) 'Speech to the National Academy of Sciences', 7 December.

Austin, J. (1975) *How to do things with words*. Cambridge, MA: Harvard University Press.

—— (1971) 'Performative-constative,' in J. R. Searle, *Philosophy of language*, Oxford: Oxford University Press.

—— (1970) *Philosophical papers*, ed. by J. O. Urmson and G. J. Warnock, Oxford: Oxford University Press.

—— (1962) *How to do things with words: The William James lectures delivered at Harvard University in 1955*, Oxford: Clarendon Press.

Australian Broadcasting Corporation (2005) *Wolfensohn hands over World Bank reins*, TV program Transcript, interview with Kerry O'Brian 2005-0530. Online. Available HTTP: www.abc.net.au/7.30/content/2005/s1380527.htm (accessed 6 March 2009).

Avdeeva, E. (2005) 'Miting v Bishkeke: ruki proch or Kulova!' [trans. 'Protest in Bishkek: Hands off Kulov!'], *Belyi parakhod KG*, 2(1).

Ayer, A. J. (1936) *Language, truth and logic*, London: Gollancz.

Bächler, G. (1999) *Violence through environmental discrimination*, Dordrecht: Kluwer.

—— (1998) 'Why environmental transformation causes violence: A synthesis', *Environmental Change and Security Project Report*.

Bächler, G. *et al* (1996), *Kriegsursache Umweltzerstörung. Environmental degradation as a cause of war*. Vol. I–III. Zurich: Rüegger Verlag.

Bakhtin, M. M. (1986) 'The problem of speech genre', in Caryl Emerson and Michael Holquist (eds) *Speech genre and other late essays*, Austin: University of Texas Press.

Balzacq, T. (2005a) 'Constructivism and securitization studies', in V. Mauer and M. Dunn Cavelty (eds) *Handbook of Security Studies*, London: Routledge.

—— (2009b) 'Trust: From securitization to de-securitization, and back', PhD seminar, Aberystwyth, University of Wales.

—— (2008) 'The policy tools of securitization: Information exchange, EU foreign and interior policies', *Journal of common Market Studies*, 46(1): 75–100.

—— (2005) 'The three faces of securitization: Political agency, audience and context', *European Journal of International Relations*, 11(2): 171–201.

—— (2004) 'The pragmatic act of security: Politics and methods.' Unpublished manuscript.

—— (2003) 'Constructivism, pragmatism and security studies,' PhD Thesis, University of Cambridge.

Balzacq, T., and Carrera, S. (2006) *Security versus freedom? A challenge for Europe's future*, Aldershot: Ashgate.

—— (2005) 'Migration, borders, and asylum: Trends and vulnerabilities' in *EU Politics*, Brussels: Centre for European Policy Studies.

Barnett, J. (2001) *The meaning of environmental security: Ecological politics and policy in the new security era*, New York: Zed Books.

Barnett, T. and Prins, G. (2006) 'HIV/AIDS and security: fact, fiction and evidence – A report to UNAIDS', *International Affairs*, 82(2): 359–68.

Barthwal-Datta, M. (2009) 'Securitizing threats without the state: A case study of misgovernance as a security threat in Bangladesh', *Review of International Studies*, 35(2): 277–300.

Bar-Tal, D. (2000) *Shared beliefs in a society: Social psychological analysis*, Thousand Oaks, CA: Sage.

Bateson, P. (2000) 'What must be known in order to understand imprinting?', in C. Heyes and L. Huber (eds) *The evolution of cognition*, Cambridge, MA: MIT Press.

BBC News (2003) 'Setback for UK at EU summit', 19 June.

Bechtel, W. (1988) *Philosophy of science*, London: Lawrence Erlbaum.

Beck, U. (2002) 'The terrorist threat. World risk society revisited', *Theory, Culture & Society*, 19(4): 39–55.

—— (2000) *What is globalization?* Cambridge: Polity Press.

—— (1999) *World risk society*, Malden, MA: Polity Press.

—— (1992) *Risk society: Towards a new modernity*, Thousand Oaks: Sage.

Beer, F. A., Sinclair, G. P., Healy, A. F., and Bourne, L. E. Jr. (1995). 'Peace agreement, intractable conflict, escalation trajectory: A psychological laboratory experiment', *International Studies Quarterly*, 39(3): 297–312.

Behnke, A. (2006) 'No way out: Desecuritization, emancipation and the eternal return of the political – a reply to Aradau', *Journal of International Relations and Development*, 9(1): 62–69.

Beishenova, M. (2005) 'Deputaty, vozmushchennye bespomoshchnostyu silovikov, sozdali svoyu komissiyu' [trans. 'Deputies concerned by the helplessness of the law enforcement bodies, have created their own commission'], *Litsa*, 21 (62): 3, 27 October.

Bell, A. (1991) *The language of news media*, Oxford: Blackwell.

Bendrath, R., Erikson, J., and Giacomello, G. (2007) 'From "cyberterrorism" to "cyberwar", back and forth – how the United States securitized cyberspace', in J. Erikson and G. Giacomello (eds) *International relations and security in the digital age*, London: Routledge.

Bennett, W. L. (1990) 'Toward a theory of press–state relations in the United States', *Journal of Communication*, 40(2), 103–25.

Berdal, M. R. and Malone, D. M. (2000) *Greed and grievance: Economic agendas in civil wars*, Boulder, CO: Lynne Rienner.

Berger, T. U. (1998) *Cultures of antimilitarism: National security in Germany and Japan*, Baltimore, MD: Johns Hopkins University Press.

Best, J. (2007) 'Why the economy is often an exception to politics as usual theory', *Culture and Society*, 24(4): 83–105.

Betts, A. (2004) 'The international relations of the "new" extraterritorial approaches to refugee protection: Explaining the policy initiatives of the UK government and UNHCR', *Refugee*, 22(1): 58–70.

Bigo, D. (2008) 'International political sociology', in P. Williams (ed.) *Security studies: An introduction*, London: Routledge.

—— (2005) 'La mondialisation de l'(in)sécurité? Réflexion sur le champ des professionnels de la gestion des inquiétudes et analytique de la transnationalisation des processus d'(in)sécurisation', *Cultures et Conflits*, Elise Special Issue: *Suspicion et exception* (58): 53–101. Online. Available HTTP: www.conflits.org/document1813.html (accessed 25 June 2007)

—— (2002) 'Security and immigration: Toward a critique of the governmentality of unease', *Alternatives*, 27 (Supp/1): 63–92 (Special English language Issue of Cultures & Conflits)

—— (2001) 'The Mobius Ribbon of internal and external security(ies)', in M. Albert, D. Jacobson, and Y. Lapid (ed) *Identities, borders, orders: Rethinking international relations theory*, Minneapolis: University of Minnesota Press.

—— (2000) 'When two become one: Internal and external securitisations in Europe', in M. Kelstrup and M. C. Williams (eds) *International relations theory and the politics of European integration, power, security and community*, London: Routledge.

—— (1994) 'The European internal security field: Stakes and rivalries in a newly developing area of police intervention', in M. A. Anderson and M. den Boer (eds) *Policing across national borders*, London: Pinter.

—— (1986) *Polices en réseaux*, Paris: Presses de Sciences Po.

Bigo, D. and Tsoukala, A. (2008) *Terror, insecurity and liberty. Illiberal practices of liberal regimes after 9/11*, New York: Routledge.

Bigo, D., Bonelli, L., and Olsson, C. (2007) *Mapping of the field of the EU Internal Security Agencies*, Paris: L'Harmattan.

Bishop, I. (2004) 'Nuisance nonsense: Rudy rages at Kerry's crack on slashing level of terror', *New York Post*, p. 7, October 12.

Biyalinov, A. (2005) 'Kriminalno-politicheskii krizis v Kyrgyzstane — chto nas zhdet vperedi?' [trans. 'Criminal-political crisis in Kyrgyzstan — What awaits Us?'], *ResPublica*, 39(605): 1

Blits, H (1989) 'Hobbesian fear', *Political Theory*, 17(3): 417–31.

Booth, K. (2007) *Theory of world security*, Cambridge: Cambridge University Press.

—— (1991) 'Security and emancipation', *Review of International Studies*, 17(4): 313–26.

Boswell, C. (2007) 'Migration control in Europe after 9/11: Explaining the absence of securitization?', *Journal of Common Market Studies*, 45(3): 589–610.

—— (2003) 'Burden-sharing in the European Union: Lessons from the German and UK experience', *Journal of Refugee Studies*, 16(3): 316–35.

Boucher, R. (2000), Daily Press Briefing, 19 June.

Bourdieu, P. (1991) *Language and symbolic order*, Cambridge: Polity Press.

—— (1990) *The logic of practice*, Cambridge: Polity Press.

—— (1984) *Language and symbolic power*, Cambridge: Polity Press.

—— (1979) 'Symbolic power', *Critique of Anthropology*, 4(13–14): 77–85.

Bowen, W. Q., and Dunn, D. H. (1995) *American security policy in the 1990s: Beyond containment*, Brookfield: Dartmouth.

Bradford, R. (ed.) (1993) *The state of theory*, London: Routledge.

Brady, H. E. and Collier, D. (eds) (2004) *Rethinking social enquiry: Diverse tools, shared standards*, Lanham, MD: Rowman & Littlefield.

Braml, J. (2004) *Die religiöse Rechte in den USA. Basis der Bush-Administration?* Berlin: Stiftung Wissenschaft und Politik.

Brand, M. (1984) *Intending and acting: Toward a naturalized action theory*, Cambridge, MA: MIT Press.

Briggs, A. and Burke, P. (2002) *A social history of the media: From Gutenberg to the Internet*, Cambridge: Polity Press.

Brauch, H. G. (2003) 'Security and environment linkages on the Mediterranean space', in Hans Günter Brauch *et al.* (eds) *Security and environment in the Mediterranean: Conceptualising security and environmental conflicts*, Berlin: Springer.

Bristow, M. (2007) *China tightens grip ahead of congress*. Online. Available HTTP: http://news.bbc.co.uk/2/hi/asia-pacisfic/6992946.stm (accessed 14 September 2007).

BT (Bundestag) (2001) 14. Wahlperiode, 158. Sitzung, 15 March.

Bubandt, N. (2005) 'Vernacular security: The politics of feeling safe in global, national and local worlds', *Security Dialogue*, 36(3): 275–96.

Buffalo News/Associated Press (1998a), *Clinton vows to help nations fight AIDS, especially in Africa*, 1 December.

Buffalo News/Los Angeles Times (1998b), *Spread of AIDS in S. Africa threat to social order, reports say*, 1 December.

Buhl, D. (1998) 'Die verwundbare Weltmacht', *Die ZEIT*, 13 August.

Burke, K. (1955) *A rhetoric of motives*, Berkeley: University of California Press.

Bush, G. W. (2002a) 'Graduation speech at West Point', 1 June.

—— (2002b) 'Remarks by the President on Iraq at the Cincinnati Museum Center', 7 October.

—— (1990) 'Remarks at the Aspen Institute Symposium in Aspen', 2 August.

Buzan, B. (1997) 'Rethinking security after the Cold War', *Cooperation and Conflict*, 32(1): 5–28.

—— (1983) *People, states, and fear: The national security problem in international relations*, Chapel Hill: University of North Carolina Press.

Buzan, B. and Hansen, L. (2009) *The evolution of international security studies*, Cambridge: Cambridge University Press.

Buzan, B. and Little, R. (2001) 'Why International Relations has failed as an intellectual project and what to do about it', *Millennium*, 30(1): 19–39.

Buzan, B. and Waever, O. (2009) 'Macro-securitization and security constellations: reconsidering scale in securitization theory', *Review of International Studies*, 35(2), 253–76.

—— (2003) *Regions and powers*, Cambridge: Cambridge University Press.

—— (1997) 'Slippery? Contradictory? Sociologically untenable? The Copenhagen school replies', *Review of International Studies*, 23(2), 241–50.

Buzan, B., Waever, O., and De Wilde, J. (1998) *Security: A new framework for analysis*, Boulder. CO: Lynne Rienner.

Bynander, F. (2001) 'Securitizing submarine intrusions', in J. Eriksson (ed.), *Threat politics: New perspectives on security, risk and crisis management*, Aldershot: Ashgate.

Campbell, D. (1993) *Writing security: United States foreign policy and the politics of identity*, 2nd edn, Minneapolis: University of Minnesota Press.

—— (1992) *Writing security: United States foreign policy and the politics of identity*, Minneapolis: University of Minnesota Press.

Carey, J. (2002) 'American journalism on, before, and after September 11', in B. Zelizer and S. Allan (eds) *Journalism after September 11*, New York: Routledge.

—— (1988) *Communication as culture: Essays on media and society*, Boston: Unwin Hyman.

Carroll, D. R. (ed.) (1990) *The states of 'theory': History, art, and critical discourse*, New York: Columbia University Press.

Cavell, S. (2002) *Must we mean what we say?* Cambridge: Cambridge University Press.

CCTV (2001) *The lesson and price of evil cult. Video compact disk*, Beijing: Central China Television.

Ceyhan, A. and Tsoukala, A. (2002) 'The securitization of immigration in Western societies: Ambivalent discourses and policies', *Alternatives*, 27(suppl.): 21–39.

Chang, M. (2004) *Falun Gong – The end of days*, New Haven: Yale University Press.

Chauvistre, E. (1998) 'Schurken sind die Länder mit schlechten Beziehungen zu den USA. Die neue US-Militärdoktrin nach dem Zweiten Weltkrieg und die Politik gegenüber Irak', *Frankfurter Rundschau*, 4 February.

Checkel, T. (2008) 'Process tracing', in A. Klotz and D. Prakash (eds) *Qualitative methods in International Relations*, Basingstoke, UK: Palgrave Macmillan: 114–30.

—— (2005) 'International institutions and socialization in Europe', *International Organization*, 59(4): 801–26.

—— (2001) 'Why comply? Social learning and European identity change', *International Organization*, 55(3): 553–88.

Checkel, J. T. (1999) 'Norms, institutions, and national identity in contemporary Europe', *International Studies Quarterly*, 43(1): 83–114.

Chen, S., Duckworth, K., and Chaiken, S. (2000) 'Motivated heuristic and systematic processing', *Psychological Inquiry*, 10(1), 44–49.

Chicago Sun-Times (1993) *HIV entry ban isn't illogical*, 23 February.

ChinaOnline (1999) *Decision of the Standing Committee of the National People's Congress on Banning Heretical Cult Organizations, and Preventing and Punishing Cult Activities*. Online. Available HTTP: http://www.chinaonline.com/refer/legal/Mmeyer_laws/pdf/pdf_e/c9111570e. pdf (accessed 25 May 2009).

Cimbala, S. J. (1996) *Clinton and post-war defense*, New York: Praeger.

Ciuta, F. (2009) 'Security and the problem of context: a hermeneutical critique of securitisation theory', *Review of International Studies*, 35(2): 301–26.

Clifton, H. (2003) 'Harsh criticism stymies future of Pentagon's futures market', Online. Available HTTP: http://www.prweekus.com/MEDIA-WATCH-Harsh-criticism-stymies-future-of-Pentagons-futures-marketarticle/47712/ (accessed 12 May 2009).

Clinton, B. (1996) *Presidential Decision Directive.NSTC-7, 12 June*. Online. Available HTTP: http://www.geis.fhp.osd.mil/GEIS/aboutGEIS/historicaldocs/NSTC-7.asp (accessed 15 April 2009).

—— (1993) *President Clinton's Inaugural Speech, 20 January*. Online. Available HTTP: www.history.com (accessed 10 April 2009).

Clinton, B. and Gore, A. (1992) *Putting people first. How we can all change America*, New York: Three Rivers Press.

CNN (2000) *US steps up global fight against AIDS*. Online. Available HTTP: http://archives.cnn.com/2000/US/01/10/aids.africa.02 (accessed 22 September 2008).

Cobb, M. D. (2005) 'Framing effects on public opinion about nanotechnology', *Science Communication*, 27(2): 221–39.

Cochran, M. (2002) 'Deweyan pragmatism and post-positivist social science in IR', *Millennium*, 31(3): 525–48.

Coleman, R. and Thorson, E. (2002) 'The effect of news stories that put crime and violence into context: Testing the public health model of reporting', *Journal of Health Communication*, 7(5): 401–25.

Collier, D. and Mahoney, J. (1996) 'Insights and pitfalls: Selection bias in qualitative work', *World Politics*, 49(1): 56–91.

Corollier, C. (2010) 'Nationalité. Preuves par l'absurde', *Libération*, 2–4.

Coupland, R. (2007) 'Security, insecurity and health', *Bulletin of the World Health Organization*, 85(3): 181–84.

Crawford, (2004) 'Understanding discourse: A method of ethical argument analysis', *Qualitative Methods*, 2(1): 22–25.

Creswell, J. W. (2006) *Qualitative inquiry and research design: Choosing among five approaches*, Thousand Oaks, CA: Sage.

Crotty, M. (1998) *The foundations of social research: Meaning and perspective in the research process*, Thousand Oaks, CA: Sage.

Culler, J. (1986) *Ferdinand de Saussure*, 2nd edn, New York: Cornell University Press.

Curley, M. G. (2004) *Security and illegal migration in Northeast Asia*, Monterey, CA: Monterey Institute of International Affairs.

Dabelko, G. and Simmons, P. J. (1997) 'Environment and security: Core ideas and US government initiatives', *SAIS Review*, 17(1): 127–46.

Daily News (1999) *Hit at UN, urges a global AIDS fight*, 2 December.

Dalby, S. (2001) 'Environmental change and human security: Rethinking the context of sustainable development', paper presented at the Canadian Institute of International Affairs National Policy Conference on "The Environmental Balance Sheet", Chateau Laurier, Ottawa, October 2001.

—— (1999) 'Threats from the South? Geopolitics, equity, and environmental security', in D. Deudney and A. Matthew (eds), *Contested grounds: Security and conflict in the new environmental politics*, Albany: SUNY Press.

Dalgaard-Nielsen, A. (2006) *Germany, pacifism and peace enforcement*, Manchester: Manchester University Press.

Danto, A. R. (ed.) (1968) *The philosophy of action*, London: Oxford University Press.

Das, P. and Samarasekera, U. (2008) 'What next for UNAIDS?', *The Lancet*, 372(9656): 2099–2102.

Davidson, D. (1982) *Essays on actions and events*, Oxford: Oxford University Press.

—— (1963) 'Actions, reasons and causes', *The Journal of Philosophy*, 60(23): 685–700.

De Bruijn, A. and Hufen, H. A. M. (1998) 'The traditional approach to policy instruments', in B. G. Peters and F. K. M. V. Nispen (eds), *Public policy instruments: Evaluating the tools of public administration*, New York: Edward Elgar.

Dellmayr, F. (1984) *Language and politics*, Notre Dame, IN: University of Notre Dame Press.

Denzin, N. K. and Lincoln, Y. S. (1994) *Handbook of qualitative research*, Thousand Oaks, CA: Sage.

Der Derian,J. (2001) 'Global events, national security, and virtual theory', *Millennium: Journal of International Studies*, 30(3): 669–90.

—— (1995) 'The value of security: Hobbes, Marx, and Baudrillard', in R. Lipschutz (ed.), *On security*. New York: Columbia University Press.

Derrida,J. (1988) *Limited Inc*, Evanston: Northwestern University Press.

—— (1982) *Positions*, Chicago: University of Chicago Press.

—— (1977) 'Signature Event Context,' *Glyph: Johns Hopkins Textual Studies*, Baltimore: Johns Hopkins University Press.

Der Spiegel (1997) 'Zeichen für Liebesentzug', 23: 142–43.

Deutsche Presse-Agentur (1995) *US turns Cold War energies to AIDS control*, 7 August.

De Vreese, C. H. (2005) 'News framing: Theory and typology', *Information Design Journal & Document Design*, 13(1): 51–62.

—— (2004) 'The effects of frames on political television news on issue interpretation and frame salience', *Journalism and Mass Communication Quarterly*, 81(1): 36–52.

De Vreese, C. H. and Elenbaas, M. (2008) 'Media in the game of politics: Effects of strategic metacoverage on political cynicism', *The International Journal of Press/Politics*, 13(3): 285–309.

De Wilde, J. (2008) 'Environmental security deconstructed', in H. G. Brauch, J. Grin, C. Mesjasz, N. C. Behera, B. Chourou, U. Oswald Spring, P. H. Liotta, and P. Kameri-Mbote, (eds), *Globalisation and environmental challenges: Reconceptualizing security in the 21st Century*, Berlin: Springer.

Dewulf, A. Gray, B., Putnam, L., Lewicki, R., Aarts, N., Bouwen, R., and van Woerkum, C. (2009) 'Disentangling approaches to framing in conflict and negotiation research: A meta-paradigmatic perspective', *Human Relations*, 62(2): 155–93.

Die ZEIT (1998) *De verwundbare Weltmacht*, 13 August.

Dillon, M. (1996) *Politics of security: Towards a political philosophy of Continental thought*, London: Routledge.

Doty, R. L. (2007) 'States of exception on the Mexico-U.S. border: Security, decisions, and civilian border patrols', *International Political Sociology*, 1(2): 113–37.

—— (1998/1999) 'Immigration and the Politics of Security', *Security Studies*, 8(2/3): 71–93.

Dror, Y. (1971) *Crazy states: A counterconventional strategic problem*, New York: Kraus Reprint.

Druckman,J. N. (2001) 'On the limits of framing effects: Who can frame?', *Journal of Politics*, 63(4): 1041–66.

Duffield,J. S. (1998) *World power forsaken: Political culture, international institutions and German security policy after unification*, Stanford, CA: Stanford University Press.

Duffield, M. and Waddell, N. (2006) 'Securing humans in a dangerous world', *International Politics*, 43(1): 1–23.

Duffy, G., Federking, B. K., and Tucker, S. A. (1998) 'Language games: Dialogical analysis of INF negotiations', *International Studies Quarterly*, 42(2): 271–94.

Dunford, R. and Jones, D. (2000) 'Narrative in strategic change', *Human Relations* 53(9): 1207–26.

Dunn, N., Moore, M., and Nosek, B. A. (2005) 'The war of the words: How linguistic differences in reporting shape perceptions of terrorism', *Analyses of Social Issues and Public Policy*, 5(1): 67–86.

Dunn Cavelty, M. (2008) *Cyber-security and threat politics: US efforts to secure the information age*, London: Routledge.

Duranti, A. and Goodwin, C. (1992) 'Editors' introduction,' in A. Duranti and C. Goodwin (eds) *Rethinking context: Language as an interactive phenomenon*, Cambridge: Cambridge University Press.

Dutton, M. (2005) *Policing Chinese politics – A history*, Durham, NC: Duke University Press.

Eagly, A. H., Chen, S., Chaiken, S., and Shaw-Barnes, K. (1999) 'The impact of attitudes on memory: An affair to remember', *Psychological Bulletin*, 125(1): 64–89.

Eckard, R. (1990) 'The concept of action', in A. Burkhardt (ed.) *Speech acts, meaning and intentions: Critical approaches to the philosophy of John R. Searle*, Berlin: Walter de Gruyter.

Eckstein, H. (1975) 'Case studies and theory in political science', in F. Greenstein and N. Polsby (eds), *Handbook of political science*, Reading, MA: Addison-Wesley: 79–138.

Edelman, M. (1988) *Constructing the political spectacle*, Chicago: The University of Chicago Press.

Einwohner, R. L. (2002) 'Bringing the outsiders in: Opponents' claims and the construction of animal rights activists' identity', *Mobilization*, 7(3): 253–67.

Ekeus, R. (2004) 'Reassessment: The IISS strategic dossier on Iraq's weapons of mass destruction', *Survival*, 46(2): 73–88.

Elbe, S. (2006) 'Should HIV/AIDS be securitized? The ethical dilemmas of linking HIV/AIDS and security', *International Studies Quarterly*, 50(1): 119–44.

Elhefnawy, N. (2004) 'Societal complexity and diminishing returns in security', *International Security*, 29(1): 152–74.

Emirbayer, M. (1997) 'Manifesto for a relational sociology', *American Journal of Sociology*, 103(2): 281–317.

Emirbayer, M. and Mische, A. (1998) 'What is agency?' *The American Journal of Sociology*, 103(4): 962–1023.

Emmers, R. (2004) *Non-traditional security in the Asia-Pacific: The dynamics of securitisation*, Singapore: Marshall Cavendish.

—— (2003) 'ASEAN and the securitization of transnational crime in Southeast Asia', *The Pacific Review*, 16(3): 419–38.

Entman, R. M. (2004) *Projections of power: Framing news, public opinion and U.S. foreign policy*, Chicago: University of Chicago Press.

—— (1991) 'Framing U.S. coverage of international news: Contrasts in narratives in the KAL and Iran Air incidents', *Journal of Communication*, 41(4): 6–26.

—— (1993) 'Framing: Toward clarification of a fractured paradigm', *Journal of Communication*, 43(4): 51–58.

Eriksson, J. (ed.) (2001) *Threat politics: New perspectives on security, risk and crisis management*, Aldershot: Ashgate.

—— (1999a) 'Observers or advocates? On the political roles of security analysts', *Cooperation and Conflict*, 34(3): 311–30.

—— (1999b) *Agendas, threats, and politics: Securitization in Sweden*, paper presented at the ECPR Joint Sessions, Mannheim, 26–31 March.

Erlandson, D. A., Harris, E. L., Skipper, B. L., and Allen, S. D. (1993) *Doing naturalistic enquiry*, London: Sage.

EU Observer (2003) *Germany attacks UK's refugee "camp" plan*, 31 March.

Fairclough, N. (1995) *Critical discourse analysis: The critical study of language*, London: Longman.

—— (1992) *Discourse and social change*, Cambridge: Polity Press.

Fairclough, N. and Wodak, R. (1997) 'Critical discourse analysis', in T. Van Dijk (ed.), *Discourse as social interaction*, London: Sage, 258–84.

Fazhi, Ribao (1999) 'Laws exist for the banning of Falun Gong', *Chinese Law and Government*, 32(5): 43–45.

Fearon, J. (1999) *What is identity (as we now use the word)?* Unpublished manuscript, Stanford University, Stanford.

Fee, E. and Parry, M. (2008) 'Jonathan Mann, HIV/AIDS, and human rights', *Journal of Public Health Policy*, 2008 (29), 54–71.

Feingold, R. (1999a) *Debate in Senate regarding African Growth and Opportunity Act*. Online. Available HTTP: www.thomas.gov (accessed 15 April 2009).

—— (1999b) *Debate in Senate regarding Hope for Africa Bill*. Online. Available HTTP: www.thomas.gov (accessed 30 March 2009).

Ferree, M.M. (2005) 'Soft repression: Ridicule, stigma, and silencing in gender-based movements', in C. Davenport, H. Johnston and C. Mueller (eds) *Repression and mobilization*, Minneapolis: University of Minnesota Press.

Fierke, K. M. (1998) *Changing games, changing strategies: Critical investigations in security*, Manchester: Manchester University Press.

Financial Times (2003) *UK moots 'zones of protection' for refugees*, 16 June.

Finnemore, M. and Sikkink, K. (1998) 'International norm dynamics and political change', *International Organization*, 52(4): 887–917.

Floyd, R. (2007) 'Towards a consequentialist evaluation of security: bringing together the Copenhagen and the Welsh Schools of security studies', *Review of International Studies*, 33(2): 327–50.

Forguson, L. W. (1969) 'Austin's philosophy of action', in K. T. Fann (ed.) *Symposium on J. L. Austin*, London: Routledge & Kegan Paul.

Fotion, N. (2000) *John Searle*, Princeton: Princeton University Press.

Foucault, M. (1980) *Power/Knowledge*, New York: Pantheon Books.

Gamson, W. (1988) 'Political discourse and collective action', in B. Klandermans, H. Kriesi and S. Tarrow (eds) *International social movement research – From structure to action: Comparing social movement research across cultures*, London: JAI Press.

Gamson, W. and Modigliani, A. (1989) 'Media discourse and public opinion on nuclear power: A constructionist approach', *American Journal of Sociology*, 95(1): 1–37.

Garcia, M.J., Margaret, M. L. and Todd, T. (2005) *Immigration: Analysis of the major provisions of the REAL ID act of 2005*, Congressional Research Service.

Gazeta.kg (2005a) *Okolo tysyachi chelovek sobralos na tsentralnoi ploshchadi Bishkeka* [trans. *Around a thousand people gather on Bishkek's central square*]. Online. Available HTTP: http://older.gazeta.kg/view.php?i = 17284 (accessed 27 August 2008).

—— (2005b) *V Bishkeke prokhodit miting s trebovaniem otstavki Kulova. Rysbek [sic] Akmatbaev obyavil Feliksu Kulovu dzhikhad* [trans. *Protest in Bishkek demands Kulov's resignation. Rysbek [sic] declares jihad on Feliks Kulov*]. Online. Available HTTP: http://older.gazeta.kg/view.php?i = 17286 (accessed 27 August 2008).

Gecas, V. (2000) 'Value identities, self-motives, and social movement', in S. Stryker, T. J. Owens and R. W. White (eds) *Self, identity, and social movement*, Minneapolis: University of Minnesota Press.

Geddes, A. (2005) 'Getting the best of both worlds? Britain, the EU and migration policy', *International Affairs*, 81(4): 723–40.

232 *References*

Geddes, B. (1990) 'How the cases you choose affect the answers you get: Selection bias in comparative politics', *Political Analysis*, 2(1): 131–50.

Geertz, C. (1973) *The interpretation of cultures: Selected essays*, New York: Basic Books.

—— (1968) *Islam observed: Religious development in Morocco and Indonesia*, New Haven: Yale University Press.

GEIS (2009) *Fact page*. Online. Available HTTP: http://www.geis.fhp.osd.mil/ (accessed 15 April 2009).

George, A. L. and Bennett, A. (2005) *Case studies and theory development in the social sciences*, Cambridge, MA: MIT Press.

Gerring, J. (2006) *Case study research: Principles and practice*, Cambridge: Cambridge University Press.

Giddens, A. (1979) *Central problems in social theory: Action, structure and contradiction in social analysis*, London: Macmillan.

Gill, R. (1993) 'Justifying insjustice: Broadcasters account of inequality on radio', in I. Parker and E. Burman (eds) *Discourse analytic research*, London: Macmillan.

Gitlin, T. (2003). *The whole world is watching: Mass media in the making and unmaking of the New Left*, Berkeley: University of California Press.

Goffman, E. (1959) *The presentation of the self in everyday life*, New York: Doubleday.

Goldstone, J. (1991) *Revolution and rebellion in the early modern world*, Berkeley: University of California Press.

Gore, A. (1996) 'Emerging infections threaten national and global security', *American Society for Microbiology*, 62(9): 448–49.

Gow, J. (2002) 'The HIV/AIDS epidemic in Africa: Implications for US policy', *Health Affairs*, 21(3): 57–69.

Grabe, M. E. and Kamhawi, R. (2006) 'Hard wired for negative news? Gender differences in processing broadcast news', *Communication Research*, 33(5): 346–69.

Grace, G. W. (1987) *The linguistic construction of reality*, London: Croom Helm.

Greenberg, J., Solomon, S., Pyszczynski, T., and Steinberg, L. (1988) 'A reaction to Greenwald, Pratkanis, Leippe, and Baumgardner (1988): Under what conditions does research obstruct theory progress?', *Psychological Review*, 95(4): 566–71.

Greenwald, A. G., Leippe, M. R., Pratkanis, A. R., and Baumgardner, M. H. (1986) 'Under what conditions does theory obstruct research progress', *Psychological Review*, 93(2): 216–29.

Guitter, E. P. (2008) 'Military activities within national boundaries: The French case', in D. Bigo and A. Tsoukala (eds), *Terror, insecurity and liberty*, London: Routledge, 121–45.

Gusfield, J. R. (1981) *The culture of public problems: Drinking-driving and the symbolic order*, Chicago: The University of Chicago Press.

Gusterson, H. (2008) 'Ethnographic research', in A. Klotz and D. Prakesh (eds), *Qualitative methods in International Relations: A pluralist guide*, London: Palgrave Macmillan-ECPR.

Haar, B. J. (2002) 'China's inner demons: The political impact of the demonological paradigm', in W. L. Chong (ed.) *China's great proletarian cultural revolution—Master narratives and post-Mao counternarratives*, New York: Rowman & Littlefield.

Habermas, J. (1984) *Theory of communicative action, Vol. 1: Reason and rationalization of society*. Boston, MA: Beacon Press.

Hajer, M. A. (2005) 'Setting the stage: A dramaturgy of policy deliberation', *Administration and Society*, 36(6): 624–47.

—— (1995) *Politics of environmental discourse*, Oxford: Oxford University Press.

Hancock, D. R. and Algozzine, B. (2006) *Doing case study research: A practical guide for beginning researchers*, New York, NY: Teachers College Press.

Hansen, L. (2007) 'The clash of the cartoons? The clash of civilizations? Visual securitization and the Danish 2008 cartoon crisis', paper presented at the International Studies Association Conference, Chicago, 28 February–3 March.

—— (2006) *Security as practice: Discourse analysis and the Bosnian war*, London: Routledge.

—— (2000) 'The Little Mermaid's silent security dilemma and the absence of gender in the Copenhagen School', *Millennium: Journal of International Studies*, 29(2): 285–306.

Hanson, R. D. (2006) 'Designing real terrorism futures', *Public Choice*, 128(1–2): 257–74.

Hardy, C. (2004) 'Scaling up and bearing down in discourse analysis: Questions regarding textual agencies and their contexts', *Organization*, 11(3): 415–425.

—— (2001) 'Researching organizational discourse', *International Studies in Management and Organization*, 31(3): 25–47.

Hardy, C., Harley, B., and Philipps, N. (2004) 'Discourse analysis and content analysis: Two solitudes?', *Qualitative Methods*, 2(1): 19–22.

Harkavy, R. E. (1981) 'Pariah states and nuclear proliferation', *International Organization*, 35(1): 135–63.

—— (1977) 'The pariah state syndrome', *Orbis*, 21(3): 623–49.

Harnisch, S. and Maull, H. W. (2001) *Germany as a civilian power? The foreign policy of the Berlin Republic*, Manchester: Manchester University Press.

Harris, P. G. (2001) *The environment, international relations, and U.S. foreign policy*, Washington DC: Georgetown University Press.

Hauge, W. and Ellingsen, T. (2001) 'Causal pathways to conflict', in P. Diehl and N. P. Gleditsch (eds), *Environmental conflict*, Boulder, CO: Westview Press.

Havel, V. (1992) *Open letters: Selected writings 1965–1990*, New York: Vintage Books.

Health Resources and Services Administration/US Department of Health and Human Services (2008) *The HIV/AIDS programs: Who was Ryan White?*. Online. Available HTTP: http://hab.hrsa.gov/about/ryanwhite.htm (accessed 8 September 2008).

Heath, L. and Tindale, R. S. (1994) 'Heuristics and biases in applied settings: An introduction', in Heath, L., Tindale, R. S., Edwards, J., Posavac, E. J., Bryant, F. B., Henderson-King, E., Suarez-Balcazar, Y., and Myers, J. (eds), *Applications of heuristics and biases to social issue*, New York: Plenum.

Hedstroem, P. and Swedberg, R. (eds) (1998) *Social mechanisms: An analytical approach to social theory*, Cambridge: Cambridge University Press.

Henriksen, T. H. (2001) 'The rise and decline of rogue states', *Journal of International Affairs*, 54(2): 349–73.

Henry J. Kaiser Family Foundation (2007) *The HIV/AIDS epidemic in the United States*, Menlo Park, CA: The Henry J. Kaiser Family Foundation.

Herek, G. M., Capitanio, J. P., and Widaman, K. F. (2002) 'HIV-related stigma and knowledge in the United States: Prevalence and trends, 1991–99', *American Journal Of Public Health*, 92(3): 371–77.

Herman, E. S. and Chomsky, N. (1989) *Manufacturing consent: The political economy of the mass media*, New York: Pantheon Books.

Hermann, M. G. (2008) 'Content analysis', in *Qualitative methods in International Relations: A pluralist guide*, New York: Palgrave Macmillan.

Herrera, Y. M. and Braumoeller, B. F. (2004) 'Symposium: Discourse and content analysis', *Newsletter of the American Political Science Association Organized Section on Qualitative Methods*, 2(1): 15–39.

Heymann, D. L. (2003) 'The evolving infectious disease threat: Implications for national and global security', *Journal of Human Development*, 4(2): 191–207.

Hils, J. and Wilzewski, J. (2004) 'Zwischen Imperium und Republik: Die Außenpolitik der

USA von Clinton zu Bush', in H. J. Puhle, S. Schreyer and J. Wilzewski (eds) *Supermacht im Wandel: Die USA von Clinton zu Bush*, Frankfurt: Campus.

Holm, U. (2004) 'Algeria: Securitization of state/regime, nation and Islam', in S. Guzzini and D. Jung (eds) *Contemporary security analysis and Copenhagen peace research*, London: Routledge.

Holsti, O. R. (1969) *Content analysis for the social sciences and the humanities*, Reading, MA: Addison Wesley.

Homer-Dixon, T. F. (1999) *Environment, scarcity, and violence*, New Haven: Princeton University Press.

—— (1994) 'Environmental scarcities and violent conflict', *International Security*, 19(1): 5–40.

—— (1991) 'On the threshold: Environmental changes as causes of conflict', *International Security*, 16(2): 76–116.

Homer-Dixon, T. F. and Blitt, J. (1998) *Ecoviolence: Links among environment, population, and security*, Lanham, MD: Rowman & Littlefield.

Honig, B. (2005) 'Bound by Law? Alien rights, administrative discretion and the politics of the technicality: Lessons from Louis Post and the First Red Scare', in A. Sarat, L. Douglas and M. M. Umphrey (eds) *The limits of the law*, Stanford, CA: Stanford University Press.

Hopf, T. (2002) *Social construction of international politics. Identities and foreign policies, Moscow, 1955 and 1999*, Ithaca, NY: Cornell University Press.

Hoyt, C. (2008): 'Separating the terror and the terrorists', *The New York Times*, December 14, p. WK10.

Hua, S. and Xia, M. (1999) 'Guest editors' introduction', *Chinese Law and Government*, 32(6), 172–80.

Hunt, S. A., Benford, R. D., and Snow, D. A. (1994) 'Identity fields: Framing process and the social construction of movement identities', in E. Laraña, H. Johnston and J. R. Gusfield (eds) *New social movements: From ideology to identity*, Philadelphia: Temple University Press.

Huysmans, J. (2008) 'The jargon of exception – On Schmitt, Agamben and the absence of political society', *International Political Sociology*, 2(2): 165–83.

—— (2006) *The politics of insecurity: Fear, migration and asylum in the EU*, London: Routledge.

—— (2004) 'Minding exceptions. Politics of insecurity and liberal democracy', *Contemporary Political Theory* 3(3): 321–41.

—— (2002) 'Defining social constructivism in security studies: The normative dilemma of writing security', *Alternatives*, 27, Special Issue: 41–62.

—— (2000) 'The European Union and the securitization of migration', *Journal of Common Market Studies*, 38(5): 751–777.

—— (1998 a) 'Revisiting Copenhagen: Or, on the creative development of a security agenda in Europe', *European Journal of International Relations*, 4(4): 479–505.

—— (1998b) 'Security! What do you mean? From concept to thick signifier', *European Journal of International Relations*, 4(2): 226–55.

—— (1995) 'Migrants as security problem: Dangers of securitizing societal issues', in R. Miles and D. Thränhardt (eds) *Migration and European integration: The dynamics of inclusion and exclusion*, London: Pinter.

Ingram, H. and Schneider, A. (1991) 'Target population and policy design', *Administration and Society*, 23(3): 233–56.

—— (1990) 'Behavioral assumptions of policy tools', *Journal of Politics*, 52 (2): 510–29.

Jackson Jr., J. (1999a) *AIDS Testimony* (*Subcommittee on Criminal Justice, Drug Policy and Human Resources*). Online. Available HTTP: http://www.jessejacksonjr.org/ (accessed 15 April 2009).

—— (1999b) *Hope for Africa Legislative Outline*. Online. Available HTTP: http://www.jessejacksonjr.org/ (accessed 15 April 2009).

Jackson, N. J. (2006) 'International organizations, security dichotomies and the trafficking of persons and narcotics in post-Soviet Central Asia: A critique of the securitization framework', *Security Dialogue*, 37(3): 299–317.

Jervis, R. (2005) *American foreign policy in a new era*, New York: Routledge.

John, P. (1998) *Analysing public policy*, London: Continuum.

Johnson, K. E. (2002) 'AIDS as a US national security threat: Media effects and geographical imaginations', *Feminist Media Studies*, 2(1): 81–96.

Johnson-Laird, P. (1983) *Mental models: Towards a cognitive science of language, inference and consciousness*, Cambridge: Cambridge University Press.

Jones, J. M. (2002) 'Bush averages near-record 86% job approval rating in Fourth Quarter', *Gallup Poll Analyses*, 17 January.

Jorgensen, D. L. (1989) *Participant observation: A methodology for human sciences*, New York: Sage.

Judis, J. B. (2005) 'The chosen nation: The influence of religion on U.S. foreign policy', *Carnegie Endowment for International Peace Policy Brief*, 37(5).

Junker, D. (2003) *Power and mission: Was Amerika antreibt*, Freiburg: Herder.

Jutersonke, O. (forthcoming) *Images of law and reality in the realism of Hans J. Morgenthau*, Cambridge: Cambridge University Press.

K.A. (2005) 'Mirnye grazhdane protiv kriminala' – tak nazyvaetsya novoe dvizhenie' [trans. 'New movement called "Peaceful Citizens Against Criminals"'], *Slovo Kyrgyzstana*, 109 (21870): 5.

Kagan, R. (2003) *Paradise and power: America and Europe in the new world order*, London: Atlantic.

Kamuf, P. (1991) *A Derrida reader: Between the blinds*, Columbia: Columbian University Press.

Kaplan, R. D. (1994) 'The coming anarchy', *The Atlantic Monthly*, 273(2): 44–76.

Karimov, D. and Satybekov, E. (2005) 'Komu Kulov ne avtoritet, ili Kak Ryspek novuyu kyrgyzskuyu elitu napugal' [trans. 'For whom is Kulov not an *avtoritet*, or how Ryspek frightened the new Kyrgyz elite'], *Vechernii Bishkek*, 205(8879): 4.

Kasper, G. (1990) 'Linguistic politeness: Current research issues', *Journal of Pragmatics*, 14: 187–218.

Kaufman, S. J. (1996) 'Spiralling to ethnic war: Elites, masses, and Moscow in Moldova's Civil War', *International Security*, 21(2): 108–38.

Kegley, C. W. and Wittkopf, E. R. (1996) *American foreign policy: Pattern and process*, New York: St. Martin's Press.

Kennedy, Paul M. (1988) *The rise and fall of the great powers: Economic change and military conflict from 1500 to 2000*, London: Unwin Hyman.

Kent, A. (2006) 'Reconfiguring security: Buddhism and moral legitimacy in Cambodia', *Security Dialogue*, 37(3): 343–61.

Khokhlova, N. (2005) 'Plakaty, povara i tualety' [trans. 'Placards, cooks and toilets'], *Vechernii Bishkek*, 203(8877): 1.

Khokhlova, N. and Lokteva, S. (2005) 'Deputata Akmatbaeva rasstrelyali zeki' [trans. 'Deputy Akmatbaev shot by prisoners'], *Vechernii Bishkek*, 202(8876): 1.

King, J., Rothand, R., and Salvatore, S. (2000) *US steps up global fight against AIDS*. Online. Available HTTP: http://archives.cnn.com/2000/US/01/10/aids.africa.02 (accessed 22 September 2008).

Kingdon, J. W. (2003) *Agendas, alternatives and public policies*, 2nd edn, New York: Longman.

—— (1984) *Agenda, alternatives, and public policies*, Boston: Little Brown.

Kitcher, P. (1995) *The advancement of science*, Oxford: Oxford University Press.

Klare, M. (1995) *Rogue states and nuclear outlaws: America's search for a new foreign policy*, New York: Hill and Wang.

Klotz, A. (2008) 'Introduction', in Klotz Audie and Prakash Deepa (eds), *Qualitative methods in International Relations: A pluralist guide*, New York: Palgrave Macmillan.

Kluver, A. R. (1996) *Legitimating the Chinese economic reforms – A rhetoric of myth and orthodoxy*, Albany: State University of New York Press.

Knudsen, O. F. (2001) 'Post-Copenhagen security studies: Desecuritizing securitization', *Security Dialogue* 32(3): 355–68.

Kojomkulov, T. (2005) 'Politicheskii terror po-kyrgyzski' [trans. 'Kyrgyz-style political terror'], *ResPublica*, 39(605): 7.

Krause, J. (2006) 'Wie ernst ist die Krise? Atomare Proliferation und internationale Ordnung', *Internationale Politik*, 61: 6–15.

—— (2000) 'Streit um Raketenabwehr. Ursachen der neuen transatlantischen Krise', *Internationale Politik*, 55: 37–42.

—— (1998) *Strukturwandel der Nichtverbreitungspolitik – Die Verbreitung von Massenvernichtungswaffen und die weltpolitische Transformation*, München: Oldenbourg.

Krause, K. and Williams, M. C. (1997) 'From strategy to security: Foundations of critical security studies', in K. Krause and M. C. Williams (eds) *Critical security studies: Concepts and cases*, Minnesota: University of Minnesota Press.

—— (1996) 'Broadening the agenda of security studies: Politics and methods', *Mershon International Studies Review*, 40(2): 229–54.

Kress, G. (1995) 'The social production of language: History and structures of domination', in P. Fries and M. Gregory (eds), *Discourse analysis in society: Systemic functional perspectives*, Norwood: Ablex.

Kull, S., Ramsay, C., and Lewis, E. (2003) 'Misperceptions, media, and the Iraq war', *Political Science Quarterly*, 118(4): 569–98.

Laclau, E. and Mouffe, C. (1985) *Hegemony and socialist strategy: Towards a radical democratic politics*, London: Verso.

Laffey, M., and Weldes, J. (2004) 'Methodological reflections on discourse analysis', *Qualitative Methods*, 2(1): 28–31.

Lai, H. H. (2006) 'Religious politics in post-totalitarian china: Maintaining political monopoly over reviving society', *Journal of Chinese Political Science*, 11(1): 55–77.

Lake, A. (1994) 'Confronting backlash states', *Foreign Affairs*, 73(2): 45–55.

—— (1993) 'From containment to enlargement – remarks by Anthony Lake at Johns Hopkins University', 21 September.

Lam, W. W. (2000) 'Jiang compares sect's threat to solidarity', *South China Morning Post*, 12(2).

Larsen, H. (1997) *Foreign policy and discourse analysis: France, Britain and Europe*, London: Routledge.

Lascoumes, P. and Le Galès, P. (2004) 'L'action publique saisie par les instruments', in P. Lascoumes and P. Le Galès (eds) *Gouverner par les instruments*, Paris: Presses de la FNSP.

Lausten, C. B. and Wæver, O. (2000) 'In defense of religion: Sacred referent objects of securitization', *Millennium: Journal of International Studies*, 29(3): 705–40.

Lee, C. K. (2003) 'Pathways of labour insurgency', in E. J. Perry and M. Selden (eds) *Chinese society: Change, conflict and resistance*, 2nd edn, London: Routledge Curzon.

Léonard, S. (2007) 'The "securitization" of asylum and migration in the European Union: Beyond the Copenhagen School's framework', PhD thesis, Aberystwyth: University of Wales.

Levinson, S. C. (1983) *Pragmatics*, Cambridge: Cambridge University Press.

Levy, M. and Wall, S. S. (2004) 'Terrorism information and prevention system', *Law and Society* 31(2): 200–201.

Li, H. (2007) *Further remarks on 'politics'*. Online. Available HTTP: http://www.clearwisdom.net/emh/articles/2007/2/22/82932.html (accessed 25 May 2009).

—— (2005) *We are not 'getting political'*. Online. Available HTTP: http://www.clearwisdom.net/emh/articles/2005/1/29/57020.html (accessed 25 May 2009).

—— (2004a) *Stop the evil acts with righteous thoughts*. Online. Available HTTP: http://www.clearwisdom.net/emh/articles/2004/2/15/45145.html (accessed 25 May 2009).

—— (2004b) *Eliminate the dark minions with righteous thoughts*. Online. Available HTTP: http://www.clearwisdom.net/emh/articles/2004/3/17/46155.html (accessed 25 May 2009).

—— (2003) *Teaching and explaining the Fa at the Metropolitan New York Fa Conference*. Online. Available HTTP: http://www.falundafa.org/book/eng/jw_93.htm (accessed 25 May 2009).

—— (2001a) *Falun Gong (Law Wheel Qigong)*. Online. Available HTTP: http://www.falundafa.org/book/chibig/pdf/flg_2001.pdf (accessed 25 May 2009).

—— (2001b) *Fa-rectification and cultivation*. Online. Available HTTP: http://www.clearwisdom.net/emh/articles/2001/7/8/12052.html (accessed 25 May 2009).

—— (2001c) *Beyond the limits of forbearance*. Online. Available HTTP: http://www.clearwisdom.net/emh/articles/2001/1/2/6668.html (accessed 25 May 2009).

—— (2000a) *Suffocate the evil*. Online. Available HTTP: http://www.clearwisdom.net/emh/articles/2000/10/23/9116.html (accessed 25 May 2009).

—— (2000b) *Drive out interference*. Online. Available HTTP: http://www.clearwisdom.net/emh/articles/2000/7/7/9120.html (accessed 25 May 2009).

—— (2000c) *Teaching the Fa at the Western U.S. Fa Conference October 21, 2000 in San Francisco*. Online. Available HTTP: http://www.clearwisdom.net/emh/articles/2000/11/5/9115.html (accessed 25 May 2009).

—— (1999a) 'Letter to the Chinese communist party's central committee and to the leadership', *Chinese Law and Government*, 32(6): 24–25.

—— (1999b) *A brief statement of mine*. Online. Available HTTP: http://www.falundafa.ca/library/english/jw/jw9907221e.html (accessed 25 May 2009).

—— (1999c) 'My statement', *Chinese Law and Government*, 32(6): 26–27.

—— (1997) *Falun fofa (zai Meiguo jiangfa)* [trans. *Buddha Fa (Lectures in the United States)*]. Online. Available HTTP: http://www.falundafa.org/book/chbig/mglf.htm (accessed 25 May 2009).

—— (1996): *Zhuan Falun* [trans. *Turning the Law-wheel*]. Online. Available HTTP: http://www.falundafa.org/book/chibig/zfl.htm (accessed 25 May 2009).

Lietzmann, K. M. and Vest, G. D. (2001) *Environmental change and security project report – Environmental security in an international context: Executive summary report*, Washington DC: The Woodrow Wilson Center.

Linder, S. and Peters, B. G. (1984) 'From social theory to policy design', *Journal of Public Policy*, 4 (3), 237–59.

Lindsay, J. M. (2003) 'Apathy, interest, and the politics of American foreign policy', in B. May and M. Hönicke-Moore (eds) *The uncertain superpower: Domestic dimensions of U.S. foreign policy after the Cold War*, Opladen: Leske & Budrich.

Lippmann, W. (1922/1997) *Public opinion*, New York: Free Press.

Lipset, S. M. (1997) *American exceptionalism. A double-edged sword*, New York: Norton.

Litfin, K. T. (1994) *Ozone discourses: Science and politics in global environmental cooperation*, New York: Columbia University Press.

Lissa (2005) *Grazhdanskii sektor trebuet prezidenta privjat ikh. Bakiev po suti potreboval diktatorskikh polnomochii* [trans. *Civil sector demands that the President receives them. In effect Bakiev has demanded dictatorial powers*], 27 October.

Little, R. (1991) 'International Relations and the methodological turn', *Political Studies* 39(3): 463–78.

Litwak, R. S. (2000) *Rogue states and U.S. foreign policy: Containment after the Cold War*, Washington: Woodrow Wilson Center Press.

Longhurst, K. (2004) *Germany and the use of force: The evolution of German security policy 1990–2003*, Manchester: Manchester University Press.

Looney, R. E. (2004) 'DARPA's policy analysis market for intelligence: Outside the box or off the wall?', *International Journal of Intelligence and Counterintelligence*, 17(3): 405–19.

Lorenz, K. (1981) *The foundation of ethology*, New York: Springer-Verlag.

Lu, Y. (2005) 'Entrepreneurial logics and the evolution of falun gong', *Journal for the Scientific Study of Religion*, 44(2): 173–85.

Luke, S. (1974) *Power: A radical view*, New York: Macmillan.

Lupia, A. and McCubbins, M. D. (1998) *The democratic dilemma: Can citizens learn what they need to know?*, Cambridge: Cambridge University Press.

Lupovici, A. (2009) 'Constructivist methods: A plea and manifesto for pluralism', *Review of International Studies*, 35(1): 195–218.

McAdam, D. (1994) 'Culture and social movements', in E. Laraña, H. Johnston and J. R. Gusfield (eds) *New social movements: From ideology to identity*, Philadelphia: Temple University Press.

McCombs, M. (2004) *Setting the agenda: The mass media and public opinion*, Malden, MA: Blackwell.

McDonald, M. (2008) 'Securitization and the construction of security', *European Journal of International Relations*, 14(4): 563–87.

MacFarlane, S. N. and Torjesen, S. (2005) '"A wash with weapons"? The case of small arms in Kyrgyzstan', *Central Asian Survey*, 24(1): 5–19.

McGinn, M. (1997) *Wittgenstein and Philosophical Investigation*, London: Routledge.

McInnes, C. (2006) 'HIV/AIDS and security', *International Affairs*, 82(2): 315–26.

McLaughlin, P. (2001) *What functions explain: Functional explanation and self-reproducing systems*, Cambridge: Cambridge University Press.

Madsen, D. (1998) *American exceptionalism*, Edinburgh: Keele University Press.

Major, L. H. (2009) 'Break it to me harshly: The effects of intersecting news frames in lung cancer and obesity coverage', *Journal of Health Communication*, 14(2): 174–88.

Malevanaya, D. (2005a) '"Rekviem" so stvolami' [trans. '"Requiem" with gun barrels'], *Moya stolitsa novosti*, 123(314): 1.

—— (2005b) 'Ryspekovtsy ukhodyat. No nadolgo li?' [trans. 'Ryspekites leave. But for how long?'], *Moya stolitsa novosti*, 125(316): 2.

—— (2005c) 'Narod skazal net kriminalu!' [trans. 'People say no to criminals'], *Moya stolitsa novosti*, 126(317): 9.

Markoff, J. (2002) 'Pentagon plans a computer system that would peek at personal data of Americans', *The New York Times*, 9 November, Online Available. www.nytimes. com/2002/11/09/politics09COMP.html?ex=1170824400&en=3c391fde4069f97&ei=5070

Mathews, J. T. (1989) 'Redefining security', *Foreign Affairs*, 68(2): 162–77.

Matthew, R. (2002) 'In defense of environment and security research', *Environmental Change and Security Project*, 8: 109–24.

Mauws, M. K. (2000) 'But is it art? Decision making and discursive resources in the field of cultural production', *Journal of Applied Behavioral Science*, 36(2): 229–44.

Maxwell, T. A. (2005) 'Information policy, data mining, and national security: False positives and unidentified negatives', *Proceedings of the 38th Hawaii International Conference on System Sciences*.

Mead, G. H. (1934) *Mind, self, and society: From the standpoint of a social behaviorist*, Chicago: University of Chicago Press.

Meirowitz, A. and Joshua, A. T. (2004) 'Learning from terrorism markets', *Perspectives on Politics*, 2(2): 331–36.

Melanson, R. A. (1996) *American foreign policy since the Vietnam war: The search for consensus from Nixon to Clinton*, London: M.E. Sharpe.

Melucci, A. (1996) *Challenging codes: Collective action in the information age*, New York: Cambridge University Press.

Memorandum (2001) 'Memorandum zur Zukunft der transatlantischen Beziehungen: Die USA und Europa am Beginn einer neuen Präsidentschaft'. Online. Available HTTP: http://www.bdi-online.de (accessed 25 May 2009).

Merson, M. H. (2006) 'The HIV-AIDS pandemic at 25 – The global response', *New England Journal of Medicine*, 354(23): 2414–17.

Mey, J. L. (2001) *Pragmatics: An introduction*, Oxford: Blackwell.

Meynaud, H. Y. (2007) *Les sondages d'opinion*, Paris: La Découverte.

Migration News Sheet (2003a) *Persons arrested in connection with a terrorist plot using a highly dangerous and toxic chemical include three asylum-seekers*, February.

—— (2003b) *All-time record of asylum applications recorded last year*, March.

—— (2003c) *Prime Minister holds firm on his promise to reduce the number of asylum-seekers by half even though his Home secretary described the target as 'undeliverable'*, March.

—— (2003d) *UK is forced to withdraw proposal to set up 'Transit processing centres'*, July.

Mille, A. (2007) Hu Jintao and the Sixth Plenum, China Leadership Monitor 20.

Milliken, J. (1999) 'The study of discourse in International Relations: A critique of research and methods', *European Journal of International Relations*, 5(2): 225–54.

Milwaukee Journal Sentinel (1999a) *Feingold urges more attention to Africa, especially on AIDS*, 15 December.

—— (1999b) *Feingold joins Holbrooke on trip to African nations. Goals include assessing situation in the Congo and UN's role on the continent*, 1 December.

Milwaukee Journal Sentinel/New York Times/Associated Press (1996) *3 million new HIV cases seen this year. 23 million live with virus; 6.4 million dead*, 29 November.

Mintz, A. and Geva, N. (1993) 'Why don't democracies fight each other? An experimental study', *Journal of Conflict Resolution*, 37(3): 484–503.

Mintz, A., Redd, S. B., and Vedlitz, A. (2006) 'Can we generalize from student experiments to the real world in political science, military affairs, and international relations?', *Journal of Conflict Resolution*, 50(5): 757–76.

Monahan, T. (2006) 'Securing the homeland: Torture, preparedness, and the right to let die', *Social Justice*, 33(1): 95–105.

Morris, P. (1987) *Power: A philosophical analysis*, Manchester: Manchester University Press.

Moural, J. (2002) 'Searle's theory of institutional facts', in G. Grewendorf and G. Meggle (eds) *Speech acts, mind and social reality. Discussions with John R. Searle*, Dordrecht: Kluwer Academic Publishers.

Moya stolitsa novosti (2005) 'Zayavlenie' [trad. 'Statement'],123(314): 1

Moyser, G. and Wagstaffe, M. (1987) *Research methods for elite studies*, London: Allen and Unwin.

Mueller, J. (1973) *War, presidents, and public opinion*, New York: Wiley.

Mukashev, K. (2005) 'General, narod s toboi!' [trans. 'General, the people are with you!'], *Vechernii Bishkek*, 205(8879): 1.

Müller, H. (1995a) 'Rüstungs-und Zerstörungspotential als Herausforderung der internationalen Politik', in K. Kaiser and H. W. Maull (eds) *Deutschlands neue Außenpolitik – Band 2: Herausforderungen*, München: Oldenbourg.

240　*References*

—— (1995b) 'Die (Nicht-)Weiterverbreitung von Massenvernichtungswaffen: Internationale Regime und ihre Wirksamkeit', in H. G. Wehling (ed.) *Sicherheitspolitik unter geänderten weltpolitischen Rahmenbedingungen*, Stuttgart: Kohlhammer.

Munro, R. (1989) 'Syncretic sects and secret societies: Revival in the 1980s', *Chinese Sociology and Anthropology*, 21(4): 10–11.

Neal, A. W. (2009) 'Securitization and risk at the EU border: The origins of FRONTEX?', *Journal of Common Market Studies*, 47(2): 333–356.

Neergaard, H. and Ulhoi, J.P. (eds) (2007) *Handbook of qualitative research methods in entrepreneurship*, Cheltenham: Edward Elgar Publishing Ltd.

Neuendorf, K. (2002) *The content analysis guidebook*, Thousand Oaks, CA: Sage.

Neumann, I. B. (2008) 'Discourse analysis', in A. Klotz, and D. Prakash (eds) *Qualitative methods in International Relations*, Basingstoke, UK: Palgrave Macmillan: 61–77.

Neumann, I. B. and Heikka, H. (2005) 'Grand strategy, strategic culture, practice: The social roots of Nordic defence', *Cooperation and Conflict*, 40(1): 5–23.

Nightingale, D. and Cromby, J. (2002) 'Social constructionism as ontology: Exposition and Example', *Theory & Psychology*, 12(5): 701–13.

Nordstrom, C. (2004) *Shadows of war: Violence, power, and international profiteering in the twenty-first century*, Berkeley: University of California Press.

Norris, P., Kern, M., and Just, M. (2003) *Framing terrorism: The news media, the government and the public*, New York: Routledge.

Nyers, P. (2006) 'The accidental citizen: acts of sovereignty and (un)making citizenship', *Economy and Society*, 35(1): 22–41.

Oakeshott, M. (1975) 'Dr. Leo Strauss on Hobbes', in Oakeshott, *Hobbes On Civil Association*, Indianapolis: Liberty Fund.

O'Brien, K. J. (1996) 'Rightful resistance', *World Politics*, 49(1): 31–55.

Onuf, N. (1989) *World of our making: Rules and rules in social theory and international relations*, Columbia: University of South Carolina Press.

O'Reilly, C. (2008) 'Primetime patriotism: News media and the securitization of Iraq', *Journal of Politics and Law*, 1(3): 66–72.

Orlova, T. (2005a) 'Kriminalitet ne budet diktovat usloviya prezidentu' [trans. 'Criminals will not dictate terms to the President'], *Moya stolitsa novosti*, 123(314): 2.

Orlova, T. (2005b) *Ne boites skazat pravdu!* [trans. *Don't be afraid to tell the truth!*]. Online. Available HTTP: http://www.msn.ru/ru/news/11740 (accessed 11 June 2008).

Orlova, T. (2005c) 'Kriminal i poteri tandema' [trans. 'Criminals and the tandem's losses'], *Moya stolitsa novosti*, 126(317): 7.

Ostergaard, R. L. (2007) *HIV/AIDS and the threat to national and international security*, Basingstoke, UK: Palgrave Macmillan.

—— (2002) 'Politics in the hot zone: AIDS and national security in Africa', *Third World Quarterly*, 23(2): 333–50.

Pachur, T. and Hertwig, R. (2006) 'On the psychology of the recognition heuristic: Retrieval primacy as a key determinant of its use', *Journal of Experimental Psychology: Learning, Memory, and Cognition*, 32(5): 983–1002.

Paltema, L. and Vuori, J. A. (2009) 'Regime transition and the Chinese politics of technology: From mass science to the controlled internet', *Asian Journal of Political Science*, 17(1): 1–23.

—— (2006) 'How cheap is identity talk? A framework of identity frames and security discourse for the analysis of repression and legitimization of social movements in mainland China', *Issues and Studies*, 42(3): 47–86.

Parker, S. L. (1995) 'Toward an understanding of "rally" effects: Public opinion in the Persian Gulf war', *Public Opinion Quarterly*, 59(4): 526–46.

Peirce, C. S. (1931–1958) *Collected papers of Charles Sanders Peirce*, 8 vols. Vols. I–IV ed. by C. Hartshorne and P. Weiss. Vols V–VIII ed. by W. Burks, Cambridge, MA: Harvard University Press.

Penny, B. (2003) 'The life and times of li hongzhi: Falun gong and religious biography', *The China Quarterly*, (644–61): 14–23.

People's Daily (2007) *Carrying forward Buddhism or fuelling evil cults?* Online. Available HTTP: http://english.people.com.cn/90001/90780/6279537.html (accessed 25 May 2009).

Perelman, C. (1988) *L'empire rhétorique – Rhétorique et argumentation*, Paris: Vrin.

Perinbanayagam, R. S. (1985) *Significant acts: Structure and meanings in everyday life*, Cambridge: Polity Press.

Perrow, C. (1984) *Normal accidents: Living with high risk technologies*, New York: Basic Books.
—— (1999) *Normal accidents: Living with high risk technologies*, 2nd edn, Princeton: Princeton University Press.

Perry, E. J. (2000) 'Moving the masses: Emotion work in the Chinese revolution', *Mobilization*, 5(1): 198–99.

Perry, E. J. and Selden, M. (2003) 'Introduction: Reform and resistance in contemporary China', in E. J. Perry and M. Selden (eds) *Chinese society*, 2nd edn, London: Routledge – Curzon.

Peters, G. B. (2002) 'The politics of tool choice', in L. Salamon (ed.) *The tools of government: A guide to the new governance*, Oxford: Oxford University Press.

Peters, G. B. and Van Nispen, F. K. M. (eds) (1998) *Public policy instruments, evaluating the tools of public administration*, Cheltenham: Edward Elgar.

Peterson, S. (2002) 'Epidemic disease and national security', *Security Studies*, 12(2): 43–81.

Pfaff, S. (1996) 'Collective identity and informal groups in revolutionary mobilization in east Germany 1989', *Social Forces*, 75(1): 91–118.

Philips, N. and Hardy, C. (2002) *Discourse analysis: Investigating processes of social construction*, Thousand Oaks, CA: Sage.

Pieke, F. N. (1994) 'The use of making history: Chinese traditions of protest', *Issues and Studies*, 30(1): 13–36.

Pittsburgh Post-Gazette/Miami Herald (1993) *Clinton to let Haitian refugees enter US. HIV-infected will be allowed to leave Cuba, be brought in for political asylum*, 10 June.

Pittsburgh Post-Gazette/The Associated Press (1995) *AIDS, abortion spark defense debate: Dornan pushes anti-gay, anti-abortion agenda while GOP boosts Pentagon spending*, 25 May.

Pittsburgh Post-Gazette/Reuters News Service (1997) *Global survey: Many ignore AIDS threat*, 29 November.

Pleasants, N. (1999) *Wittgenstein and the idea of Critical Theory*, London: Routledge.

Poindexter, J., Robert, P., and Brian, S. (2003) 'Total Information Awareness (TIA)', *IEEE Explore*, 6(2938): 1–8.

Polletta, F. and Jasper, J. M. (2001) 'Collective identity and social movements', *New York Annual Review of Sociology*, 27(285): 283–305.

Ponemann, D. B. (1998) 'The United States, Europe, and the "rogue states"', in M. Dembinski and K. Gerke (eds) *Cooperation or conflict? Transatlantic relations in transition*, Frankfurt: Campus.

Popp, R. and Poindexter, J. (2006) 'Countering terrorism through information and privacy protection technologies', *IEEE Security & Privacy*, November/December: 18–27.

Porta, D. (1996) 'Social movements and the state: Thoughts on the policing of protest', in D. McAdam, J. McCarthy and M. Zald (eds) *Comparative perspectives on social movements*, Cambridge: Cambridge University Press.

Pouliot, V. (2008) 'The logic of practicality: A theory of practice of security communities', *International Organization*, 62(2): 257–88.

Price, V., Tewksbury, D., and Powers, E. (1997) 'Switching trains of thought: The impact of news frames on readers' cognitive responses', *Communication Research*, 24(5): 481–506.

Price-Smith, A. T. (2002) *The health of nations: Infectious disease, environmental change, and their effects on national security and development*, Cambridge, MA: MIT Press.

Prins, G. (2004) 'AIDS and global security', *International Affairs*, 80(5): 931–52.

Prins, G. and Stamp, R. (1991) *Top guns and toxic whales: The environment and global security*, London: Earthscan.

Program on International Policy Attitudes/Knowledge Networks Poll (2004) *Americans on detention, torture, and the war on terrorism*. Online. Available HTTP: http://www.pipa.org/OnlineReports/Terrorism/Torture_Jul04/Torture_Jul04_rpt.pdf (accessed 4 August 2009).

Rabinow, P. and Dreyfus, H. L. (1982). *Michel Foucault: Beyond structuralism and hermeneutics*, Chicago: University of Chicago Press.

Radaelli, C. (1999) *Technocracy in the European Union*, London: Longman.

Radnitz, S. (2005) 'Networks, localism and mobilization in Aksy, Kyrgyzstan', *Central Asian Survey* 24(4): 405–24.

Rahn, P. (2002) 'The chemistry of conflict: The Chinese government and the Falun gong', *Terrorism and Political Violence*, 14(4): 321–49.

Reagan, R. (1986) 'The President's News Conference', 7 May.

—— (1985) 'Remarks at the Annual Convention of the American Bar Association', 8 July.

Reckwitz, A. (2002) 'Toward a theory of social practices: A development in culturalist theorizing', *European Journal of Social Theory*, 5(2): 243–63.

Reese, S. D. (2007) 'The framing project: A bridging model for media research revised', *Journal of Communication*, 57(1): 148–54.

Renmin Ribao (1999a) *Li Hongzhi qiren qishi* [trans. *Li Hongzhi: the man and his deeds*], 23 July.

—— (1999b) *Gedi ganbu qunzhong jianjue yonghu dang he zhengfu chuli 'Falungong' jueding chongshan kexue pochu mixin weihu wending* [trans. *Cadres and the masses in various areas firmly support the party and the governments handling of 'Falungong' by upholding science, removing superstitions, and safeguarding stability*], 23 July.

—— (1999c) *Tongbao Zhongyangchuli "Falungong" wenti de wenjian jingshen* [trans. *Notification from Wang Zhaoguo Regarding the Essence of the Central Government Documents on Handling the 'Falun Gong' Issue*], 24 July.

—— (1999d) *Sanbai duoci weigong de zhengzhi mudi* [trans. *The political objective of over 300 attacks*], 5 August.

Ricoeur, P. (1981) *Hermeneutics and the human sciences: Essays on language, action and interpretation*, Cambridge: Cambridge University Press.

Rielly, J. E. (1995) *American public opinion and US foreign policy*, Chicago: Chicago Council on Foreign Relations.

Rinehart, J. F. (2006) *Apocalyptic faith and political violence: Prophets of terror*, New York: Palgrave Macmillan.

Ringmar, E. (1996) *Identity, interests, and action: A cultural explanation of Sweden's intervention in the Thirty Years' War*, Cambridge: Cambridge University Press.

Risse, T. (2000) '"Let's argue!": Communicative action in world politics', *International Organization* 54(1): 1–40.

Roberts, C. (1995) *The logic of historical explanation*, University Park: Pennsylvania State University Press.

Robin, C. (2005). *The politics of fear*, Oxford: Oxford University Press.

Roe, P. (2008) 'Actor, audience(s) and emergency measures: Securitization and the UK's decision to invade Iraq', *Security Dialogue*, 39(6): 615–35.

Rokeach, M. (1979) *Understanding human values: Individual and societal*, New York: Free Press.

Rosati, J. and Twing, S. (1998) 'The presidency and US foreign policy after the Cold War', in J. A. Scott (ed.) *After the end: Making US foreign policy in the post-Cold War world*, Durham: Duke University Press.

Rudolf, P. (1999) 'Stigmatisierung bestimmter Staaten. Europa bevorzugt den politischen Dialog', *Internationale Politik*, 54(6): 15–22.

Ruzicka, J. (2009) 'Have you seen a failure recently? Why failed cases of securitization matter', paper presented at the Annual Convention of the International Studies Association (ISA), New York City, NY: 15–18 February.

Safire, W. (2009). 'I don't do "do."', *The New York Times Magazine*, April 10, p. 14.

—— (2003) 'Privacy invasion curtailed', *New York Times*, February 13.

Salamon, L. (2002) The new governance and the tools of public action: An introduction', in L. Salamon (ed.) *The tools of government: A guide to the new governance*, Oxford: Oxford University Press.

Sartori, G. (1970) 'Concept misformation in comparative politics', *American Political Science Review*, 64(4): 1033–53.

Salter, M. B. (2008) 'Securitization and desecuritization: A dramaturgical analysis of the Canadian Air Transport Security Authority', *Journal of International Relations and Development*, 11(4): 321–49.

San Antonio Express-News (1998) *US HIV scorecard is mixed*, 1 December.

Sapir, E. (1934) 'Symbolism' in *Encyclopaedia of Social Sciences*, London: Macmillan.

Sarkesian, S. C., Williams, J. A., and Cimbala, S. J. (1995) *US national security: Policymakers, processes, and politics*, Boulder, CO: Lynne Rienner.

Sarup, M. (2003) *An introductory guide to post-structuralism and postmodernism*, Hemel Hempstead, UK: Prentice Hall.

Saunders, A. N. W. (1970) *Greek political oratory*, London: Penguin Books.

Schegloff, E. A. (1992) 'In another context', in A. Duranti and C. Goodwin (eds) *Rethinking context: Language as an interactive phenomenon*, Cambridge: Cambridge University Press.

Scherrer, A. (2009) *G8 against transnational organized crime*, Farnham, UK: Ashgate.

Scheufele, D. A. (1999) 'Framing as a theory of media effects', *Journal of Communication*, 49(1): 103–22.

Scheuerman, W. (1999). 'Another hidden dialogue: Hans Morgenthau and Carl Schmitt', in W. Scheuerman, *Carl Schmitt: The end of law*, New York: Rowan and Littlefield: 225–52.

Schiffrin, D. (1994) *Approaches to discourse*, Oxford: Blackwell Publishers.

Schlör, W. F. (1993) *German security policy: An examination of the trends in German security policy in a new European and global context*, London: Brassey's.

Schmitt, C. (1985) *Political theology: Four chapters on the concept of sovereignty*, Cambridge, MA: MIT Press.

—— (1996) *The concept of the political*, Chicago: University of Chicago Press.

Schmitchen, D. and Stritzel, H. (2008) 'Unterschiedliche "Sprachen" in Deutschland und den USA? Ein Vergleich transatlantischer Sicherheitsdiskurse am Beispiel der "Rogue States"', *Internationale Politik und Gesellschaft*, 1: 52–67.

Schneider, A. and Ingram, H. (1993) 'Social construction of target populations: Implications for politics and policy', *American Political Science Review*, 87(2): 334–37.

Schön, D. and Rein, M. (1994) *Frame reflection: Toward the resolution of intractable controversies*, New York: Basic Books.

Schrader, L. (2002) 'Unilateralismus versus Global Governance: Die so genannten Schurkenstaaten als Problem der internationalen Sicherheitspolitik', in M. Behrens (ed) *Globalisierung als politische Herausforderung: Global Governance zwischen Utopie und Realität*, Wiesbaden: VS Verlag.

Schudson, M. (2007) 'The anarchy of events and the anxiety of story-telling', *Political Communication*, 24(3): 253–57.

—— (2003) *The sociology of news*, New York: Norton.

—— (2002) 'What's unusual about covering politics as usual', in B. Zelizer and S. Allam (eds), *Journalism after September 11*, New York: Routledge.

—— (1978). *Discovering the news: A social history of America's newspapers*, New York: Basic Books.

Schuster, L. (2005) 'A sledgehammer to crack a nut: Deportation, detention and dispersal in Europe', *Social Policy & Administration*, 39(6): 606–621.

—— (2003a) *The use and abuse of political asylum in Britain and Germany*, London: Frank Cass.

—— (2003b) 'Asylum seekers: Sangatte and the tunnel', *Parliamentary Affairs*, 56(3): 506–22.

Schwartz-Shea, P. and Yanow, D. (2002) '"Reading" "methods" "texts": How research methods texts construct political science', *Political Research Quarterly*, 55(2): 461.

Schwarz, H. P. (2003) 'Von Elefanten und Bibern. Die Gleichgewichtsstörungen deutscher Außenpolitik', *Internationale Politik*, 58: 21–30.

Searle, J. R. (1995) *The construction of social reality*, New York: Free Press.

—— (1977a) 'Reiterating the differences: A reply to Derrida', *Glyph*, 1: 198–208.

—— (1977b) 'A classification of illocutionary acts', in P. Cole and J. L. Morgan (eds) *Syntax and semantics, Vol. 3: Speech acts*, New York: Academic Press.

—— (1969) *Speech acts: An essay in the philosophy of language*, Cambridge: Cambridge University Press.

Searle, J. R. and Vanderveken, D. (1985) *Foundations of illocutionary logic*, Cambridge: Cambridge University Press.

Seife, C. (2003) '"Terrorism futures" could have a future, experts say', *Science*, 301: 749.

Sepkowitz, K. A. (2006) 'One disease, two epidemics – AIDS at 25', *New England Journal of Medicine*, 354(23): 2411–14.

Seymor, J. D. (2005) 'Sizing up china's prisons', in B. Bakken (ed) *Crime, punishment, and policing in China*, Lanham, MD: Rowan & Littlefield Publishers.

Shambaugh, D. (2007) 'China's propaganda system: Institutions, processes and efficacy', *The China Journal*, 57: 25–58.

Shek, R. (1990) 'Sectarian eschatology and violence', in J. N. Lippman and S. Harrell (eds) *Violence in China. Essays in culture and counterculture*, Albany: State University of New York Press.

Shepelenko, A. (2005) 'Spros po gamburgskomu schetu' [trans. 'Demand for a Long-Term Values System'], *Slovo Kyrgyzstana*, 107(21868): 3.

Shklar, J. N. (2004). 'The liberalism of fear', in Shaun P. Young (ed) *Political liberalism*, Albany: State University of New York Press.

Shue, V. (1994) 'Legitimacy crisis in china?', in P. H. Gries and S. Rosen (eds) *State and society in 21st-century China*, London: Routledge.

Singer, P. W. (2002) 'AIDS and international security', *Survival*, 44(1): 145–58.

Siplon, P. D. (2002) *AIDS and the policy struggle in the United States*, Washington DC: Georgetown University Press.

Sjöstedt, R. (forthcoming) *When is a threat threatening? The securitization of HIV/AIDS in the United States and Russia*, Uppsala: Uppsala University Press.

—— (2008) 'Exploring the construction of threats: The securitization of HIV/AIDS in Russia', *Security Dialogue*, 39(1): 7–29.

—— (2007) 'The discursive origins of a doctrine: Norms, identity and securitization under Harry S. Truman and George W. Bush', *Foreign Policy Analysis*, 3(3): 233–54.

Skinner, Q. (2002) *Visions of politics. Vol. 1: Regarding method*, Cambridge: Cambridge University Press.

Skorodumova, E. (2005) 'Vse resheniya parlamenta dolzhny byt obosnovannym' [trans. 'All parliament's decisions must be well-founded'], *Moya stolitsa novosti*, 123(314): 4.

—— (2005) 'Ne dopustim khaosa' [trans. 'We will not permit chaos'], *Moya stolitsa novosti*, 125(316): 2.

Slashcheva, T. (2005a) 'Kogda ne bylo kvoruma . . .' [trans. 'When there was no quorum . . .'], *Slovo Kyrgyzstana*, 107(21868): 4.

—— (2005b) 'Pozitsiya sozreet cherez 20 dnei' [trans. 'The position will develop in 20 days'], *Slovo Kyrgyzstana*, 108(21869): 6.

Slotow, R. and van Dyk, G. (2004) 'Musth and elephant society'. Online. Available HTTP: http://www.und.ac.za/und/lesci/elephant/musth.htm (accessed 25 May 2009).

Slovo Kyrgyzstana (2005a) 'U bespredela net predela?' [trans. 'Is there no limit to disorder?'], 106(21867): 2.

—— (2005b) 'Strana – odna. Narod – odin. Chto delit?' [trans. 'The country is one. The people are one. What's to divide?'], 107(21868): 1.

—— (2005 c) 'Chto pokazhet sledstvie' [trans. 'What the inquiry shows'], 108(21869): 2.

Smith, S. (1999) 'The increasing insecurity of security studies: Conceptualizing security in the last twenty years', *Contemporary Security Policy*, 20(3): 72–101.

Snow, D. A. and Benford, R. D. (1992) 'Master frames and cycles of protest', in A. D. Morris and M. Mueller (eds) *Frontiers in social movement theory*, New Haven: Yale University Press.

—— (1988) 'Ideology, frame resonance, and participant mobilization', in B. Klandermans, H. Kriesi and S. Tarrow (eds) *International social movement research – From structure to action: Comparing social movement research across cultures*, London: JAI Press.

Snow, D. A. and McAdam, D. (2000) 'Identity work process in the context of social movements: Clarifying the identity/movement nexus', in S. Stryker, T. J. Owens and R. W. White (eds) *Self, identity, and social movement*, Minneapolis: University of Minnesota Press.

Snyder, J. and Ballentine, K. (1996) 'Nationalism and the market place of ideas', *International Security*, 21(2): 5–40.

Stokoe, E. H. (1998) 'Talking about gender: The conversational construction of gender categories in academic discourse', *Discourse and Society*, 9(2): 217–40.

Strauss, L. (1952) *The political philosophy of Hobbes: Its basis and genesis*, Chicago: University of Chicago Press.

Stritzel, H. (2010, forthcoming) 'Localizing threat images: Securitization as a politics of translation'.

—— (2007) 'Towards a theory of securitization: Copenhagen and beyond', *European Journal of International Relations*, 13(3): 357–83.

Strutynski, P. (2004) 'Zwischenaufenthalt Bagdad: Kriege im Zeitalter des Neoimperialismus', in Österreichisches Studienzentrum für Frieden und Konfliktlösung (ed) *Schurkenstaat und Staatsterrorismus: Die Konturen einer militärischen Globalisierung*, Münster: Agenda.

Süddeutsche Zeitung (1998) *Iran spielt fair*, 20 June.

Surowieki, J. (2004) *The wisdom of crowds: Why the many are smarter than the few and how collective wisdom shapes business, economies, societies, and nations*, New York: Doubleday.

Szabo, S. F. (2004) *Parting ways: The crisis in German-American relations*, Washington: Brookings Institution Press.

Tanter, R. (1999) *Rogue regimes*, Terrorism and proliferation, New York: St. Martin's Griffin.

Tarrow, S. (1998) *Power in movement: Social movements and contentious politics*, Cambridge: Cambridge University Press.

Taurek, R. (2006) 'Securitization theory — the story so far: Theoretical inheritance and what it means to be a post-structural realist', Mimeo.

Tenir, E. (2005) 'Kommentarii deputatov Jogorku Kenesha' [trans. 'Commentary from Jogorku Kenesh Deputies'], *Vechernii Bishkek*, 202(8876): 1.

The Atlanta Journal and Constitution (1997) *Focus on Sandra Thurman*, 30 November.

—— (1993) *An equal opportunity killer*, 11 April.

The Boston Globe (1999a) *Gates pledges AIDS vaccine effort; Gift by Microsoft chief doubles fund*, 4 May.

—— (1999b) *US leadership needed on AIDS in Africa*, 1 August.

—— (1999c) *Step up fight against AIDS, panel says*, 15 December.

—— (1999d) *Africans and Americans: We want to give the issue of AIDS and sexual behavior the same level of visibility that a previous generation gave apartheid in South Africa*, 13 January.

The Boston Herald (1993) *College students hungry for Haitian policy change*, 11 March.

The Columbus Dispatch (1998) *AIDS scorecard: Face of dread disease is changing US*, 6 July.

The Denver Post (1999) *American help urged in African AIDS war: Nations face devastation from disease, experts say*, 7 November.

The Denver Post/The New York Times (1997) *Study on HIV now focuses on ethics: Third-World mothers received placebos*, 18 September.

The Epoch Times (2004) *Nine commentaries on the Communist Party — a book that has shocked all Chinese around the world. A book that is disintegrating the Communist Party*, Gillette: Yih Chyun Corp & The Epoch Times.

The Guardian (2003) *Safe havens plan to slash asylum numbers*, 5 February.

The Guardian (2003) *Blunkett pushes for refugee safe havens*, 1 March.

The Guardian (2003) *Non-EU asylum centres 'within months'*, 8 May.

The Guardian (2003a) *Britain wavers on asylum plans*, 16 June.

The Guardian (2003b) *No plans' for asylum camps outside EU*, 16 June.

The Guardian (2003) *EU rejects asylum camps plan*, 20 June.

The Houston Chronicle (1999) *State of emergency: It's time leaders faced AIDS problem across community*, 1 December.

—— (1997) *Untenable: Stop giving placebos to HIV-infected mothers abroad*, 30 April.

The Houston Chronicle/The New York Times (1998) *AIDS in US becoming 'an epidemic of color'*, 29 June.

The Independent (2003) *Fortress Europe set to keep up barricades*, 19 June.

The Korean Times (2003a) *I Dunno*, 15 May. Available from http://times.hankooki.com/cgi-bin/hkiprn.cgi?/pa = /1page/opinion/200303/kt2003032516 4 (accessed 15 May 2003).

—— (2003b), *Pyongyang cancellation of talks*, 15 May.

The New York Post (2004) *Nuisance nonsense: Rudy rages at Kerry's crack on slashing level of terror*, 12 October.

The New York Times (2008) *Separating the terror and the terrorist*, 13 December.

—— (2003) *Privacy invasion curtailed*, 13 February.

—— (2002) *Pentagon plans a computer system that would peek at personal data of Americans*, 9 November.

—— (1996) *President finds a way to fight mandate to oust HIV troops*, 10 February.

—— (1999) *Chief American UN Delegate charts course for his month at the helm*, 21 December.

—— (1993) *Military cites wide range of reasons for its gay ban*, 27 January.

The New York Times Magazine (2009) *I don't do 'do'*, New York, 12 April.

The Virginian-Pilot/The Ledger-Star (1993) *Clinton's study must sort tough issues*, 31 January.

The Washington Post (1994) *Athlete may be deported for falsifying HIV status*, 22 June.

The Washington Post (2000) *AIDS is declared threat to security: White House fears epidemic could destabilize world*, 30 April.

—— (1999a) *AIDS activists badger Gore again*, 18 June.

—— (1999b) *The war on disease is worth fighting*, 18 June.

—— (2007) *The real verdict on Jose Padilla*, 17 August.

The White House (1996) *A national security strategy of enlargement and engagement*. Online. Available HTTP: http://www.fas.org/spp/military/docops/national/1996stra.htm (accessed 25 May 2009).

Thompson, J. B. (1991) 'Introduction', in P. Bourdieu, *Language and symbolic power*, Cambridge: Polity Press.

—— (1984) 'Editor's introduction', in P. Bourdieu, *Language and symbolic power*, ed. by J. B. Thompson, trans. by G. Raymond and M. Adamson, Cambridge: Polity Press.

Thornton, P. (2003) 'The new cybersects: Resistance and repression in the reform era', in E. J. Perry and M. Selden (eds) *Chinese society: Change, conflict and resistance*, 2nd edn, London: RoutledgeCurzon.

—— (2002) 'Framing dissent in contemporary China: Irony, ambiguity and metonymy', *China Quarterly*, 171: 661–81.

Tilly, C. (1978) *From mobilization to revolution*, Reading MA: Addison-Wesley.

Time (1993a) *Haiti or Hades*, 1 March.

—— (1993b) *Opening the boarder to AIDS*, 22 February.

Times-Picayune/Associated Press (1993) *Judge: Free HIV Haitians; Raps Bush, Clinton*, 9 June.

Todorov, T. (1983) *Symbolism and interpretation*, London: Routledge & Kegan Paul.

—— (1996) *Facing the extreme: More life in the concentration camps*, London: Metropolitan Books.

Tong, S. (2002) 'An organizational analysis of the falun gong: Structure, communications, financing', *China Quarterly*, 171: 636–60.

Turkmenov, U. (2005) 'Tragediya – vne politicheskikh schetov' [trans. 'Tragedy is beyond political scores'], *Slovo Kyrgyzstana*, 107(21868): 2.

UK Cabinet Office and Home Office (2003) *A new vision for refugees*. Online. Available HTTP: http://www.proasyl.de/texte/Europe/union/2003/UK_NewVision.pdf.

UK Government (2003) *New international approaches to asylum processing and protection*. Online. Available HTTP: http://www.statewatch.org.

UNAIDS (2008) *Information web page*. Online. Available HTTP: http://www.unaids.org/en/AboutUNAIDS/Leadership/EXD/ (accessed 21 October 2008).

—— (2004) *UNAIDS epidemic update. North America, Western and Central Europe fact sheet*, Geneva: UNAIDS.

United Nations Development Program (UNDP) (1994) *Human development report 1994*, New York: Oxford University Press.

United Nations Economic and Social Council (1996) *Resolution 1996/47*. Online. Available HTTP: http://data.unaids.org/Publications/External-Documents-Restored/ecosoc_resolution1996_en.pdf (accessed 9 March 2009).

—— (1994) *Resolution 1994/24*. Online. Available HTTP: http://data.unaids.org/Publications/External-Documents-Restored/ecosoc_resolution1994_24_en.pdf (accessed 9 March 2009).

248 *References*

United Nations Security Council (2000a) *Resolution 1308*. Online. Available HTTP: http://daccessdds.un.org/doc/UNDOC/GEN/N00/536/02/PDF/N0053602.pdf?OpenElement (accessed 4 October 2007).

United Nations Security Council (2000b) *Security Council holds debate on impact of AIDS on peace and security in Africa*. Online. Available HTTP: www.un.org/News/Press/docs/2000/20000110.sc6781.doc.html (accessed 21 November 2006).

USA Today (2002) *Former diplomat Holbrooke takes on global AIDS*, 10 June.

—— (1999a) *Africa AIDS crisis becomes a higher priority for US*, *Gore to announce today doubling of prevention and treatment funding*, 19 July.

—— (1999b) *Bill Gates, wife donate $25m for AIDS vaccine*, 4 June.

—— (1993) *Immigration-AIDS showdown looms*, 12 February.

US Department of Defense (2003) 'Report to Congress regarding the terrorism information awareness program'. Online. Available HTTP: http://www.darpa.mil/body/tia/tia_report_page.htm (accessed 25 May 2009).

US Department of Health and Human Services (2000) *HHS fact sheet: the Clinton Administration record on HIV/AIDS*. Online. Available HTTP: www.hhs.gov/news/press/2000pres/00fsaids.html (accessed 22 February 2007).

Valbjorn, M. (2004) 'Culture and IR – Culture in IR: Ignoring, introducing, up-dating or forgetting the concept of culture in international relations', paper presented at The Fifth Pan-European International Relations Conference, the Hague, Netherlands, 9–11 September 2004. (Cited with permission).

Van Dijk, T. A. (1997a) *Discourse as structure and process*, Thousand Oaks, CA: Sage.

—— (ed.) (1997b) *Discourse as social interaction*, Thousand Oaks, CA: Sage.

—— (1993) 'Principles of critical discourse analysis', *Discourse and Society*, 4(2): 249–83.

Vaughn, J. (2009) 'The unlikely securitizer: Humanitarian organizations and the securitization of indistinctiveness', *Security Dialogue*, 40(3): 263–85.

Vechernii Bishkek (2005) *Kstati* [trans. *Incidentally*], 25 October.

Vieira, M. A. (2007) 'The securitization of the HIV/AIDS epidemic as a norm: A contribution to the constructivist scholarship on the emergence and diffusion of international norms', *Brazilian Political Science Review*, 1(2): 137–81.

Violi, P. (2001) *Meaning and experience*, Bloomington: Indiana University Press.

Virilio, P. (1998) '"Is the author dead?" An Interview with Paul Virilio by James Der Derian', in J. Der Derian (ed.), *The Virilio reader*, Oxford: Blackwell.

Vladimirova, L. (2005) 'Prezident doveryaet premeru' [trans. 'The President Trusts the Prime Minster']. *Slovo Kyrgyzstana*, (21869): 3.

Vogel, H. J. (1992) 'Proliferation als Sicherheitsrisiko – Rede auf der Internationalen Konferenz für Sicherheitspolitik in München', 8 February.

Vulter, F. (2010) 'Securitization: A new approach to framing and media portrayals of the "war on terror"', *Journalism Practice*.

Vuori, J. A. (2008) 'Illocutionary logic and strands of securitisation – Applying the theory of securitisation to the study of non-democratic political orders', *European Journal of International Relations*, 14(1): 65–99.

—— (2005) 'Desecuritising the Tiananmen incidents', in R. Asikainen (ed.) *Perspectives on China*, Helsinki: Renvall Institute Publications.

Wæver, O. (2004), 'Aberystwyth, Paris, Copenhagen: New "schools" in security theory and their origins between Core and Periphery', paper presented at ISA Annual Convention, Montreal, Canada.

—— (2003) *Securitization: Taking stock of a research program in security studies*, Mimeo.

—— (2000) 'The EU as a security actor: Reflections from a pessimistic constructivist on post-sovereign security orders', in M. Kelstrup and M. C. Williams (eds) *International relations theory and the politics of European integration: Power, security and community*, London: Routledge.

—— (1997) '"Concepts of security,"' PhD thesis, University of Copenhagen, 355–357.

—— (1995) 'Securitization and desecuritization', in R. D. Lipschutz (ed.), *On security*, New York: Columbia University Press.

—— (1989) 'Conflicts of vision: Visions of conflict', in O. Wæver, P. Lemaitre and E. Tromer (eds) *European polyphony: Perspectives beyond East–West confrontation*, London: Macmillan.

Wagnsson, C. (2000) *Russian political language and public opinion on the West, NATO and Chechnya*, Stockholm: Akademitryck AB, Edsbruk.

Warren, M. (1990) 'Ideology and the self', *Theory and Society*, 19: 599–634.

WCED (1987) *Our common future*, Oxford: Oxford University Press.

Weldes, J., Laffey, M., Gusterson, H., and Duvall, R. (1999) 'Introduction: Constructing insecurity', in J. Weldes *et al.* (eds) *Cultures of insecurity: States, communities, and the production of danger*, Minneapolis: University of Minnesota Press.

Wendt, A. (1999) *Social theory of international politics*, Cambridge: Cambridge University Press.

Westby, D. L. (2002) 'Strategic imperative, ideology, and frame', *Mobilization*, 7(3): 287–304.

Wetherell, M. (2001) 'Debates in discourse research', in M. Wetherell, S. Taylor, and S. Yates (eds), *Discourse theory and practice: A reader*, Thousand Oaks, CA: Sage, 380–99.

White, E. E. (1992) *The context of human discourse: A configurational criticism of rhetoric*, Columbia, SC: University of South Carolina Press.

White, R. W. (ed.) (2000) *Self, identity, and social movement*, Minneapolis: University of Minnesota Press.

White House Press Office (2004) *Citizen Corps*. Online. Available HTTP: http://www.whitehouse.gov/news/releases/2002/04/corps.html (accessed 25 May 2009).

Whiteside, A., de Waal, A., and Gebre-Tensae, T. (2006) 'AIDS, security and the military in Africa: A sober appraisal', *African Affairs*, 105(419): 201–18.

Wiarda, H. J. (1996) *American foreign policy: Actors and processes*, New York: Harper Collins.

Wierzbicka, A. (1991) *Cross-cultural pragmatics. The semantics of human interaction*, Berlin: Mouton de Gruyter.

Wilkinson, C. (2009) 'Interpreting security: Grounding the Copenhagen School in Kyrgyzstan', unpublished thesis, University of Birmingham.

—— (2008) 'Positioning "security" and securing one's position: The researcher's role in investigating "security" in Kyrgyzstan', in C. R. Wall and P. P. Mollinga (eds) *Fieldwork in difficult environments*, Berlin: Lit Verlag.

—— (2007) 'The Copenhagen School on tour in Kyrgyzstan: Is securitization theory useable outside Europe?', *Security Dialogue*, 38(1): 5–25.

Williams, M. C. (forthcoming) 'Recasting the Hobbesian tradition in international political theory', in Raia Prokhovnic and Gabriella Slomp (eds), *International political theory after Hobbes*, London: Palgrave.

—— (2003) 'Words, images, enemies: Securitization and international politics', *International Studies Quarterly*, 47(4): 511–31.

Williams, M. J. (2005) *On Mars and Venus: Strategic culture as an intervening variable in US and European foreign policy*, Münster: Lit Verlag.

Williams, R. (1976) *Keywords: A vocabulary of culture and society*, London: Fontana.

Wittgenstein, L. (2001) *Philosophical investigations*, trans. by G. E. M. Anscombe, Oxford: Blackwell Publishers.

—— (1961) *Tractatus logico-philosophicus*, trans. by D. F. Pears and B. McGuiness, London: Routledge & Kegan Paul.

Wolfensohn, J. (2005) *Departing World Bank president Wolfensohn expresses regret in HIV/AIDS fight.* Online. Available HTTP: http://www.medicalnewstoday.com/printerfriendlynews.php?newsid=24775 (accessed 6 March 2009).

Wolfers, A. (1962) *Discord and collaboration: Essays on international politics*, Baltimore: Johns Hopkins University Press.

Wolfers, J. and Zitzewitz, E. (2004) 'Prediction markets', *The Journal of Economic Perspectives*, 18(2): 107–26.

Wong, J. and Liu, W. (1999) *The mystery of China's Falun Gong, its rise and its sociological implications*, Singapore: World Scientific/Singapore University Press.

Wright, G. H., von (1971) *Explanation and understanding*, Ithaca: Cornell University Press.

Wyn Jones, R. (1995) '"Message in a bottle?" Theory and praxis of critical security studies', *Contemporary Security Policy*, 16(3): 299–319.

Yang, C. (1961) *Religion in Chinese society: A study of contemporary social functions of religion and some of their historical factors*, Berkeley: University of California Press.

Yanow, D. (2006) 'Thinking interpretively: Philosophical presuppositions and the human sciences', in D. Yanow and P. Schwartz-Shea (eds) *Interpretation and method*, New York: M. E. Sharpe.

—— (2004) 'Translating local knowledge at organizational peripheries', *British Journal of Management*, 15: S9–S25.

—— (2003) 'Interpretive political science: What makes this not a subfield of qualitative methods', *APSA Newsletter*, 2.

—— (1996) *How does a policy mean? Interpreting policy and organizational actions*, Washington DC: Georgetown University Press.

Yin, R. K. (2008) *Case study research: Design and methods*, Beverly Hills, CA: Sage.

Young, A. J. and Valencia, M. J. (2003) 'Conflation of piracy and terrorism in Southeast Asia: Rectitude and utility', *Comparative Southeast Asia*, 25(2): 269–83.

Zand, B. (1999) 'Das Ende von Kurdistan', *Der SPIEGEL*, 9: 150–52.

Zeeck, D. (2006). Timeliness, local resonance affect what makes Page One, July 16, *Tacoma News-Tribune.* Online. Available. <http://www.thenewstribune.com/news/columnists/zeeck/story/5952919p-5240964c.html> (accessed 11 August 2006)

Zetter, R., Griffiths, D., Ferretti, S., and Pearl, M. (2003) *An assessment of the impact of asylum policies in Europe, 1990–2000. Home Office Research Study 259*, London: Home Office Research/Development and Statistics Directorate.

Index

An environmentally friendly book printed and bound in England by www.printondemand-worldwide.com

PEFC/16-33-415

PEFC Certified

This product is
from sustainably
managed forests
and controlled
sources

www.pefc.org

FSC

www.fsc.org

MIX

Paper from
responsible sources

FSC® C004959

This book is made entirely of chain-of-custody materials

#0373 - - C0 - 234/156/14 - PB